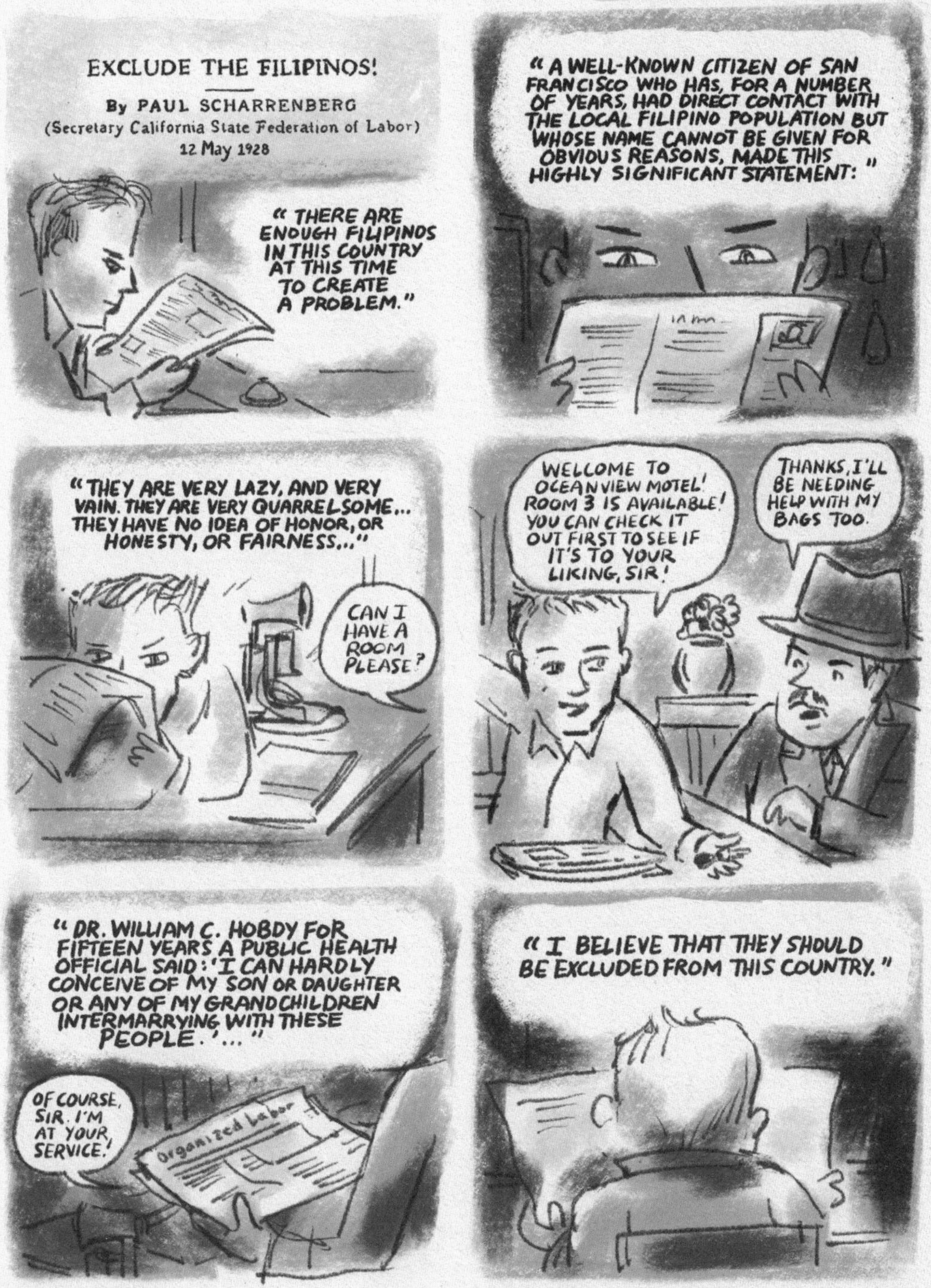
EXCLUDE THE FILIPINOS!
By PAUL SCHARRENBERG
(Secretary California State Federation of Labor)
12 May 1928
" THERE ARE ENOUGH FILIPINOS IN THIS COUNTRY AT THIS TIME TO CREATE A PROBLEM."
" A WELL-KNOWN CITIZEN OF SAN FRANCISCO WHO HAS, FOR A NUMBER OF YEARS, HAD DIRECT CONTACT WITH THE LOCAL FILIPINO POPULATION BUT WHOSE NAME CANNOT BE GIVEN FOR OBVIOUS REASONS, MADE THIS HIGHLY SIGNIFICANT STATEMENT: "
" THEY ARE VERY LAZY, AND VERY VAIN. THEY ARE VERY QUARRELSOME... THEY HAVE NO IDEA OF HONOR, OR HONESTY, OR FAIRNESS..."
CAN I HAVE A ROOM PLEASE?
WELCOME TO OCEANVIEW MOTEL! ROOM 3 IS AVAILABLE! YOU CAN CHECK IT OUT FIRST TO SEE IF IT'S TO YOUR LIKING, SIR!
THANKS, I'LL BE NEEDING HELP WITH MY BAGS TOO.
" DR. WILLIAM C. HOBDY FOR FIFTEEN YEARS A PUBLIC HEALTH OFFICIAL SAID: 'I CAN HARDLY CONCEIVE OF MY SON OR DAUGHTER OR ANY OF MY GRANDCHILDREN INTERMARRYING WITH THESE PEOPLE.'... "
OF COURSE, SIR. I'M AT YOUR SERVICE!
Organized Labor
" I BELIEVE THAT THEY SHOULD BE EXCLUDED FROM THIS COUNTRY."

"I'm Always Chasing Rainbows" on page 4 by Joseph McCarthy (lyrics), Harry Carroll (music).
"Toot, Toot, Tootsie (Goo'Bye!)" on page 33 by Gus Kahn, Ernie Erdman, Dan Russo. "When My Baby
Smiles at Me" on page 35 by Andrew B. Sterling, Ted Lewis (lyrics); Bill Munro (music). "Blue Skies"
on page 37 by Irving Berlin. "Avalon" on page 41-42 by Al Jolson, Buddy G. De Sylva, Vincent Rose.
"It Had to Be You" on page 45 by Gus Kahn (lyrics), Isham Jones (music). "You Were Meant for Me"
on page 103 by Arthur Freed (lyrics), Nacio Herb Brown (music). "I'll Always Be in Love with You" on
page 111 by Bud Green, Sam H. Stept, Herman Ruby. "Ain't Misbehavin" on page 113 by Andy Razaf
(lyrics); Thomas "Fats" Waller, Harry Brooks (music). "My Sin" on page 115-117 by Buddy G. DeSylva,
Lew Brown, Ray Henderson. "Some of These Days" on page 121-122 by Shelton Brooks (lyrics and
music), Sophie Tucker (arranger). "La Bella Filipina" on page 140 by Pedro Paterno (lyrics),
Ignacio Massaguer (music).

drawnandquarterly.com
rinaayuyang.com

ISBN 978-1-77046-666-1 · First edition: May 2023 · Printed in China · 10 9 8 7 6 5 4 3 2 1

Cataloguing data available from Library and Archives Canada

Published in the USA by Drawn & Quarterly, a client publisher of Farrar, Straus, Giroux.
Published in Canada by Drawn & Quarterly, a client publisher of Raincoast Books. Published in
the United Kingdom by Drawn & Quarterly, a client publisher of Publishers Group UK.

The MAN in the McINTOSH SUIT

by
Rina Ayuyang

- Drawn & Quarterly -

"I'm always chasing rainbows
Watching clouds drifting by
My schemes are just like all my dreams
Ending in the sky."

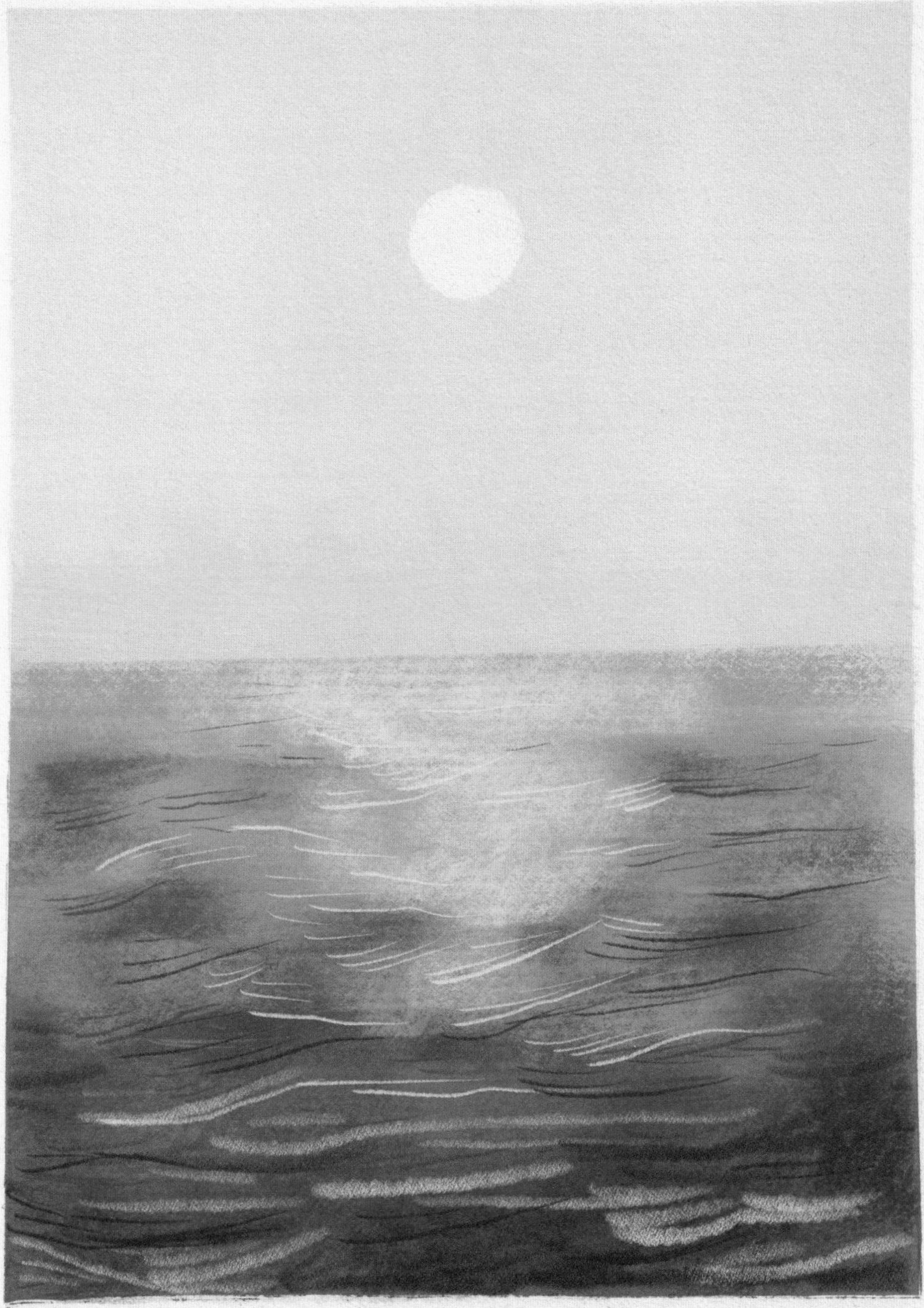

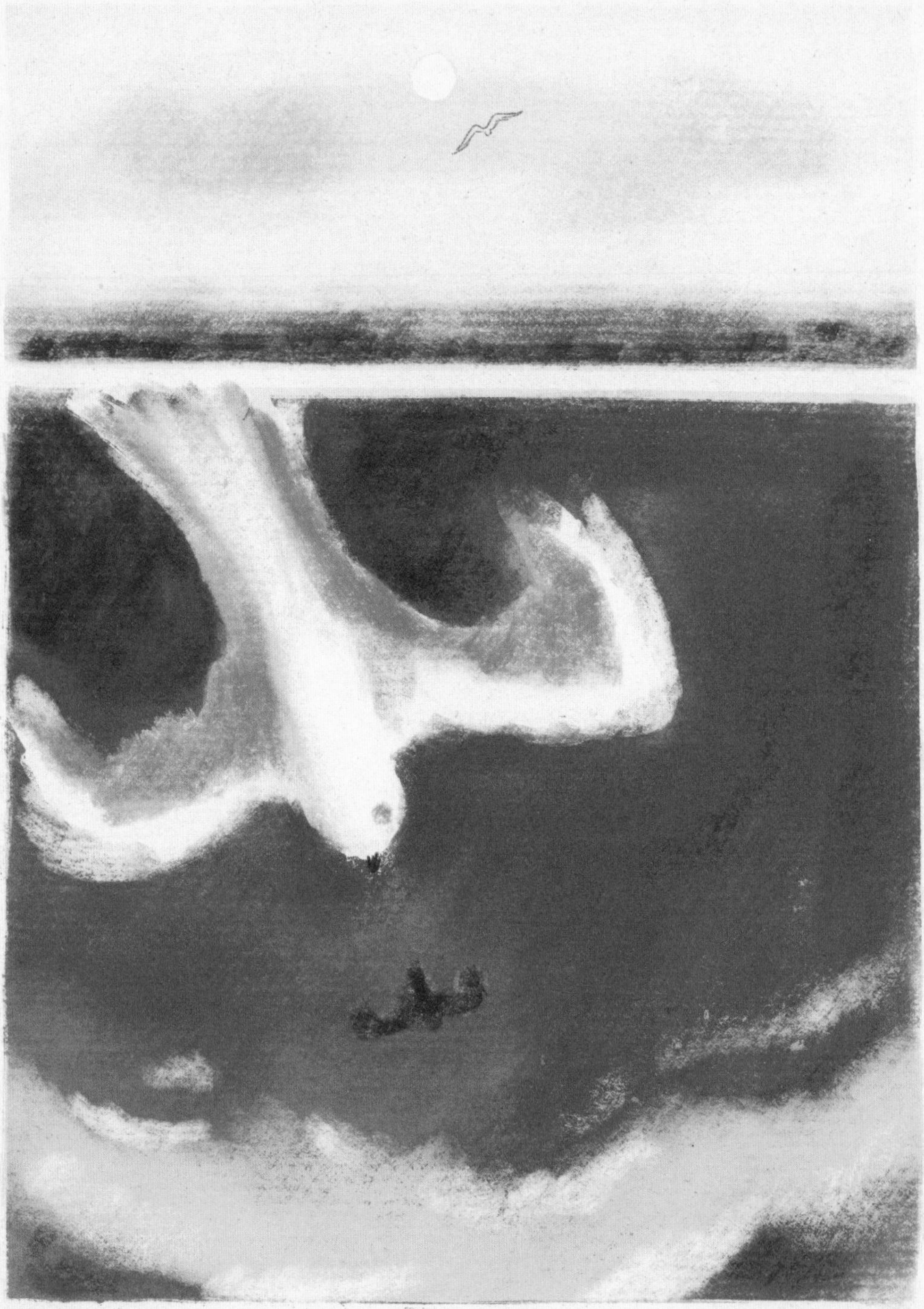

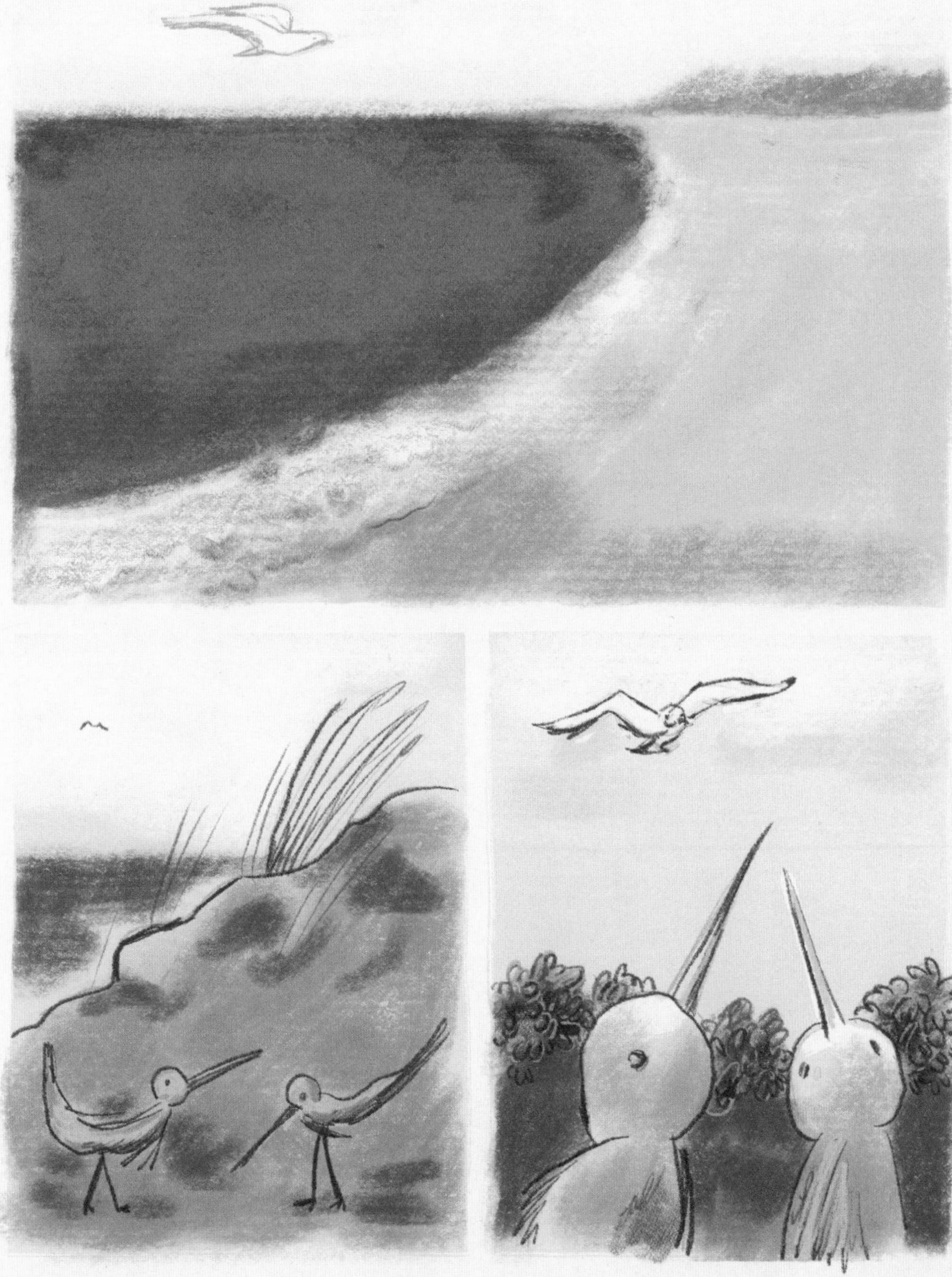

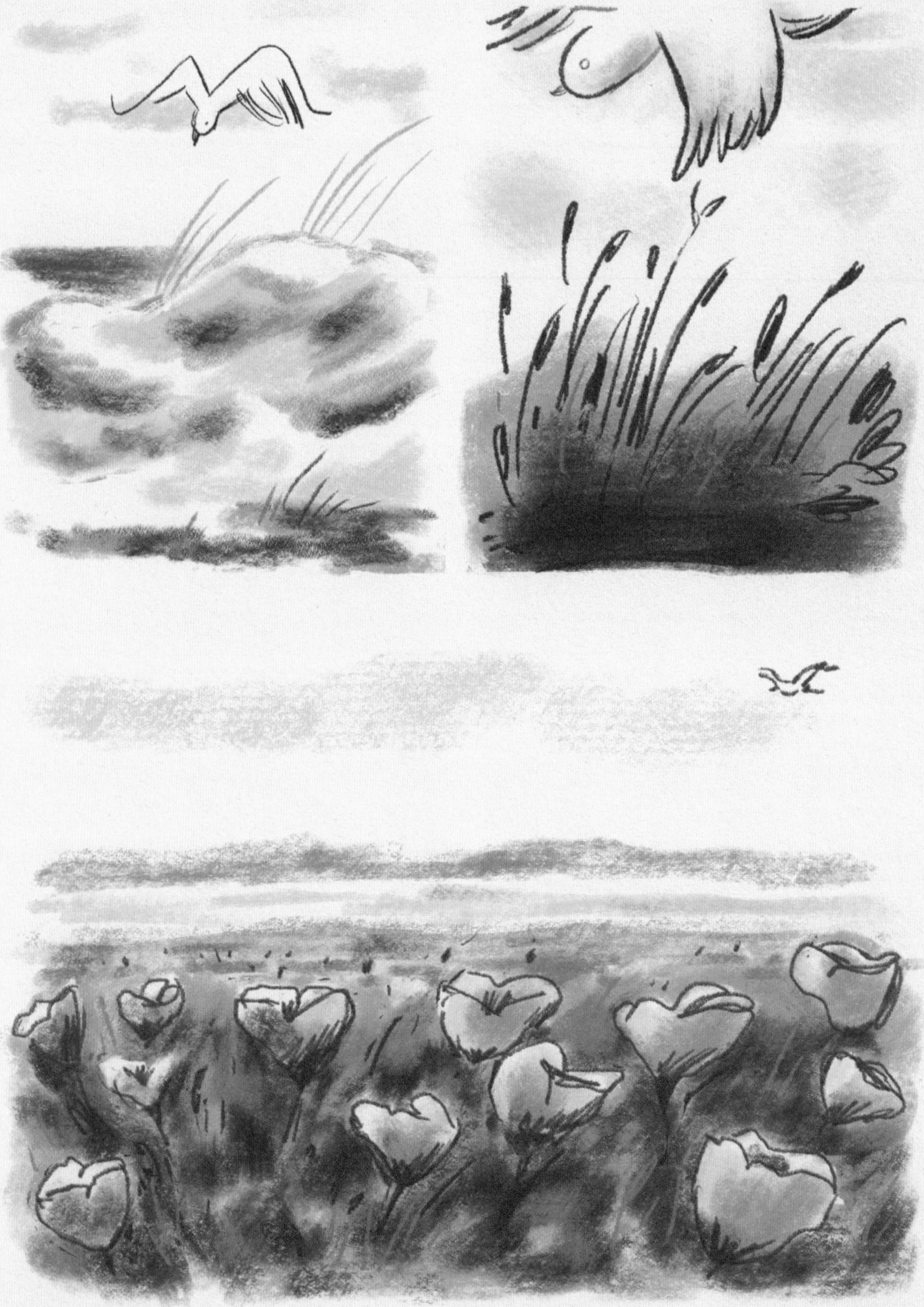

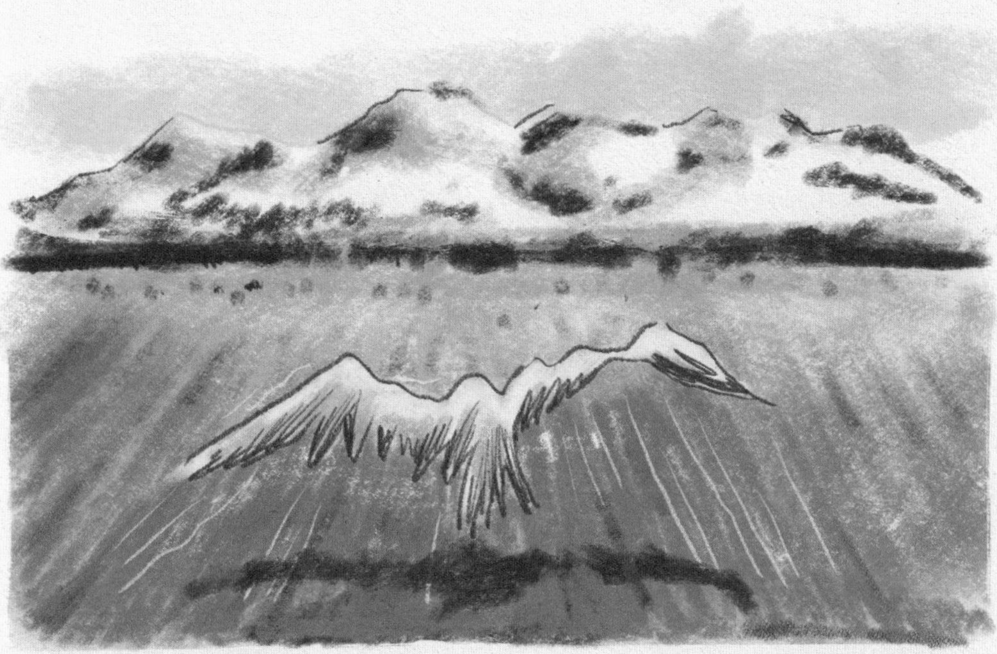

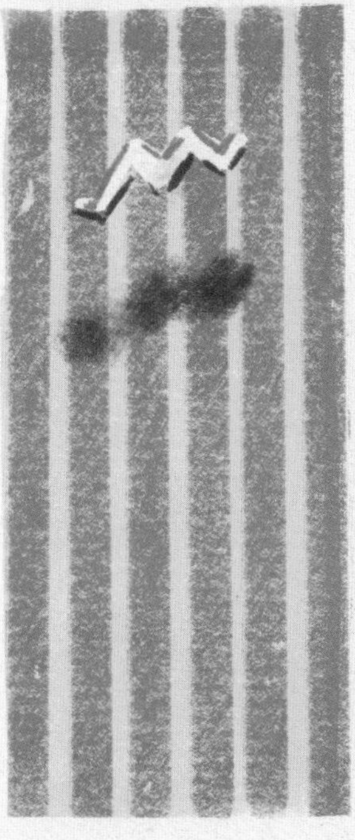

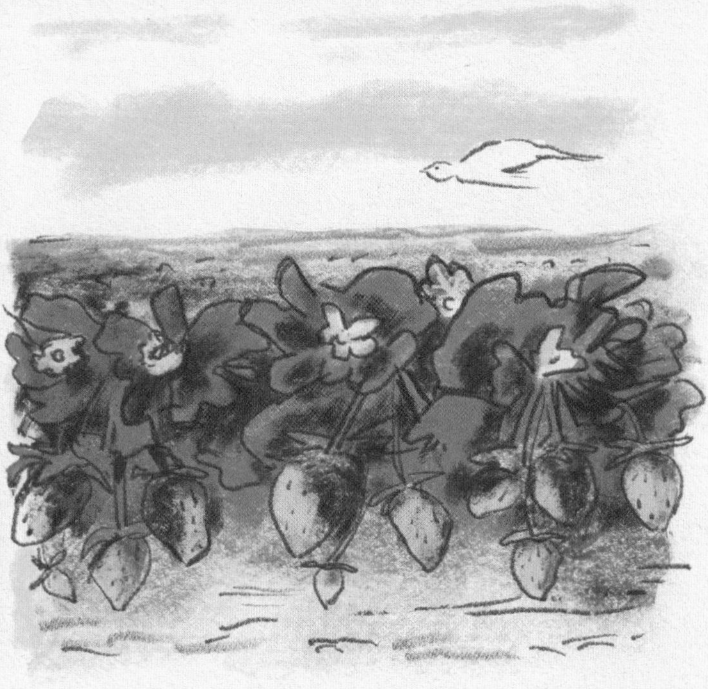

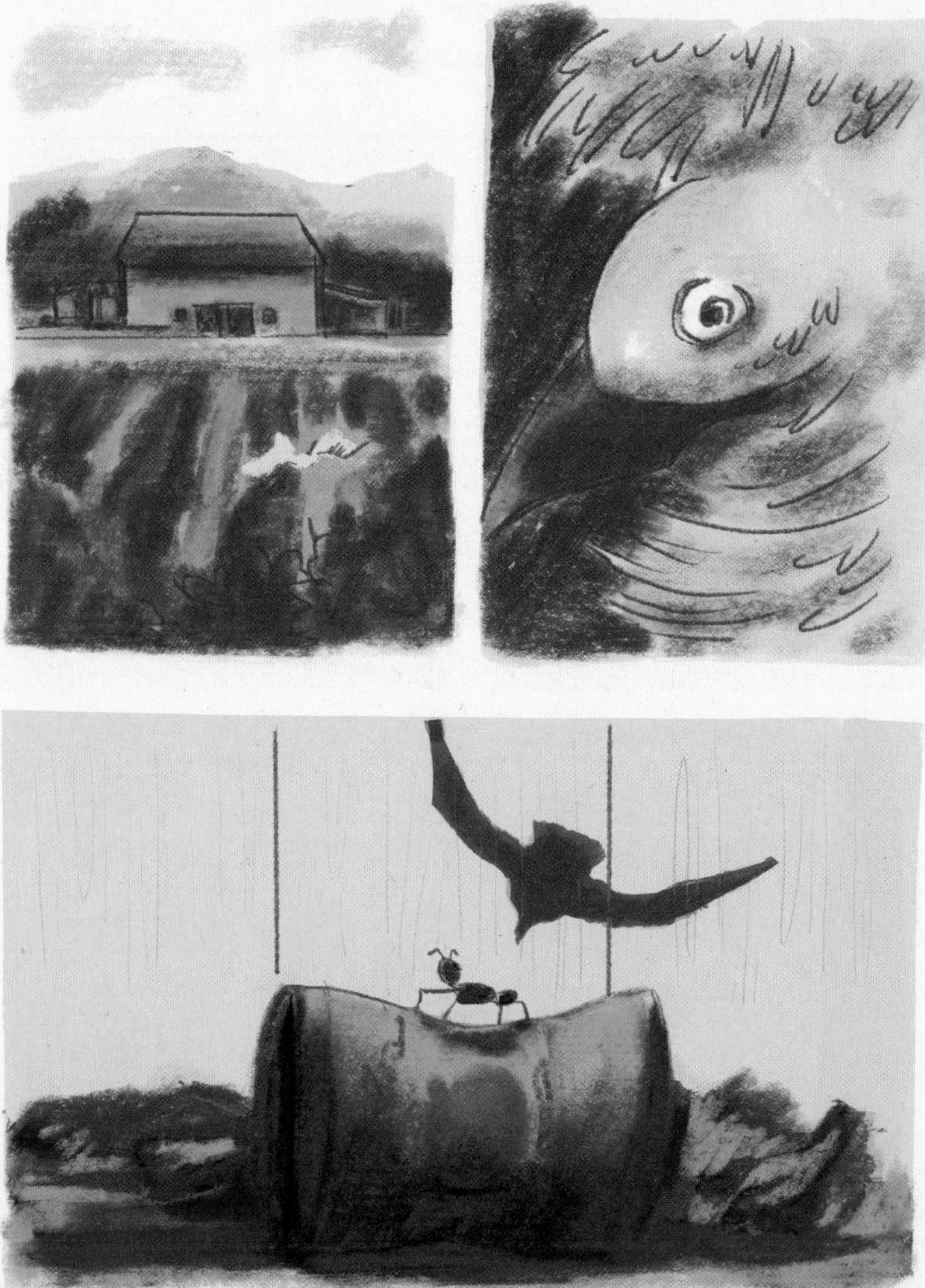

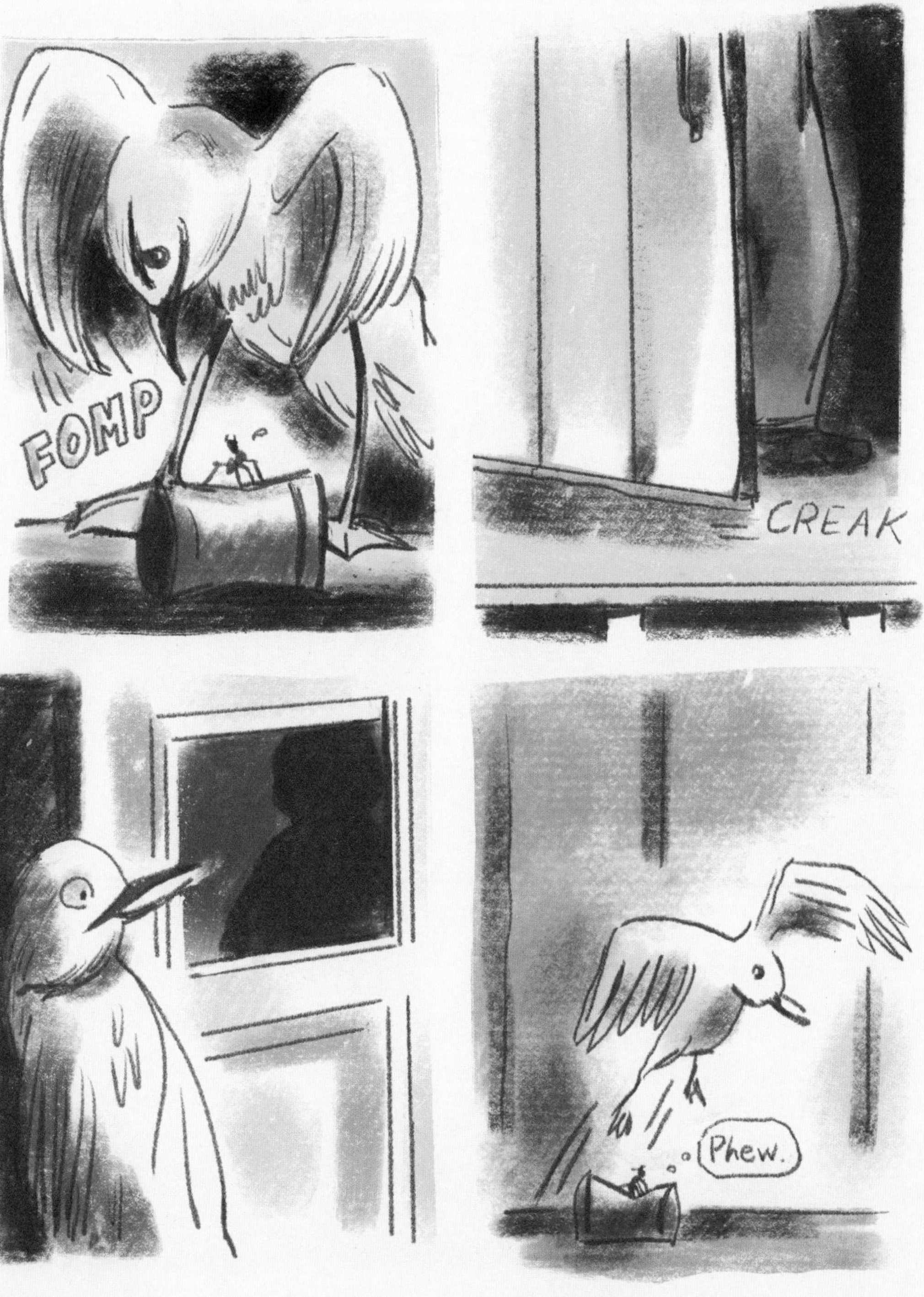
FOMP
CREAK
Phew.

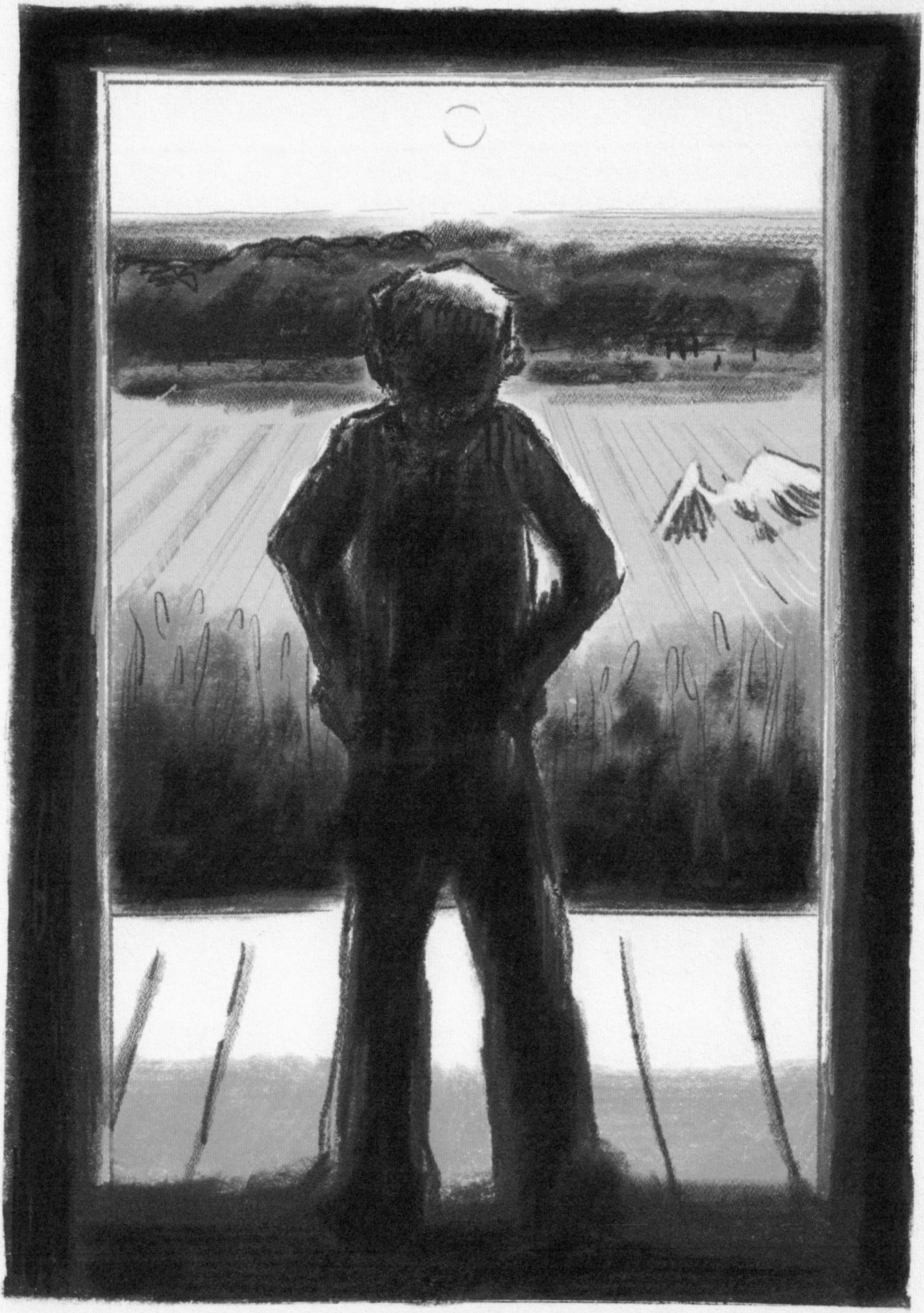

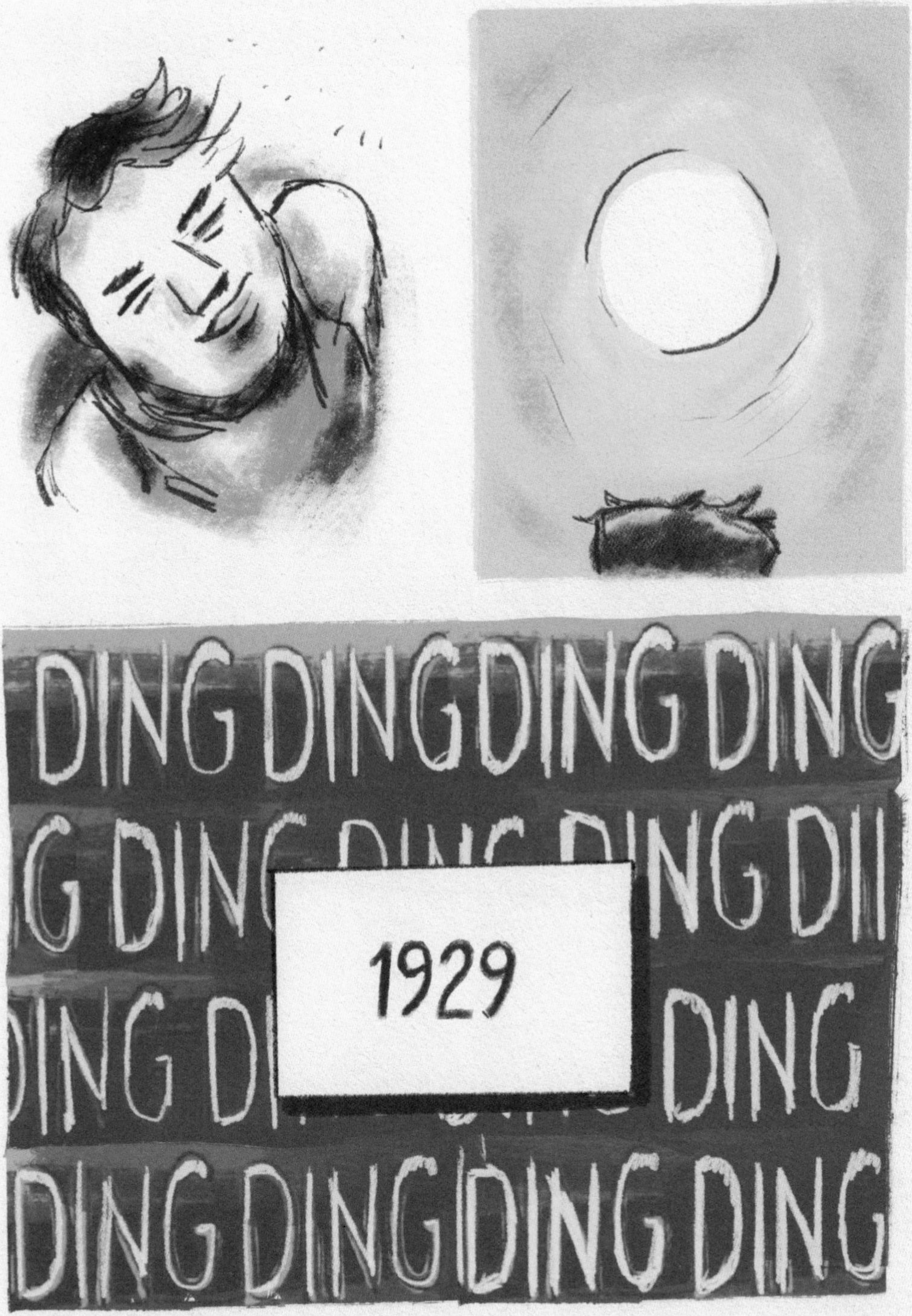
DING DING DING DING
DING
1929
DING
DING DING DING DING

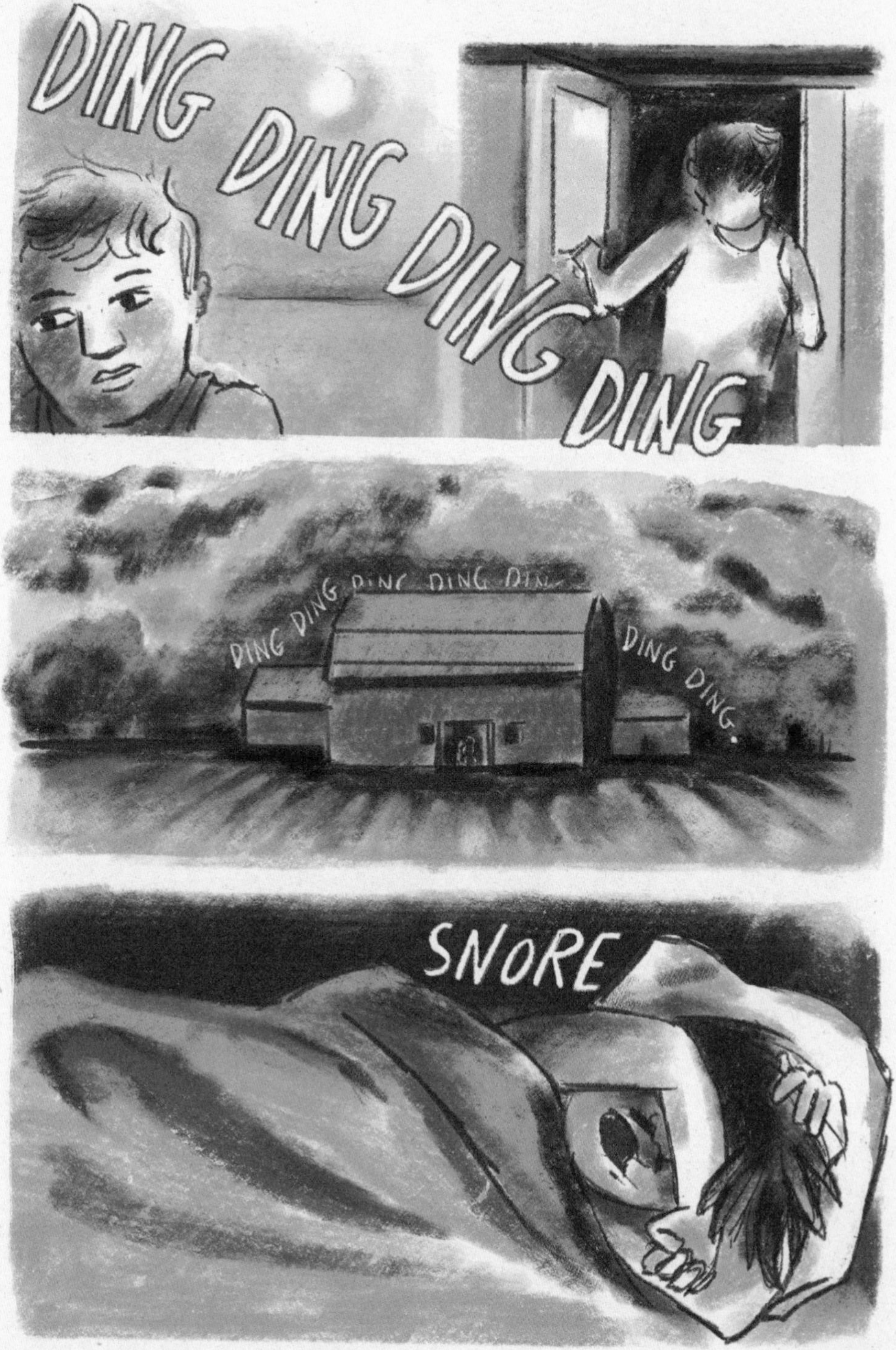
DING DING DING DING DING
DING DING
DING
DING DING
SNORE

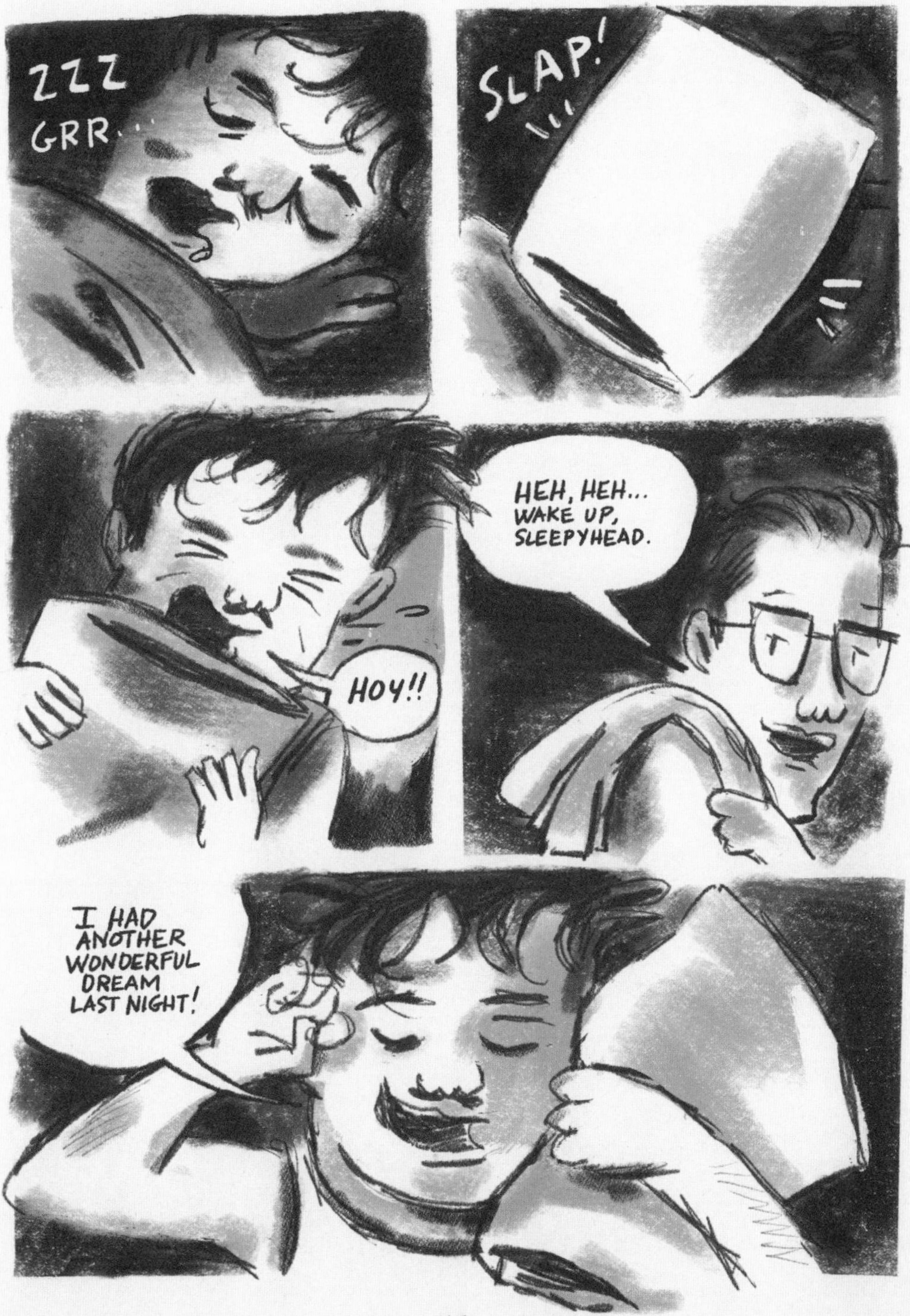
ZZZ
GRR...
SLAP!
HOY!!
HEH, HEH... WAKE UP, SLEEPYHEAD.
I HAD ANOTHER WONDERFUL DREAM LAST NIGHT!

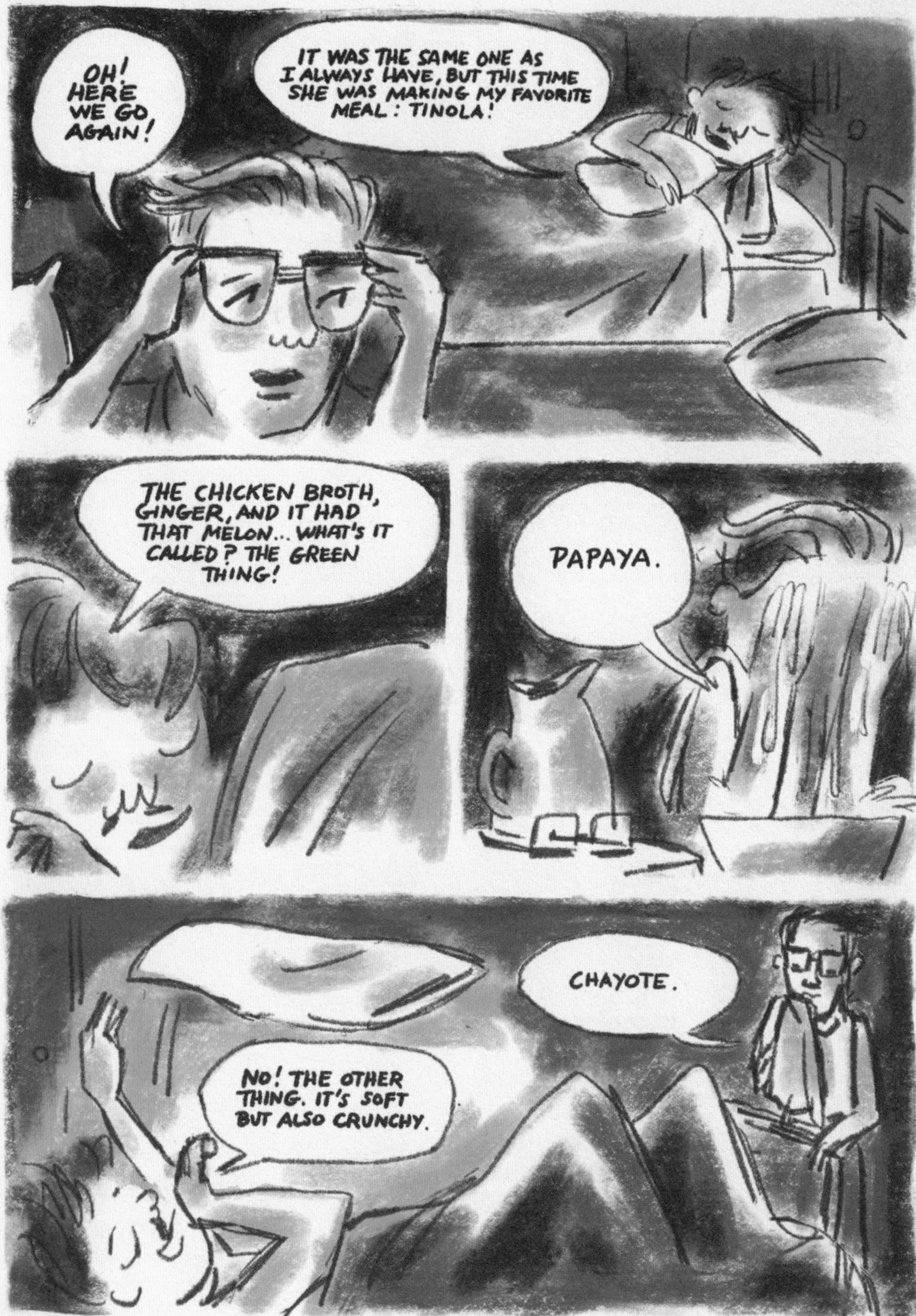
OH! HERE WE GO AGAIN!
IT WAS THE SAME ONE AS I ALWAYS HAVE, BUT THIS TIME SHE WAS MAKING MY FAVORITE MEAL: TINOLA!
THE CHICKEN BROTH, GINGER, AND IT HAD THAT MELON... WHAT'S IT CALLED? THE GREEN THING!
PAPAYA.
CHAYOTE.
NO! THE OTHER THING. IT'S SOFT BUT ALSO CRUNCHY.

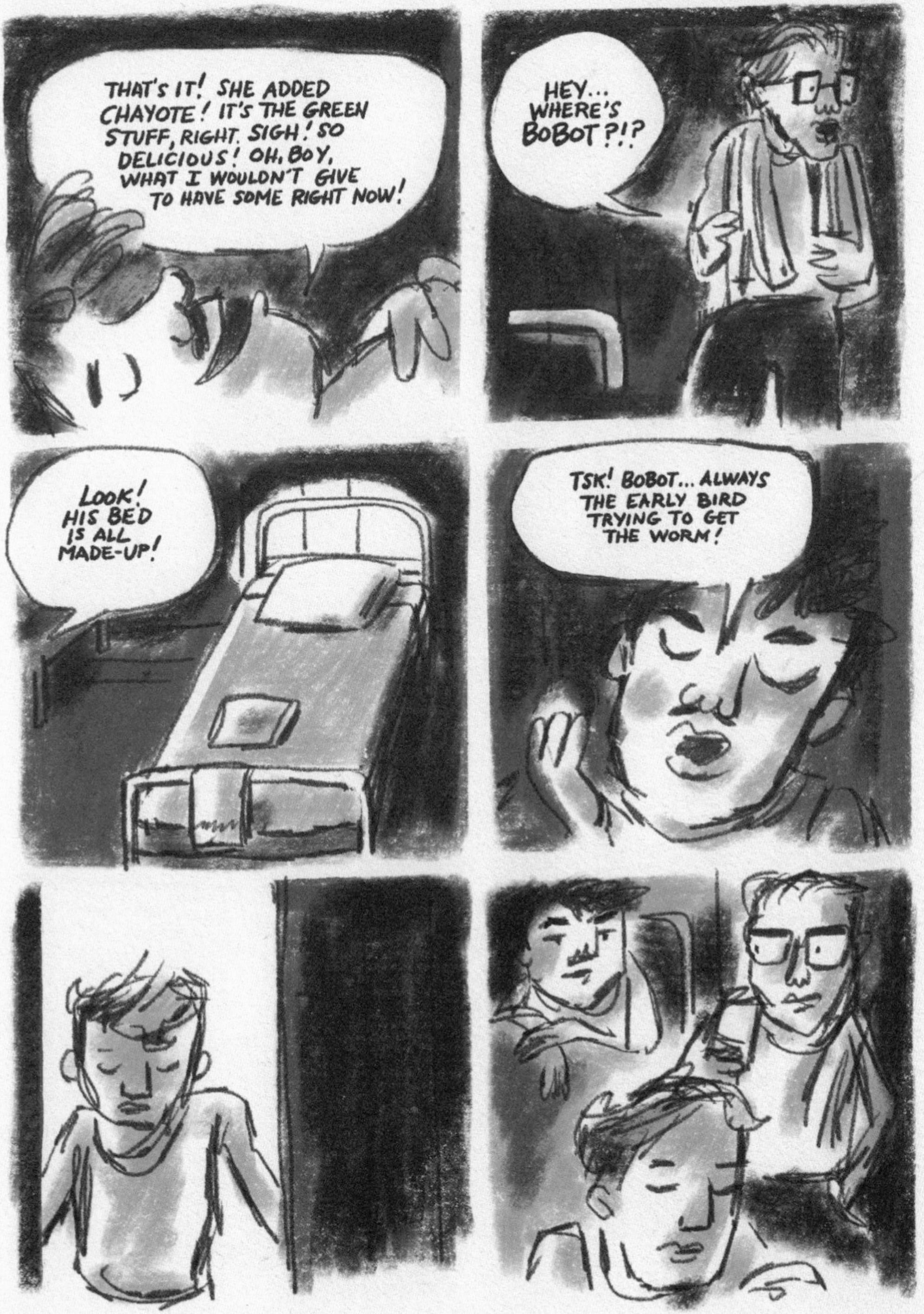
THAT'S IT! SHE ADDED CHAYOTE! IT'S THE GREEN STUFF, RIGHT. SIGH! SO DELICIOUS! OH, BOY, WHAT I WOULDN'T GIVE TO HAVE SOME RIGHT NOW!
HEY... WHERE'S BOBOT?!?
LOOK! HIS BED IS ALL MADE-UP!
TSK! BOBOT... ALWAYS THE EARLY BIRD TRYING TO GET THE WORM!

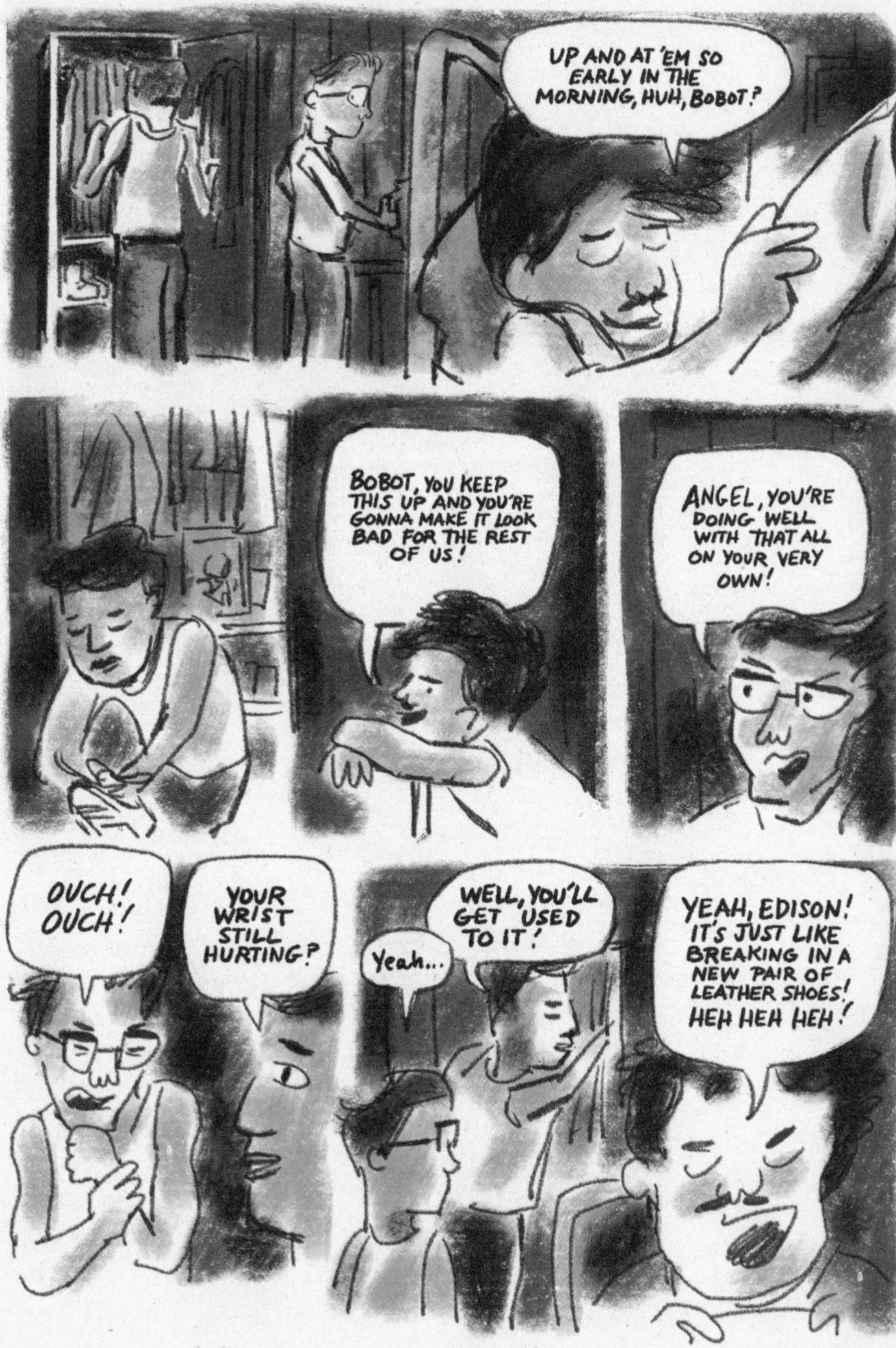
UP AND AT 'EM SO EARLY IN THE MORNING, HUH, BOBOT?
BOBOT, YOU KEEP THIS UP AND YOU'RE GONNA MAKE IT LOOK BAD FOR THE REST OF US!
ANGEL, YOU'RE DOING WELL WITH THAT ALL ON YOUR VERY OWN!
OUCH! OUCH!
YOUR WRIST STILL HURTING?
Yeah...
WELL, YOU'LL GET USED TO IT!
YEAH, EDISON! IT'S JUST LIKE BREAKING IN A NEW PAIR OF LEATHER SHOES! HEH HEH HEH!

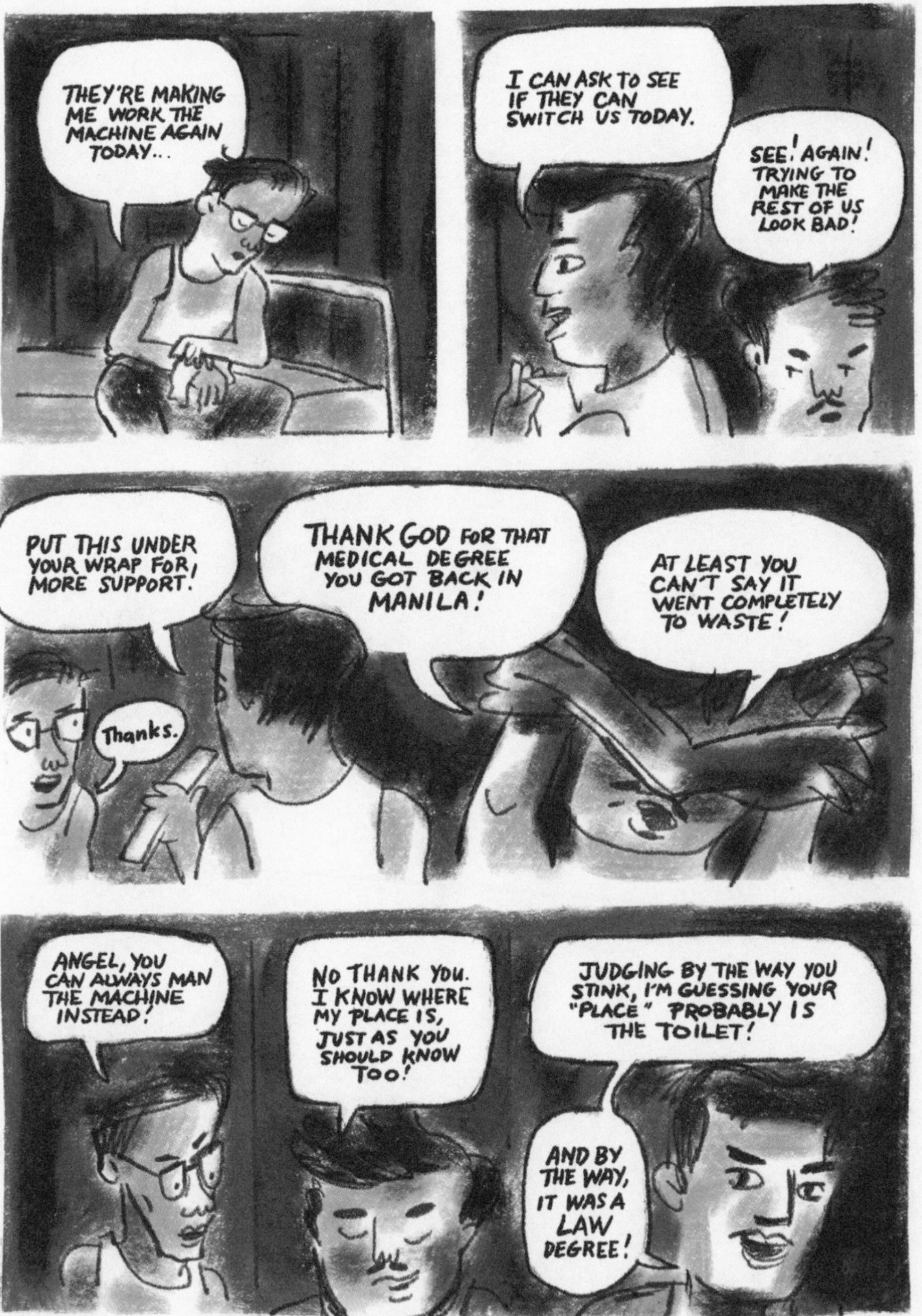
THEY'RE MAKING ME WORK THE MACHINE AGAIN TODAY...
I CAN ASK TO SEE IF THEY CAN SWITCH US TODAY.
SEE! AGAIN! TRYING TO MAKE THE REST OF US LOOK BAD!
PUT THIS UNDER YOUR WRAP FOR MORE SUPPORT.
Thanks.
THANK GOD FOR THAT MEDICAL DEGREE YOU GOT BACK IN MANILA!
AT LEAST YOU CAN'T SAY IT WENT COMPLETELY TO WASTE!
ANGEL, YOU CAN ALWAYS MAN THE MACHINE INSTEAD!
NO THANK YOU. I KNOW WHERE MY PLACE IS, JUST AS YOU SHOULD KNOW TOO!
JUDGING BY THE WAY YOU STINK, I'M GUESSING YOUR "PLACE" PROBABLY IS THE TOILET!
AND BY THE WAY, IT WAS A LAW DEGREE!

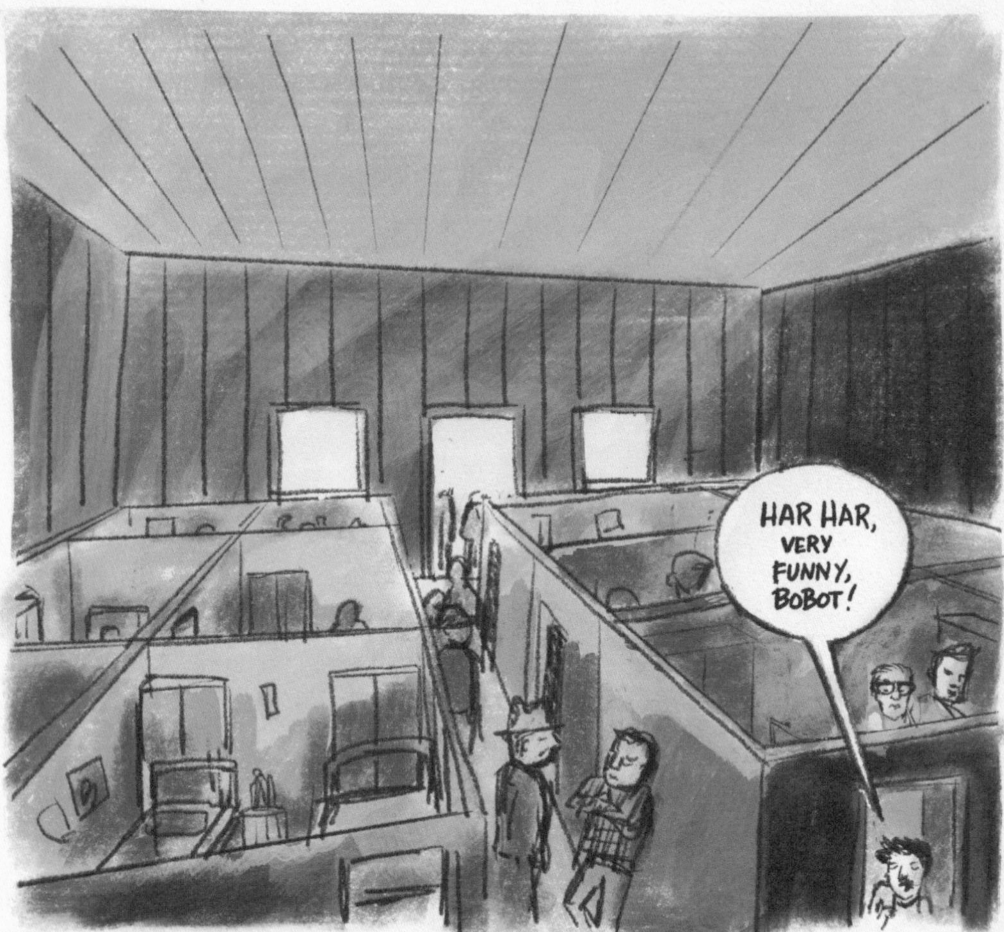
HAR HAR, VERY FUNNY, BOBOT!

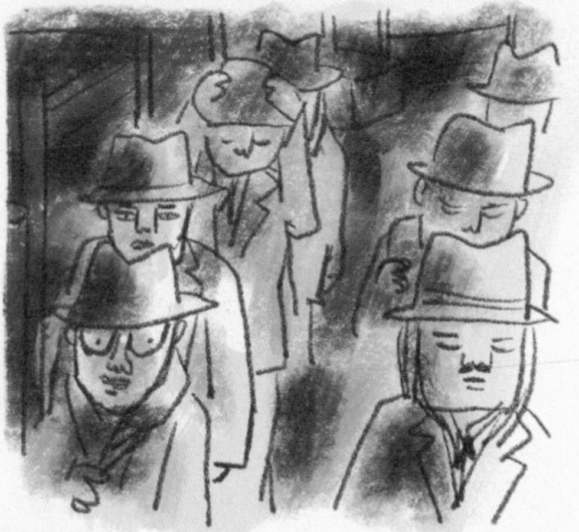

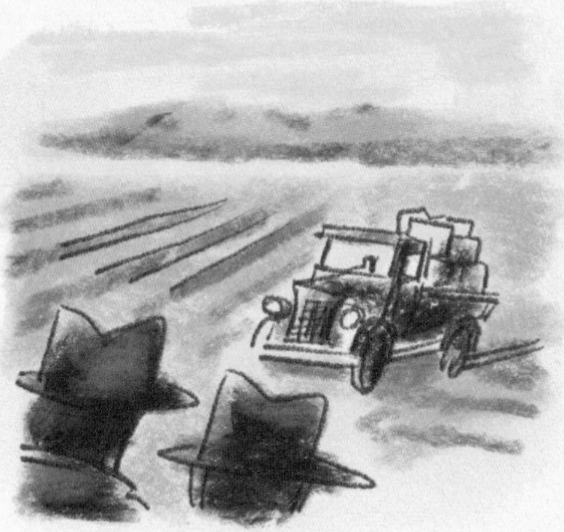

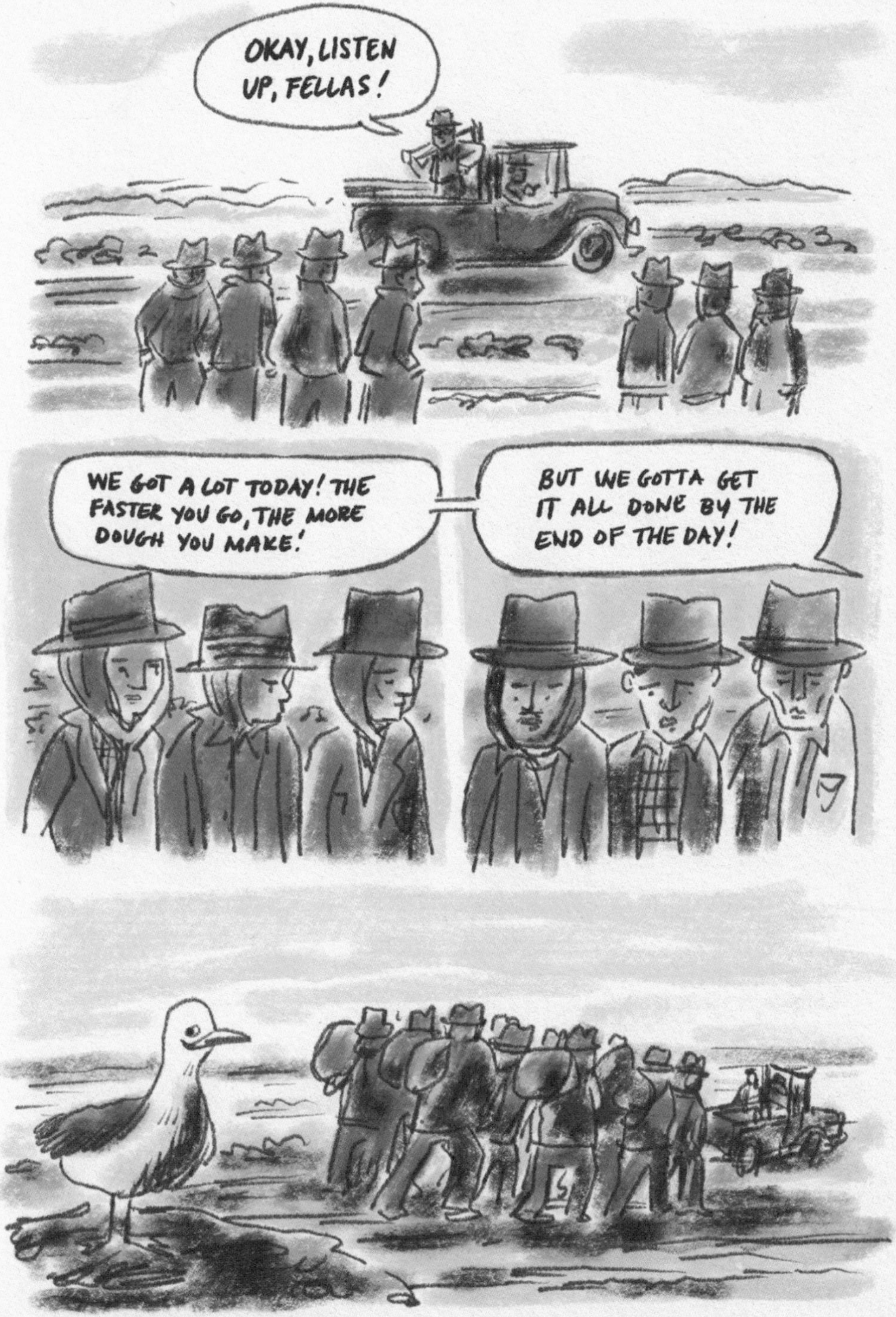
OKAY, LISTEN UP, FELLAS!
WE GOT A LOT TODAY! THE FASTER YOU GO, THE MORE DOUGH YOU MAKE!
BUT WE GOTTA GET IT ALL DONE BY THE END OF THE DAY!

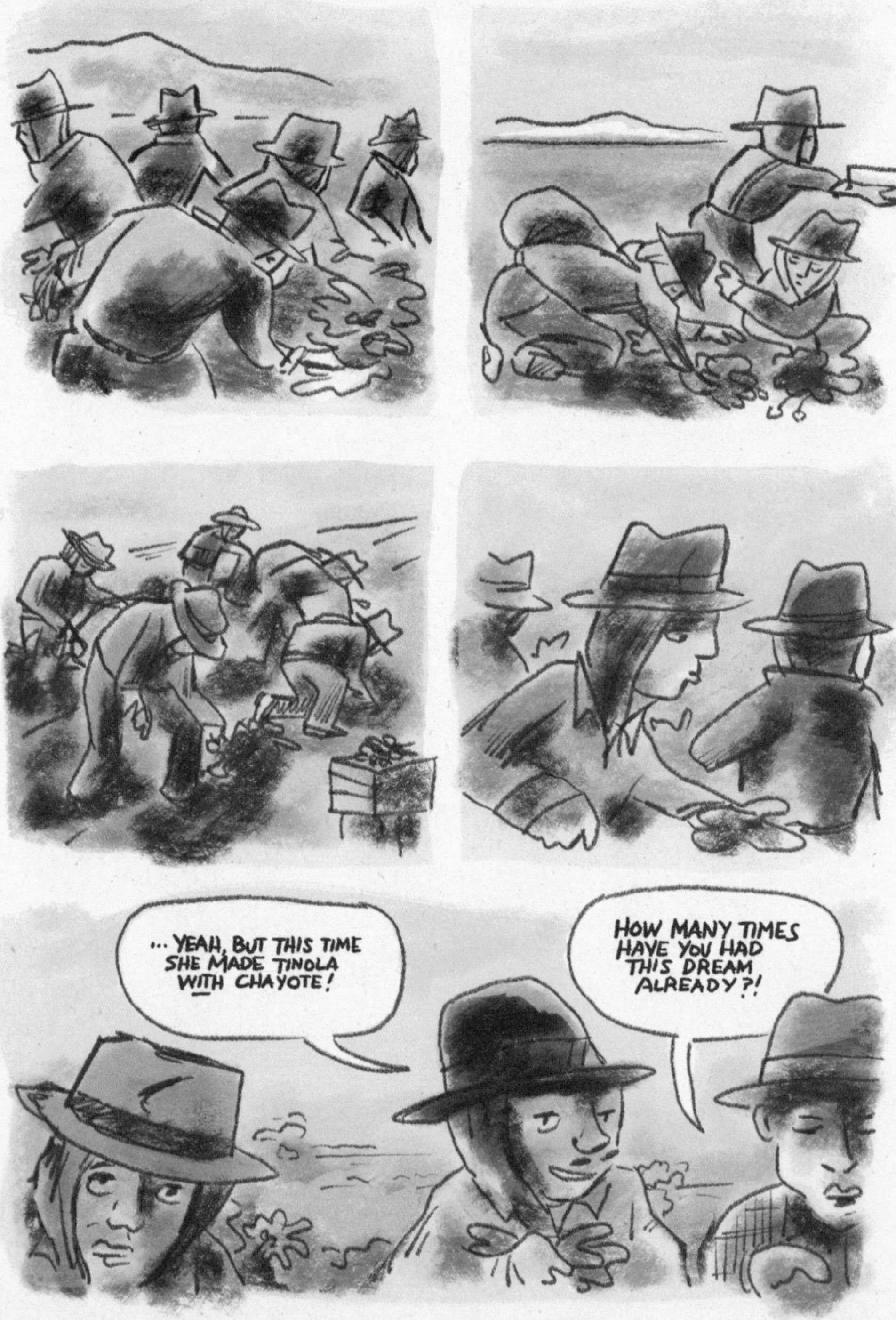
...YEAH, BUT THIS TIME SHE MADE TINOLA WITH CHAYOTE!
HOW MANY TIMES HAVE YOU HAD THIS DREAM ALREADY?!

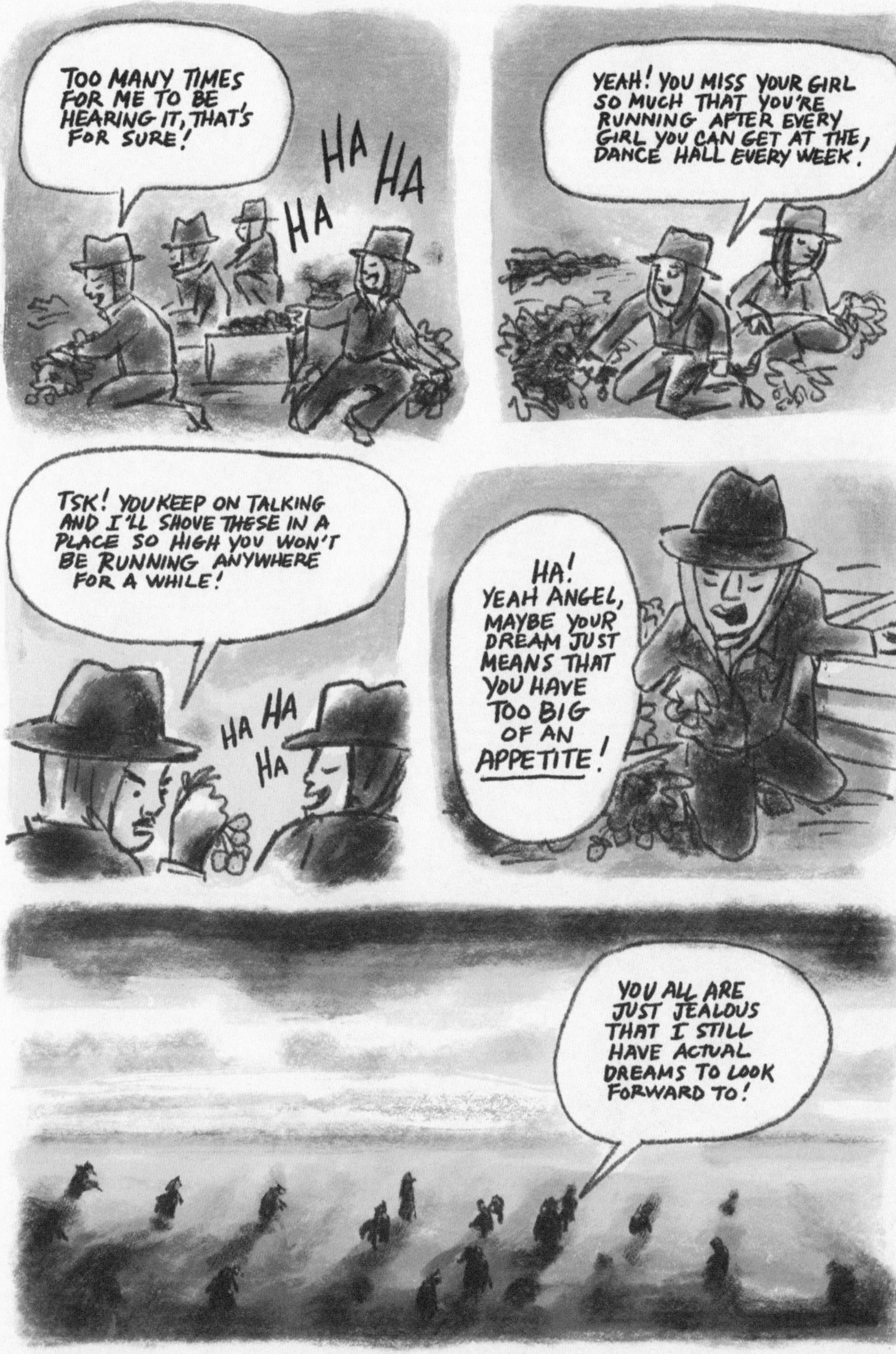
TOO MANY TIMES FOR ME TO BE HEARING IT, THAT'S FOR SURE!
HA HA HA
YEAH! YOU MISS YOUR GIRL SO MUCH THAT YOU'RE RUNNING AFTER EVERY GIRL YOU CAN GET AT THE DANCE HALL EVERY WEEK!
TSK! YOU KEEP ON TALKING AND I'LL SHOVE THESE IN A PLACE SO HIGH YOU WON'T BE RUNNING ANYWHERE FOR A WHILE!
HA HA HA
HA! YEAH ANGEL, MAYBE YOUR DREAM JUST MEANS THAT YOU HAVE TOO BIG OF AN APPETITE!
YOU ALL ARE JUST JEALOUS THAT I STILL HAVE ACTUAL DREAMS TO LOOK FORWARD TO!

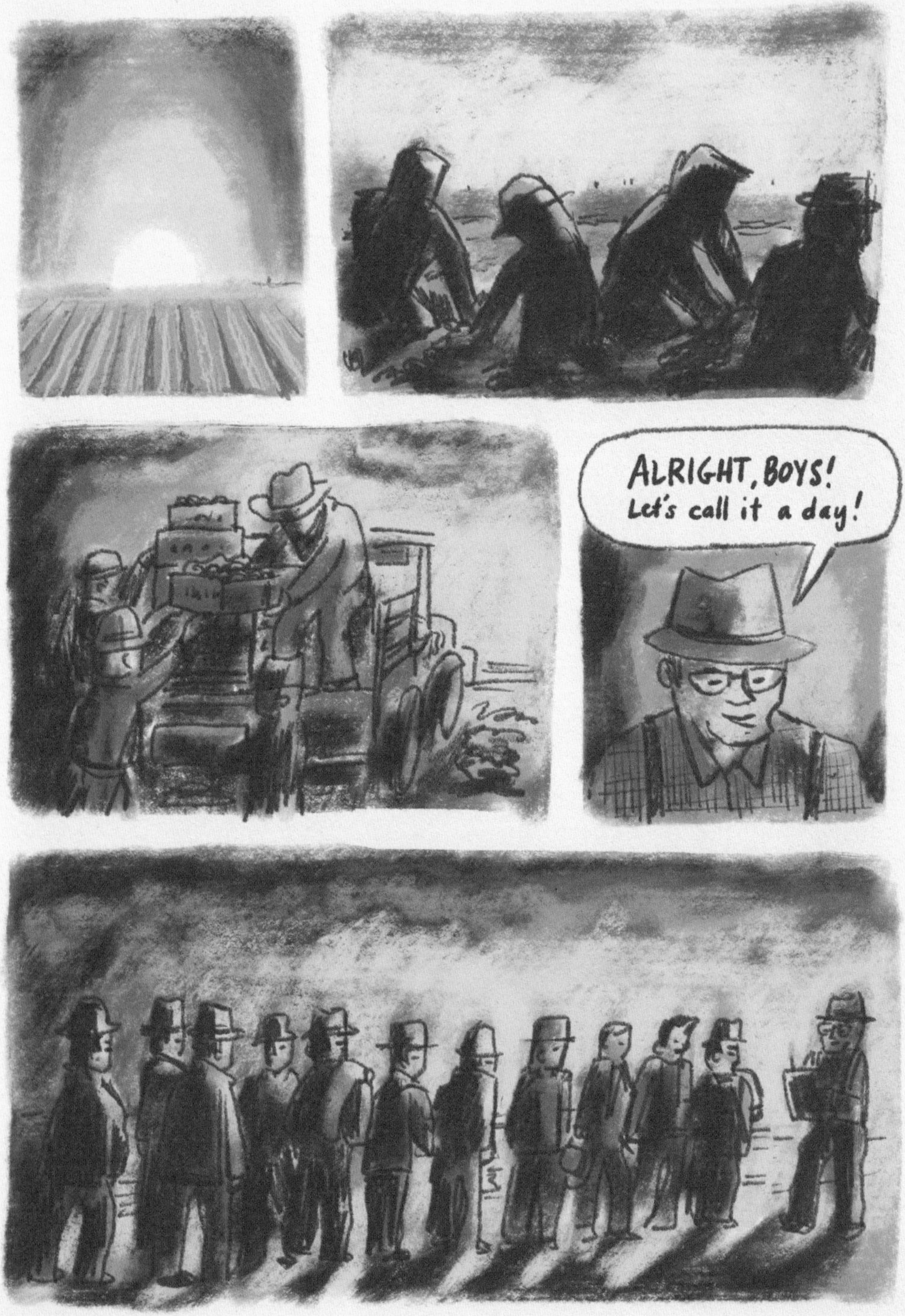
ALRIGHT, BOYS!
Let's call it a day!

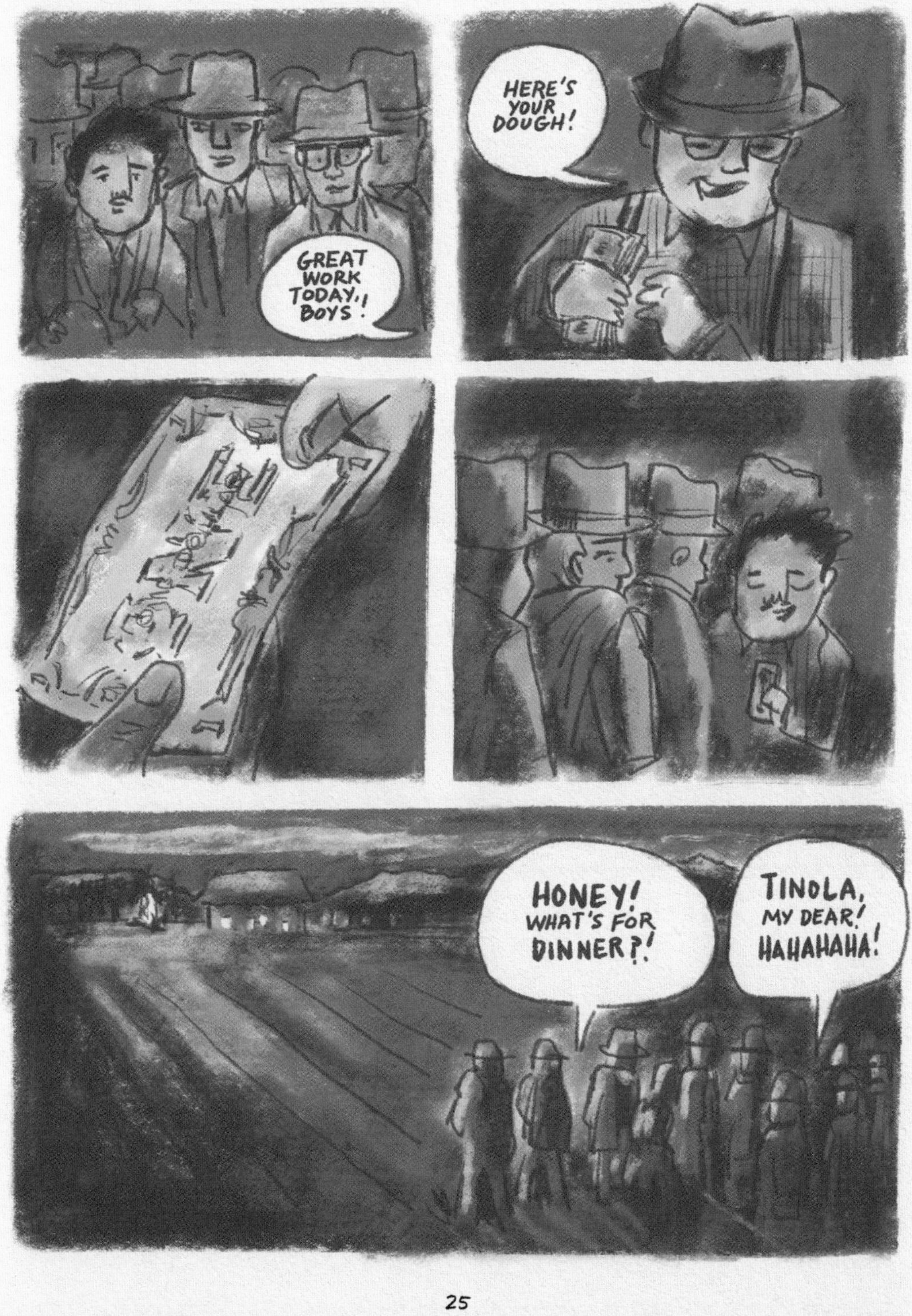
GREAT WORK TODAY, BOYS!
HERE'S YOUR DOUGH!
HONEY! WHAT'S FOR DINNER?!
TINOLA, MY DEAR! HAHAHAHA!

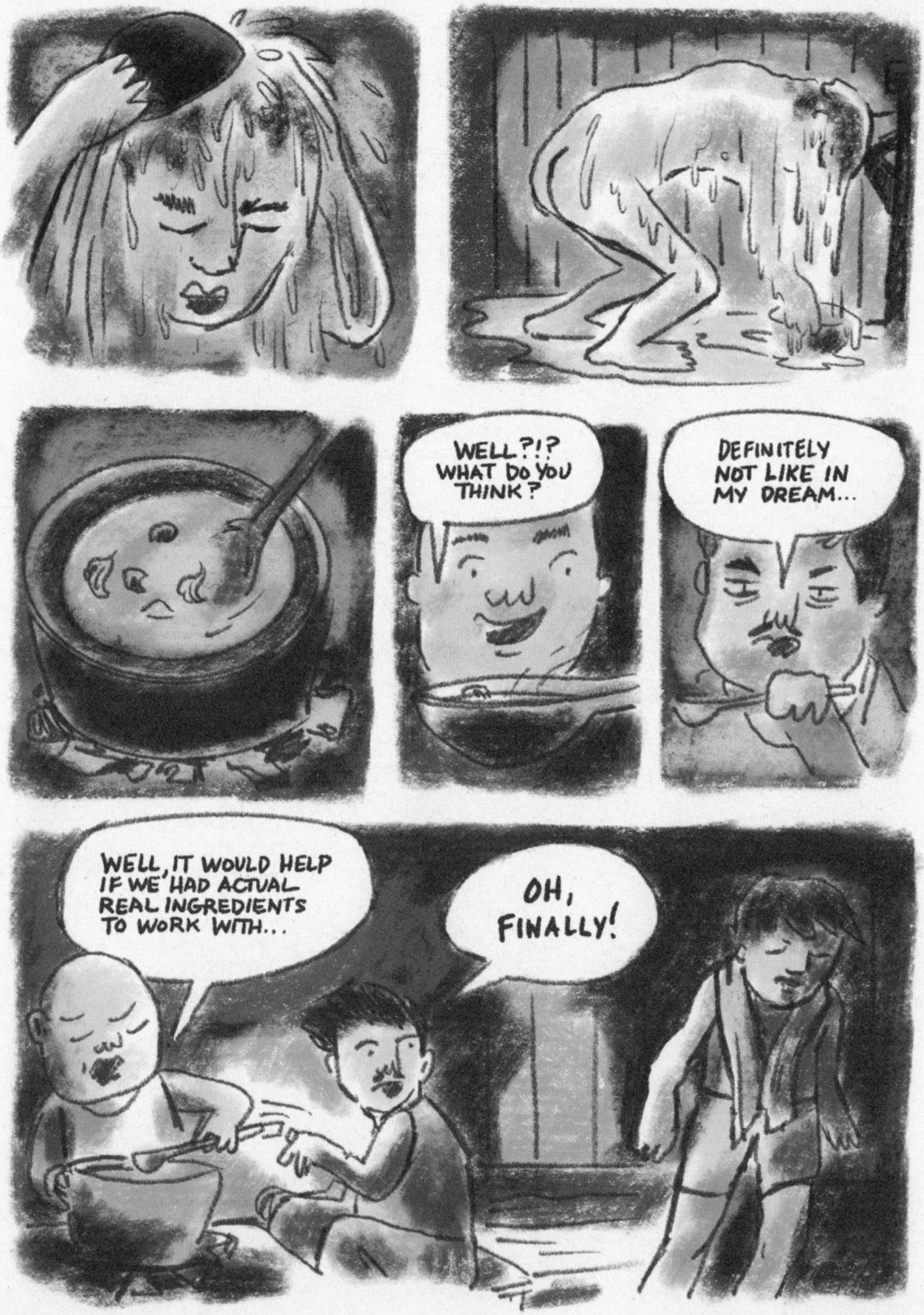
WELL?!? WHAT DO YOU THINK?
DEFINITELY NOT LIKE IN MY DREAM...
WELL, IT WOULD HELP IF WE HAD ACTUAL REAL INGREDIENTS TO WORK WITH...
OH, FINALLY!

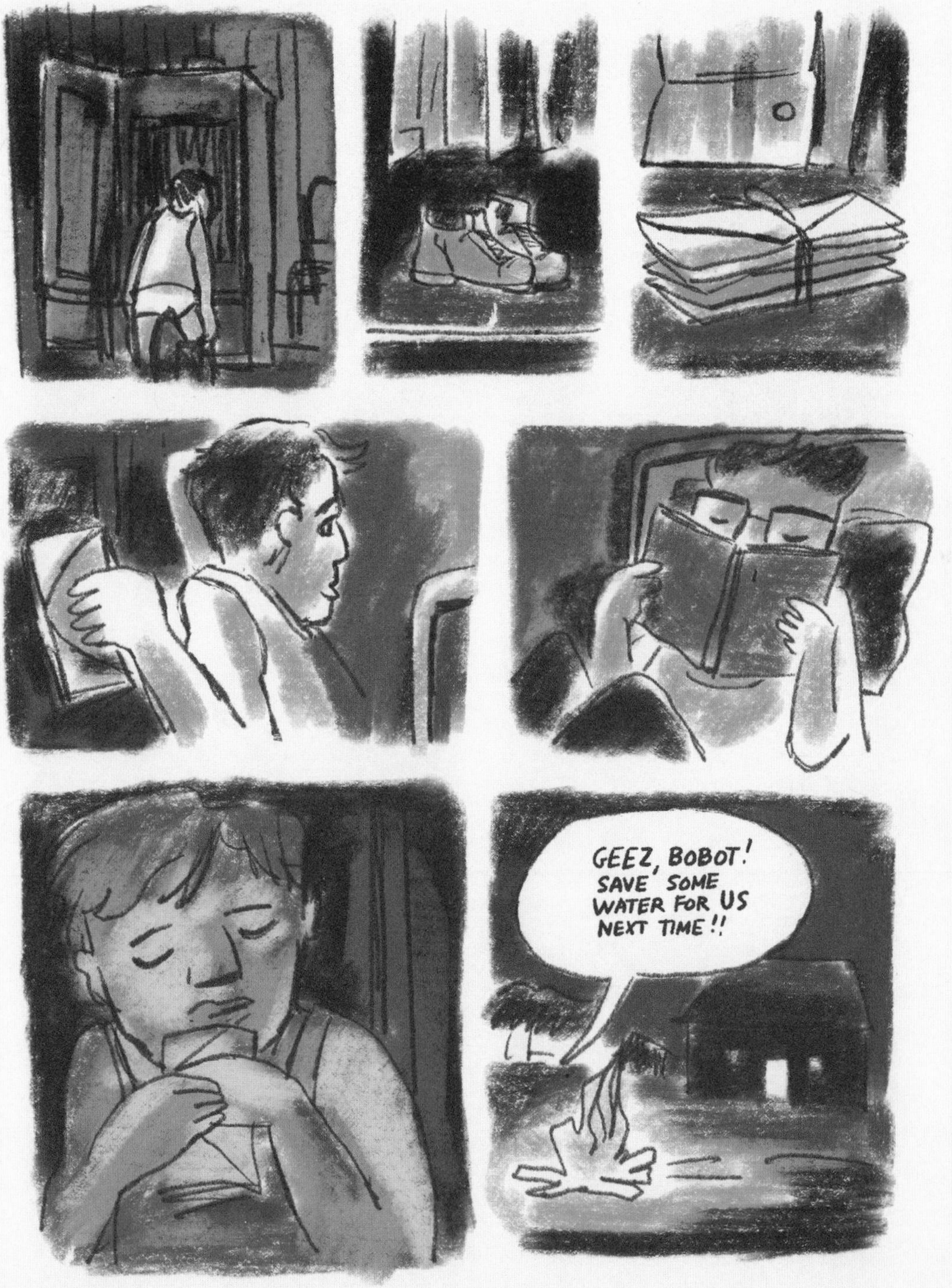
GEEZ, BOBOT! SAVE SOME WATER FOR US NEXT TIME!!

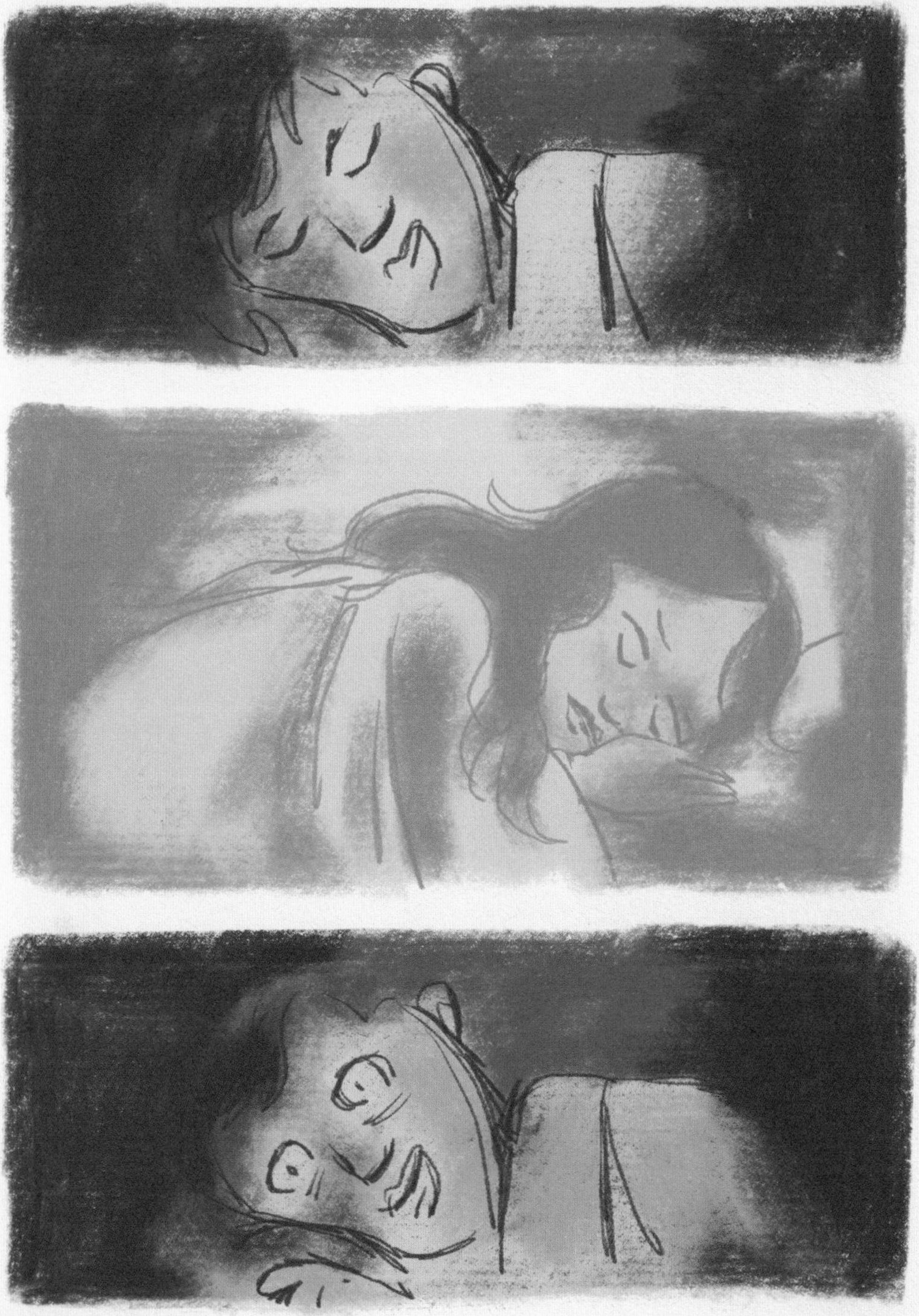

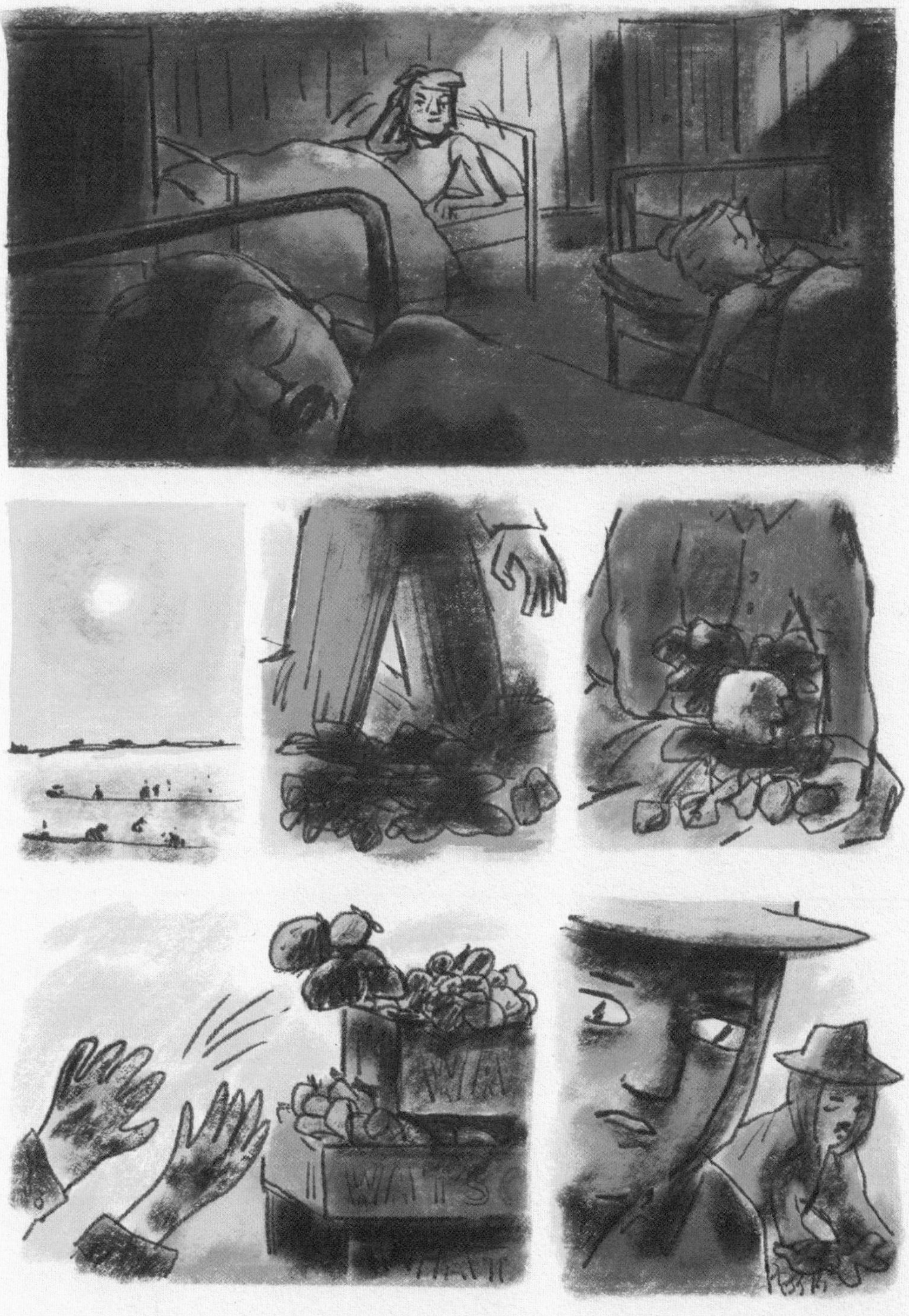

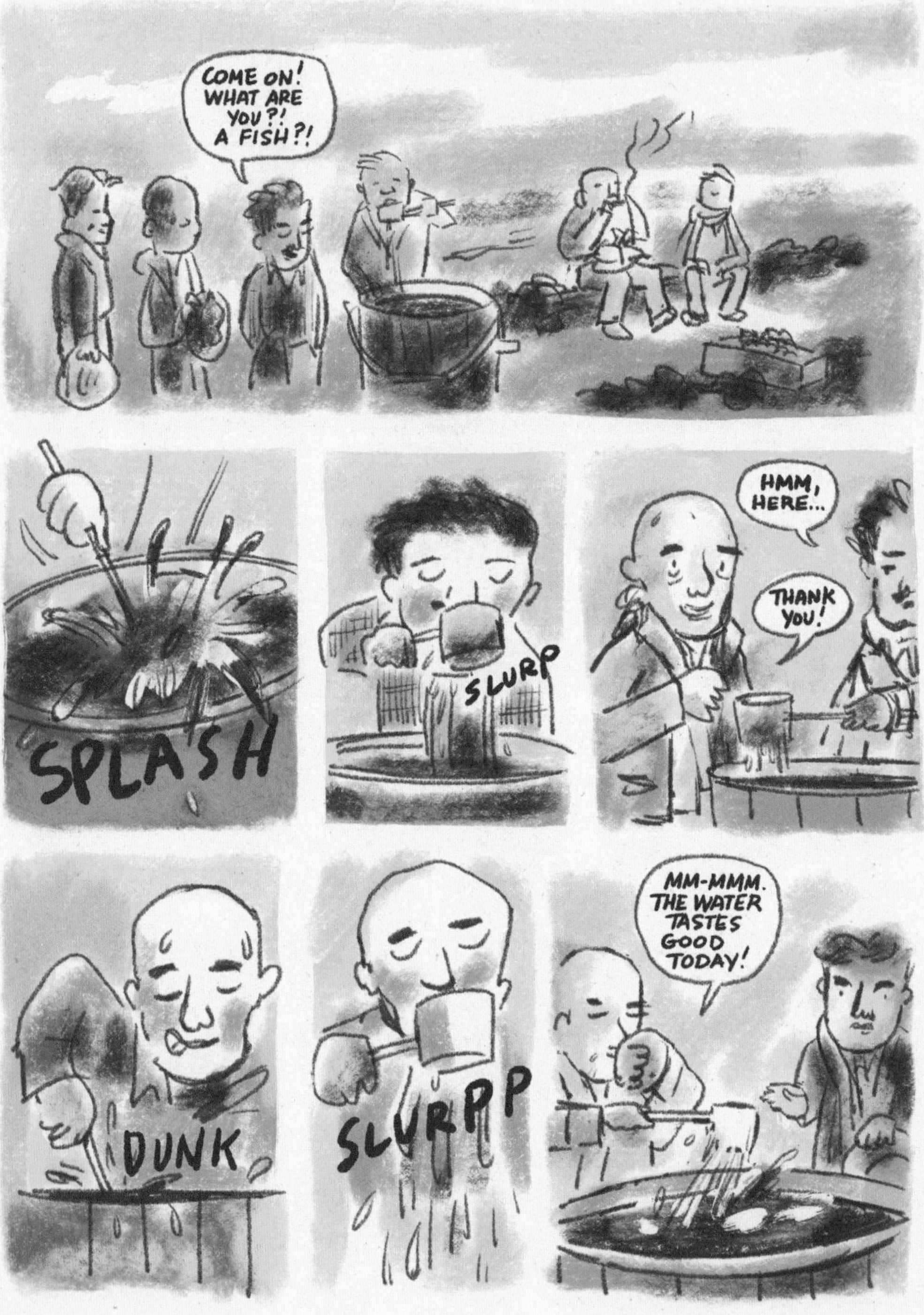
COME ON! WHAT ARE YOU?! A FISH?!
SPLASH
SLURP
HMM, HERE...
THANK YOU!
DUNK
SLURPP
MM-MMM. THE WATER TASTES GOOD TODAY!

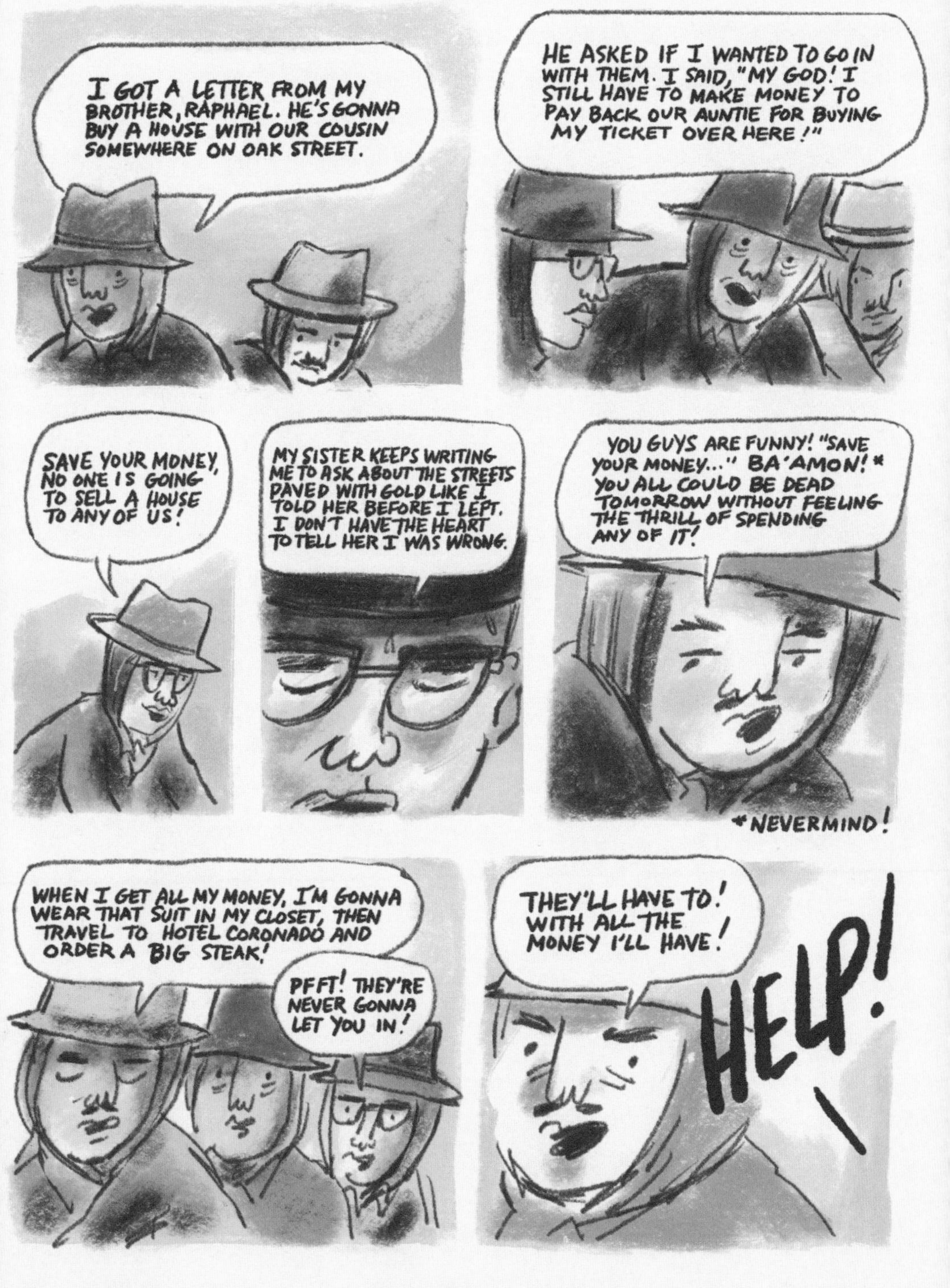
I GOT A LETTER FROM MY BROTHER, RAPHAEL. HE'S GONNA BUY A HOUSE WITH OUR COUSIN SOMEWHERE ON OAK STREET.
HE ASKED IF I WANTED TO GO IN WITH THEM. I SAID, "MY GOD! I STILL HAVE TO MAKE MONEY TO PAY BACK OUR AUNTIE FOR BUYING MY TICKET OVER HERE!"
SAVE YOUR MONEY, NO ONE IS GOING TO SELL A HOUSE TO ANY OF US!
MY SISTER KEEPS WRITING ME TO ASK ABOUT THE STREETS PAVED WITH GOLD LIKE I TOLD HER BEFORE I LEFT. I DON'T HAVE THE HEART TO TELL HER I WAS WRONG.
YOU GUYS ARE FUNNY! "SAVE YOUR MONEY..." BA'AMON! * YOU ALL COULD BE DEAD TOMORROW WITHOUT FEELING THE THRILL OF SPENDING ANY OF IT!
* NEVERMIND!
WHEN I GET ALL MY MONEY, I'M GONNA WEAR THAT SUIT IN MY CLOSET, THEN TRAVEL TO HOTEL CORONADÓ AND ORDER A BIG STEAK!
PFFT! THEY'RE NEVER GONNA LET YOU IN!
THEY'LL HAVE TO! WITH ALL THE MONEY I'LL HAVE!
HELP!

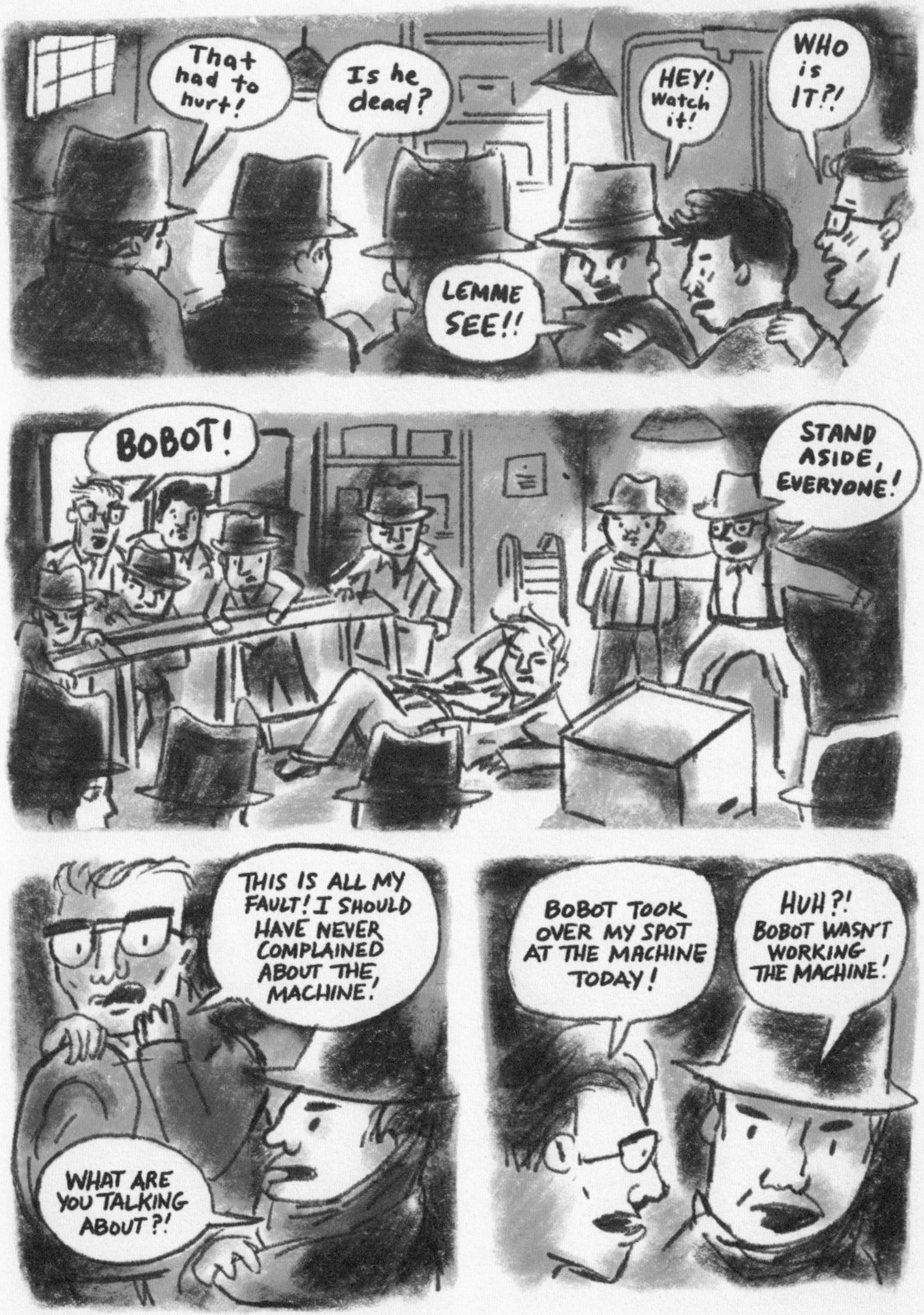
That had to hurt!
Is he dead?
HEY! Watch it!
WHO is IT?!
LEMME SEE!!
BOBOT!
STAND ASIDE, EVERYONE!
THIS IS ALL MY FAULT! I SHOULD HAVE NEVER COMPLAINED ABOUT THE MACHINE!
WHAT ARE YOU TALKING ABOUT?!
BOBOT TOOK OVER MY SPOT AT THE MACHINE TODAY!
HUH?! BOBOT WASN'T WORKING THE MACHINE!

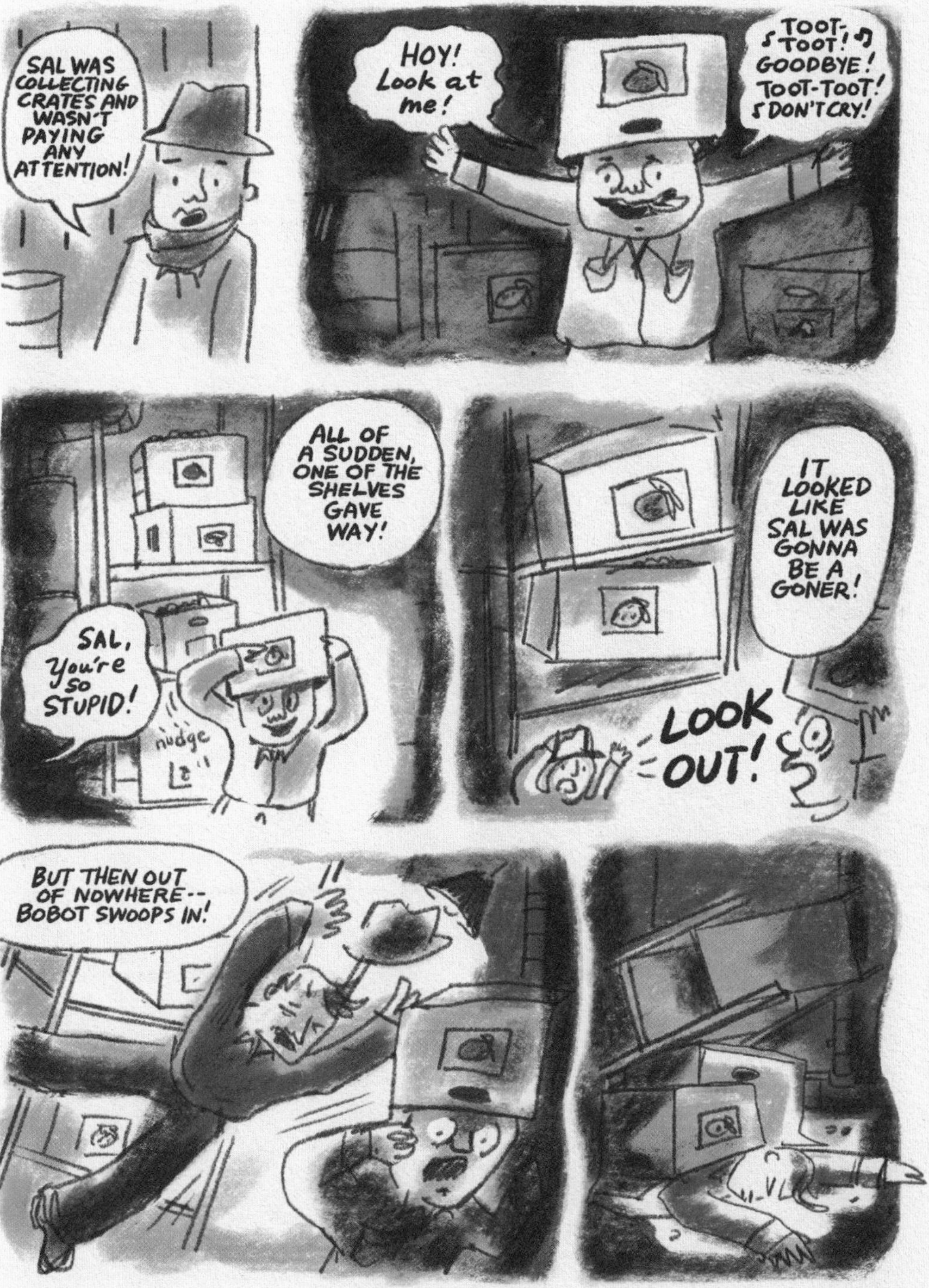

SAL WAS COLLECTING CRATES AND WASN'T PAYING ANY ATTENTION!
HOY! Look at me!
TOOT-TOOT! GOODBYE! TOOT-TOOT! DON'T CRY!
ALL OF A SUDDEN, ONE OF THE SHELVES GAVE WAY!
SAL, You're so STUPID!
nudge
IT LOOKED LIKE SAL WAS GONNA BE A GONER!
LOOK OUT!
BUT THEN OUT OF NOWHERE-- BOBOT SWOOPS IN!

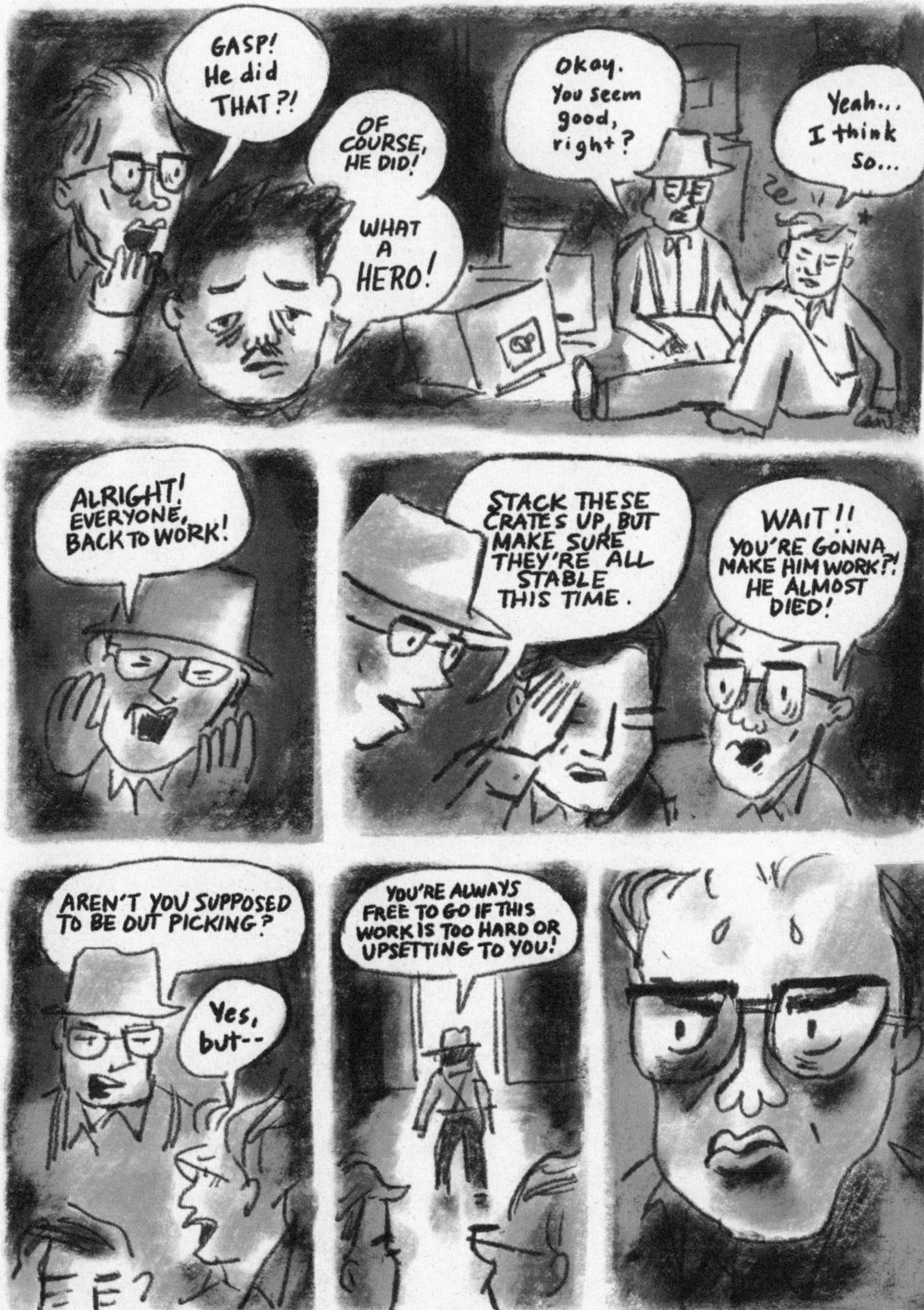
GASP! He did THAT?!
OF COURSE, HE DID!
WHAT A HERO!
Okay. You seem good, right?
Yeah... I think so...
ALRIGHT! EVERYONE, BACK TO WORK!
STACK THESE CRATES UP, BUT MAKE SURE THEY'RE ALL STABLE THIS TIME.
WAIT!! YOU'RE GONNA MAKE HIM WORK?! HE ALMOST DIED!
AREN'T YOU SUPPOSED TO BE OUT PICKING?
Yes, but--
YOU'RE ALWAYS FREE TO GO IF THIS WORK IS TOO HARD OR UPSETTING TO YOU!

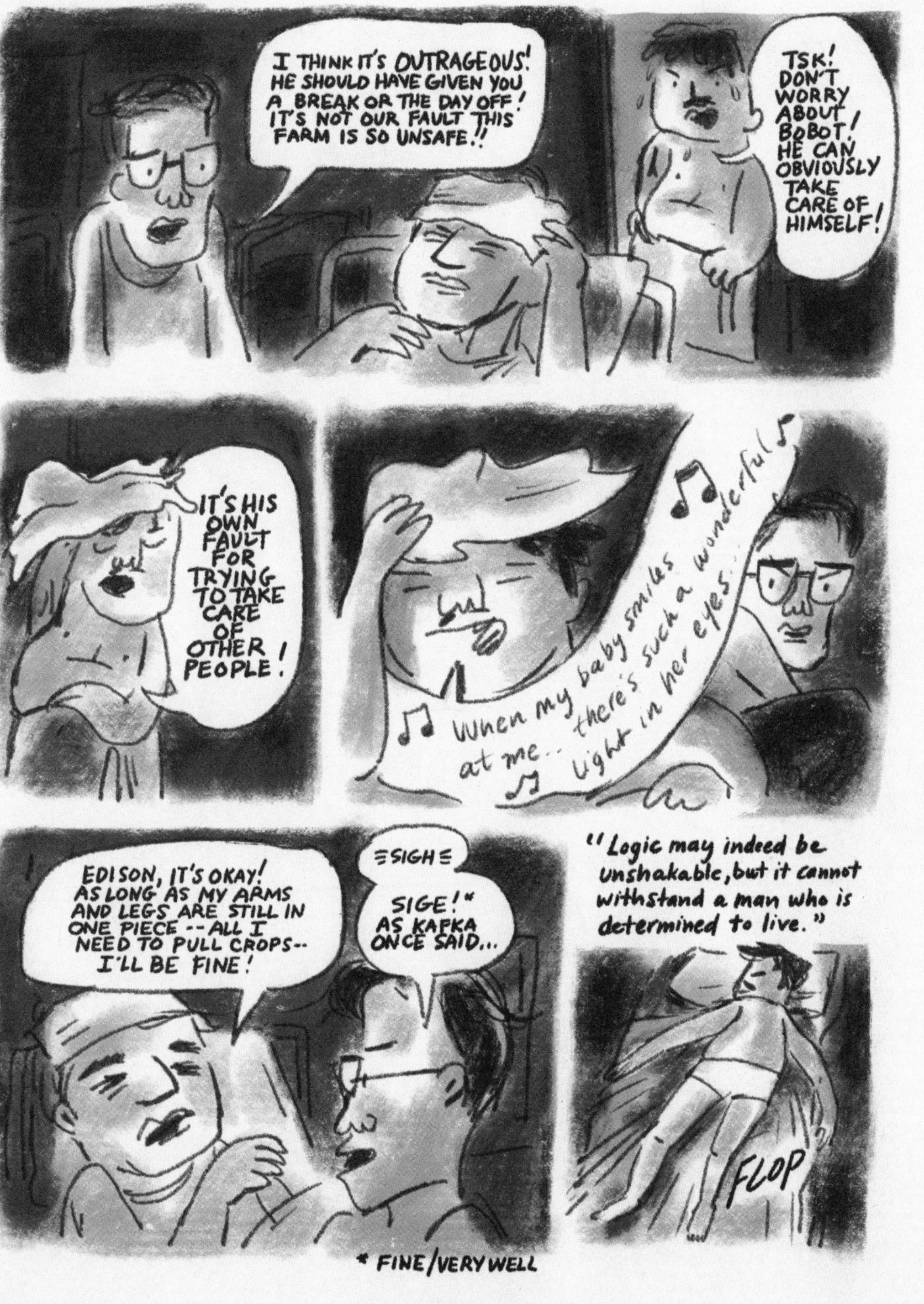
I THINK IT'S OUTRAGEOUS! HE SHOULD HAVE GIVEN YOU A BREAK OR THE DAY OFF! IT'S NOT OUR FAULT THIS FARM IS SO UNSAFE!!
TSK! DON'T WORRY ABOUT BOBOT! HE CAN OBVIOUSLY TAKE CARE OF HIMSELF!
IT'S HIS OWN FAULT FOR TRYING TO TAKE CARE OF OTHER PEOPLE!
♫ When my baby smiles at me... there's such a wonderful ♫ light in her eyes... ♫
EDISON, IT'S OKAY! AS LONG AS MY ARMS AND LEGS ARE STILL IN ONE PIECE -- ALL I NEED TO PULL CROPS -- I'LL BE FINE!
≡SIGH≡
SIGE!* AS KAFKA ONCE SAID...
"Logic may indeed be unshakable, but it cannot withstand a man who is determined to live."
FLOP
* FINE/VERY WELL

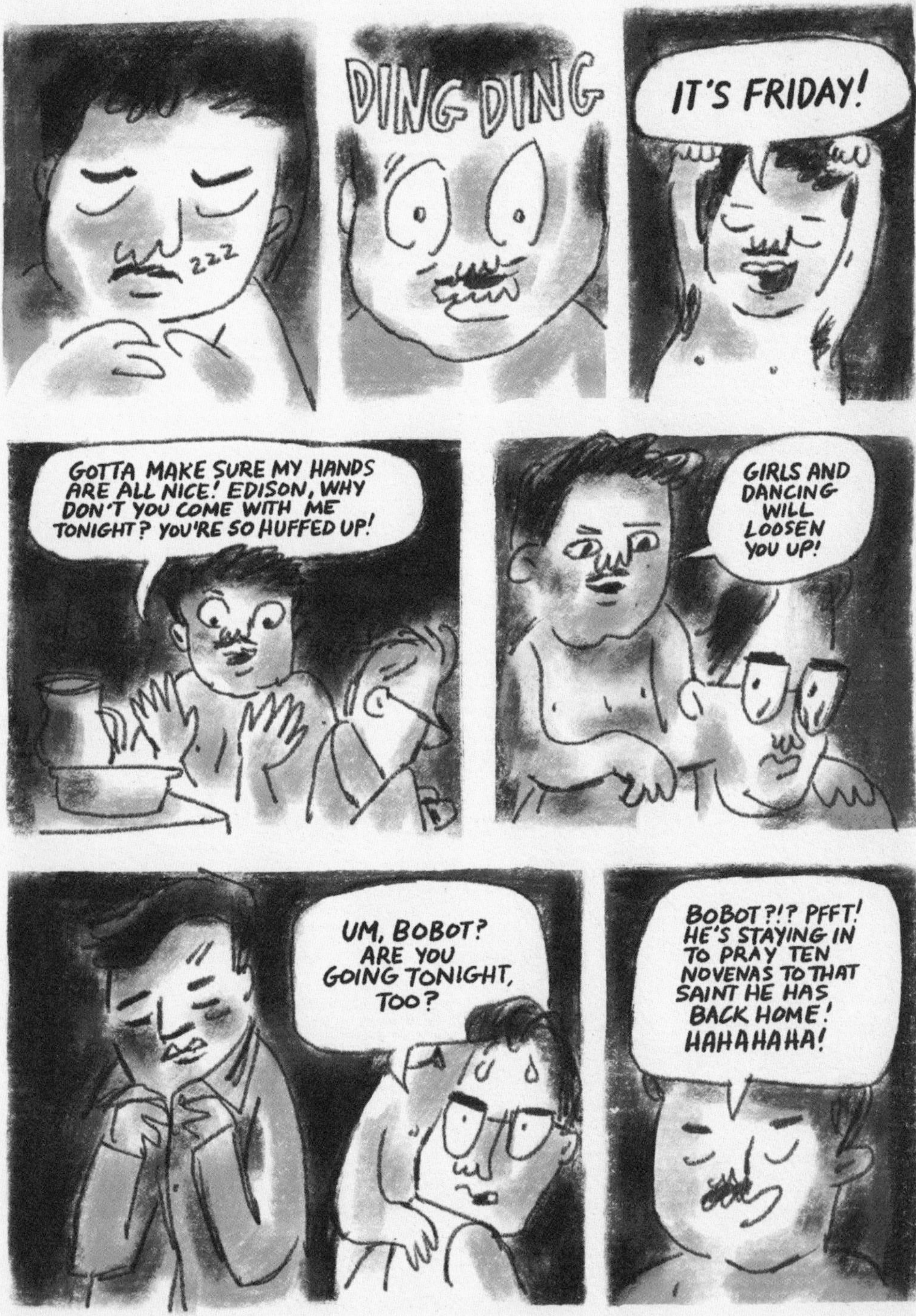
zzz
DING DING
IT'S FRIDAY!
GOTTA MAKE SURE MY HANDS ARE ALL NICE! EDISON, WHY DON'T YOU COME WITH ME TONIGHT? YOU'RE SO HUFFED UP!
GIRLS AND DANCING WILL LOOSEN YOU UP!
UM, BOBOT? ARE YOU GOING TONIGHT, TOO?
BOBOT?!? PFFT! HE'S STAYING IN TO PRAY TEN NOVENAS TO THAT SAINT HE HAS BACK HOME! HAHAHAHA!

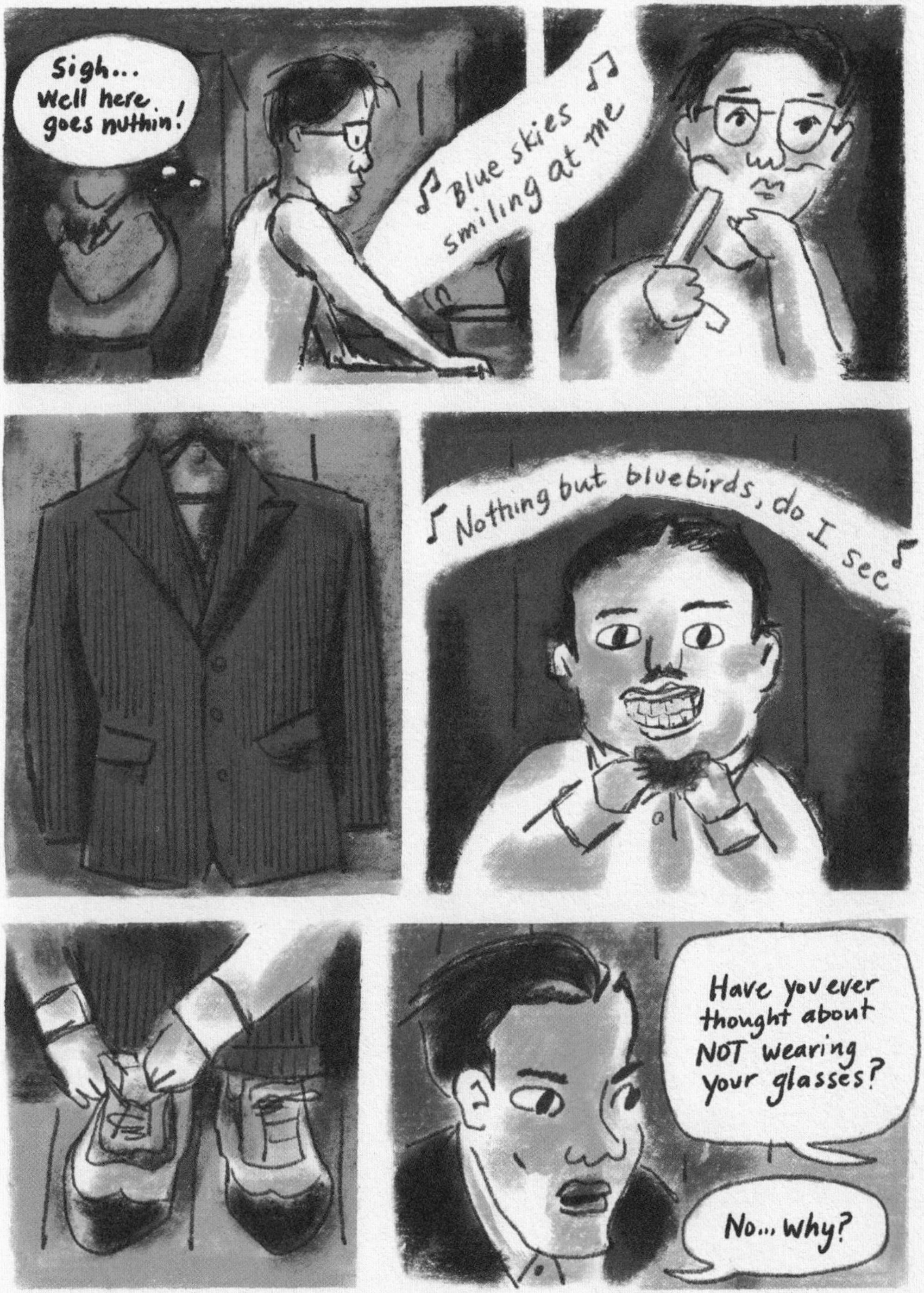
Sigh... Well here goes nuthin!
♪ Blue skies smiling at me ♪
♪ Nothing but bluebirds, do I see ♪
Have you ever thought about NOT wearing your glasses?
No... Why?

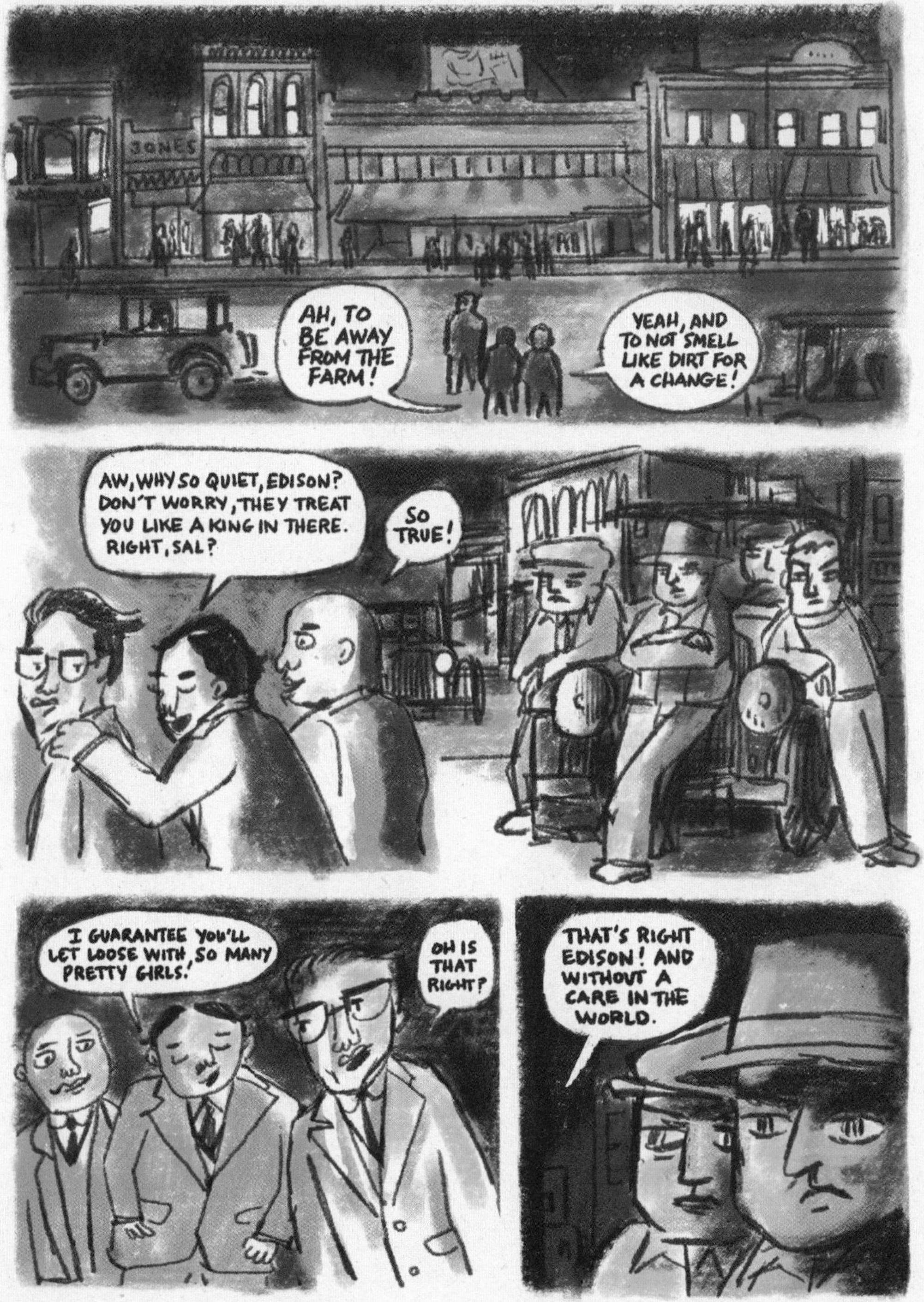
JONES
AH, TO BE AWAY FROM THE FARM!
YEAH, AND TO NOT SMELL LIKE DIRT FOR A CHANGE!
AW, WHY SO QUIET, EDISON? DON'T WORRY, THEY TREAT YOU LIKE A KING IN THERE. RIGHT, SAL?
SO TRUE!
I GUARANTEE YOU'LL LET LOOSE WITH SO MANY PRETTY GIRLS!
OH IS THAT RIGHT?
THAT'S RIGHT EDISON! AND WITHOUT A CARE IN THE WORLD.

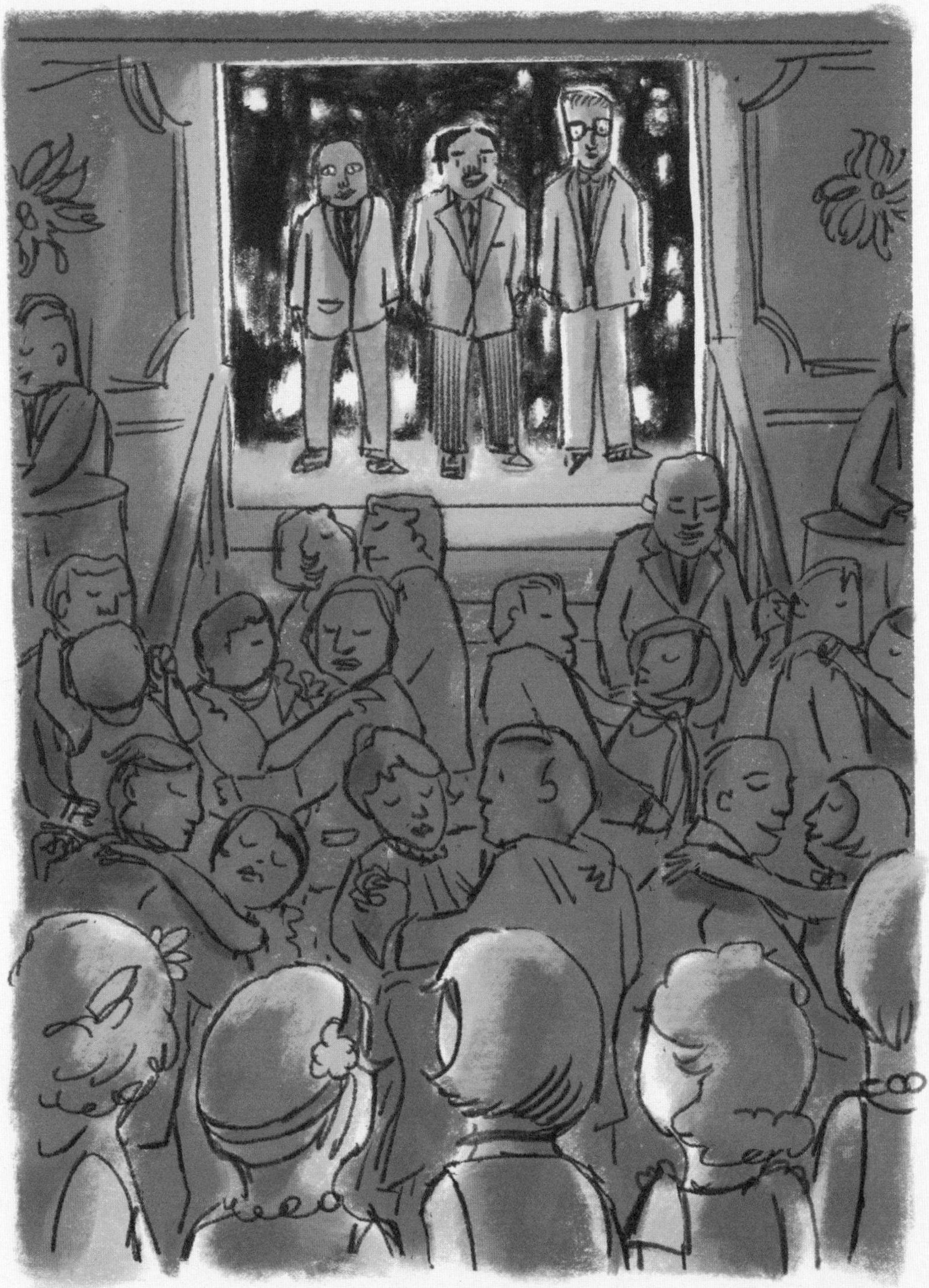

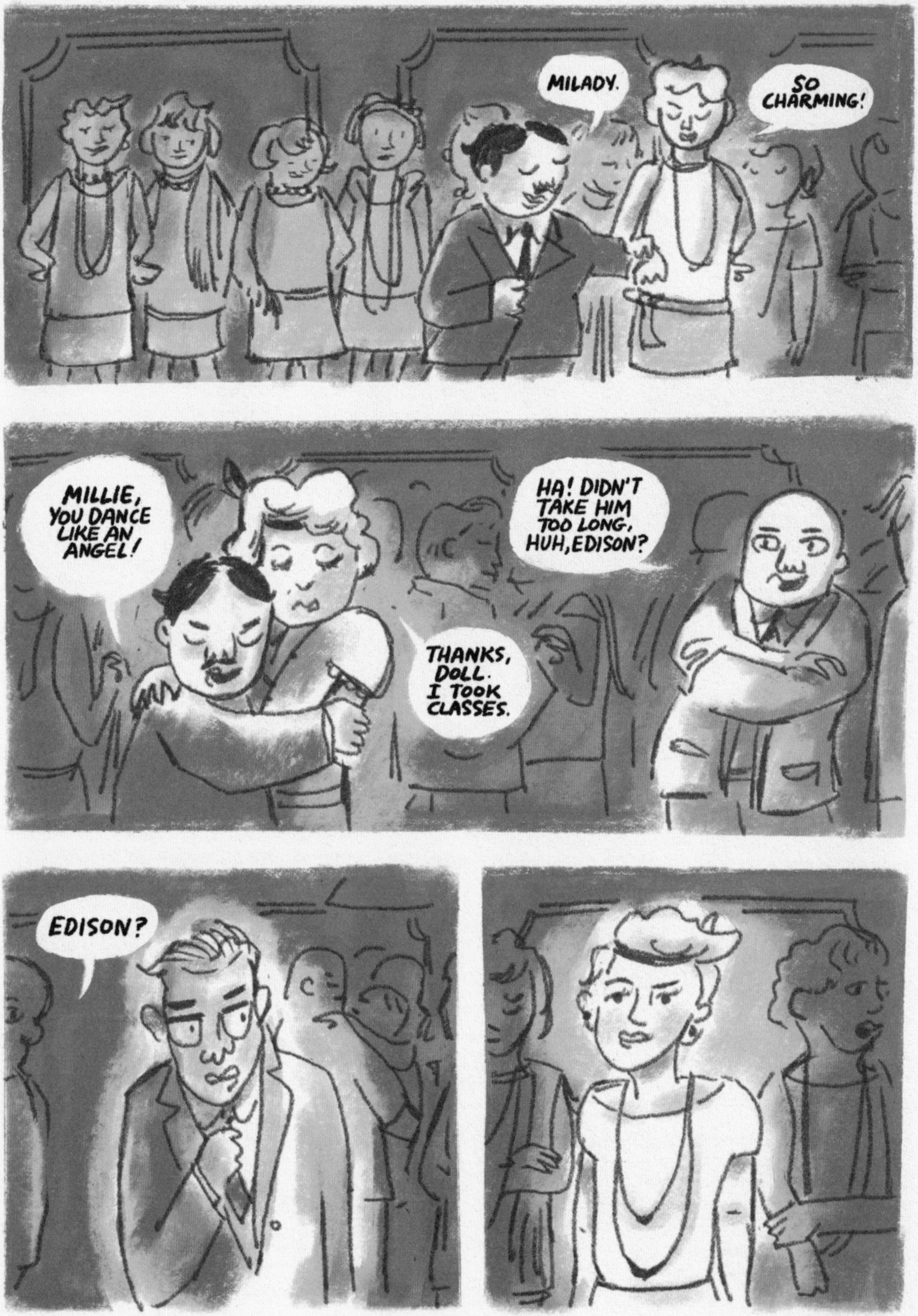
MILADY.
SO CHARMING!
MILLIE, YOU DANCE LIKE AN ANGEL!
THANKS, DOLL. I TOOK CLASSES.
HA! DIDN'T TAKE HIM TOO LONG, HUH, EDISON?
EDISON?

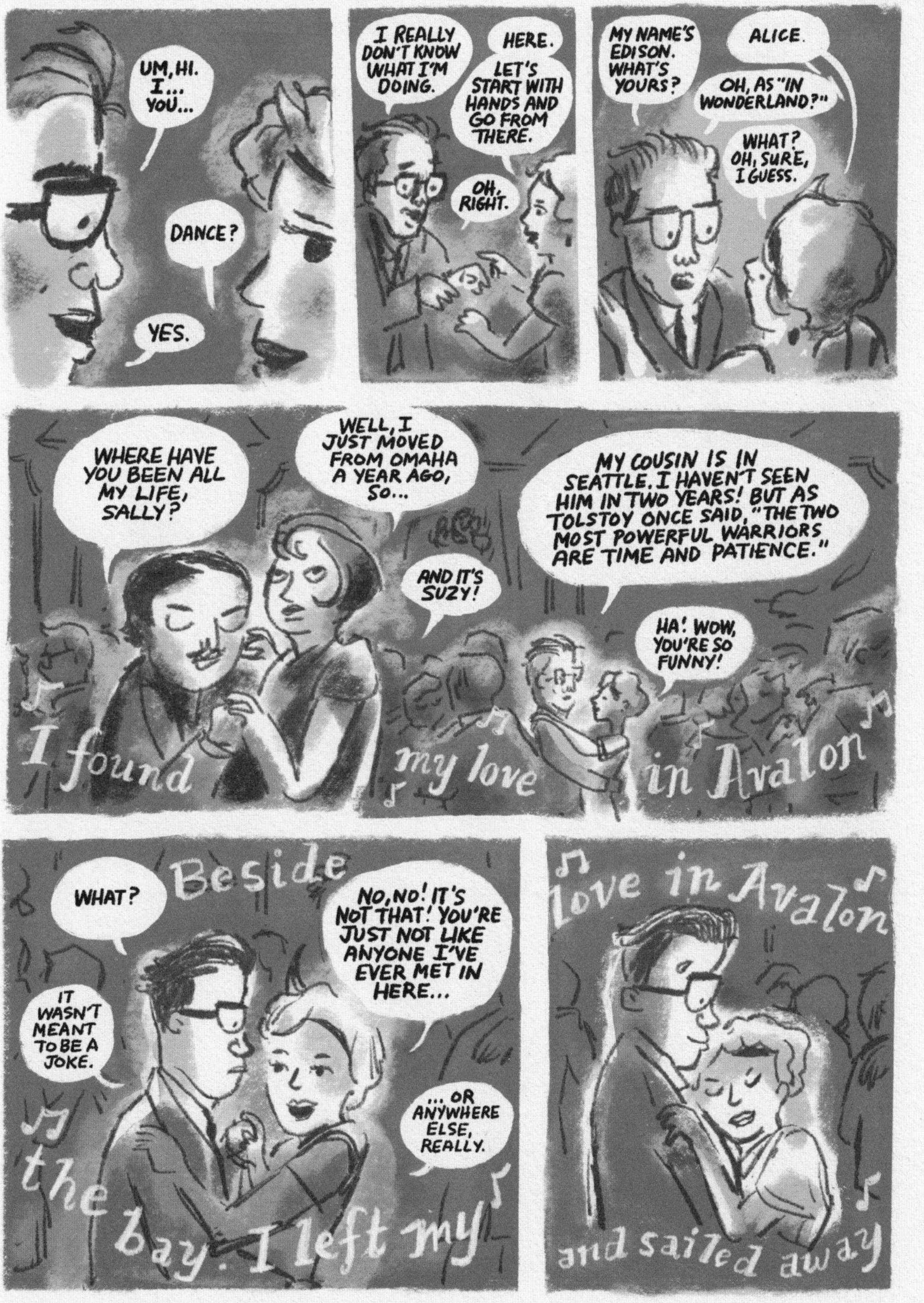

UM, HI. I... YOU...
DANCE?
YES.
I REALLY DON'T KNOW WHAT I'M DOING.
HERE.
LET'S START WITH HANDS AND GO FROM THERE.
OH. RIGHT.
MY NAME'S EDISON. WHAT'S YOURS?
ALICE.
OH, AS "IN WONDERLAND?"
WHAT? OH, SURE, I GUESS.
WHERE HAVE YOU BEEN ALL MY LIFE, SALLY?
WELL, I JUST MOVED FROM OMAHA A YEAR AGO, SO...
AND IT'S SUZY!
MY COUSIN IS IN SEATTLE. I HAVEN'T SEEN HIM IN TWO YEARS! BUT AS TOLSTOY ONCE SAID, "THE TWO MOST POWERFUL WARRIORS ARE TIME AND PATIENCE."
HA! WOW, YOU'RE SO FUNNY!
I found my love in Avalon
WHAT?
Beside
IT WASN'T MEANT TO BE A JOKE.
NO, NO! IT'S NOT THAT! YOU'RE JUST NOT LIKE ANYONE I'VE EVER MET IN HERE...
... OR ANYWHERE ELSE, REALLY.
the bay. I left my
love in Avalon
and sailed away

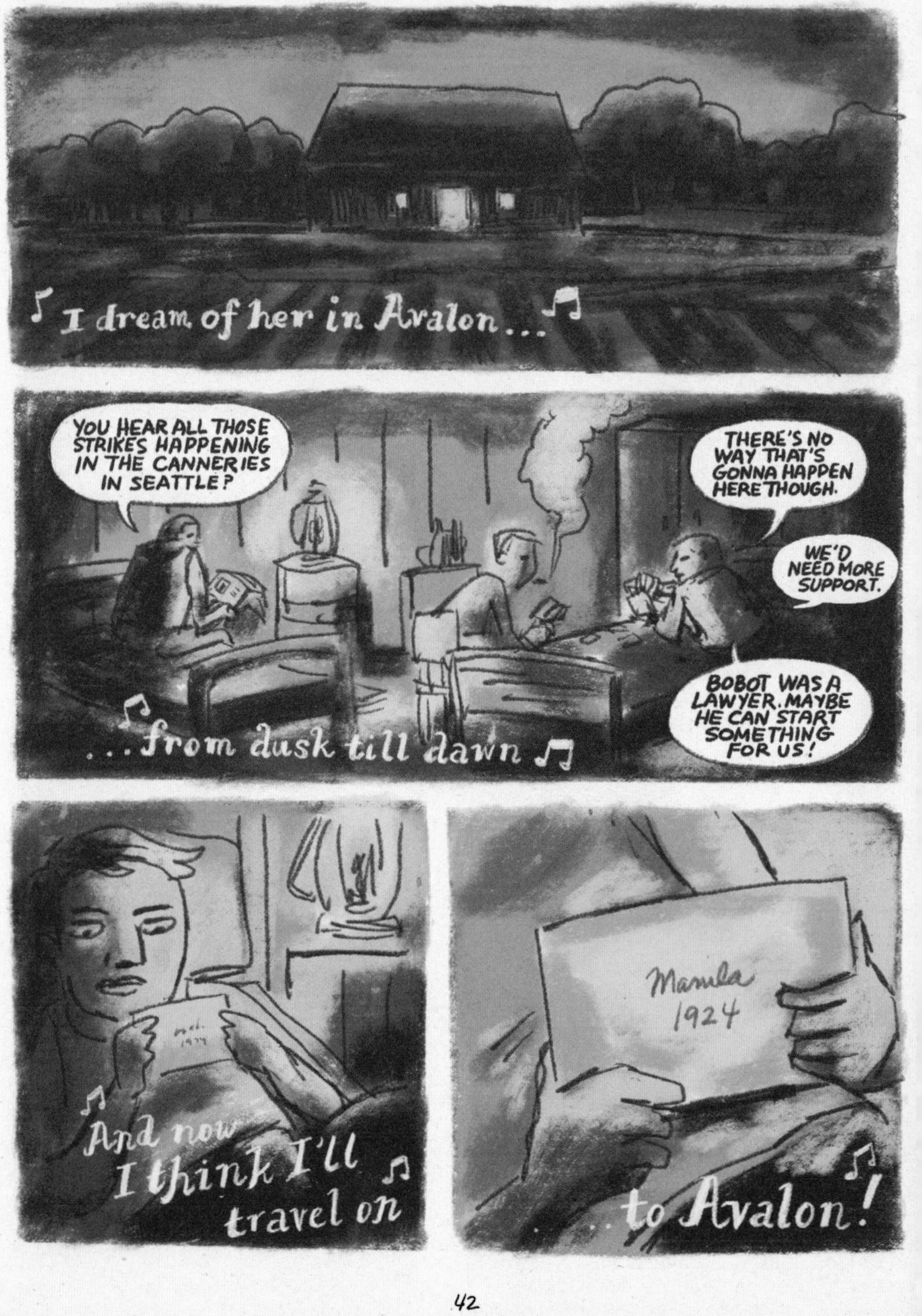
I dream of her in Avalon...
YOU HEAR ALL THOSE STRIKES HAPPENING IN THE CANNERIES IN SEATTLE?
THERE'S NO WAY THAT'S GONNA HAPPEN HERE THOUGH.
WE'D NEED MORE SUPPORT.
BOBOT WAS A LAWYER. MAYBE HE CAN START SOMETHING FOR US!
...from dusk till dawn
And now I think I'll travel on
Manila 1924
...to Avalon!

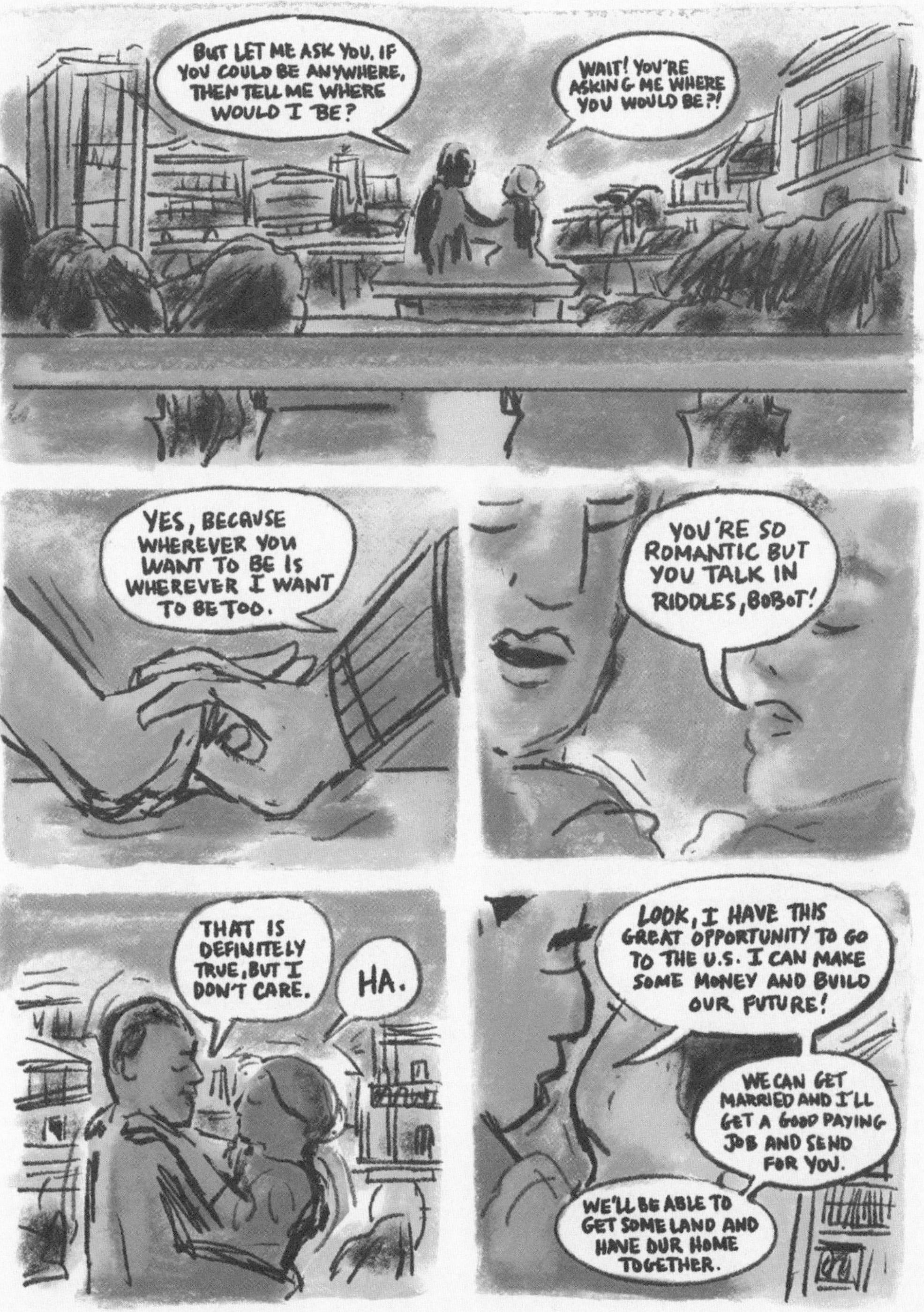
BUT LET ME ASK YOU. IF YOU COULD BE ANYWHERE, THEN TELL ME WHERE WOULD I BE?
WAIT! YOU'RE ASKING ME WHERE YOU WOULD BE?!
YES, BECAUSE WHEREVER YOU WANT TO BE IS WHEREVER I WANT TO BE TOO.
YOU'RE SO ROMANTIC BUT YOU TALK IN RIDDLES, BOBOT!
THAT IS DEFINITELY TRUE, BUT I DON'T CARE.
HA.
LOOK, I HAVE THIS GREAT OPPORTUNITY TO GO TO THE U.S. I CAN MAKE SOME MONEY AND BUILD OUR FUTURE!
WE CAN GET MARRIED AND I'LL GET A GOOD PAYING JOB AND SEND FOR YOU.
WE'LL BE ABLE TO GET SOME LAND AND HAVE OUR HOME TOGETHER.

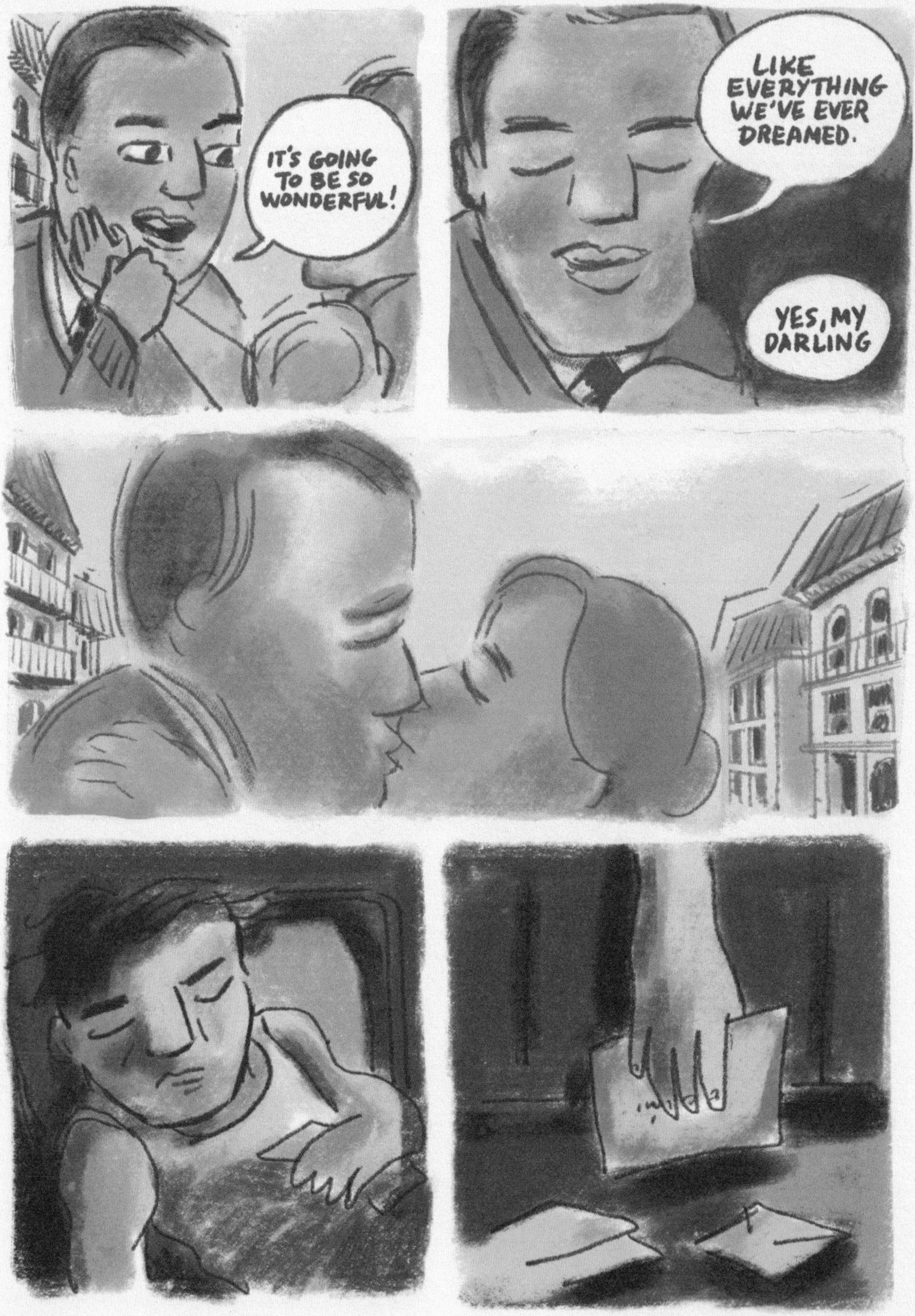
IT'S GOING TO BE SO WONDERFUL!
LIKE EVERYTHING WE'VE EVER DREAMED.
YES, MY DARLING

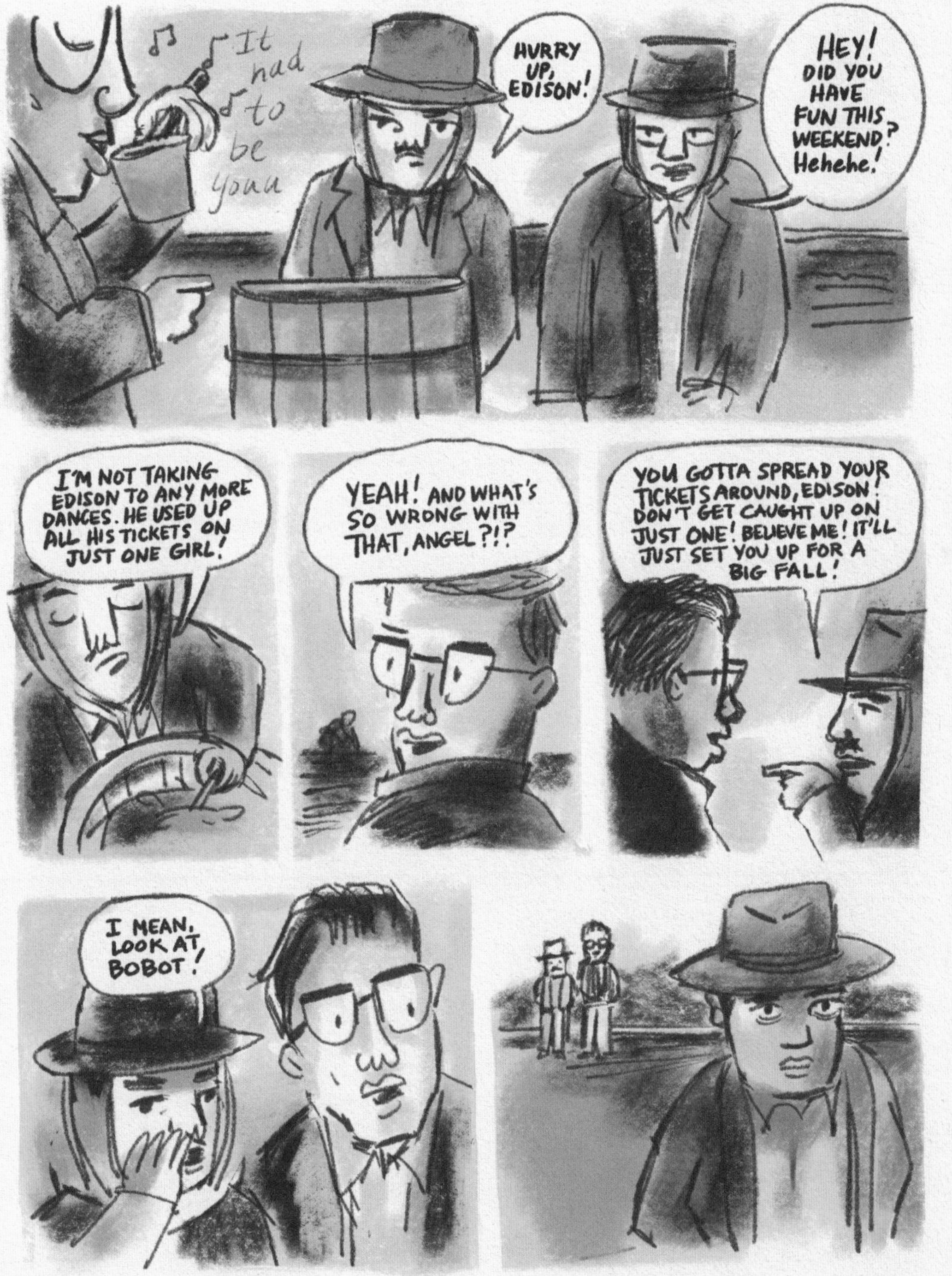
It had to be youu
HURRY UP, EDISON!
HEY! DID YOU HAVE FUN THIS WEEKEND? Hehehe!
I'M NOT TAKING EDISON TO ANY MORE DANCES. HE USED UP ALL HIS TICKETS ON JUST ONE GIRL!
YEAH! AND WHAT'S SO WRONG WITH THAT, ANGEL?!?
YOU GOTTA SPREAD YOUR TICKETS AROUND, EDISON! DON'T GET CAUGHT UP ON JUST ONE! BELIEVE ME! IT'LL JUST SET YOU UP FOR A BIG FALL!
I MEAN, LOOK AT BOBOT!

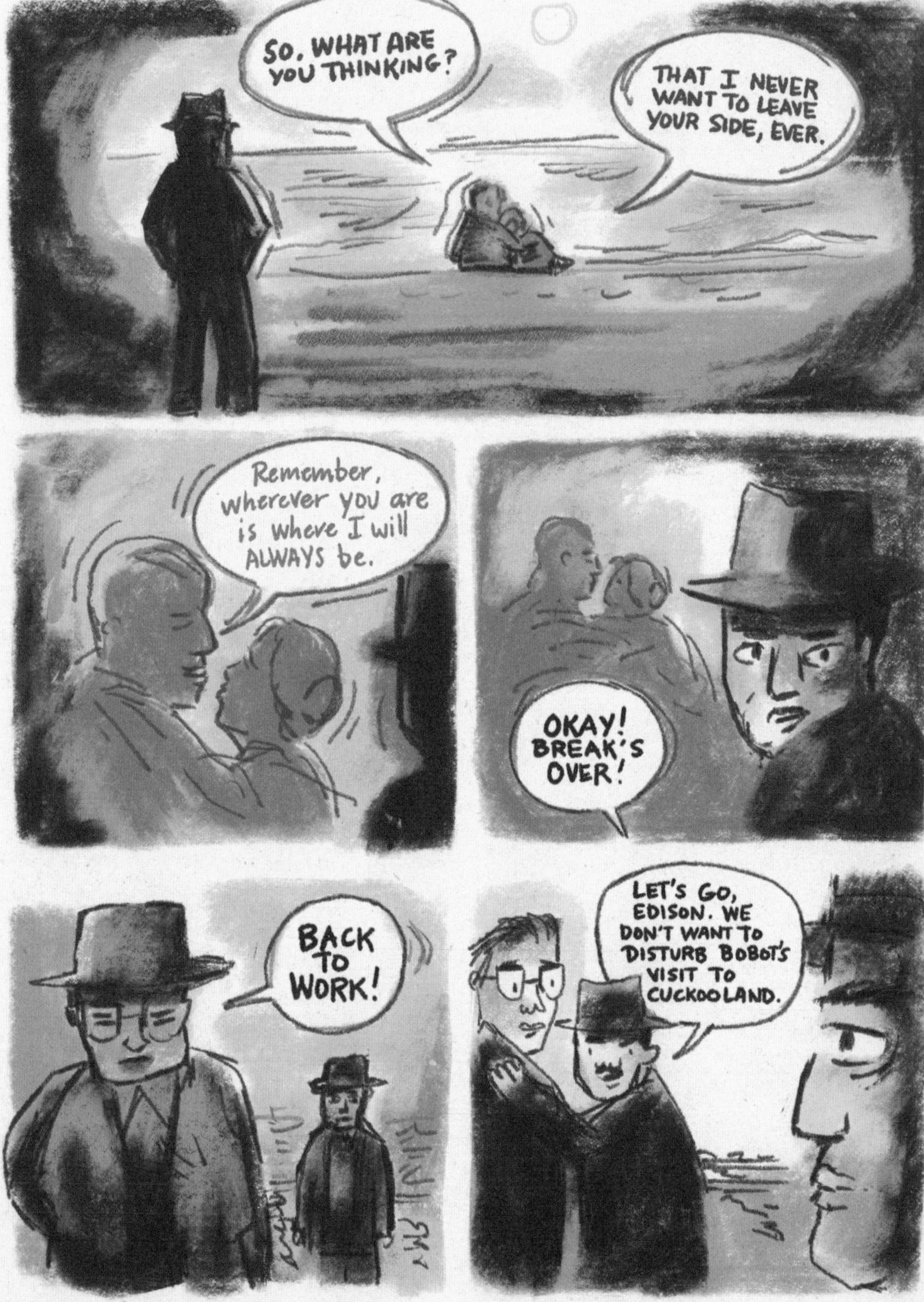
SO, WHAT ARE YOU THINKING?
THAT I NEVER WANT TO LEAVE YOUR SIDE, EVER.
Remember, wherever you are is where I will ALWAYS be.
OKAY! BREAK'S OVER!
BACK TO WORK!
LET'S GO, EDISON. WE DON'T WANT TO DISTURB BOBOT'S VISIT TO CUCKOOLAND.

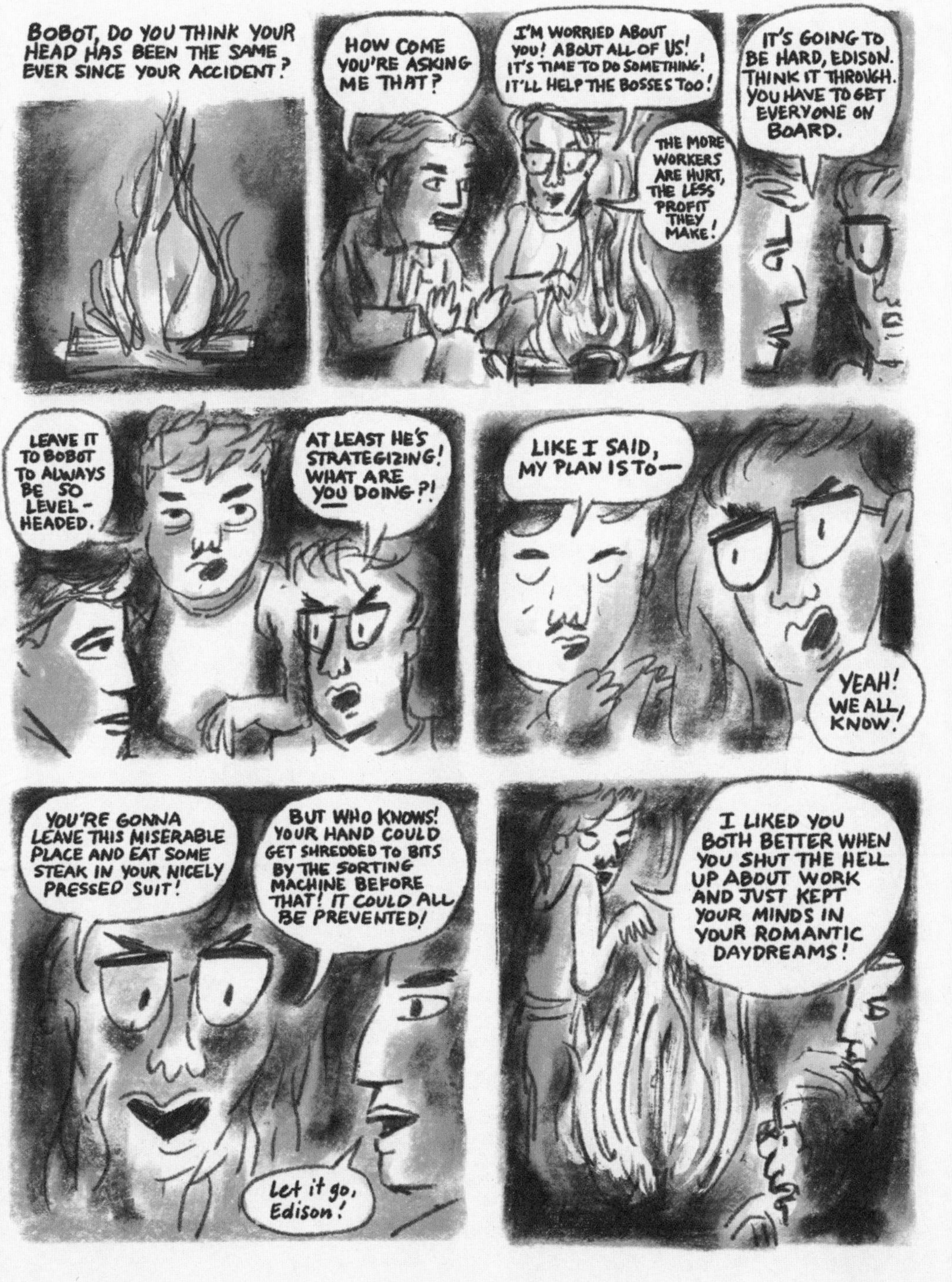
BOBOT, DO YOU THINK YOUR HEAD HAS BEEN THE SAME EVER SINCE YOUR ACCIDENT?
HOW COME YOU'RE ASKING ME THAT?
I'M WORRIED ABOUT YOU! ABOUT ALL OF US! IT'S TIME TO DO SOMETHING! IT'LL HELP THE BOSSES TOO!
THE MORE WORKERS ARE HURT, THE LESS PROFIT THEY MAKE!
IT'S GOING TO BE HARD, EDISON. THINK IT THROUGH. YOU HAVE TO GET EVERYONE ON BOARD.
LEAVE IT TO BOBOT TO ALWAYS BE SO LEVEL-HEADED.
AT LEAST HE'S STRATEGIZING! WHAT ARE YOU DOING?!
LIKE I SAID, MY PLAN IS TO—
YEAH! WE ALL KNOW!
YOU'RE GONNA LEAVE THIS MISERABLE PLACE AND EAT SOME STEAK IN YOUR NICELY PRESSED SUIT!
BUT WHO KNOWS! YOUR HAND COULD GET SHREDDED TO BITS BY THE SORTING MACHINE BEFORE THAT! IT COULD ALL BE PREVENTED!
Let it go, Edison!
I LIKED YOU BOTH BETTER WHEN YOU SHUT THE HELL UP ABOUT WORK AND JUST KEPT YOUR MINDS IN YOUR ROMANTIC DAYDREAMS!

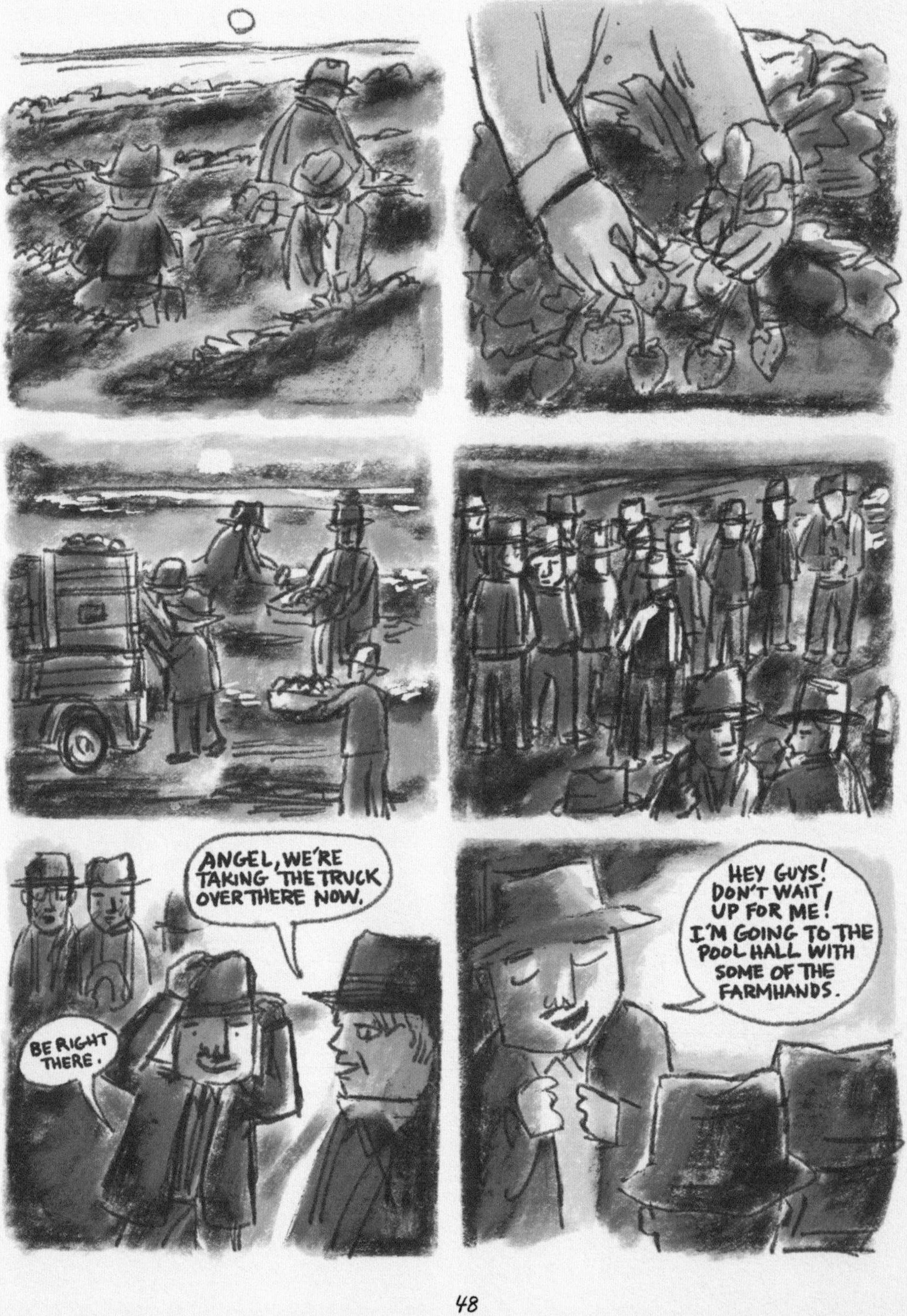
ANGEL, WE'RE TAKING THE TRUCK OVER THERE NOW.
BE RIGHT THERE.
HEY GUYS! DON'T WAIT UP FOR ME! I'M GOING TO THE POOL HALL WITH SOME OF THE FARMHANDS.

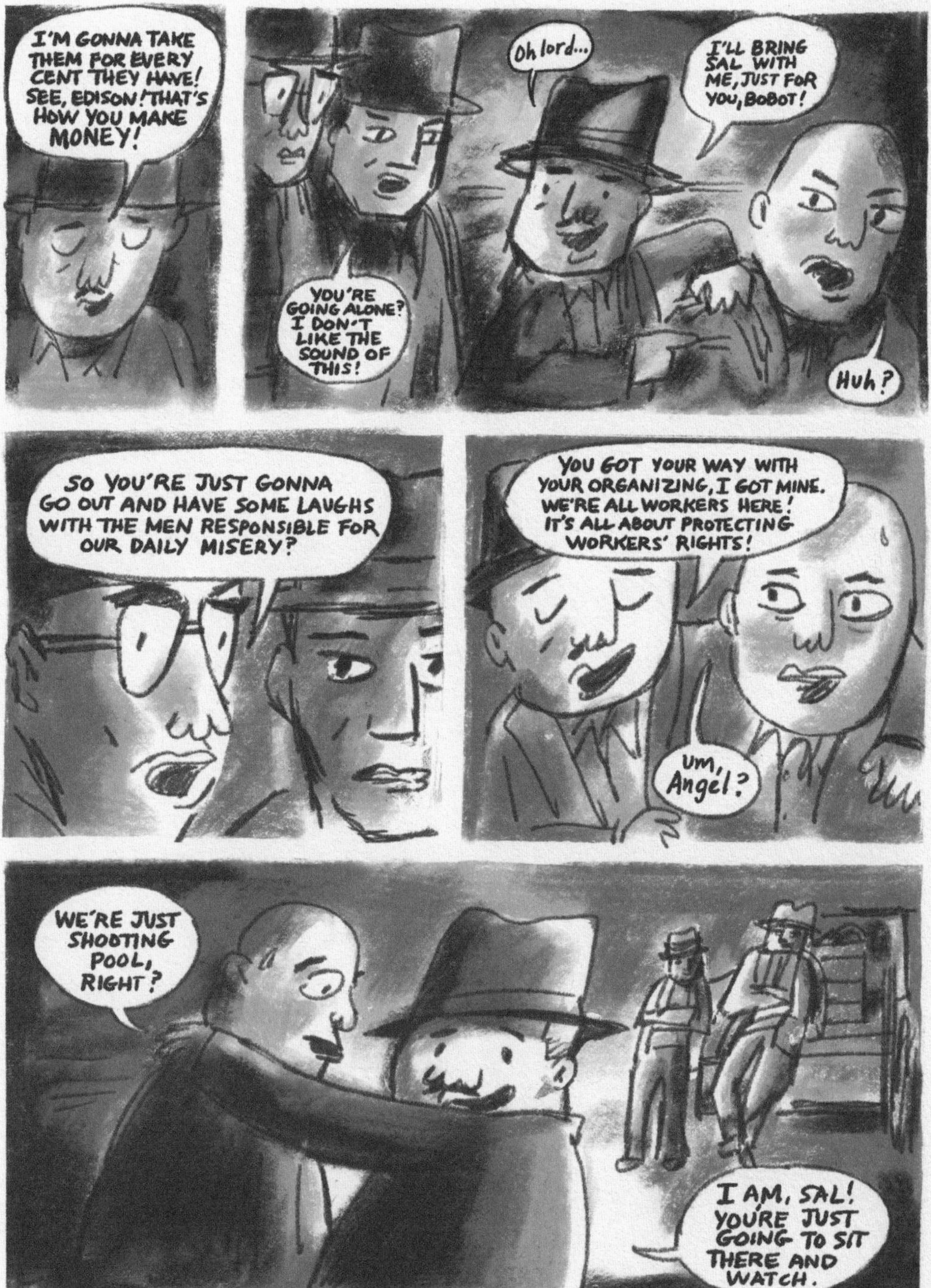
I'M GONNA TAKE THEM FOR EVERY CENT THEY HAVE! SEE, EDISON! THAT'S HOW YOU MAKE MONEY!
Oh lord...
YOU'RE GOING ALONE? I DON'T LIKE THE SOUND OF THIS!
I'LL BRING SAL WITH ME, JUST FOR YOU, BOBOT!
Huh?
SO YOU'RE JUST GONNA GO OUT AND HAVE SOME LAUGHS WITH THE MEN RESPONSIBLE FOR OUR DAILY MISERY?
YOU GOT YOUR WAY WITH YOUR ORGANIZING, I GOT MINE. WE'RE ALL WORKERS HERE! IT'S ALL ABOUT PROTECTING WORKERS' RIGHTS!
UM, Angel?
WE'RE JUST SHOOTING POOL, RIGHT?
I AM, SAL! YOU'RE JUST GOING TO SIT THERE AND WATCH.

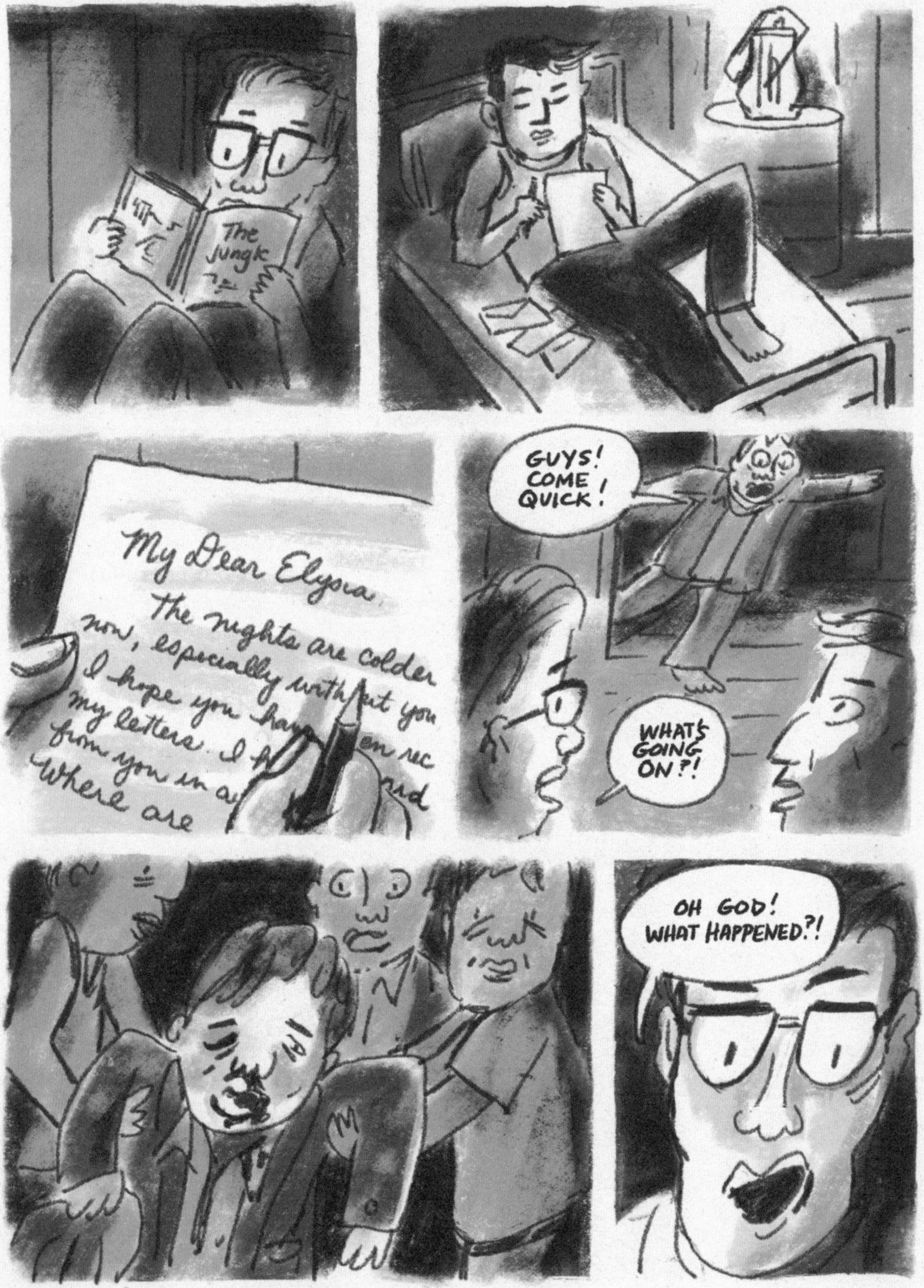
The Jungle
My Dear Elysia,
The nights are colder
now, especially with ut you
I hope you hav en rec
my letters. I h
from you in a nd
Where are
GUYS! COME QUICK!
WHAT'S GOING ON?!
OH GOD! WHAT HAPPENED?!

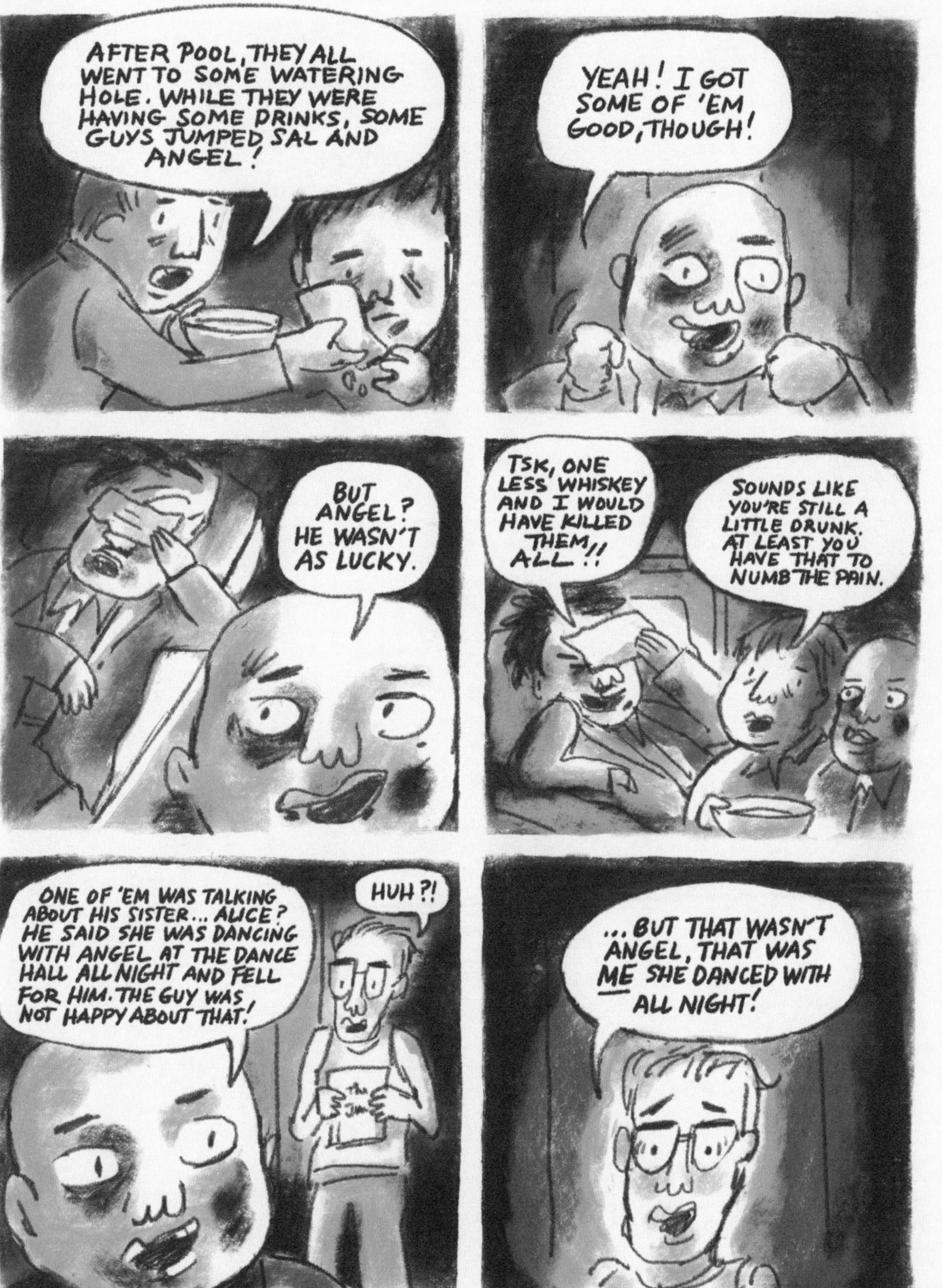
AFTER POOL, THEY ALL WENT TO SOME WATERING HOLE. WHILE THEY WERE HAVING SOME DRINKS, SOME GUYS JUMPED SAL AND ANGEL!
YEAH! I GOT SOME OF 'EM GOOD, THOUGH!
BUT ANGEL? HE WASN'T AS LUCKY.
TSK, ONE LESS WHISKEY AND I WOULD HAVE KILLED THEM ALL!!
SOUNDS LIKE YOU'RE STILL A LITTLE DRUNK. AT LEAST YOU HAVE THAT TO NUMB THE PAIN.
ONE OF 'EM WAS TALKING ABOUT HIS SISTER... ALICE? HE SAID SHE WAS DANCING WITH ANGEL AT THE DANCE HALL ALL NIGHT AND FELL FOR HIM. THE GUY WAS NOT HAPPY ABOUT THAT!
HUH?!
...BUT THAT WASN'T ANGEL, THAT WAS ME SHE DANCED WITH ALL NIGHT!

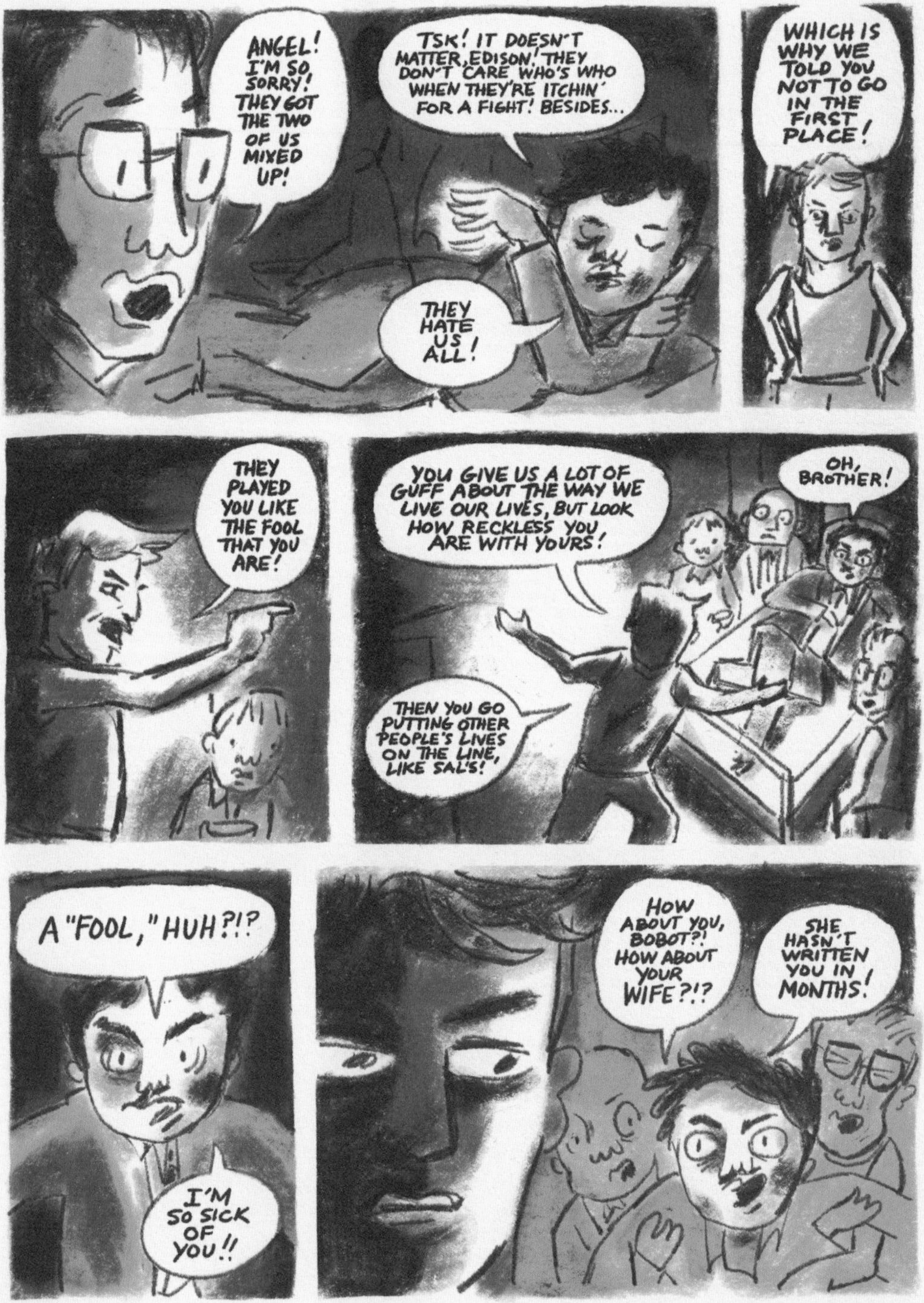
ANGEL! I'M SO SORRY! THEY GOT THE TWO OF US MIXED UP!
TSK! IT DOESN'T MATTER, EDISON! THEY DON'T CARE WHO'S WHO WHEN THEY'RE ITCHIN' FOR A FIGHT! BESIDES...
THEY HATE US ALL!
WHICH IS WHY WE TOLD YOU NOT TO GO IN THE FIRST PLACE!
THEY PLAYED YOU LIKE THE FOOL THAT YOU ARE!
YOU GIVE US A LOT OF GUFF ABOUT THE WAY WE LIVE OUR LIVES, BUT LOOK HOW RECKLESS YOU ARE WITH YOURS!
OH, BROTHER!
THEN YOU GO PUTTING OTHER PEOPLE'S LIVES ON THE LINE, LIKE SAL'S!
A "FOOL," HUH?!?
I'M SO SICK OF YOU!!
HOW ABOUT YOU, BOBOT?! HOW ABOUT YOUR WIFE?!?
SHE HASN'T WRITTEN YOU IN MONTHS!

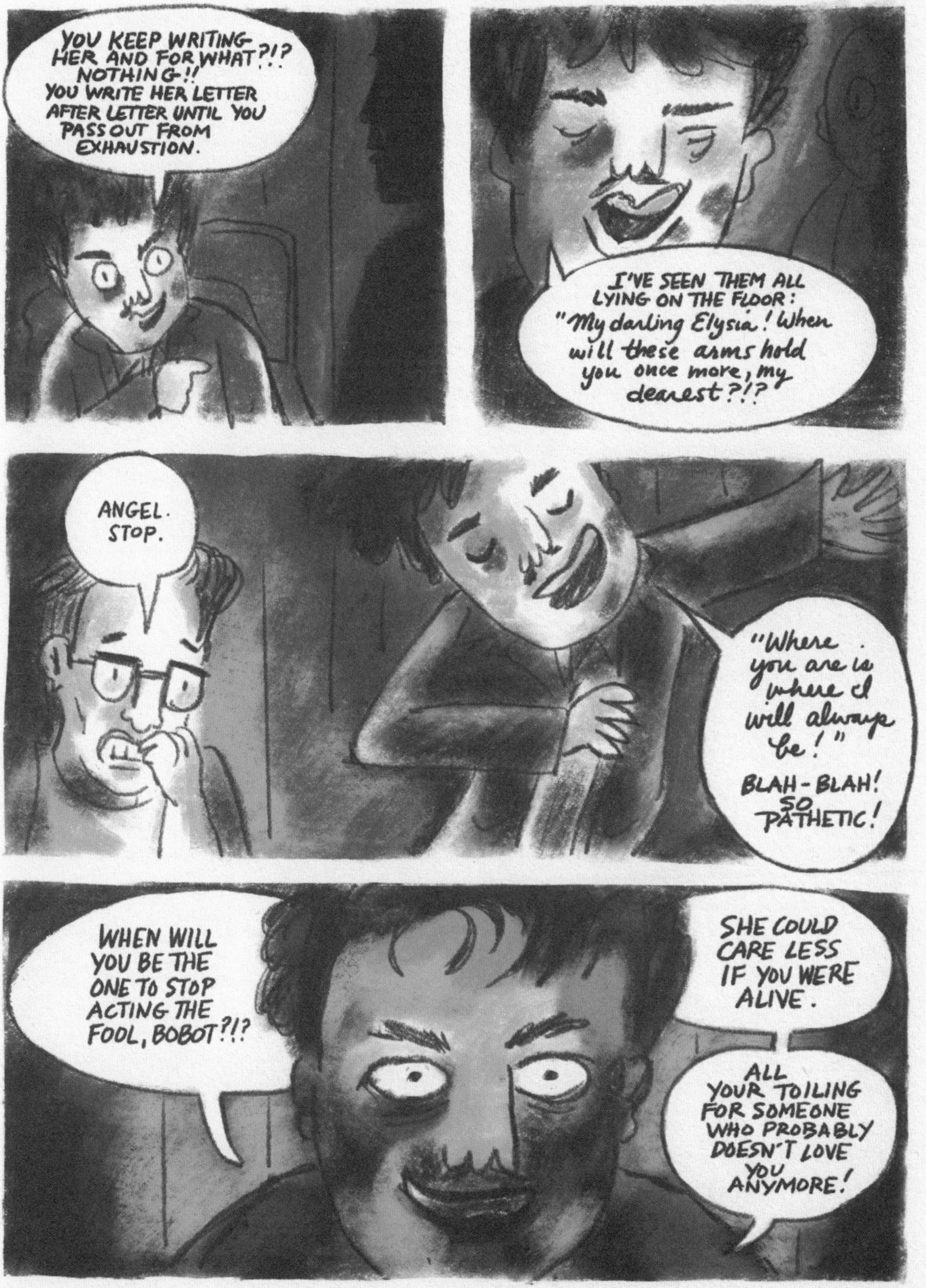
YOU KEEP WRITING HER AND FOR WHAT?!? NOTHING!! YOU WRITE HER LETTER AFTER LETTER UNTIL YOU PASS OUT FROM EXHAUSTION.
I'VE SEEN THEM ALL LYING ON THE FLOOR: "My darling Elysia! When will these arms hold you once more, my dearest?!?
ANGEL. STOP.
"Where you are is where I will always be!"
BLAH-BLAH! SO PATHETIC!
WHEN WILL YOU BE THE ONE TO STOP ACTING THE FOOL, BOBOT?!?
SHE COULD CARE LESS IF YOU WERE ALIVE.
ALL YOUR TOILING FOR SOMEONE WHO PROBABLY DOESN'T LOVE YOU ANYMORE!

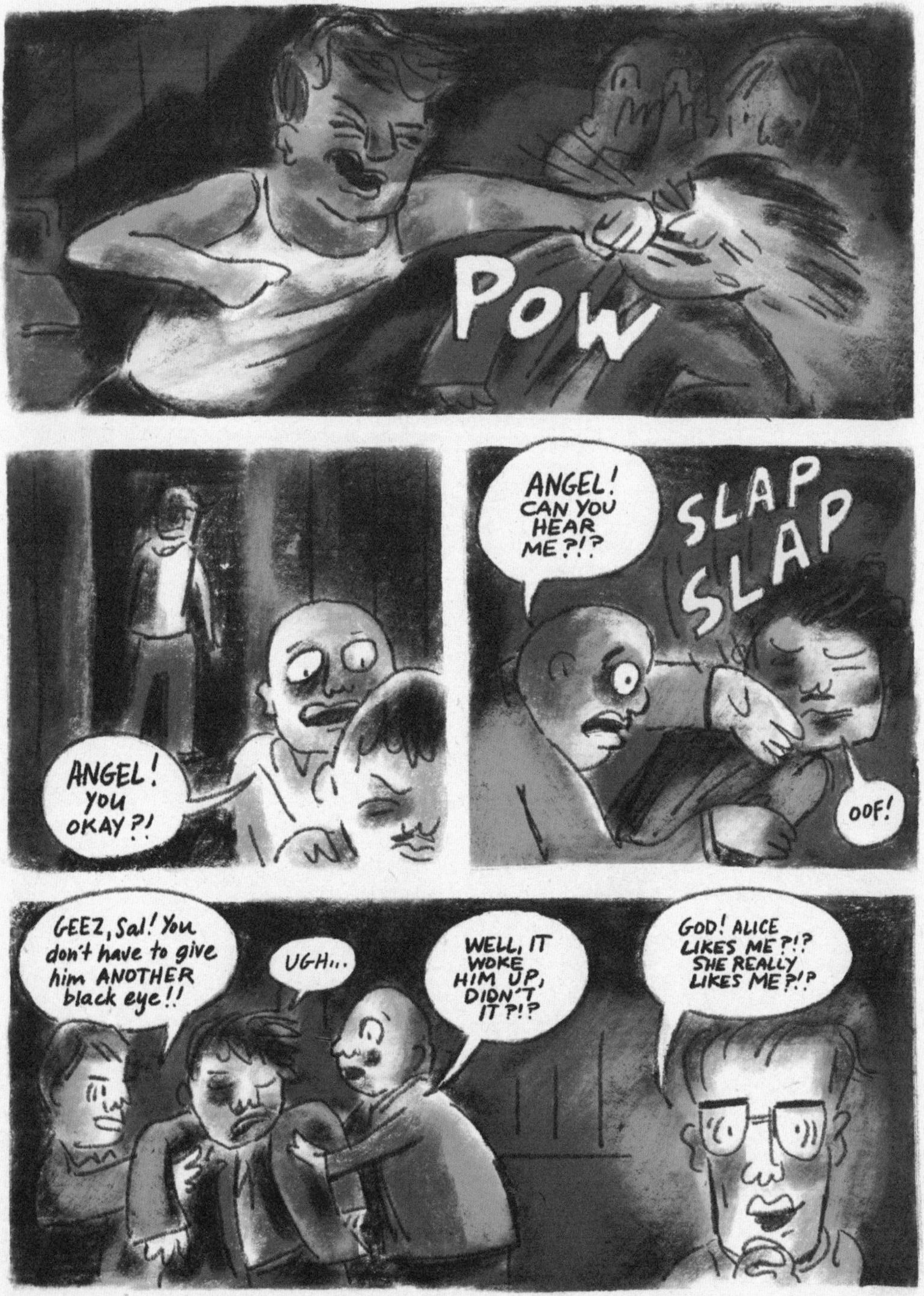
POW
ANGEL! YOU OKAY?!
ANGEL! CAN YOU HEAR ME?!?
SLAP SLAP
OOF!
GEEZ, Sal! You don't have to give him ANOTHER black eye!!
UGH...
WELL, IT WOKE HIM UP, DIDN'T IT?!?
GOD! ALICE LIKES ME?!? SHE REALLY LIKES ME?!?

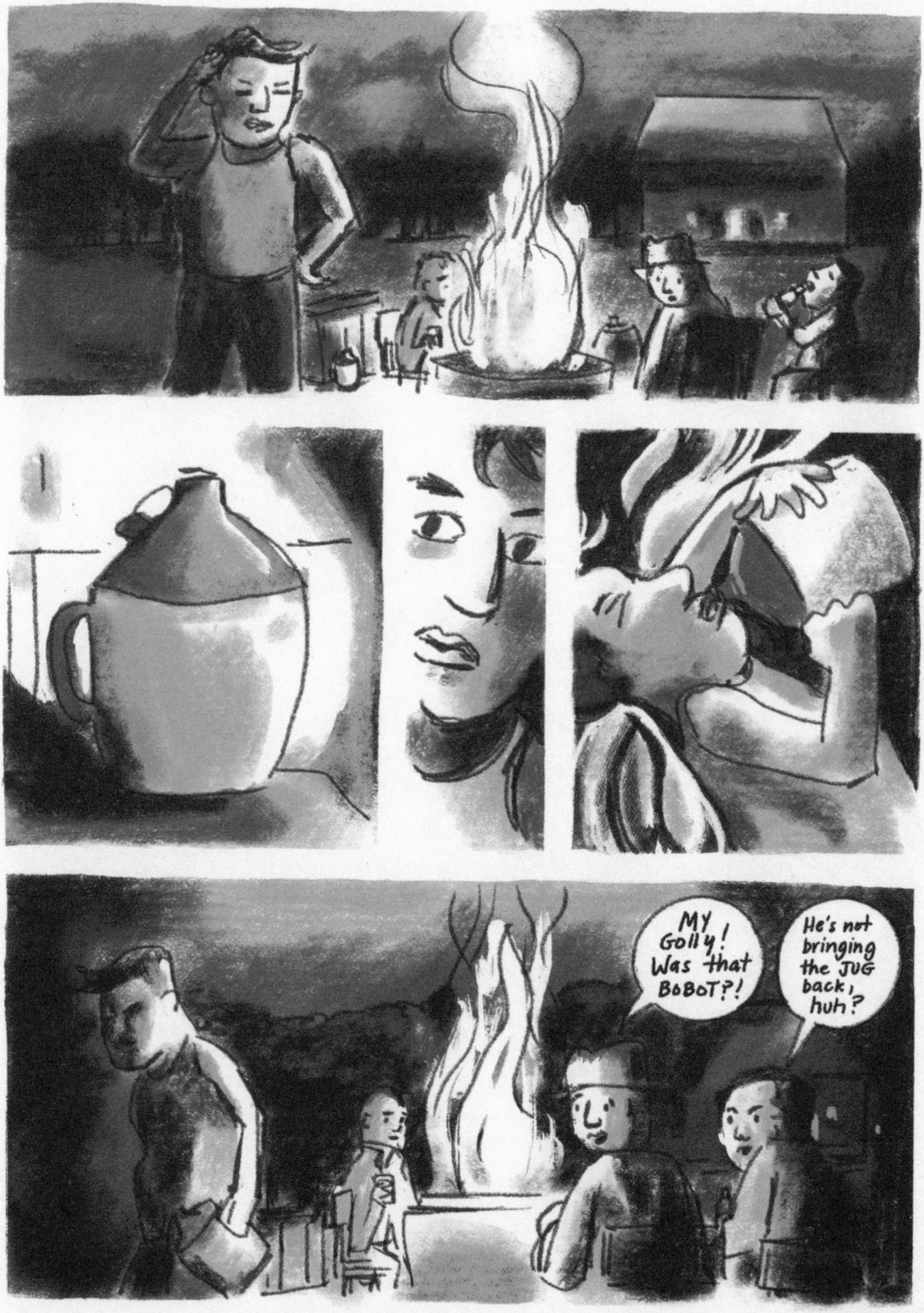
MY Golly! Was that BOBOT?!
He's not bringing the JUG back, huh?

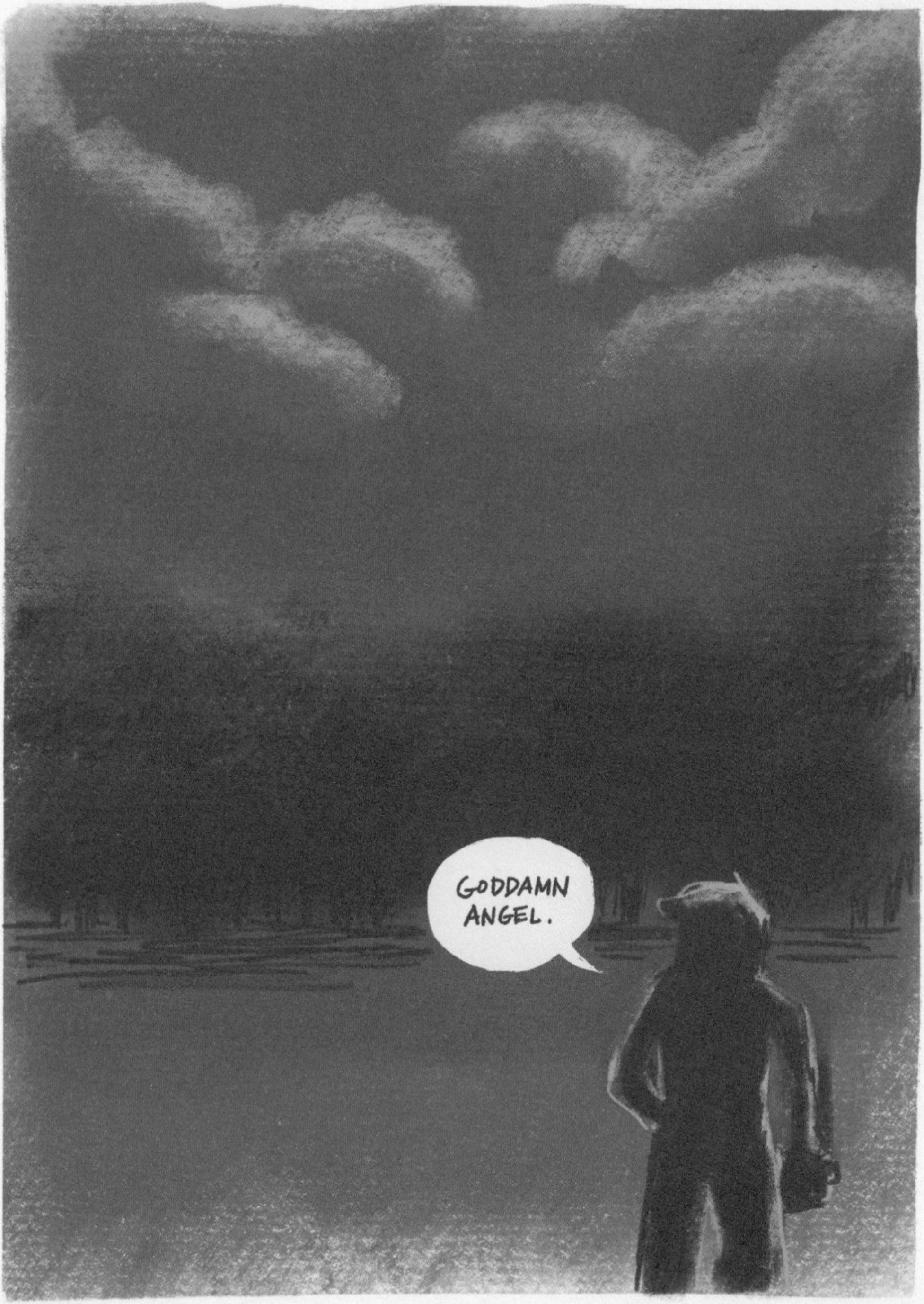
GODDAMN ANGEL.

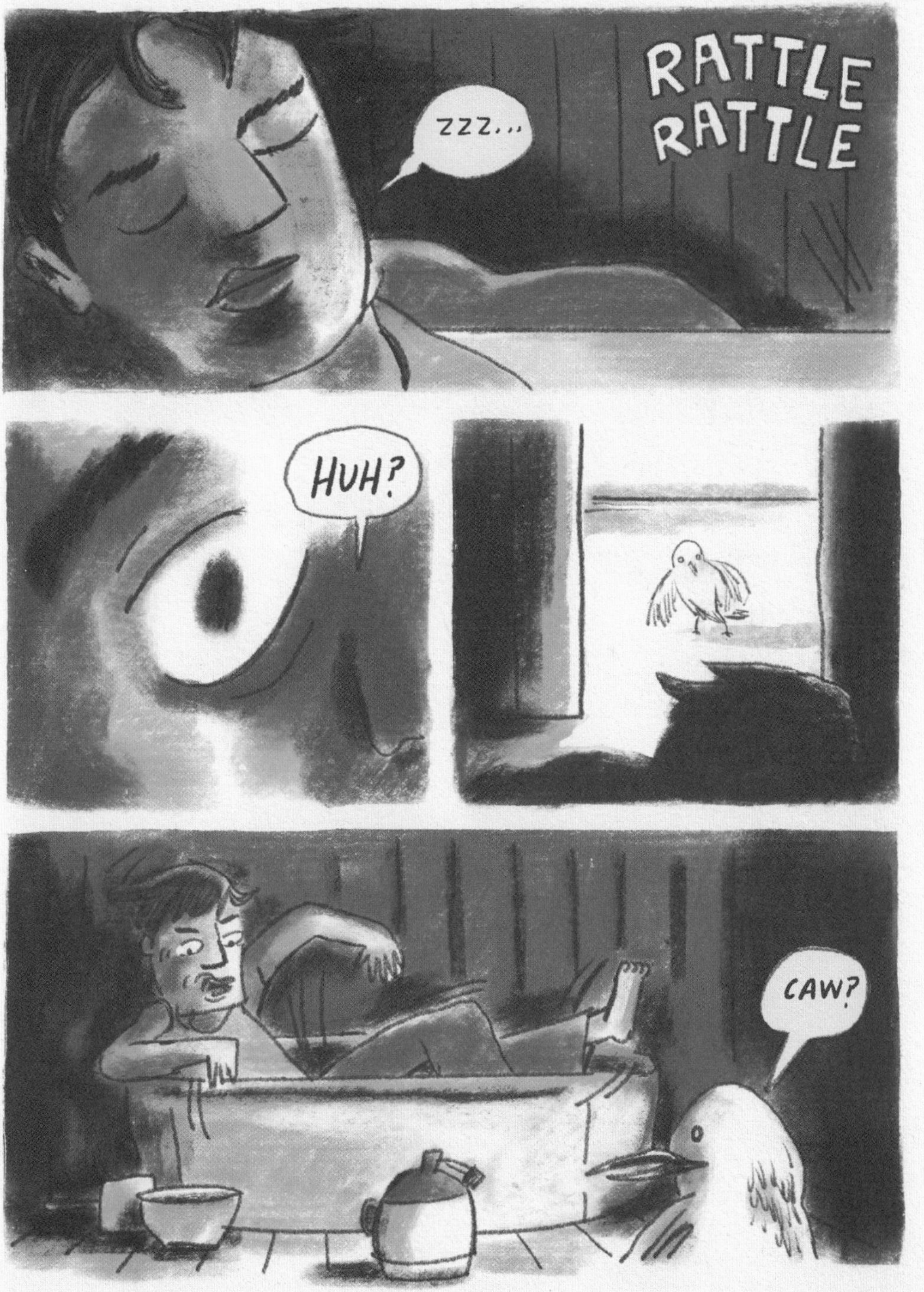
ZZZ...
RATTLE
RATTLE
HUH?
CAW?

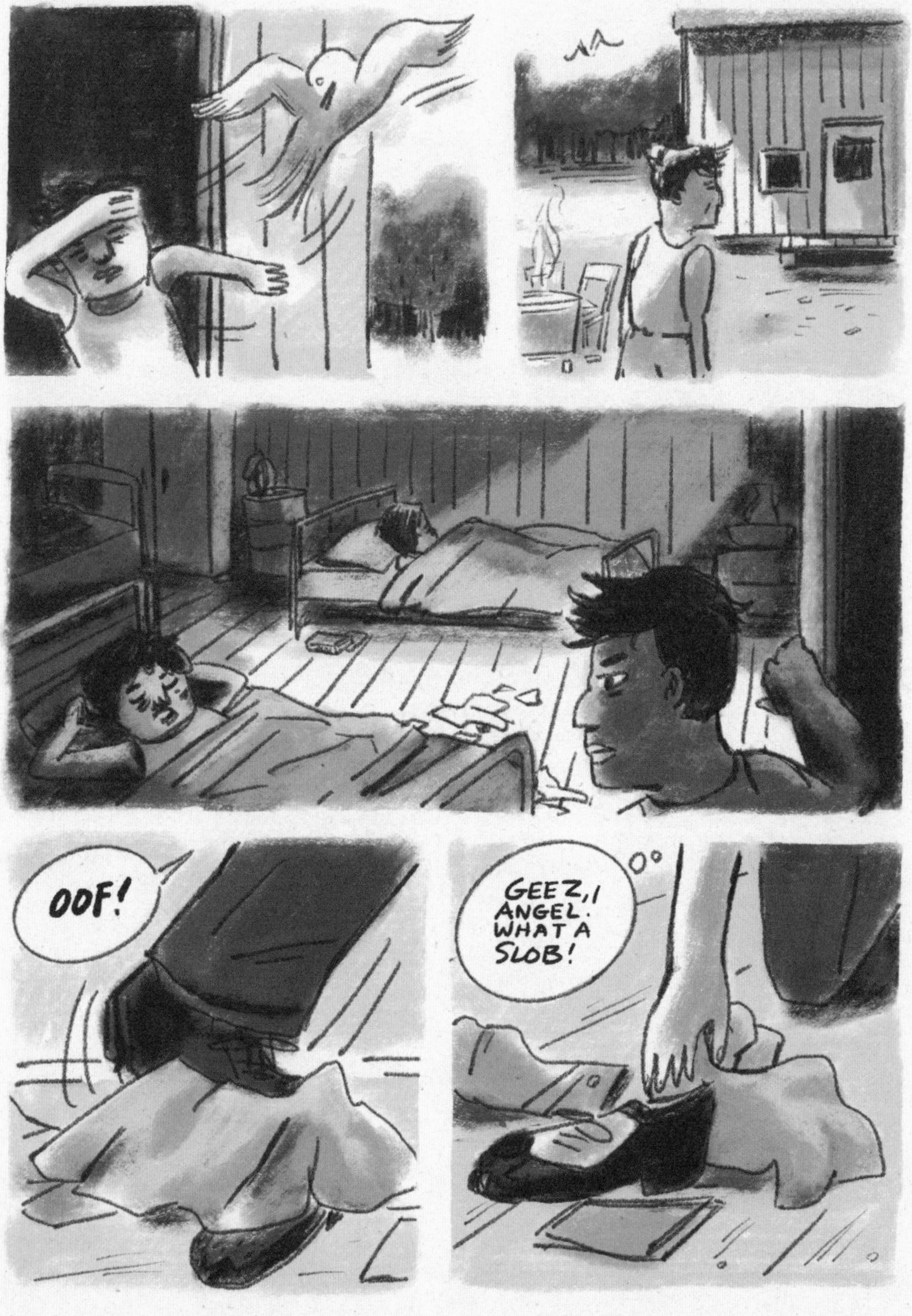
OOF!
GEEZ, ANGEL. WHAT A SLOB!

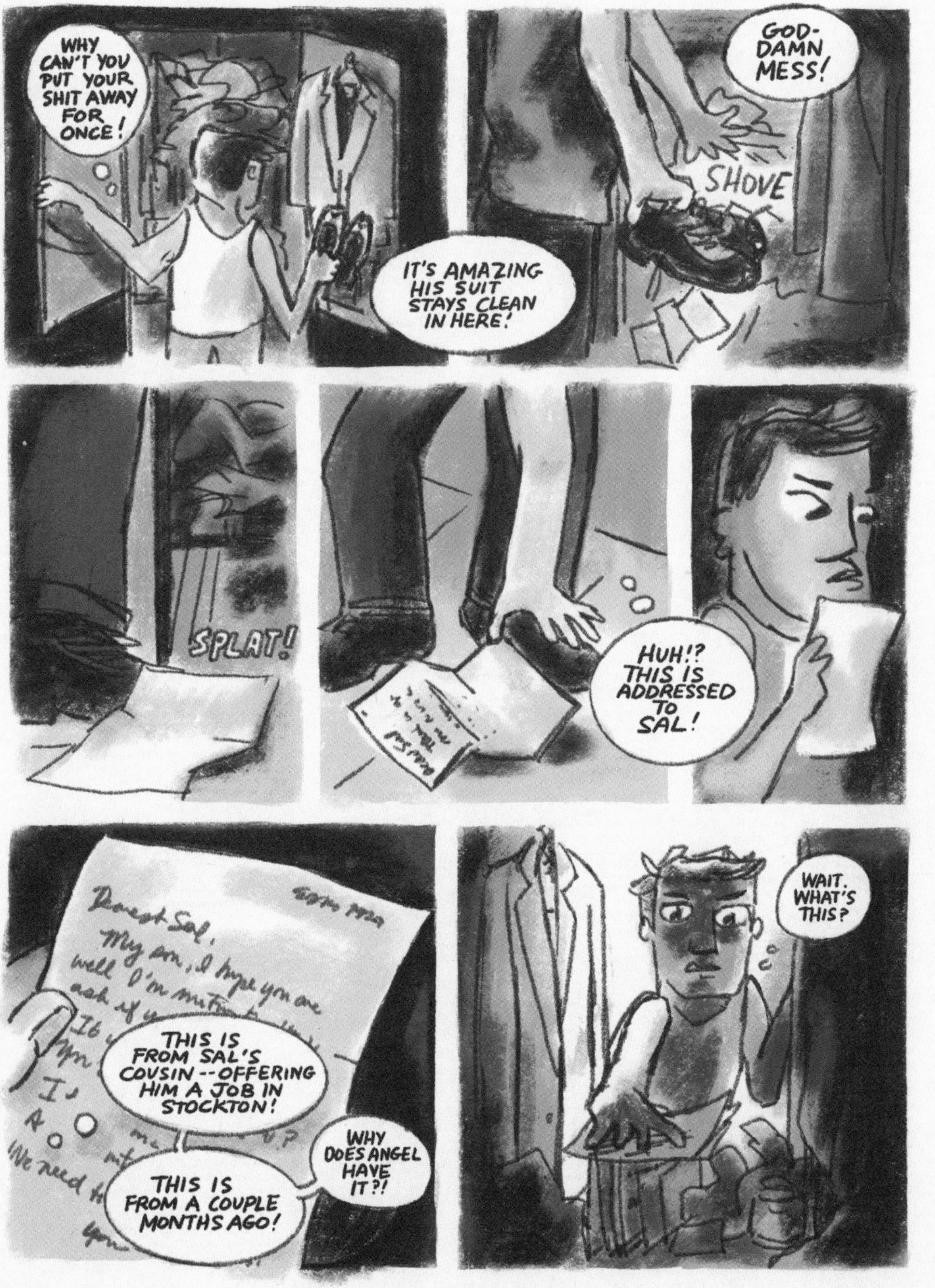
WHY CAN'T YOU PUT YOUR SHIT AWAY FOR ONCE!
GOD-DAMN MESS!
SHOVE
IT'S AMAZING HIS SUIT STAYS CLEAN IN HERE!
SPLAT!
HUH!? THIS IS ADDRESSED TO SAL!
Dearest Sal,
THIS IS FROM SAL'S COUSIN--OFFERING HIM A JOB IN STOCKTON!
THIS IS FROM A COUPLE MONTHS AGO!
WHY DOES ANGEL HAVE IT?!
WAIT. WHAT'S THIS?

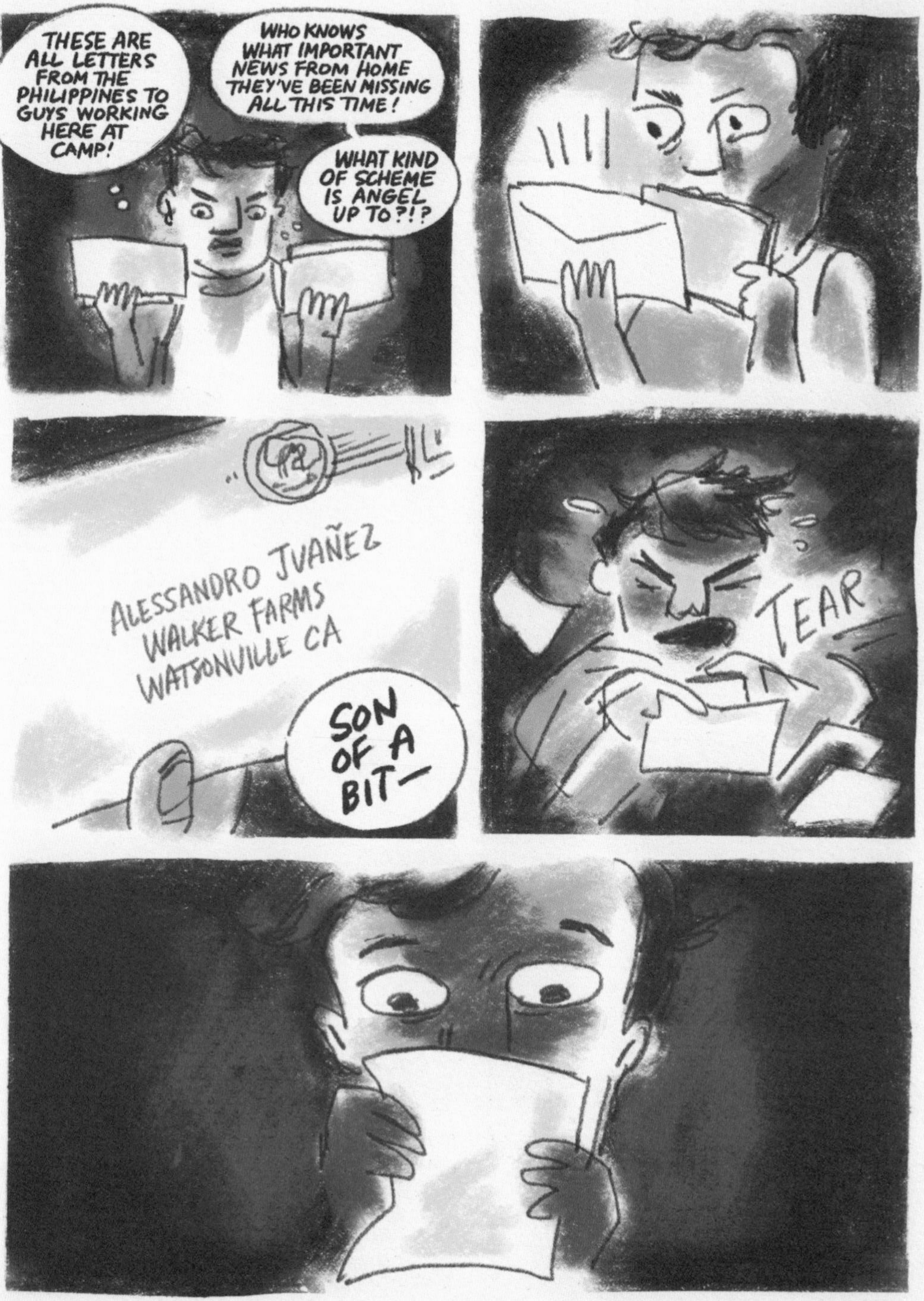
THESE ARE ALL LETTERS FROM THE PHILIPPINES TO GUYS WORKING HERE AT CAMP!
WHO KNOWS WHAT IMPORTANT NEWS FROM HOME THEY'VE BEEN MISSING ALL THIS TIME!
WHAT KIND OF SCHEME IS ANGEL UP TO?!?
ALESSANDRO JUAÑEZ
WALKER FARMS
WATSONVILLE CA
SON OF A BIT—
TEAR

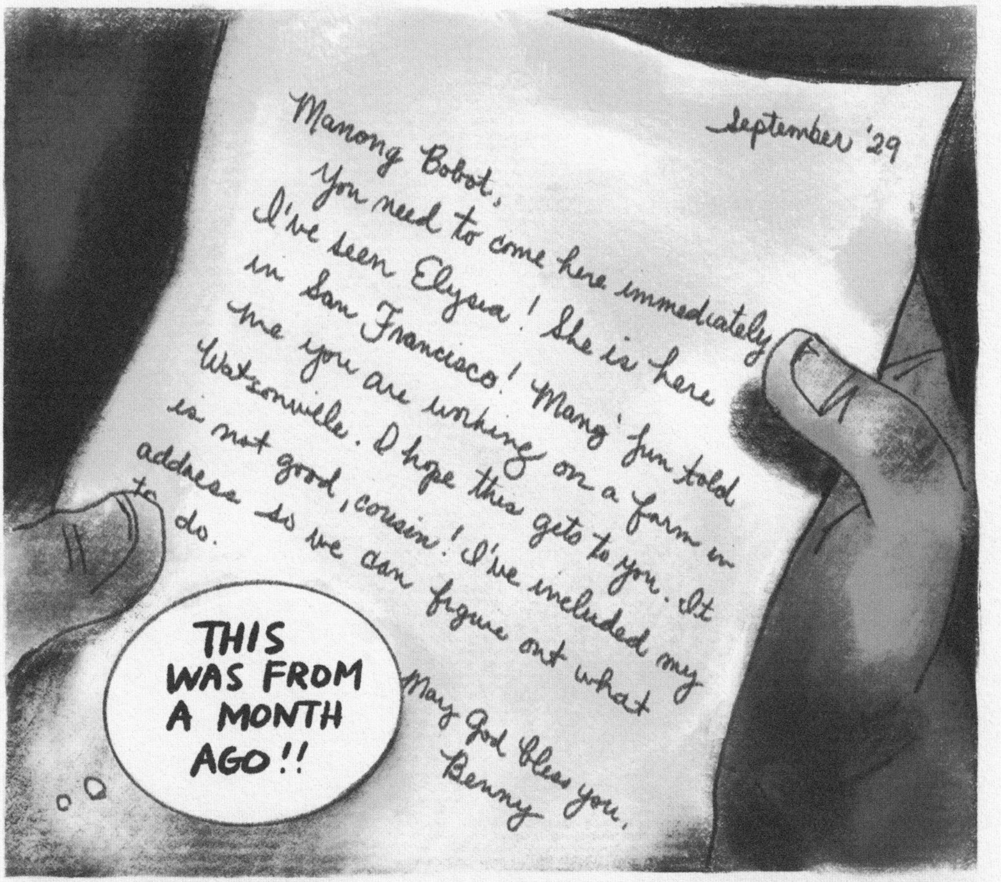
September '29
Manong Bobot,
You need to come here immediately
I've seen Elysia! She is here in San Francisco! Mang' Jun told me you are working on a farm in Watsonville. I hope this gets to you. It is not good, cousin! I've included my address so we can figure out what to do.
May God bless you,
Benny
THIS WAS FROM A MONTH AGO!!

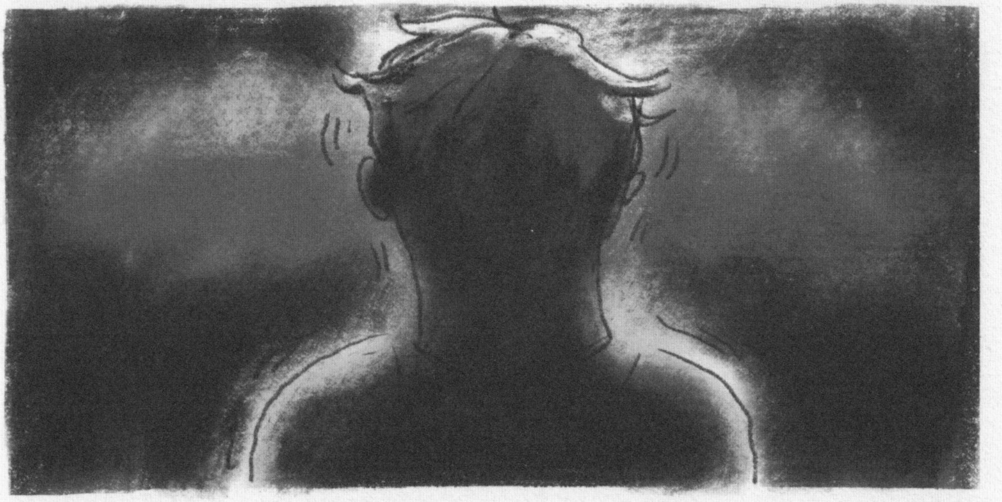

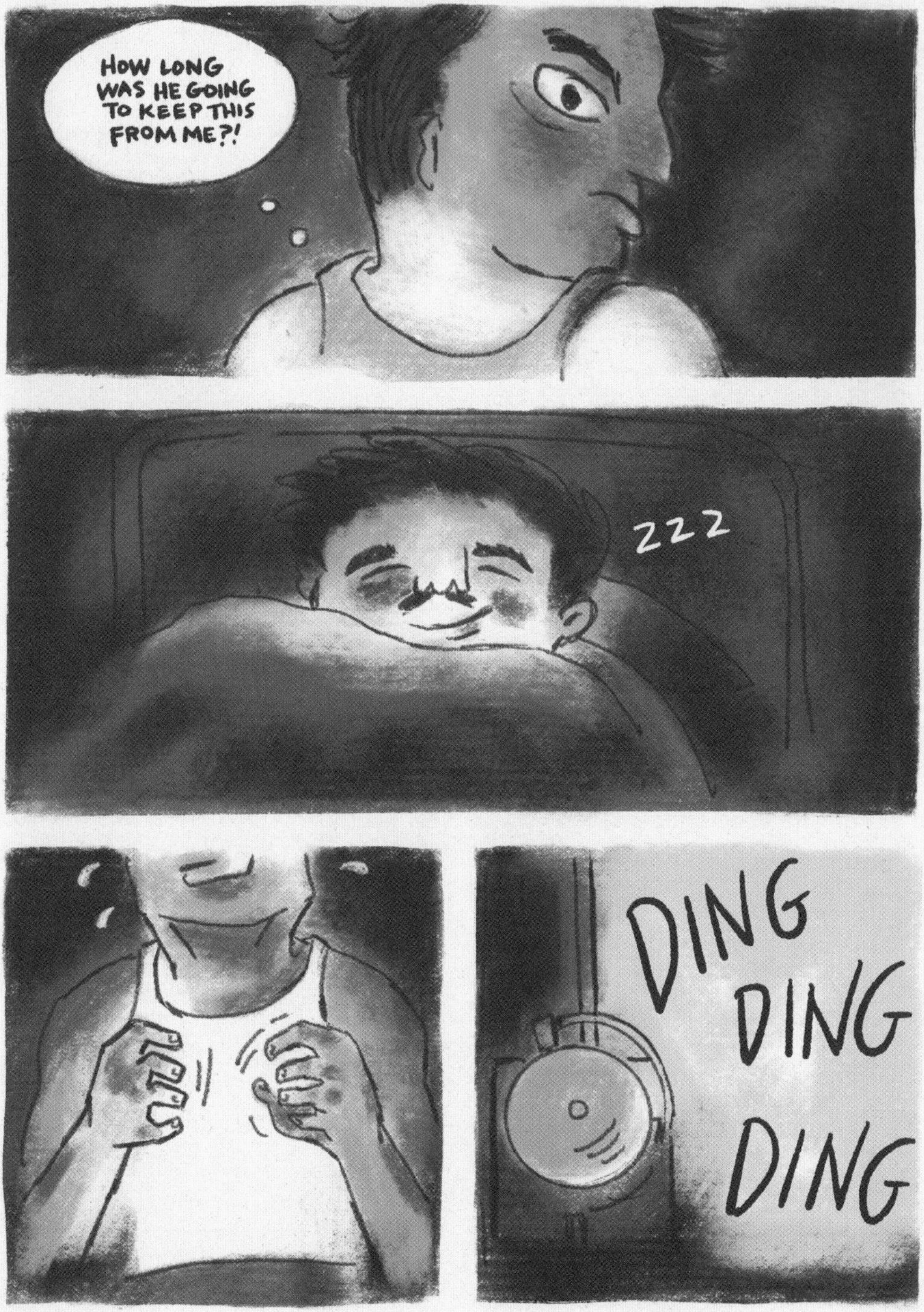
HOW LONG WAS HE GOING TO KEEP THIS FROM ME?!
ZZZ
DING DING DING

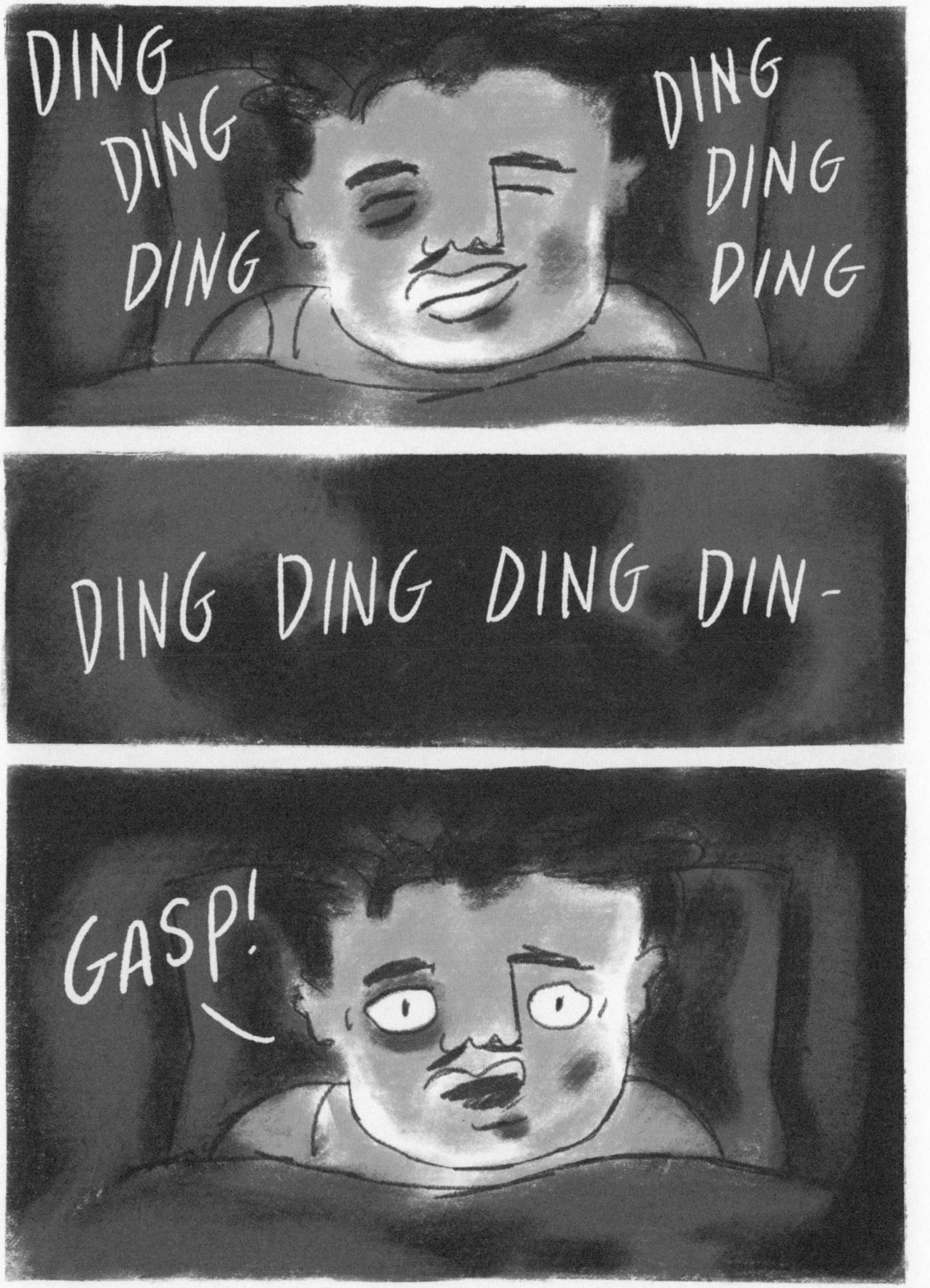
DING DING DING
DING DING DING
DING DING DING DIN-
GASP!

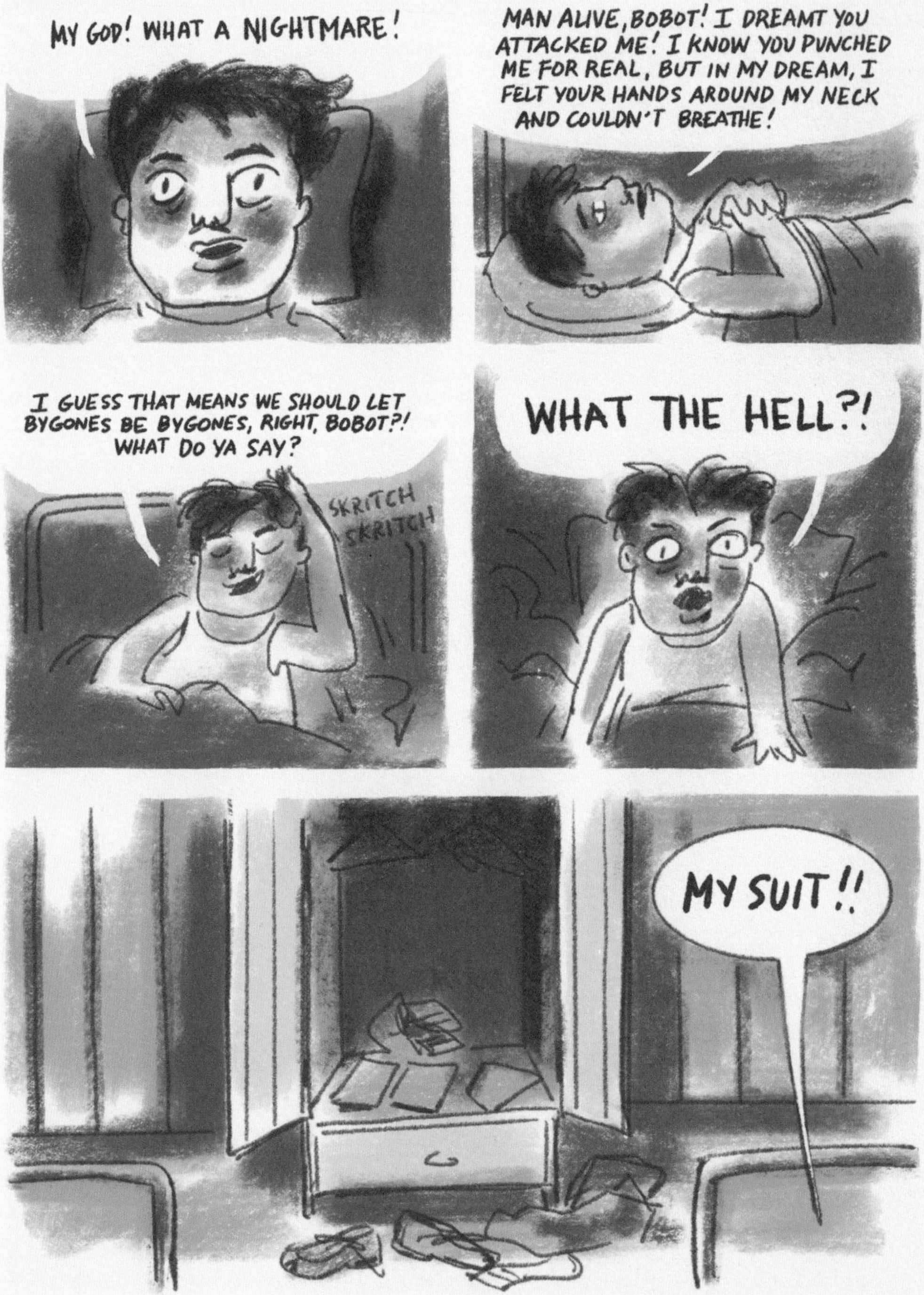
MY GOD! WHAT A NIGHTMARE!
MAN ALIVE, BOBOT! I DREAMT YOU ATTACKED ME! I KNOW YOU PUNCHED ME FOR REAL, BUT IN MY DREAM, I FELT YOUR HANDS AROUND MY NECK AND COULDN'T BREATHE!
I GUESS THAT MEANS WE SHOULD LET BYGONES BE BYGONES, RIGHT, BOBOT?! WHAT DO YA SAY?
SKRITCH SKRITCH
WHAT THE HELL?!
MY SUIT!!

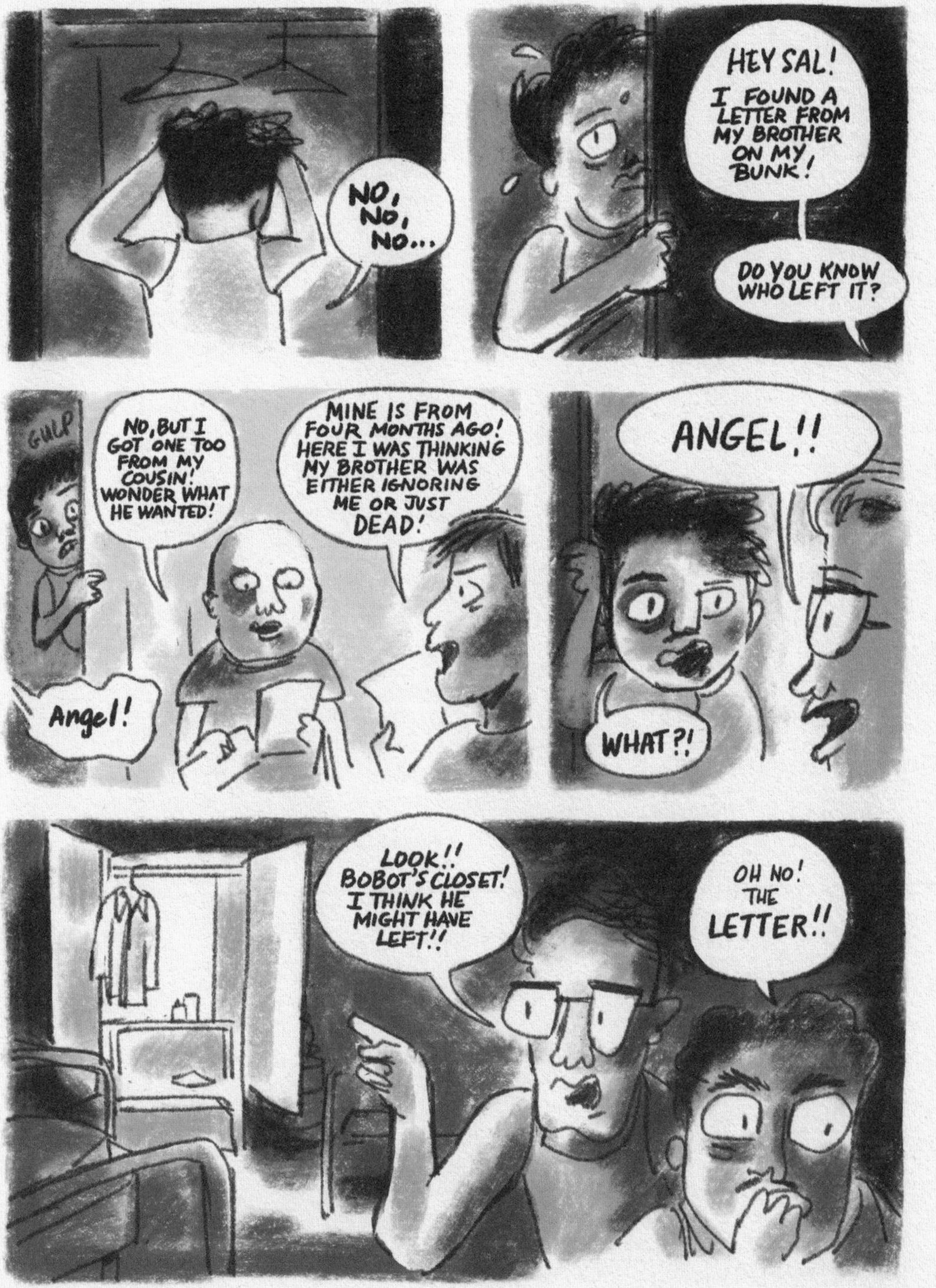
NO, NO, NO...
HEY SAL! I FOUND A LETTER FROM MY BROTHER ON MY BUNK!
DO YOU KNOW WHO LEFT IT?
GULP
NO, BUT I GOT ONE TOO FROM MY COUSIN! WONDER WHAT HE WANTED!
MINE IS FROM FOUR MONTHS AGO! HERE I WAS THINKING MY BROTHER WAS EITHER IGNORING ME OR JUST DEAD!
Angel!
ANGEL!!
WHAT?!
LOOK!! BOBOT'S CLOSET! I THINK HE MIGHT HAVE LEFT!!
OH NO! THE LETTER!!

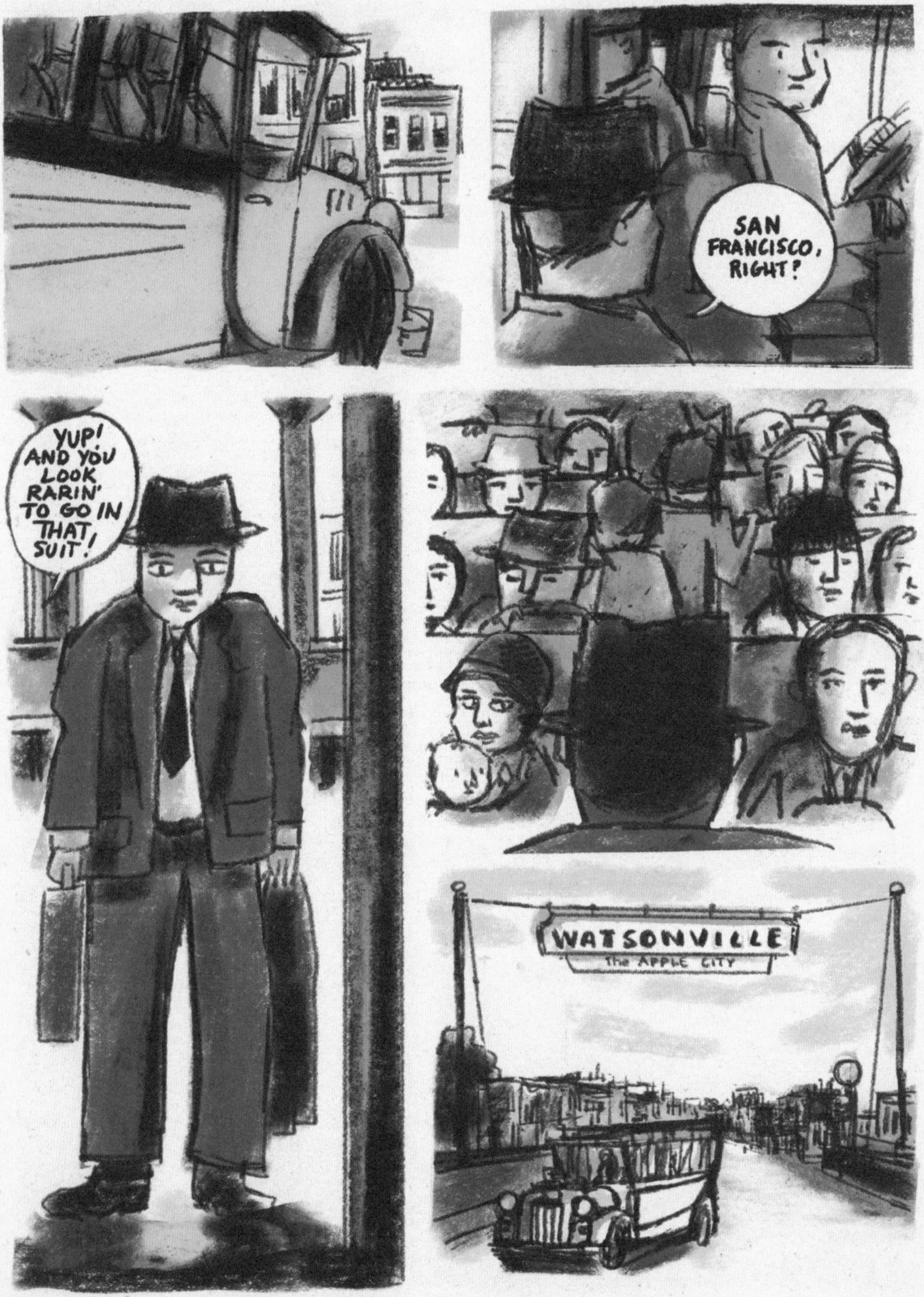

SAN FRANCISCO, RIGHT?
YUP! AND YOU LOOK RARIN' TO GO IN THAT SUIT!
WATSONVILLE
the APPLE CITY

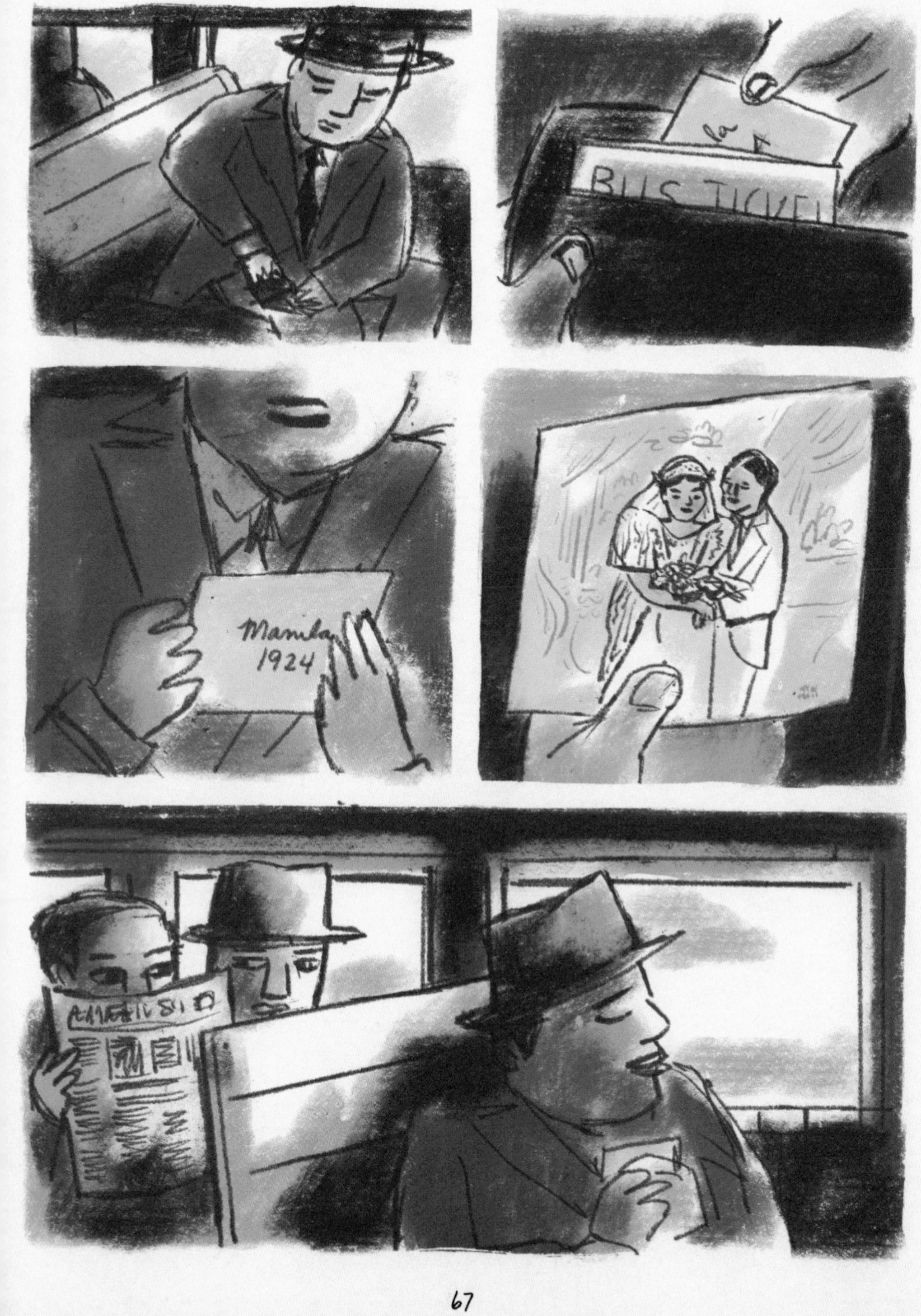
BUS TICKE
Manila
1924

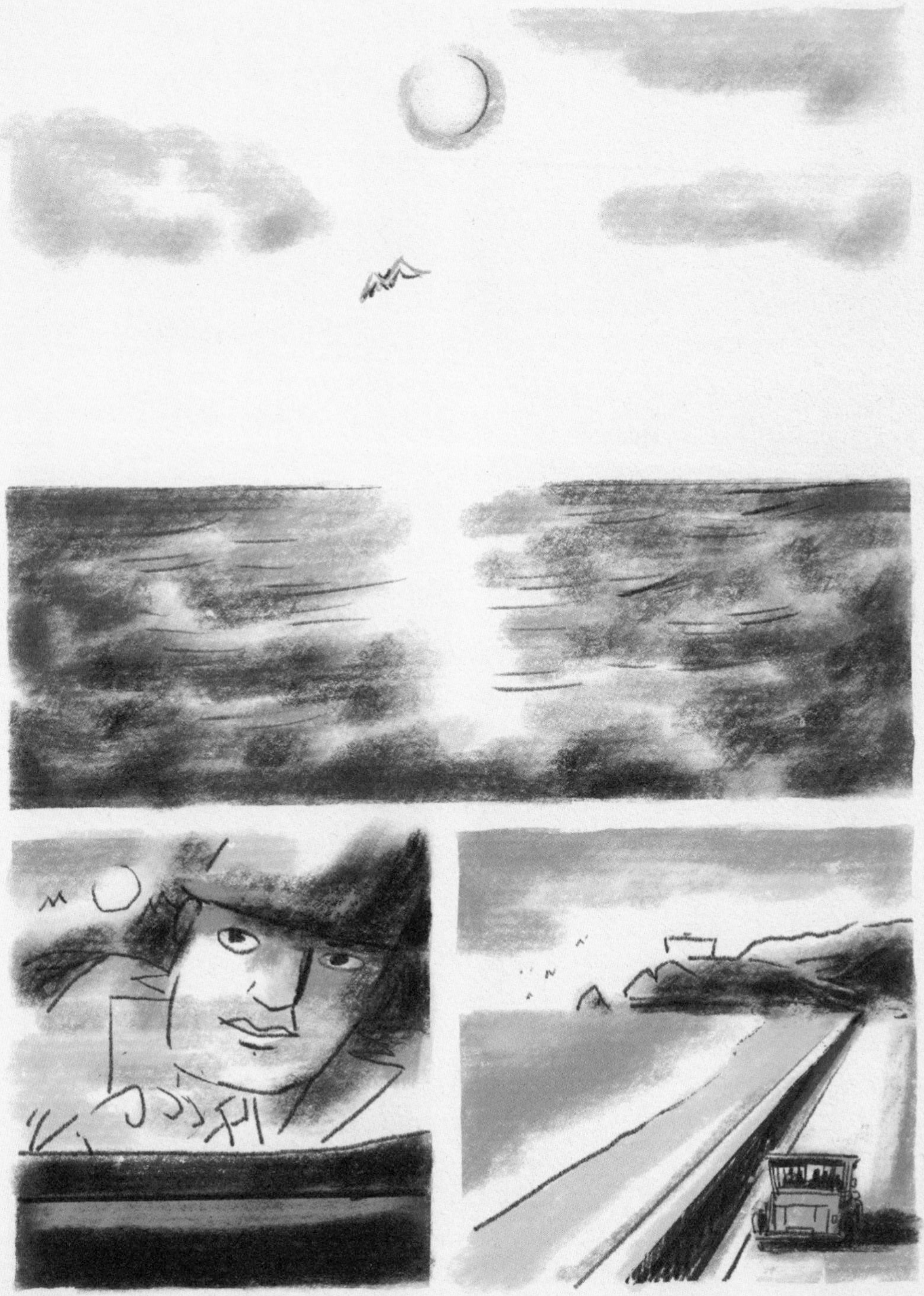

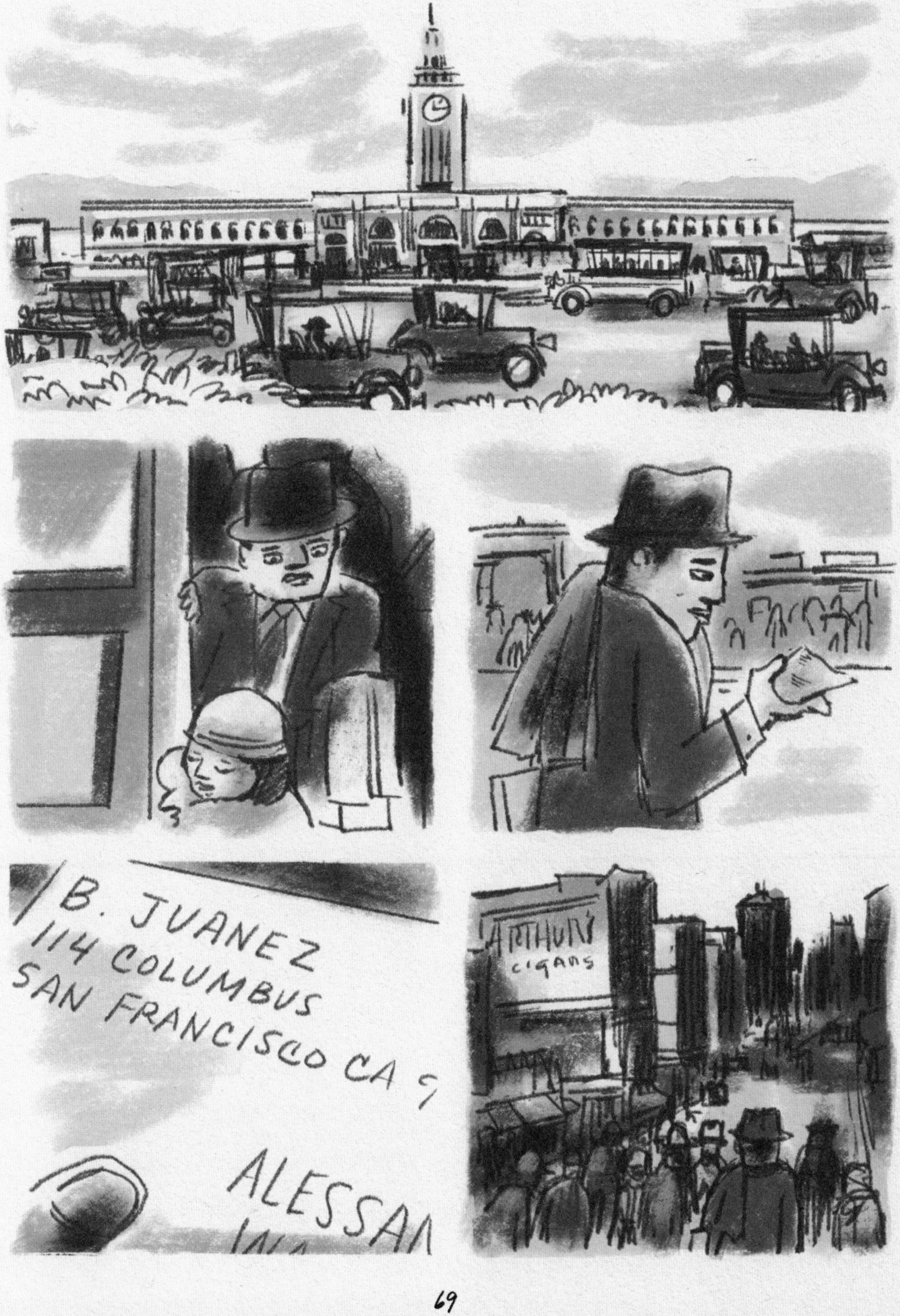
B. JUANEZ
114 COLUMBUS
SAN FRANCISCO CA
ALESSA
ARTHUR'S
CIGARS

COUPLE MORE BLOCKS.
JACKSON
ALMOST THERE.
PEOPLE SPEAKING ILOCANO NOW.
THIS IS THE RIGHT ADDRESS, BUT WHY THIS PLACE?
CAFE KALESA
COFFEE
FOOD

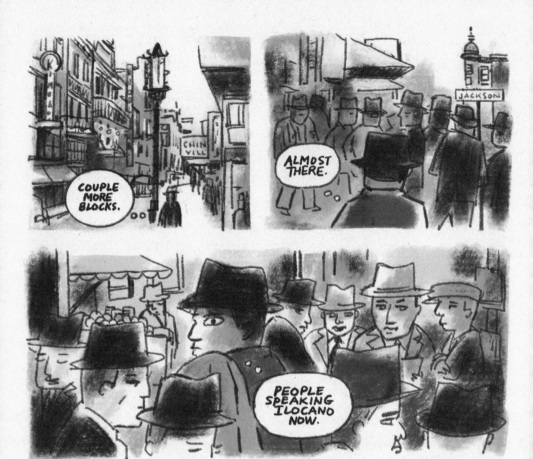

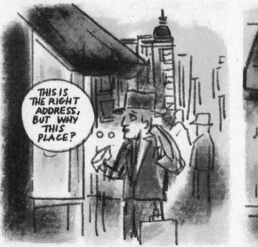

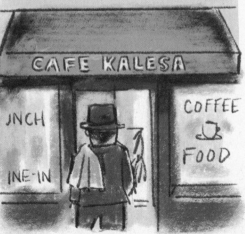

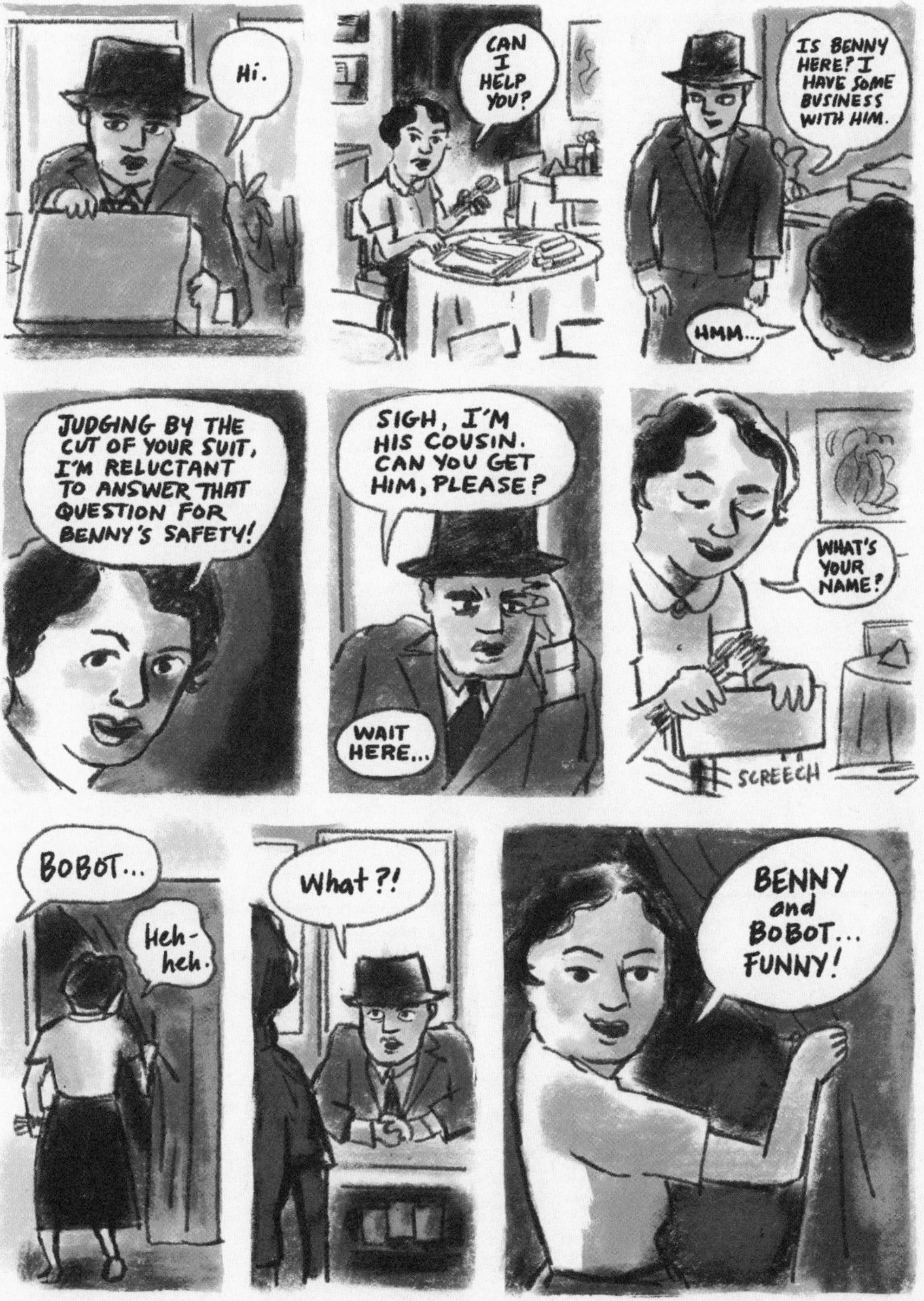
Hi.
CAN I HELP YOU?
IS BENNY HERE? I HAVE SOME BUSINESS WITH HIM.
HMM...
JUDGING BY THE CUT OF YOUR SUIT, I'M RELUCTANT TO ANSWER THAT QUESTION FOR BENNY'S SAFETY!
SIGH, I'M HIS COUSIN. CAN YOU GET HIM, PLEASE?
WAIT HERE...
WHAT'S YOUR NAME?
SCREECH
BOBOT...
Heh-heh.
What?!
BENNY and BOBOT... FUNNY!

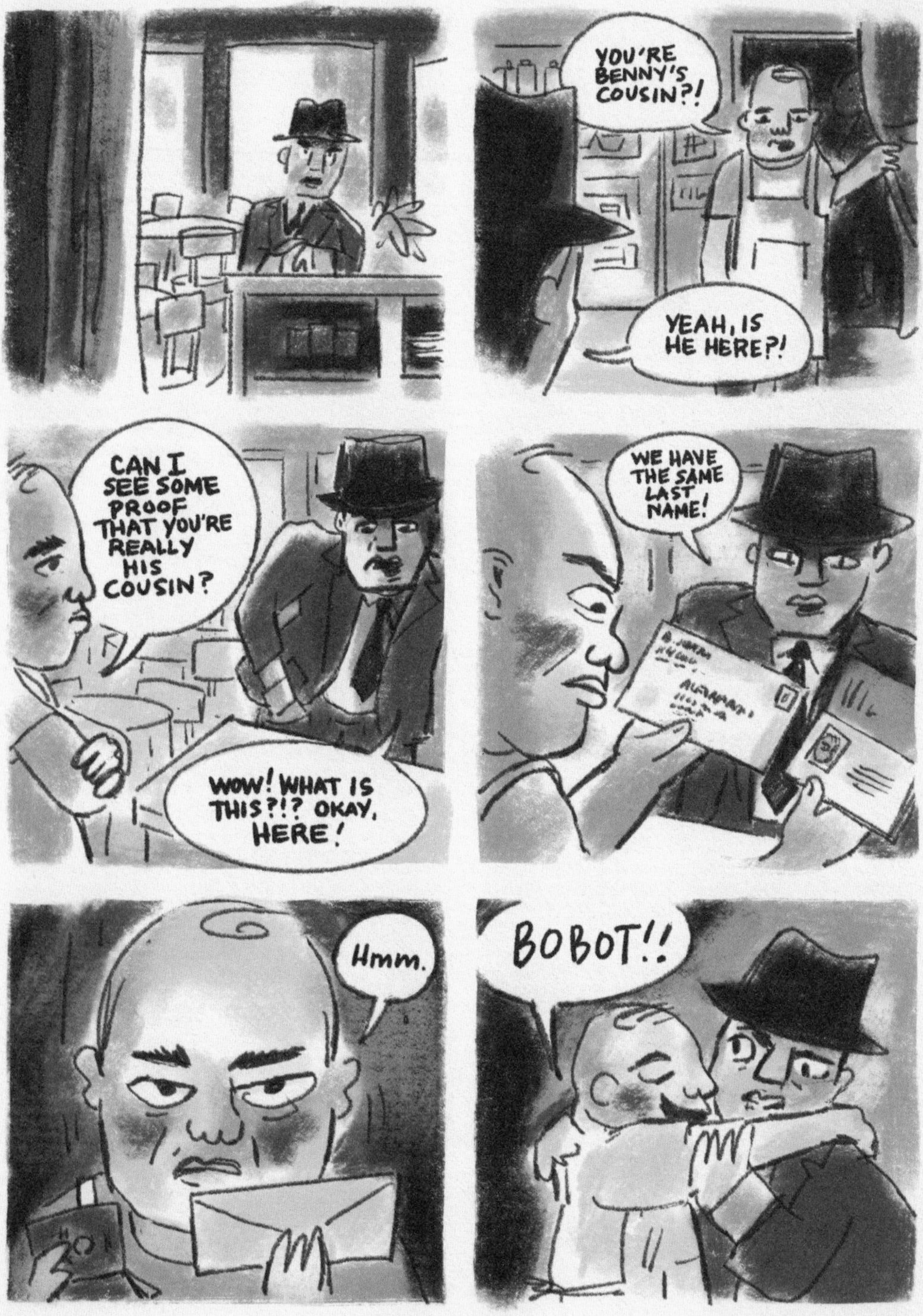
YOU'RE BENNY'S COUSIN?!
YEAH, IS HE HERE?!
CAN I SEE SOME PROOF THAT YOU'RE REALLY HIS COUSIN?
WOW! WHAT IS THIS?!? OKAY, HERE!
WE HAVE THE SAME LAST NAME!
Hmm.
BOBOT!!

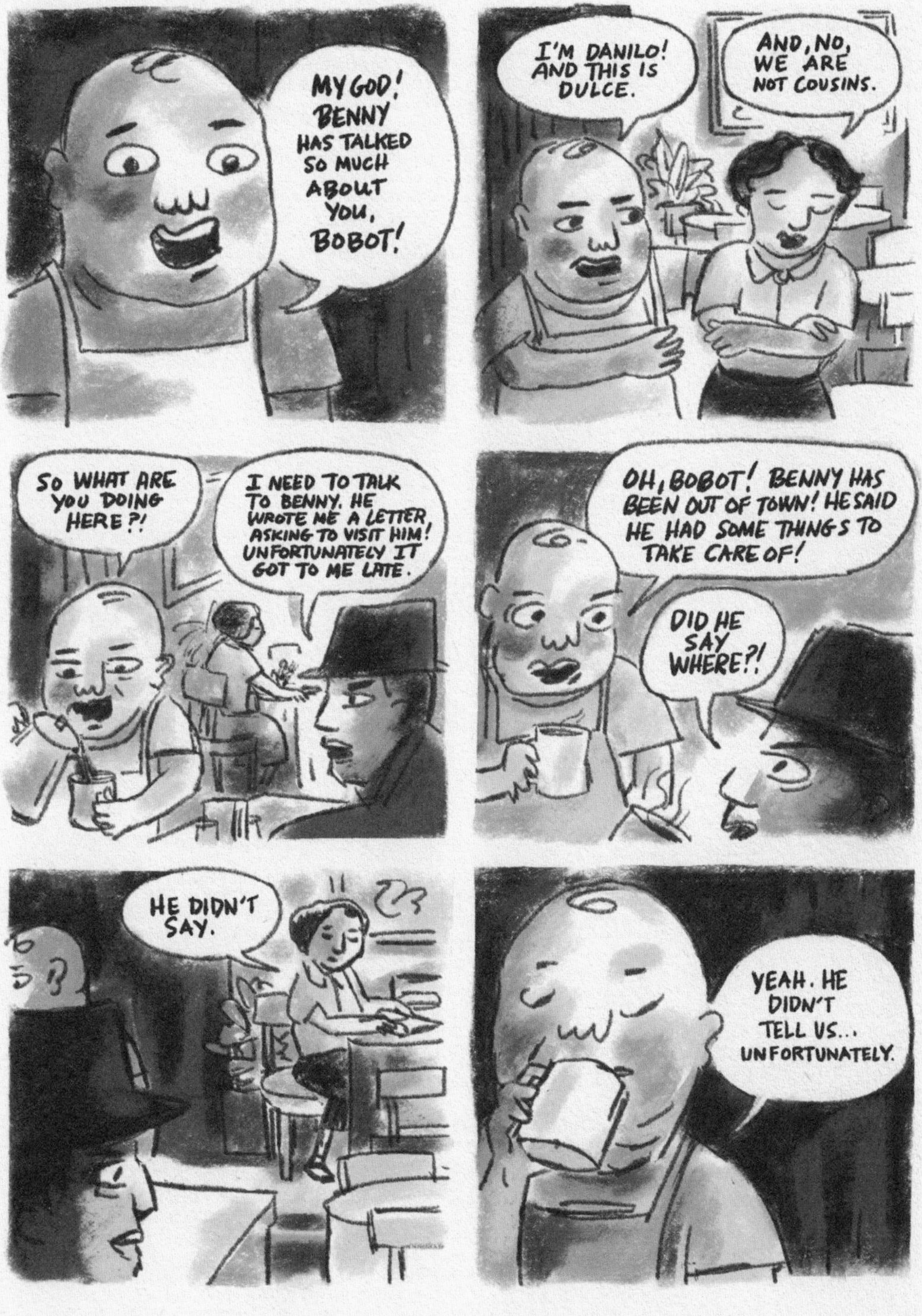
MY GOD! BENNY HAS TALKED SO MUCH ABOUT YOU, BOBOT!
I'M DANILO! AND THIS IS DULCE.
AND, NO, WE ARE NOT COUSINS.
SO WHAT ARE YOU DOING HERE?!
I NEED TO TALK TO BENNY. HE WROTE ME A LETTER, ASKING TO VISIT HIM! UNFORTUNATELY IT GOT TO ME LATE.
OH, BOBOT! BENNY HAS BEEN OUT OF TOWN! HE SAID HE HAD SOME THINGS TO TAKE CARE OF!
DID HE SAY WHERE?!
HE DIDN'T SAY.
YEAH. HE DIDN'T TELL US... UNFORTUNATELY.

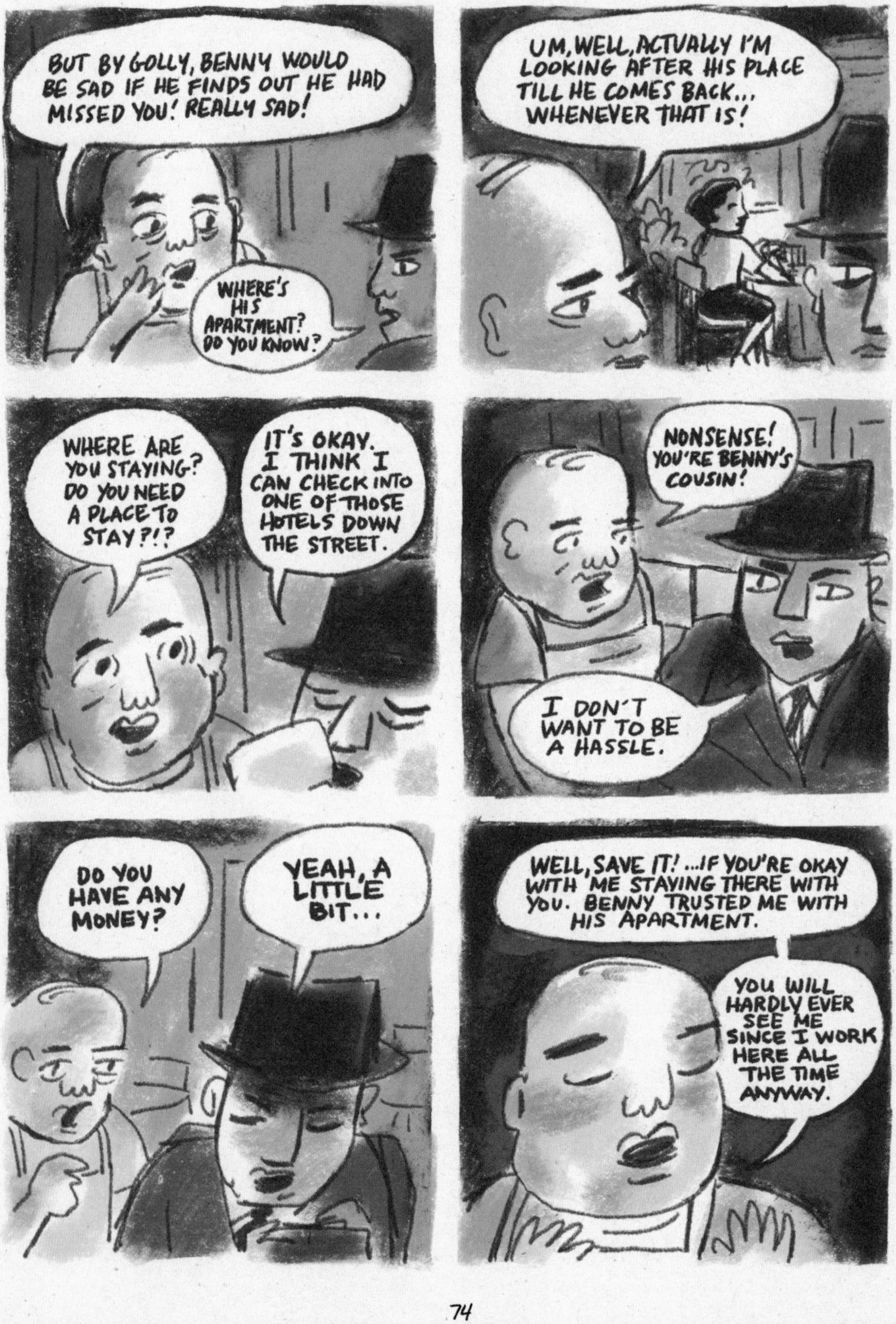
BUT BY GOLLY, BENNY WOULD BE SAD IF HE FINDS OUT HE HAD MISSED YOU! REALLY SAD!
WHERE'S HIS APARTMENT? DO YOU KNOW?
UM, WELL, ACTUALLY I'M LOOKING AFTER HIS PLACE TILL HE COMES BACK... WHENEVER THAT IS!
WHERE ARE YOU STAYING? DO YOU NEED A PLACE TO STAY?!?
IT'S OKAY. I THINK I CAN CHECK INTO ONE OF THOSE HOTELS DOWN THE STREET.
NONSENSE! YOU'RE BENNY'S COUSIN!
I DON'T WANT TO BE A HASSLE.
DO YOU HAVE ANY MONEY?
YEAH, A LITTLE BIT...
WELL, SAVE IT! ...IF YOU'RE OKAY WITH ME STAYING THERE WITH YOU. BENNY TRUSTED ME WITH HIS APARTMENT.
YOU WILL HARDLY EVER SEE ME SINCE I WORK HERE ALL THE TIME ANYWAY.

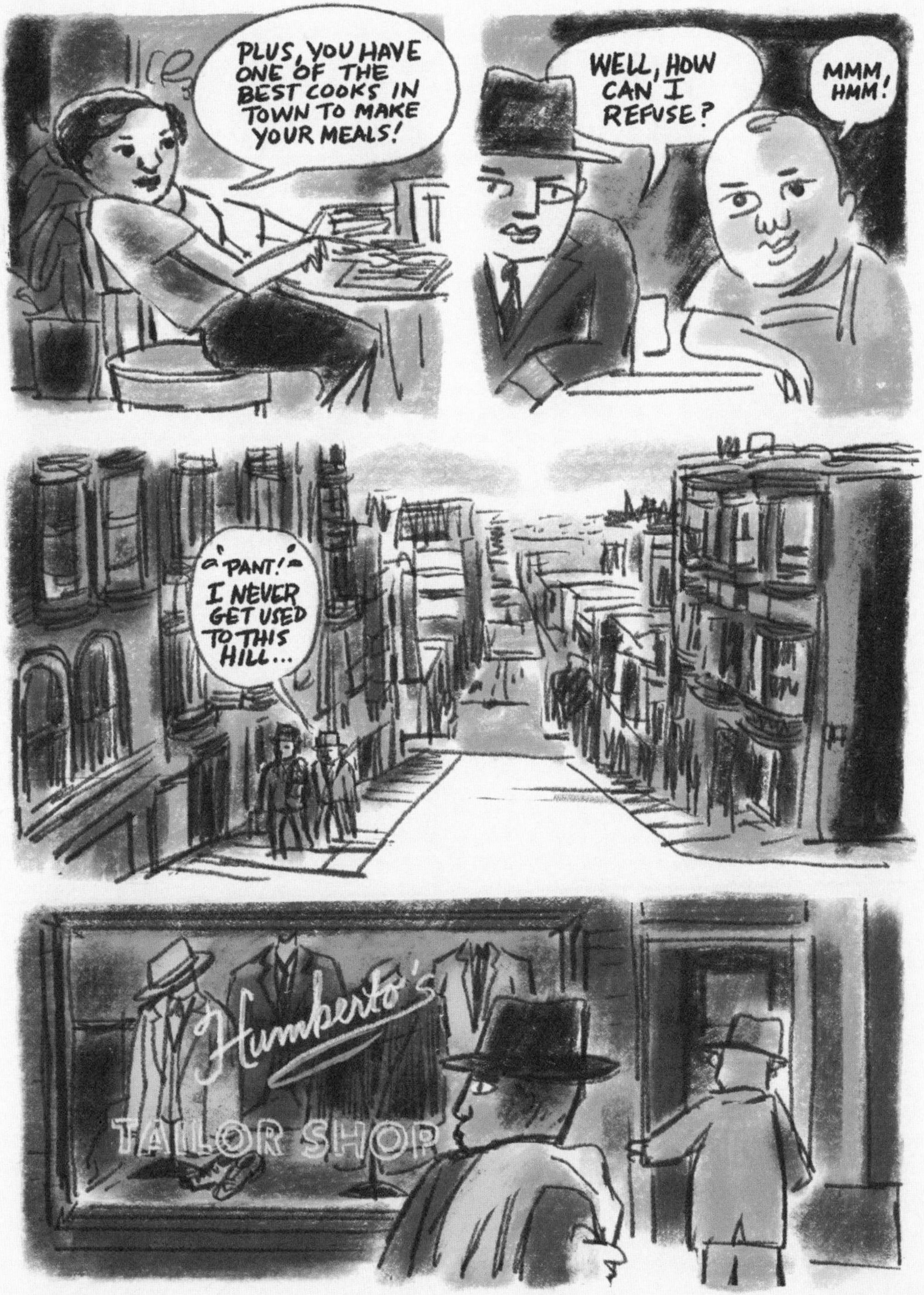
PLUS, YOU HAVE ONE OF THE BEST COOKS IN TOWN TO MAKE YOUR MEALS!
WELL, HOW CAN I REFUSE?
MMM, HMM!
PANT! I NEVER GET USED TO THIS HILL...
Humberto's
TAILOR SHOP

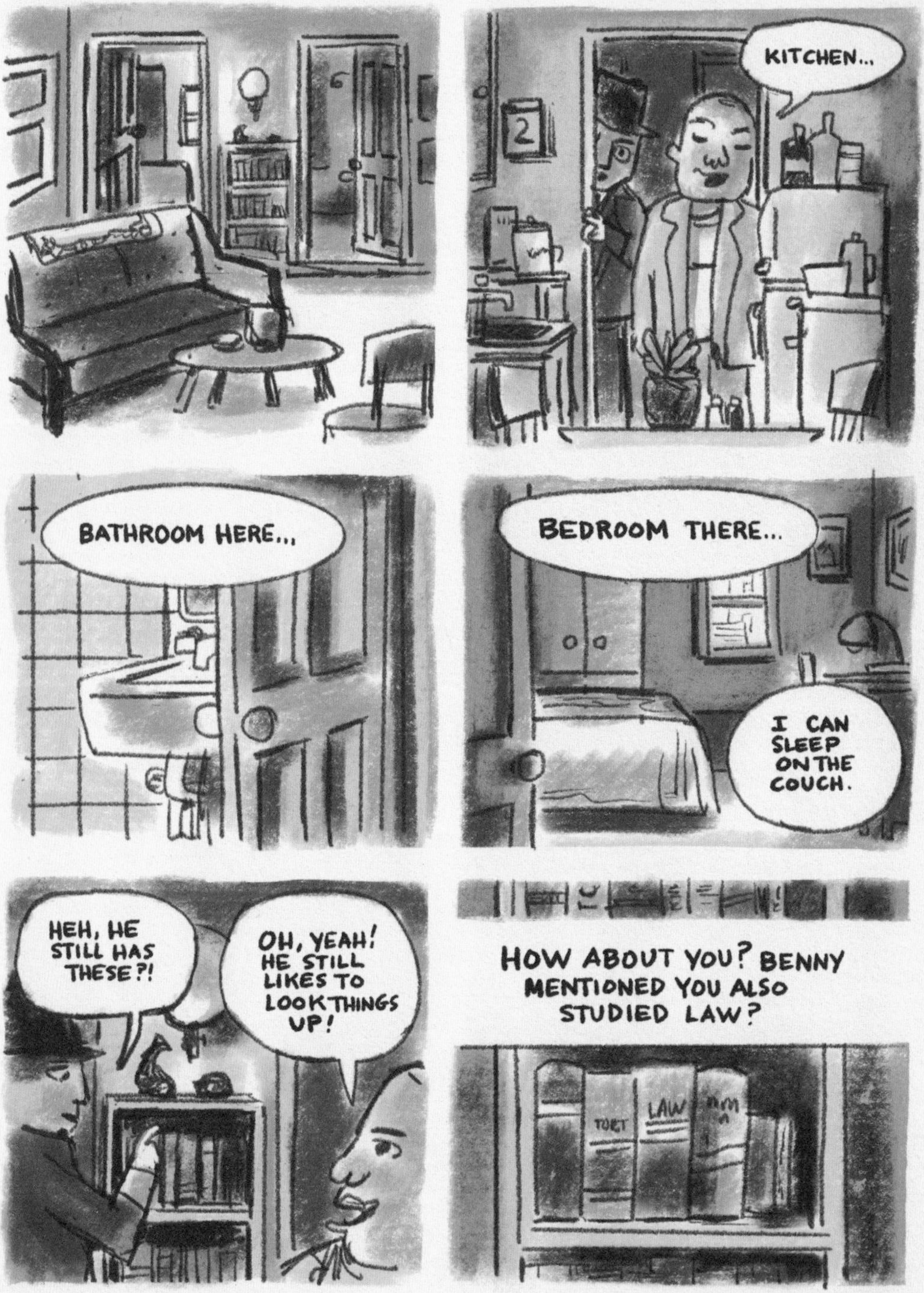
KITCHEN...
BATHROOM HERE...
BEDROOM THERE...
I CAN SLEEP ON THE COUCH.
HEH, HE STILL HAS THESE?!
OH, YEAH! HE STILL LIKES TO LOOK THINGS UP!
HOW ABOUT YOU? BENNY MENTIONED YOU ALSO STUDIED LAW?
TORT
LAW

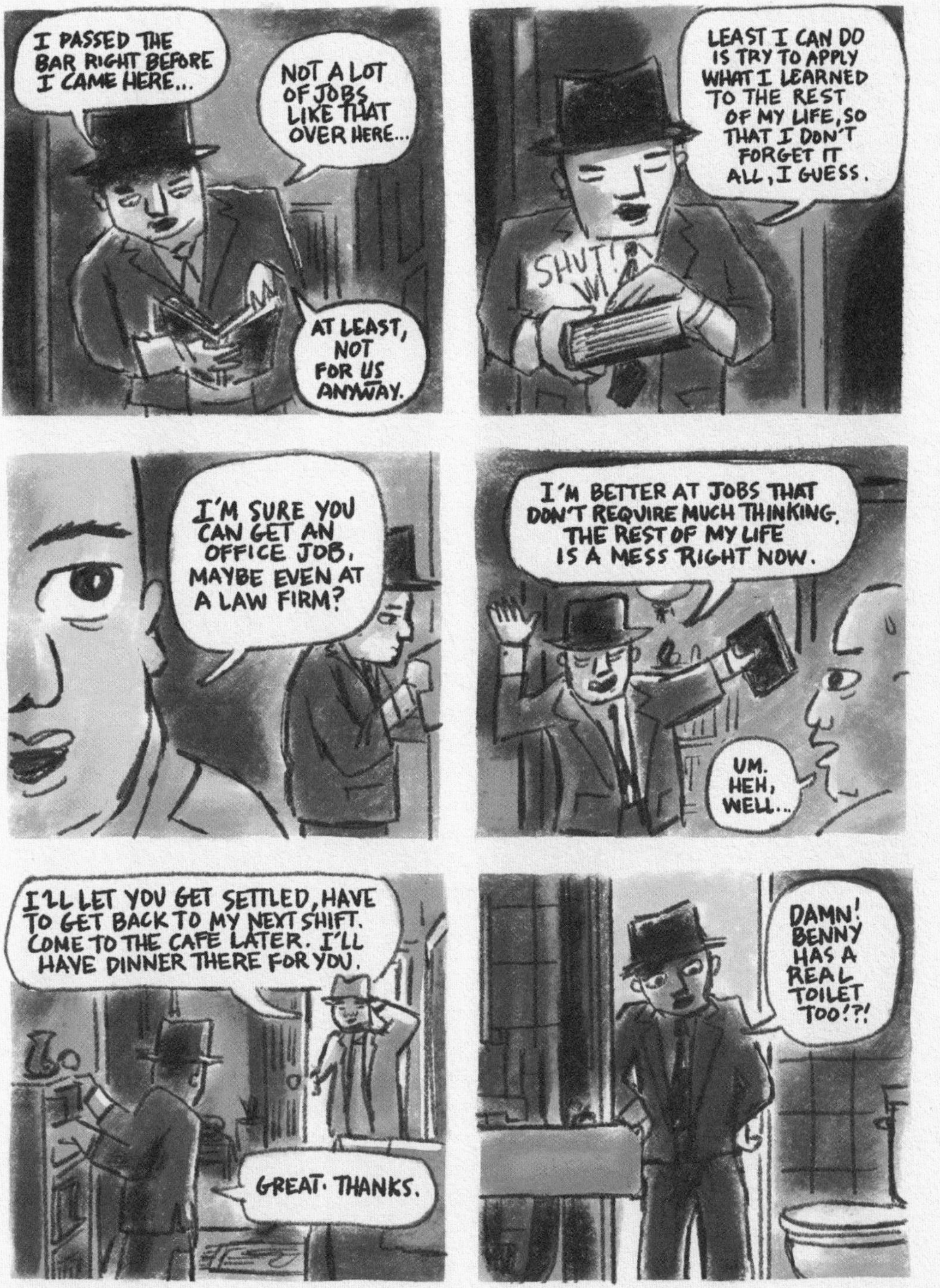
I PASSED THE BAR RIGHT BEFORE I CAME HERE...
NOT A LOT OF JOBS LIKE THAT OVER HERE...
AT LEAST, NOT FOR US ANYWAY.
LEAST I CAN DO IS TRY TO APPLY WHAT I LEARNED TO THE REST OF MY LIFE, SO THAT I DON'T FORGET IT ALL, I GUESS.
SHUT!
I'M SURE YOU CAN GET AN OFFICE JOB, MAYBE EVEN AT A LAW FIRM?
I'M BETTER AT JOBS THAT DON'T REQUIRE MUCH THINKING. THE REST OF MY LIFE IS A MESS RIGHT NOW.
UM. HEH, WELL...
I'LL LET YOU GET SETTLED, HAVE TO GET BACK TO MY NEXT SHIFT. COME TO THE CAFE LATER. I'LL HAVE DINNER THERE FOR YOU.
GREAT. THANKS.
DAMN! BENNY HAS A REAL TOILET TOO!?!

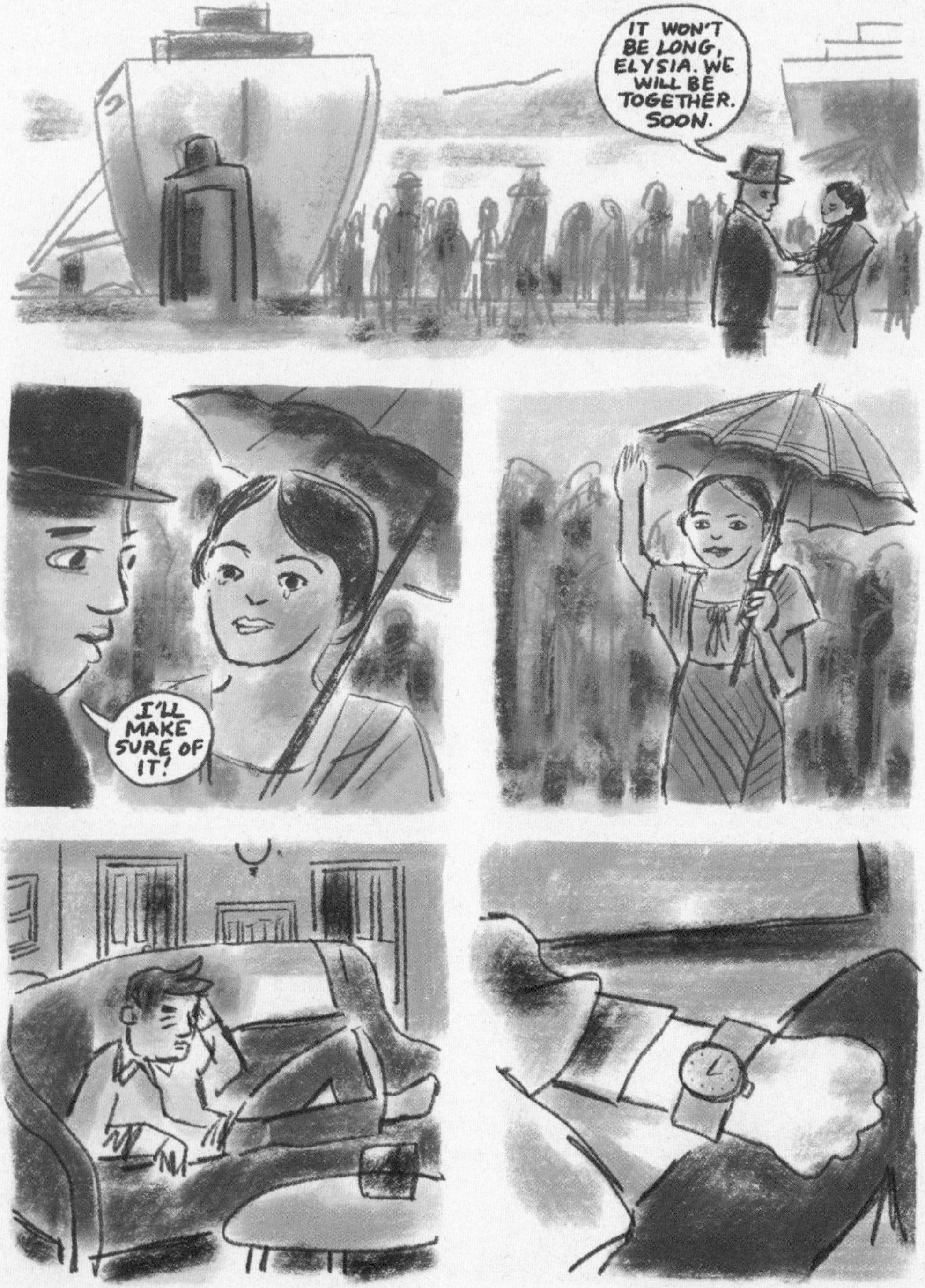
IT WON'T BE LONG, ELYSIA. WE WILL BE TOGETHER. SOON.
I'LL MAKE SURE OF IT!

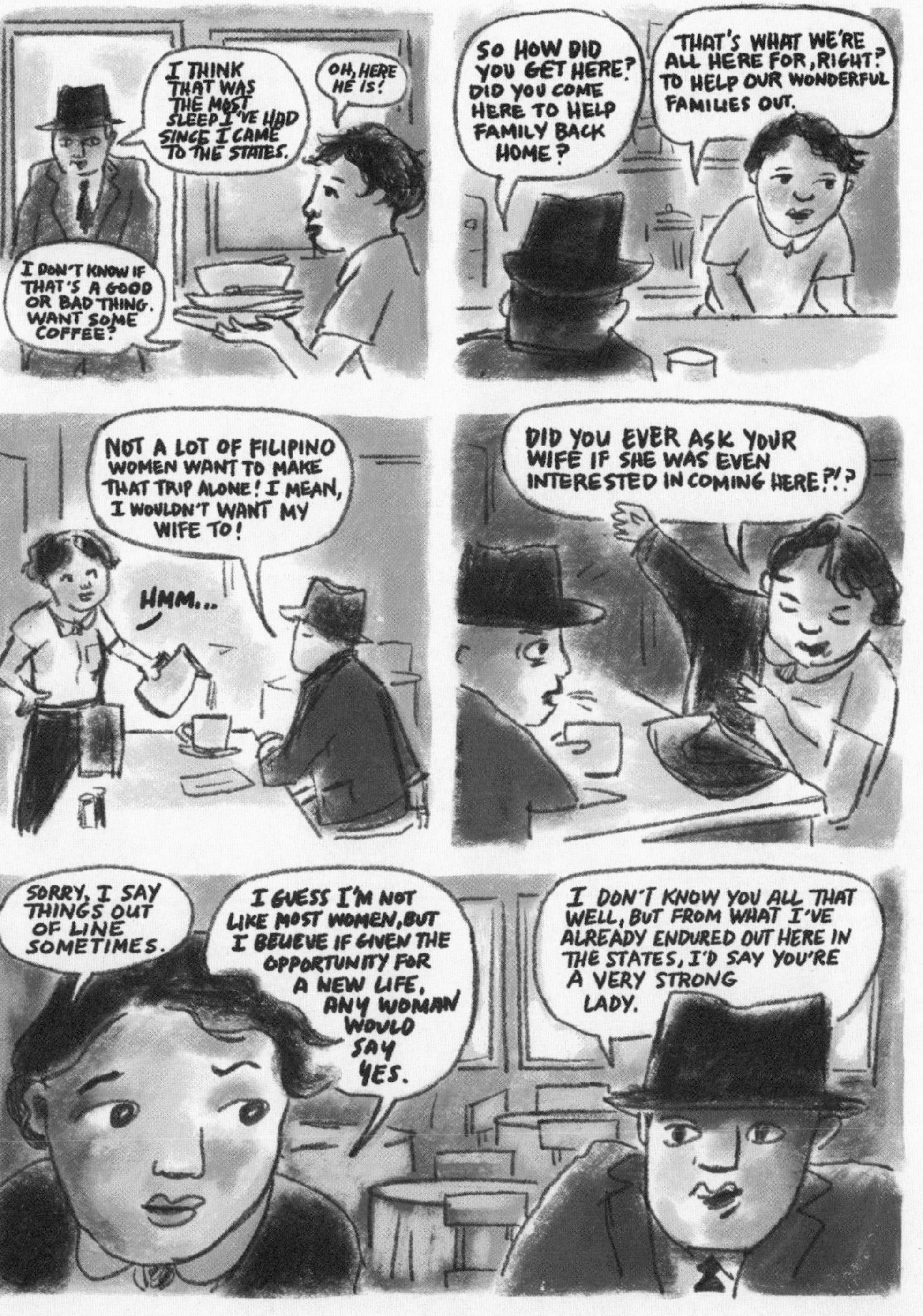
I THINK THAT WAS THE MOST SLEEP I'VE HAD SINCE I CAME TO THE STATES.
OH, HERE HE IS!
I DON'T KNOW IF THAT'S A GOOD OR BAD THING. WANT SOME COFFEE?
SO HOW DID YOU GET HERE? DID YOU COME HERE TO HELP FAMILY BACK HOME?
THAT'S WHAT WE'RE ALL HERE FOR, RIGHT? TO HELP OUR WONDERFUL FAMILIES OUT.
NOT A LOT OF FILIPINO WOMEN WANT TO MAKE THAT TRIP ALONE! I MEAN, I WOULDN'T WANT MY WIFE TO!
HMM...
DID YOU EVER ASK YOUR WIFE IF SHE WAS EVEN INTERESTED IN COMING HERE?!?
SORRY, I SAY THINGS OUT OF LINE SOMETIMES.
I GUESS I'M NOT LIKE MOST WOMEN, BUT I BELIEVE IF GIVEN THE OPPORTUNITY FOR A NEW LIFE, ANY WOMAN WOULD SAY YES.
I DON'T KNOW YOU ALL THAT WELL, BUT FROM WHAT I'VE ALREADY ENDURED OUT HERE IN THE STATES, I'D SAY YOU'RE A VERY STRONG LADY.

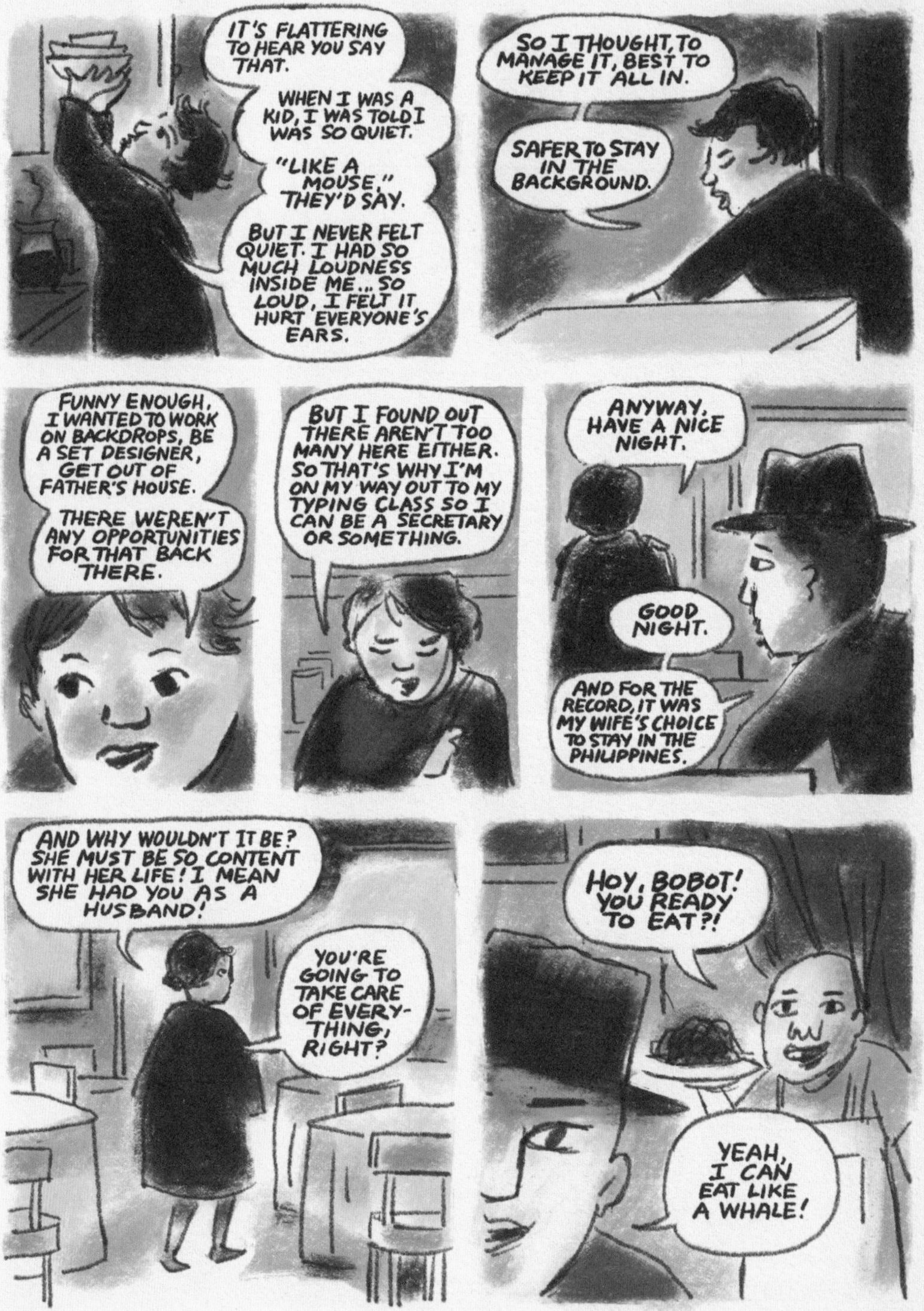

IT'S FLATTERING TO HEAR YOU SAY THAT.
WHEN I WAS A KID, I WAS TOLD I WAS SO QUIET.
"LIKE A MOUSE," THEY'D SAY.
BUT I NEVER FELT QUIET. I HAD SO MUCH LOUDNESS INSIDE ME... SO LOUD, I FELT IT HURT EVERYONE'S EARS.
SO I THOUGHT, TO MANAGE IT, BEST TO KEEP IT ALL IN.
SAFER TO STAY IN THE BACKGROUND.
FUNNY ENOUGH, I WANTED TO WORK ON BACKDROPS, BE A SET DESIGNER, GET OUT OF FATHER'S HOUSE.
THERE WEREN'T ANY OPPORTUNITIES FOR THAT BACK THERE.
BUT I FOUND OUT THERE AREN'T TOO MANY HERE EITHER. SO THAT'S WHY I'M ON MY WAY OUT TO MY TYPING CLASS SO I CAN BE A SECRETARY OR SOMETHING.
ANYWAY, HAVE A NICE NIGHT.
GOOD NIGHT.
AND FOR THE RECORD, IT WAS MY WIFE'S CHOICE TO STAY IN THE PHILIPPINES.
AND WHY WOULDN'T IT BE? SHE MUST BE SO CONTENT WITH HER LIFE! I MEAN SHE HAD YOU AS A HUSBAND!
YOU'RE GOING TO TAKE CARE OF EVERY-THING, RIGHT?
HOY, BOBOT! YOU READY TO EAT?!
YEAH, I CAN EAT LIKE A WHALE!

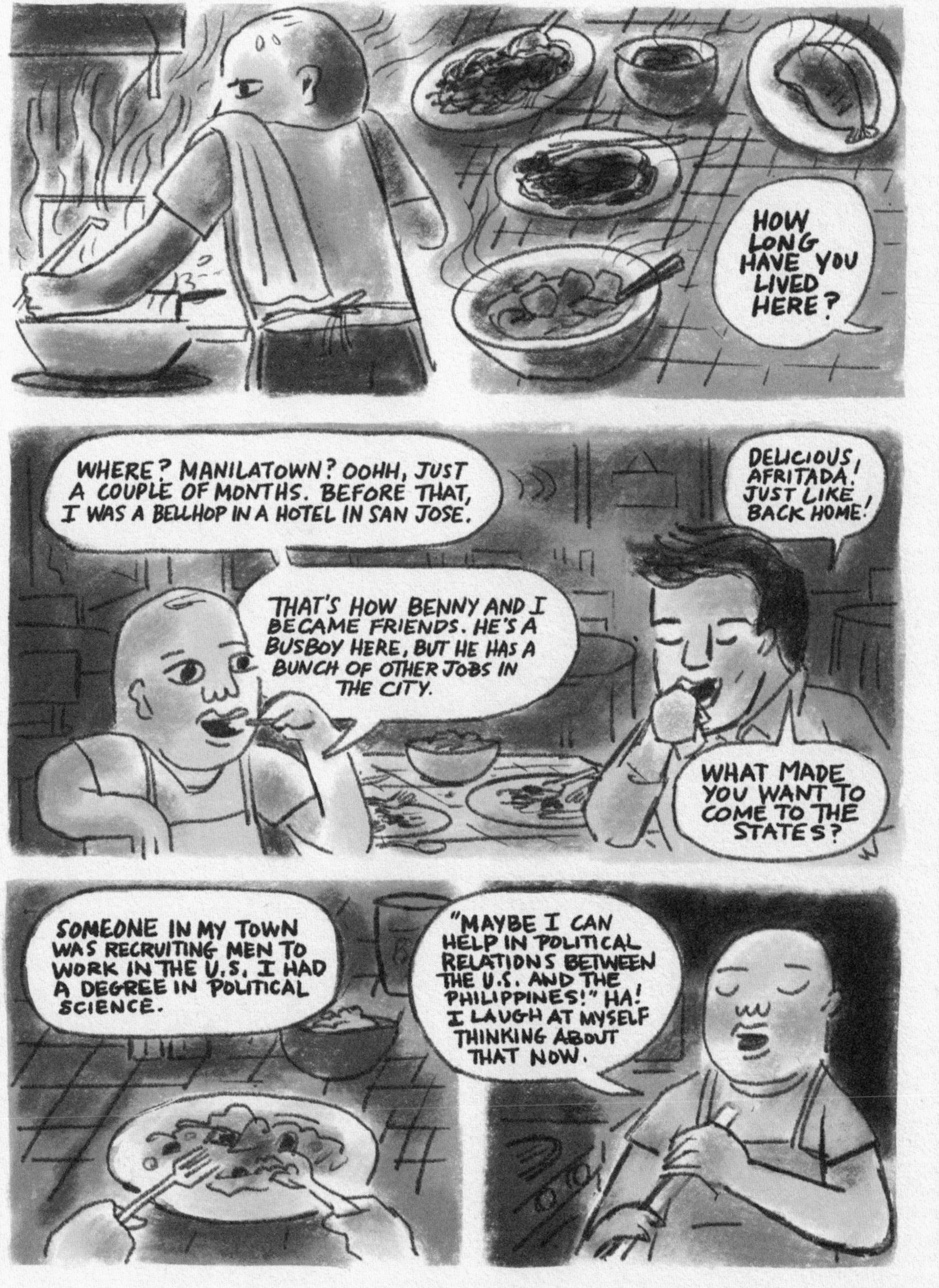
HOW LONG HAVE YOU LIVED HERE?
WHERE? MANILATOWN? OOHH, JUST A COUPLE OF MONTHS. BEFORE THAT, I WAS A BELLHOP IN A HOTEL IN SAN JOSE.
DELICIOUS, AFRITADA! JUST LIKE BACK HOME!
THAT'S HOW BENNY AND I BECAME FRIENDS. HE'S A BUSBOY HERE, BUT HE HAS A BUNCH OF OTHER JOBS IN THE CITY.
WHAT MADE YOU WANT TO COME TO THE STATES?
SOMEONE IN MY TOWN WAS RECRUITING MEN TO WORK IN THE U.S. I HAD A DEGREE IN POLITICAL SCIENCE.
"MAYBE I CAN HELP IN POLITICAL RELATIONS BETWEEN THE U.S. AND THE PHILIPPINES!" HA! I LAUGH AT MYSELF THINKING ABOUT THAT NOW.

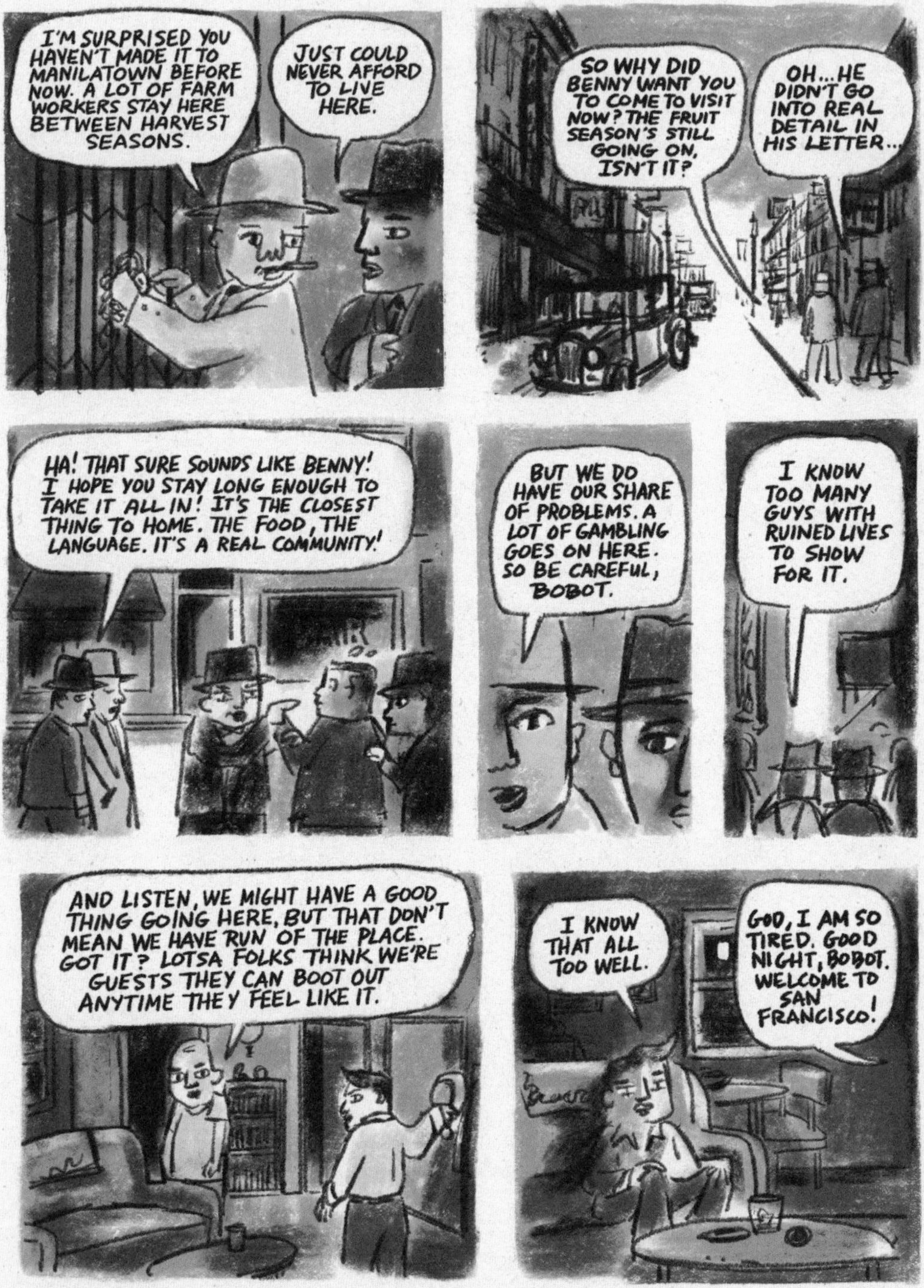
I'M SURPRISED YOU HAVEN'T MADE IT TO MANILATOWN BEFORE NOW. A LOT OF FARM WORKERS STAY HERE BETWEEN HARVEST SEASONS.
JUST COULD NEVER AFFORD TO LIVE HERE.
SO WHY DID BENNY WANT YOU TO COME TO VISIT NOW? THE FRUIT SEASON'S STILL GOING ON, ISN'T IT?
OH...HE DIDN'T GO INTO REAL DETAIL IN HIS LETTER...
HA! THAT SURE SOUNDS LIKE BENNY! I HOPE YOU STAY LONG ENOUGH TO TAKE IT ALL IN! IT'S THE CLOSEST THING TO HOME. THE FOOD, THE LANGUAGE. IT'S A REAL COMMUNITY!
BUT WE DO HAVE OUR SHARE OF PROBLEMS. A LOT OF GAMBLING GOES ON HERE. SO BE CAREFUL, BOBOT.
I KNOW TOO MANY GUYS WITH RUINED LIVES TO SHOW FOR IT.
AND LISTEN, WE MIGHT HAVE A GOOD THING GOING HERE, BUT THAT DON'T MEAN WE HAVE RUN OF THE PLACE. GOT IT? LOTSA FOLKS THINK WE'RE GUESTS THEY CAN BOOT OUT ANYTIME THEY FEEL LIKE IT.
I KNOW THAT ALL TOO WELL.
GOD, I AM SO TIRED. GOOD NIGHT, BOBOT. WELCOME TO SAN FRANCISCO!

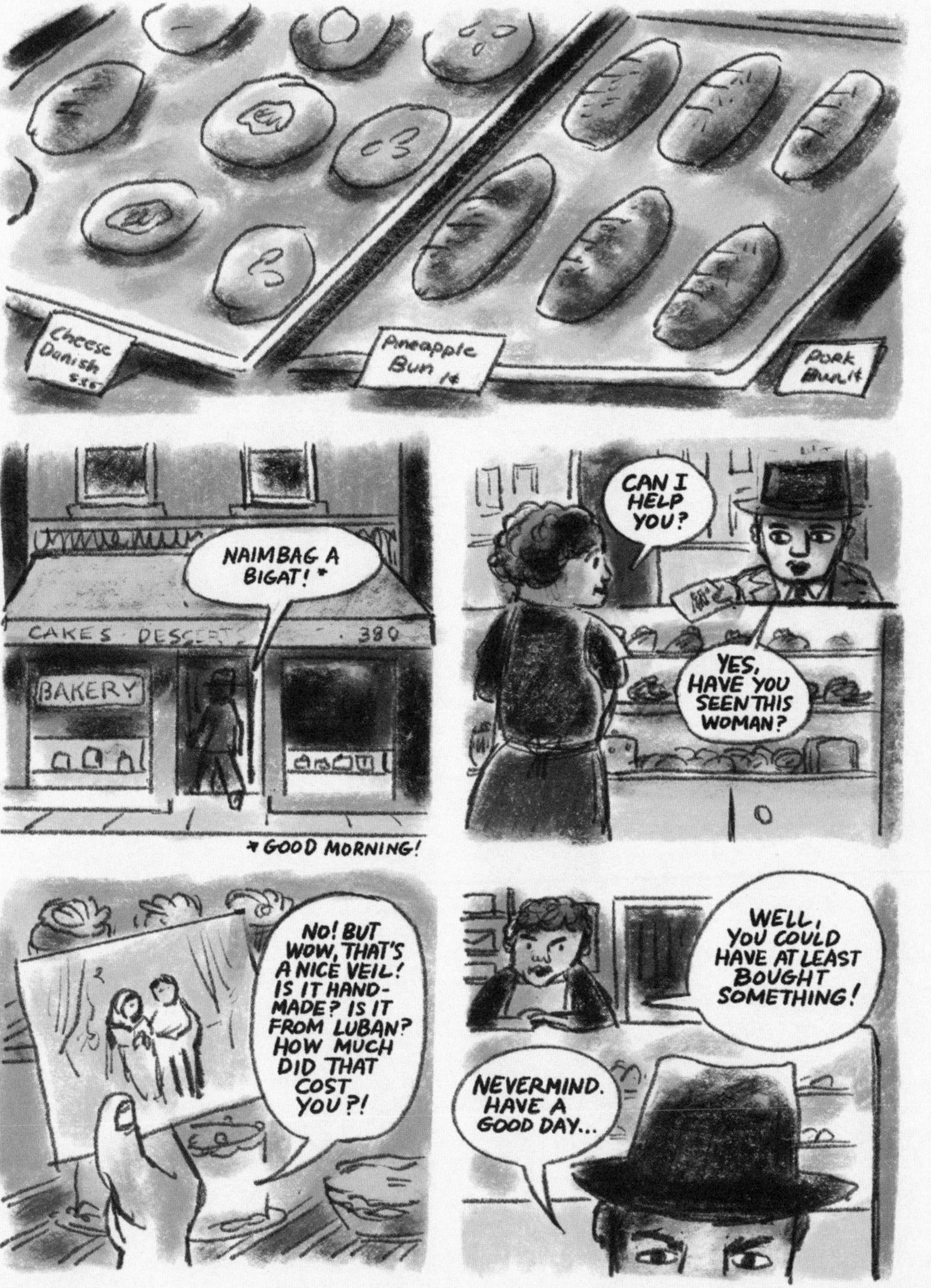

Cheese Danish
Pineapple Bun 1¢
Pork Bun
BAKERY
380
NAIMBAG A BIGAT! *
* GOOD MORNING!
CAN I HELP YOU?
YES, HAVE YOU SEEN THIS WOMAN?
NO! BUT WOW, THAT'S A NICE VEIL! IS IT HAND-MADE? IS IT FROM LUBAN? HOW MUCH DID THAT COST YOU?!
WELL, YOU COULD HAVE AT LEAST BOUGHT SOMETHING!
NEVERMIND. HAVE A GOOD DAY...

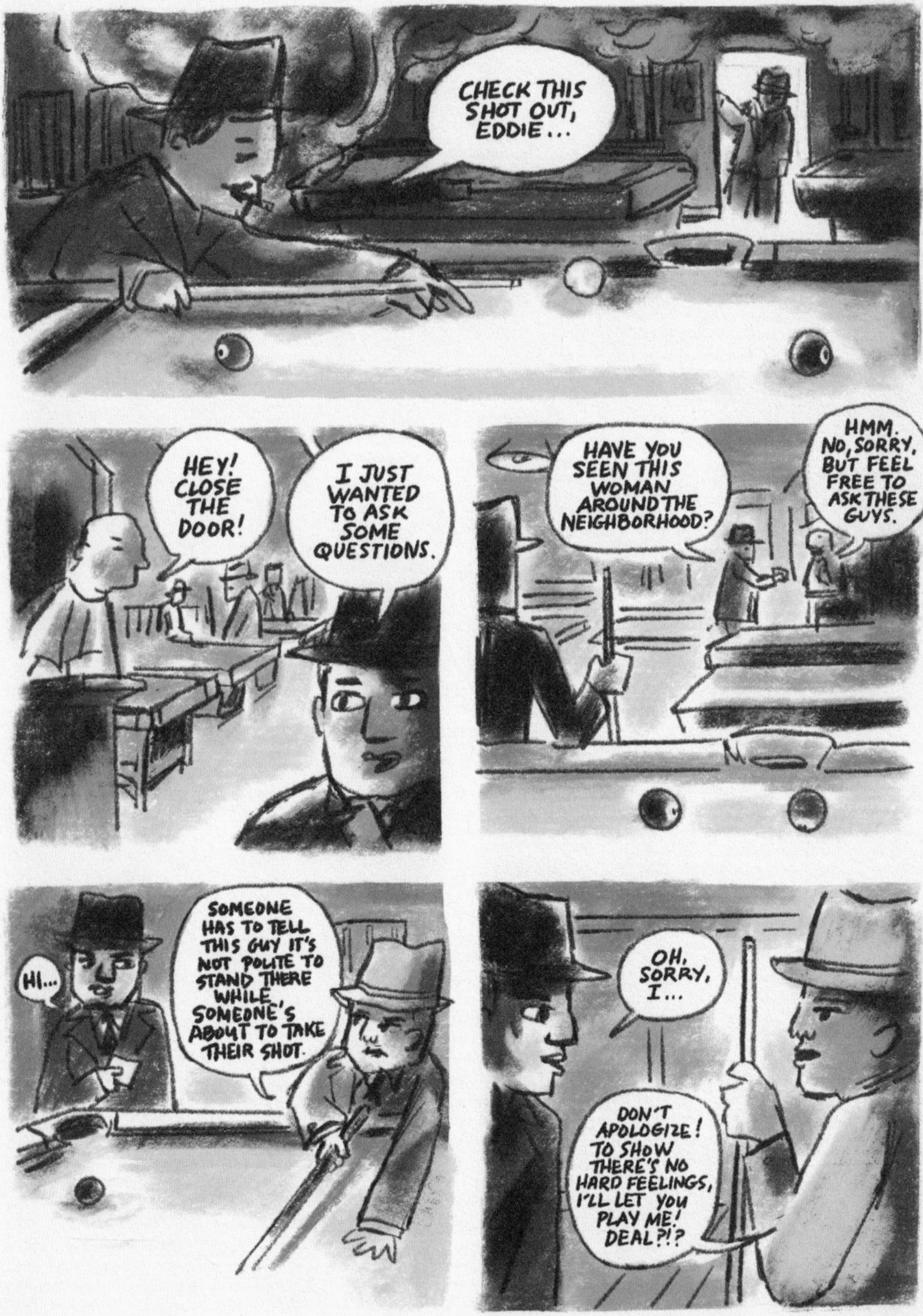
CHECK THIS SHOT OUT, EDDIE...
HEY! CLOSE THE DOOR!
I JUST WANTED TO ASK SOME QUESTIONS.
HAVE YOU SEEN THIS WOMAN AROUND THE NEIGHBORHOOD?
HMM. NO, SORRY, BUT FEEL FREE TO ASK THESE GUYS.
HI...
SOMEONE HAS TO TELL THIS GUY IT'S NOT POLITE TO STAND THERE WHILE SOMEONE'S ABOUT TO TAKE THEIR SHOT.
OH, SORRY, I...
DON'T APOLOGIZE! TO SHOW THERE'S NO HARD FEELINGS, I'LL LET YOU PLAY ME! DEAL?!?

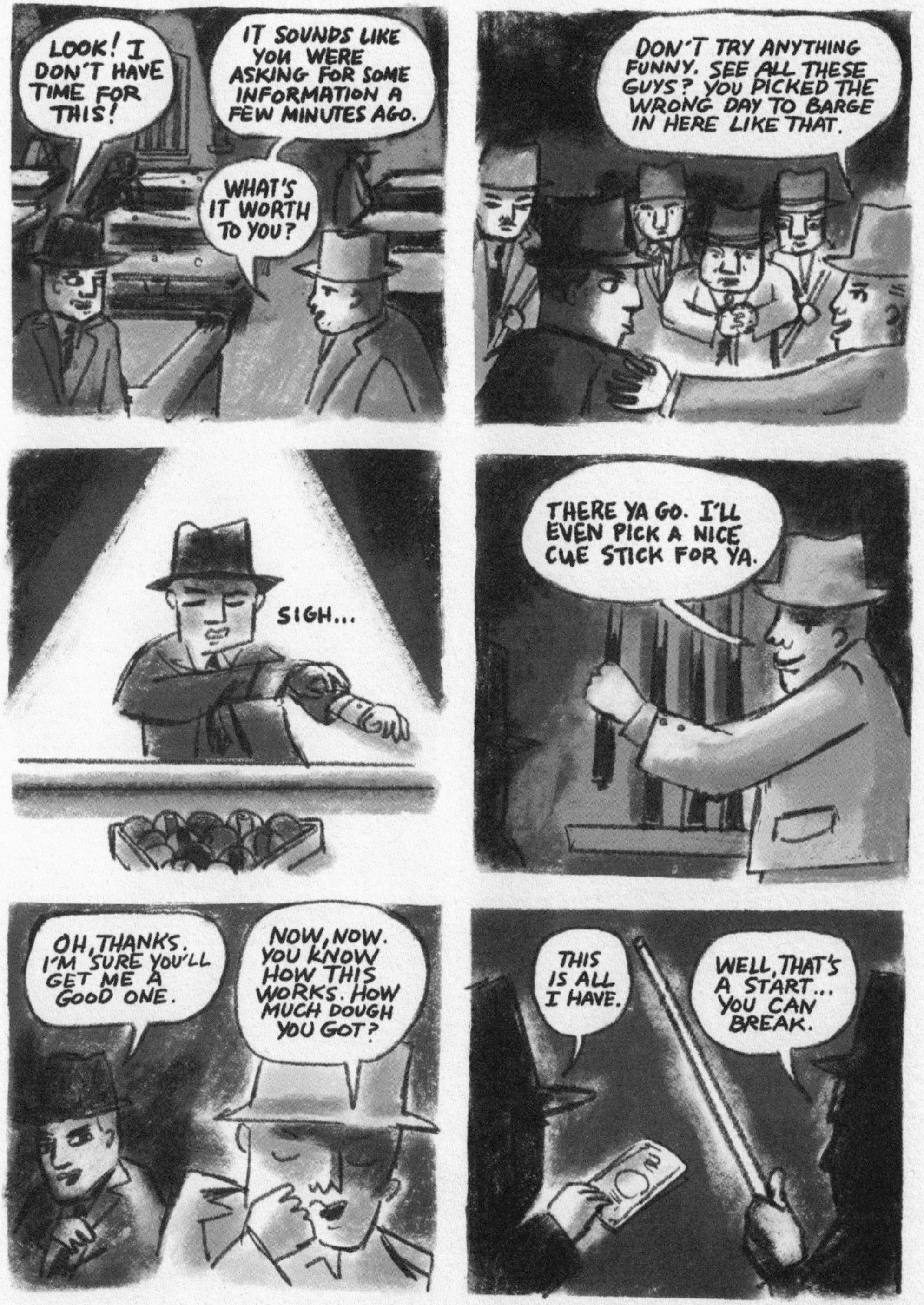
LOOK! I DON'T HAVE TIME FOR THIS!
IT SOUNDS LIKE YOU WERE ASKING FOR SOME INFORMATION A FEW MINUTES AGO.
WHAT'S IT WORTH TO YOU?
DON'T TRY ANYTHING FUNNY. SEE ALL THESE GUYS? YOU PICKED THE WRONG DAY TO BARGE IN HERE LIKE THAT.
SIGH...
THERE YA GO. I'LL EVEN PICK A NICE CUE STICK FOR YA.
OH, THANKS. I'M SURE YOU'LL GET ME A GOOD ONE.
NOW, NOW. YOU KNOW HOW THIS WORKS. HOW MUCH DOUGH YOU GOT?
THIS IS ALL I HAVE.
WELL, THAT'S A START... YOU CAN BREAK.

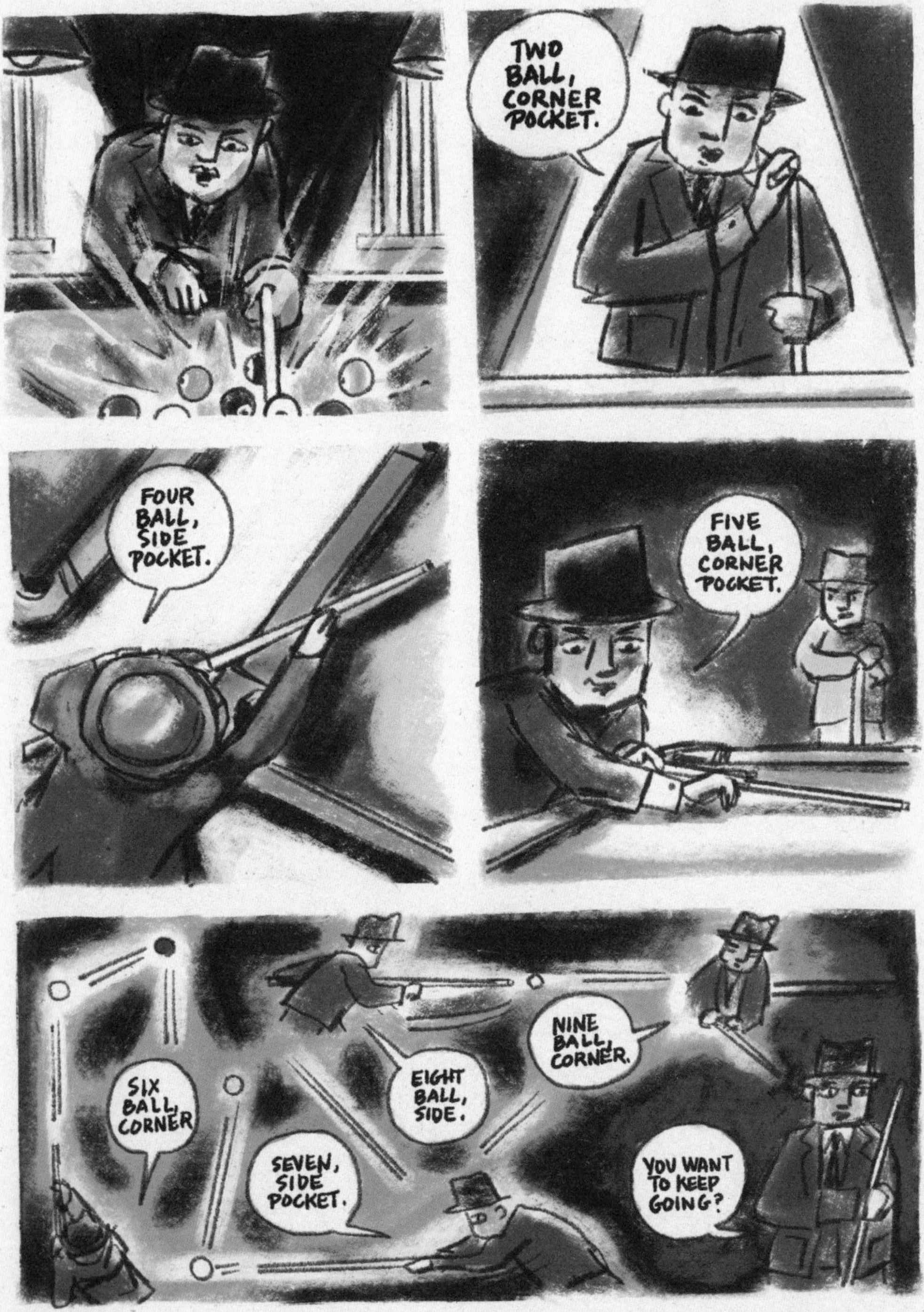
TWO BALL, CORNER POCKET.
FOUR BALL, SIDE POCKET.
FIVE BALL, CORNER POCKET.
SIX BALL, CORNER
SEVEN, SIDE POCKET.
EIGHT BALL, SIDE.
NINE BALL, CORNER.
YOU WANT TO KEEP GOING?

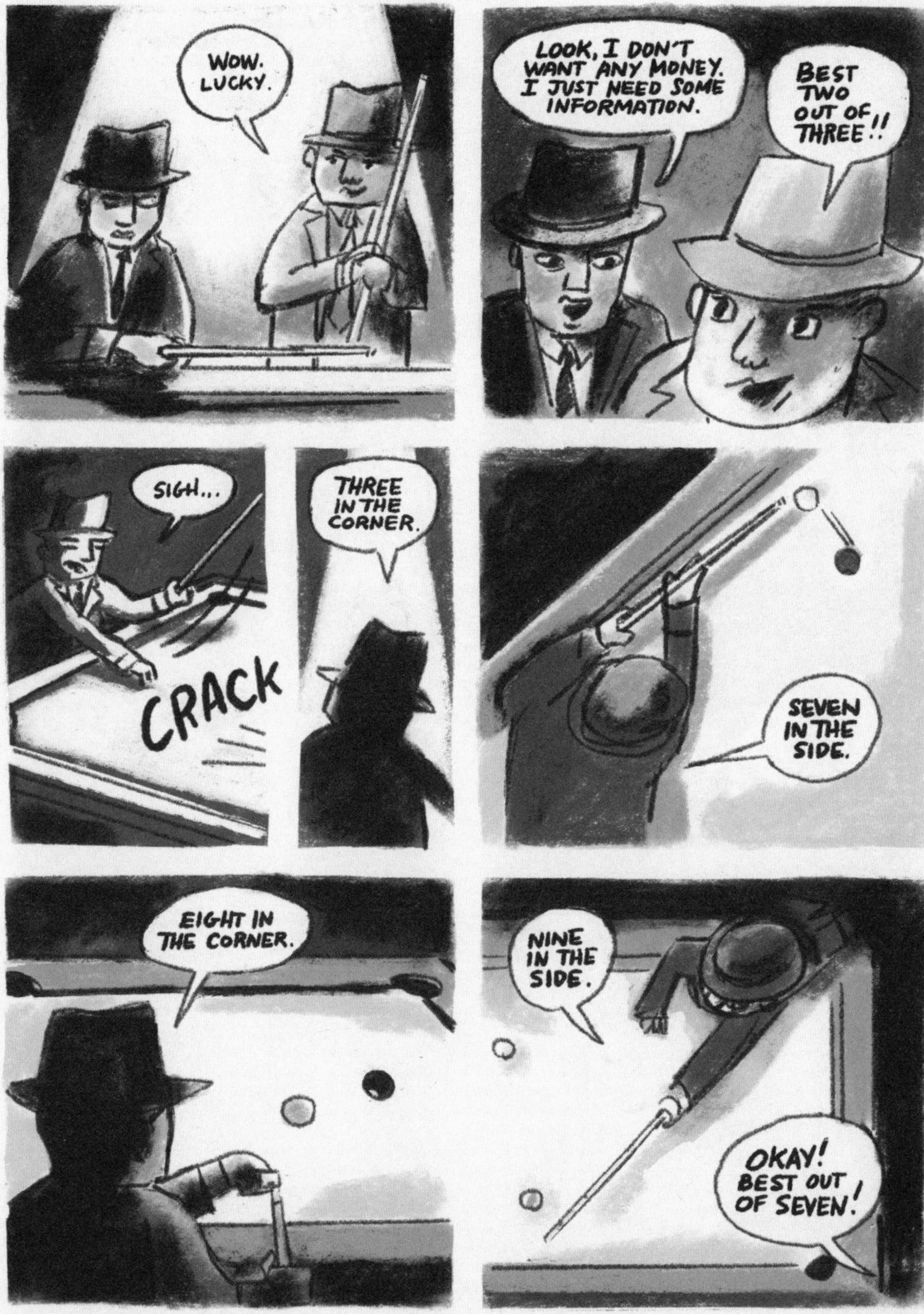
WOW. LUCKY.
LOOK, I DON'T WANT ANY MONEY. I JUST NEED SOME INFORMATION.
BEST TWO OUT OF THREE!!
SIGH...
CRACK
THREE IN THE CORNER.
SEVEN IN THE SIDE.
EIGHT IN THE CORNER.
NINE IN THE SIDE.
OKAY! BEST OUT OF SEVEN!

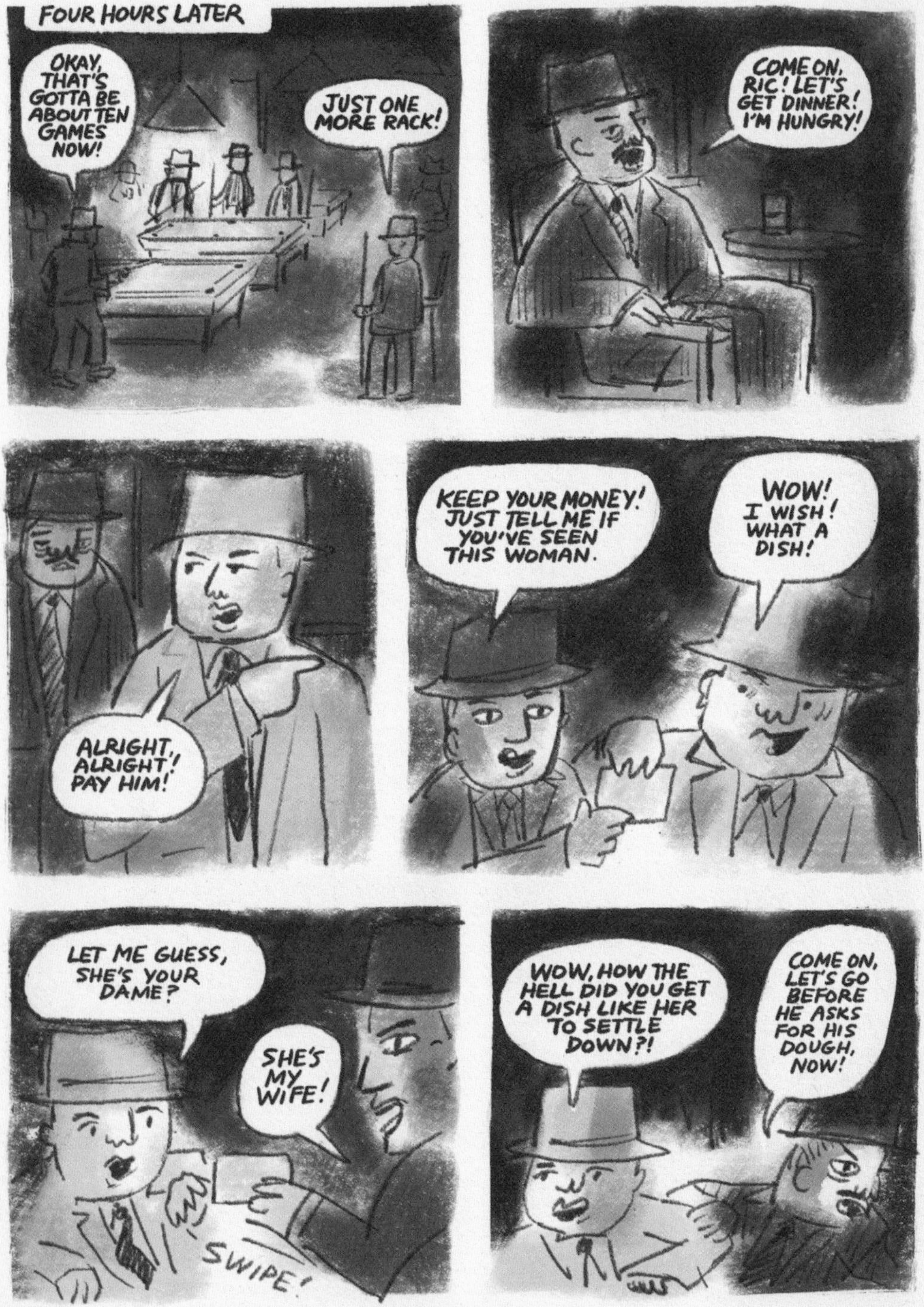
FOUR HOURS LATER
OKAY, THAT'S GOTTA BE ABOUT TEN GAMES NOW!
JUST ONE MORE RACK!
COME ON, RIC! LET'S GET DINNER! I'M HUNGRY!
ALRIGHT, ALRIGHT! PAY HIM!
KEEP YOUR MONEY! JUST TELL ME IF YOU'VE SEEN THIS WOMAN.
WOW! I WISH! WHAT A DISH!
LET ME GUESS, SHE'S YOUR DAME?
SHE'S MY WIFE!
SWIPE!
WOW, HOW THE HELL DID YOU GET A DISH LIKE HER TO SETTLE DOWN?!
COME ON, LET'S GO BEFORE HE ASKS FOR HIS DOUGH, NOW!

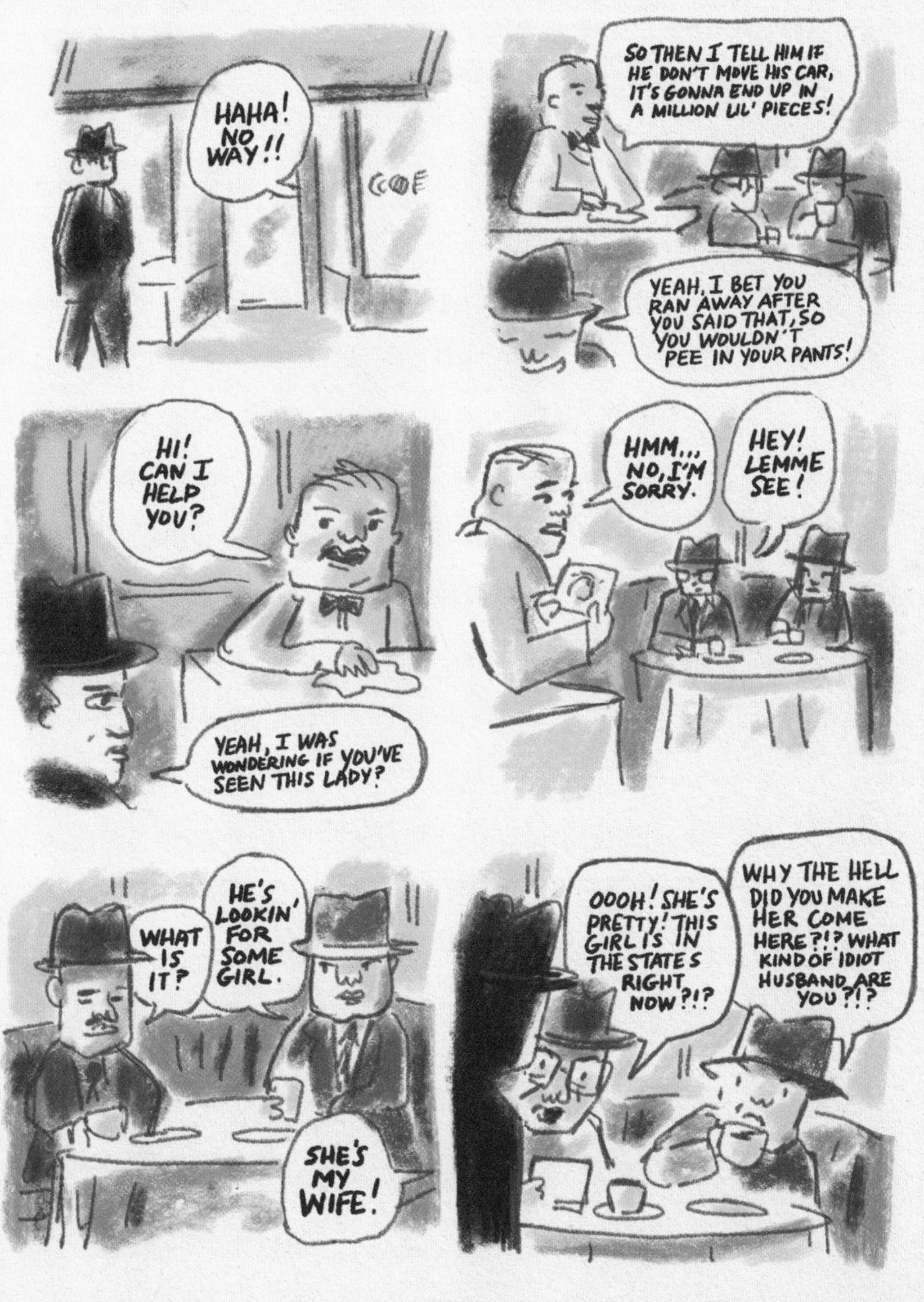
HAHA! NO WAY!!
SO THEN I TELL HIM IF HE DON'T MOVE HIS CAR, IT'S GONNA END UP IN A MILLION LIL' PIECES!
YEAH, I BET YOU RAN AWAY AFTER YOU SAID THAT, SO YOU WOULDN'T PEE IN YOUR PANTS!
HI! CAN I HELP YOU?
YEAH, I WAS WONDERING IF YOU'VE SEEN THIS LADY?
HMM.., NO, I'M SORRY.
HEY! LEMME SEE!
WHAT IS IT?
HE'S LOOKIN' FOR SOME GIRL.
SHE'S MY WIFE!
OOOH! SHE'S PRETTY! THIS GIRL IS IN THE STATES RIGHT NOW?!?
WHY THE HELL DID YOU MAKE HER COME HERE?!? WHAT KIND OF IDIOT HUSBAND ARE YOU?!?

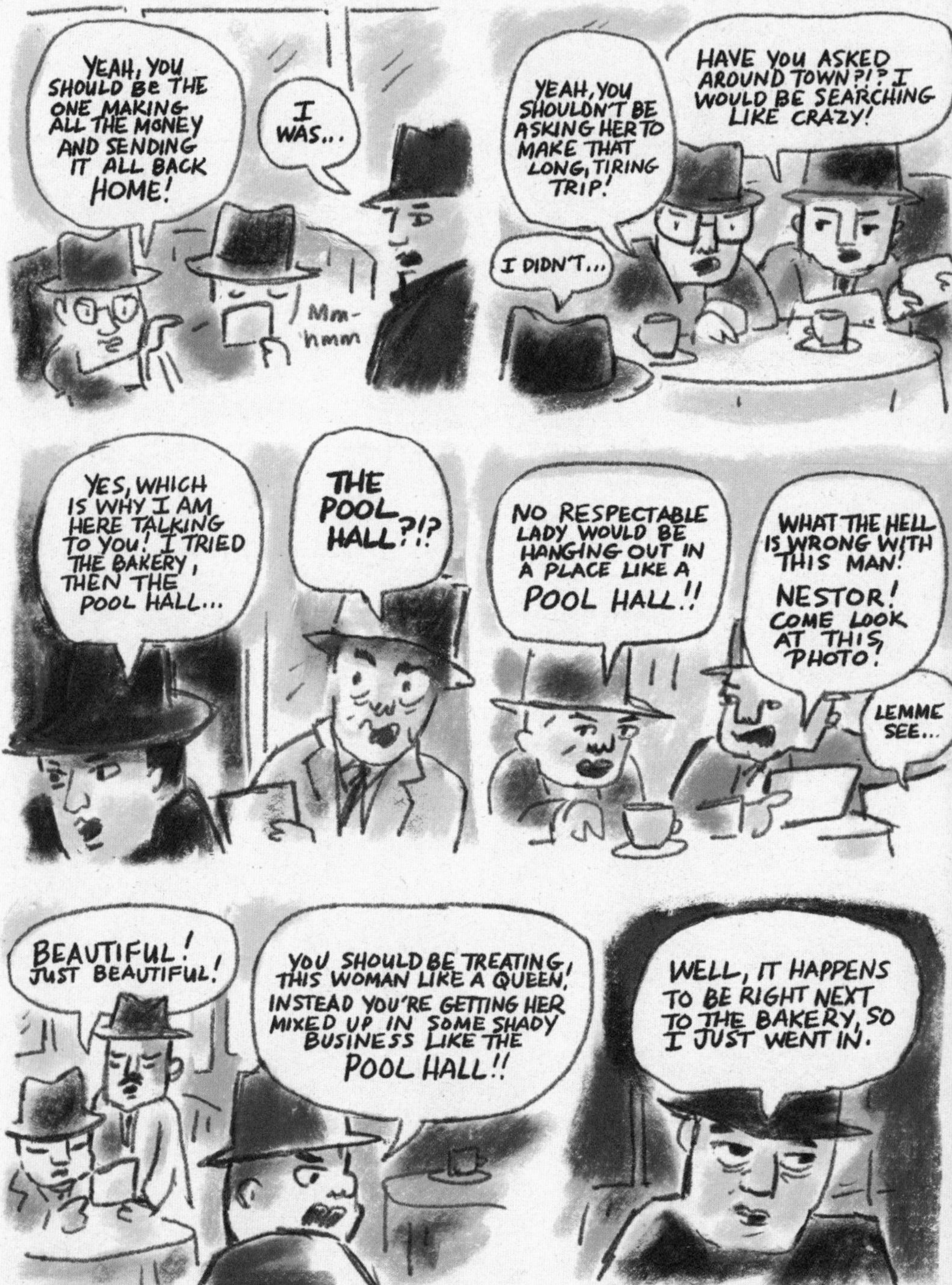
YEAH, YOU SHOULD BE THE ONE MAKING ALL THE MONEY AND SENDING IT ALL BACK HOME!
I WAS...
Mm-hmm
YEAH, YOU SHOULDN'T BE ASKING HER TO MAKE THAT LONG, TIRING TRIP!
I DIDN'T...
HAVE YOU ASKED AROUND TOWN?!? I WOULD BE SEARCHING LIKE CRAZY!
YES, WHICH IS WHY I AM HERE TALKING TO YOU! I TRIED THE BAKERY, THEN THE POOL HALL...
THE POOL HALL?!?
NO RESPECTABLE LADY WOULD BE HANGING OUT IN A PLACE LIKE A POOL HALL!!
WHAT THE HELL IS WRONG WITH THIS MAN! NESTOR! COME LOOK AT THIS PHOTO!
LEMME SEE...
BEAUTIFUL! JUST BEAUTIFUL!
YOU SHOULD BE TREATING THIS WOMAN LIKE A QUEEN! INSTEAD YOU'RE GETTING HER MIXED UP IN SOME SHADY BUSINESS LIKE THE POOL HALL!!
WELL, IT HAPPENS TO BE RIGHT NEXT TO THE BAKERY, SO I JUST WENT IN.

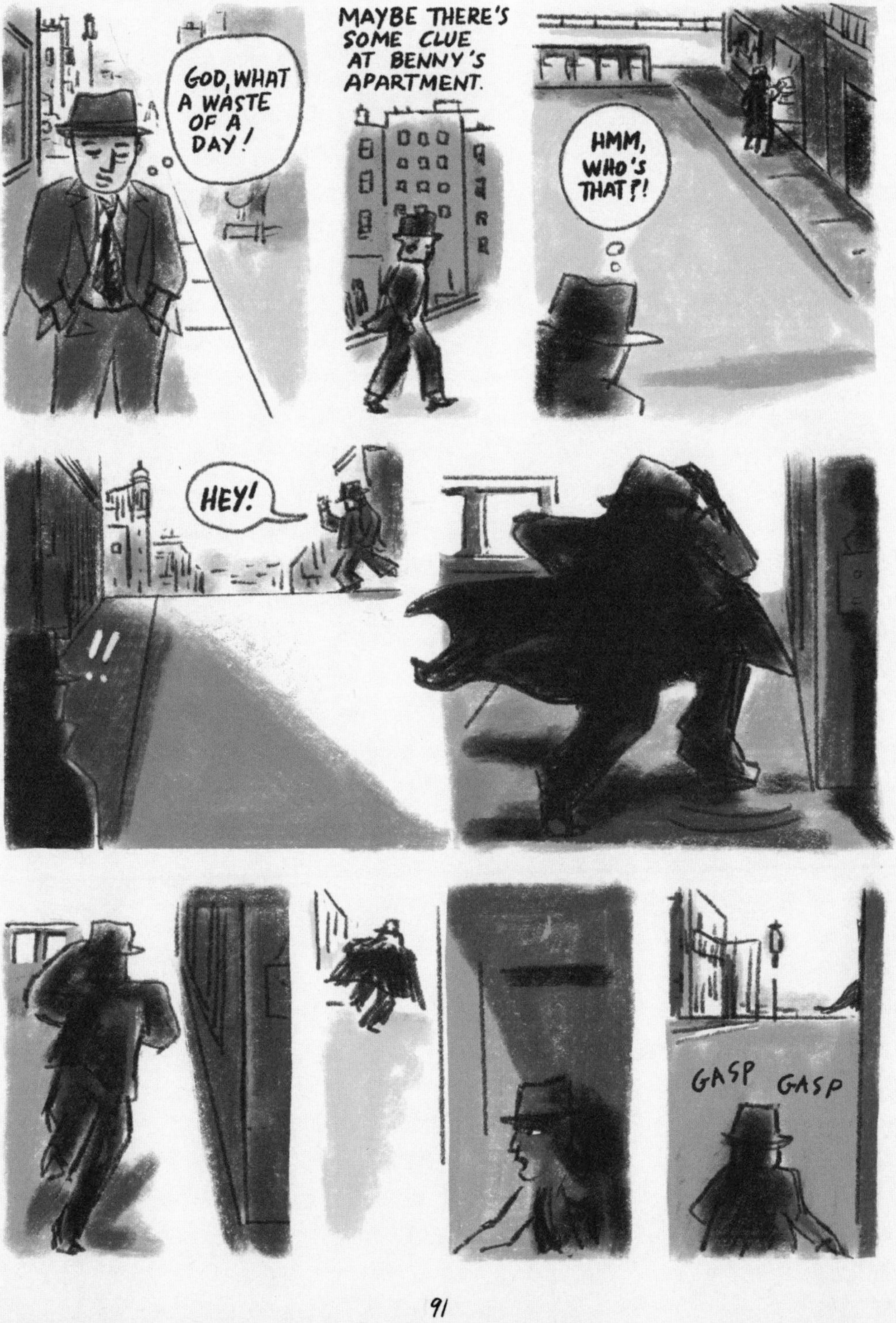
GOD, WHAT A WASTE OF A DAY!
MAYBE THERE'S SOME CLUE AT BENNY'S APARTMENT.
HMM, WHO'S THAT?!
HEY!
!!
GASP GASP

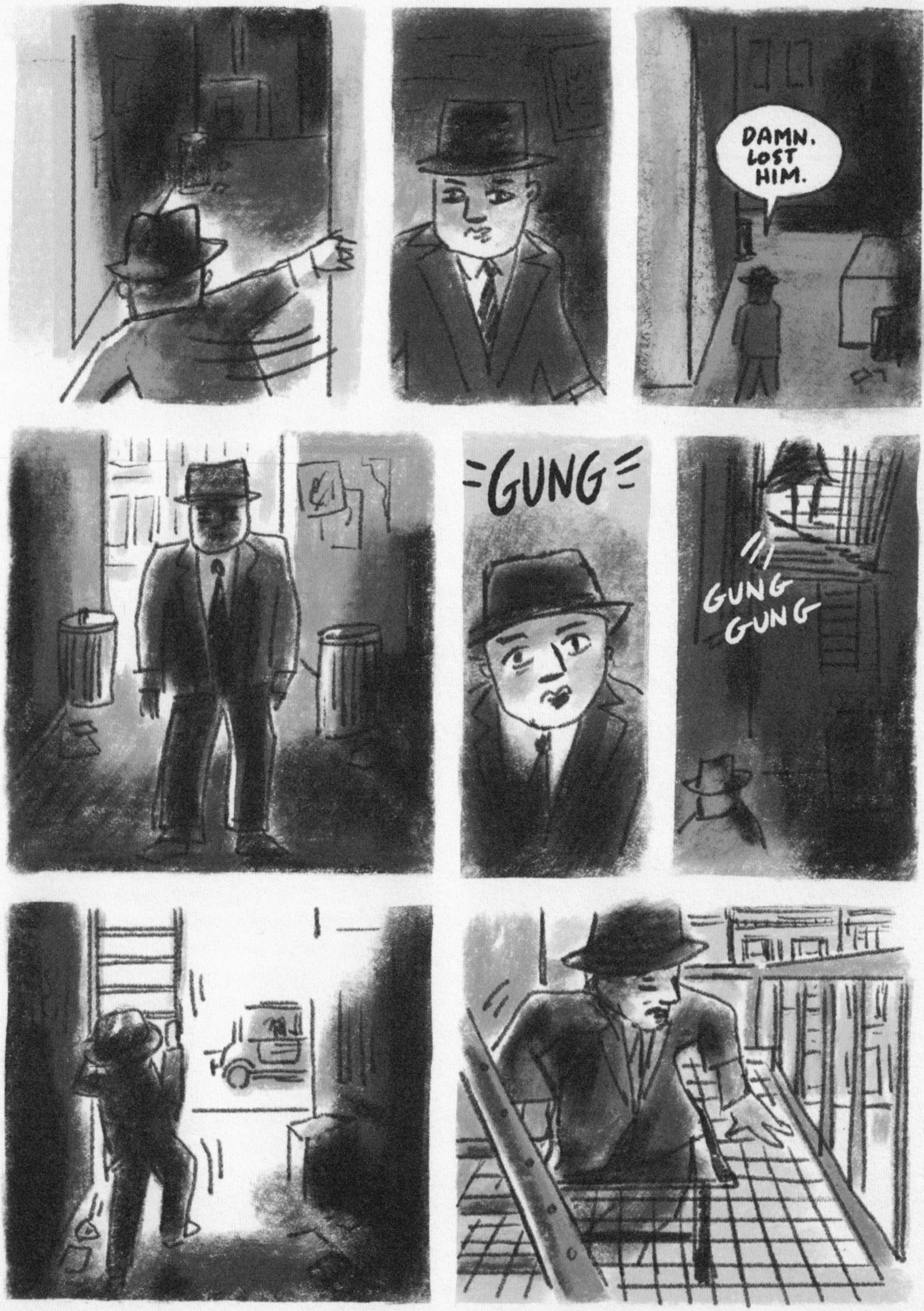
DAMN. LOST HIM.
GUNG
GUNG GUNG

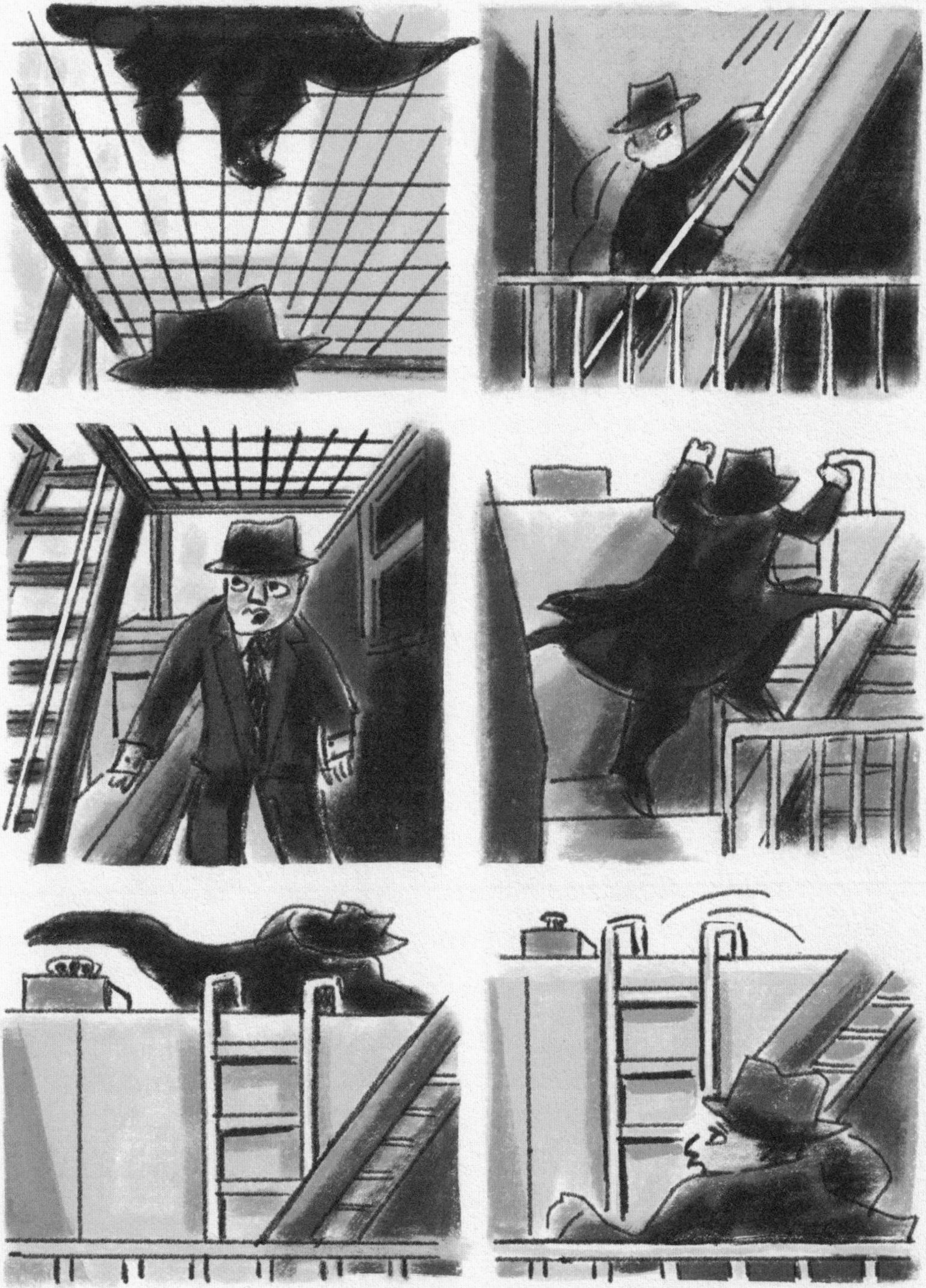

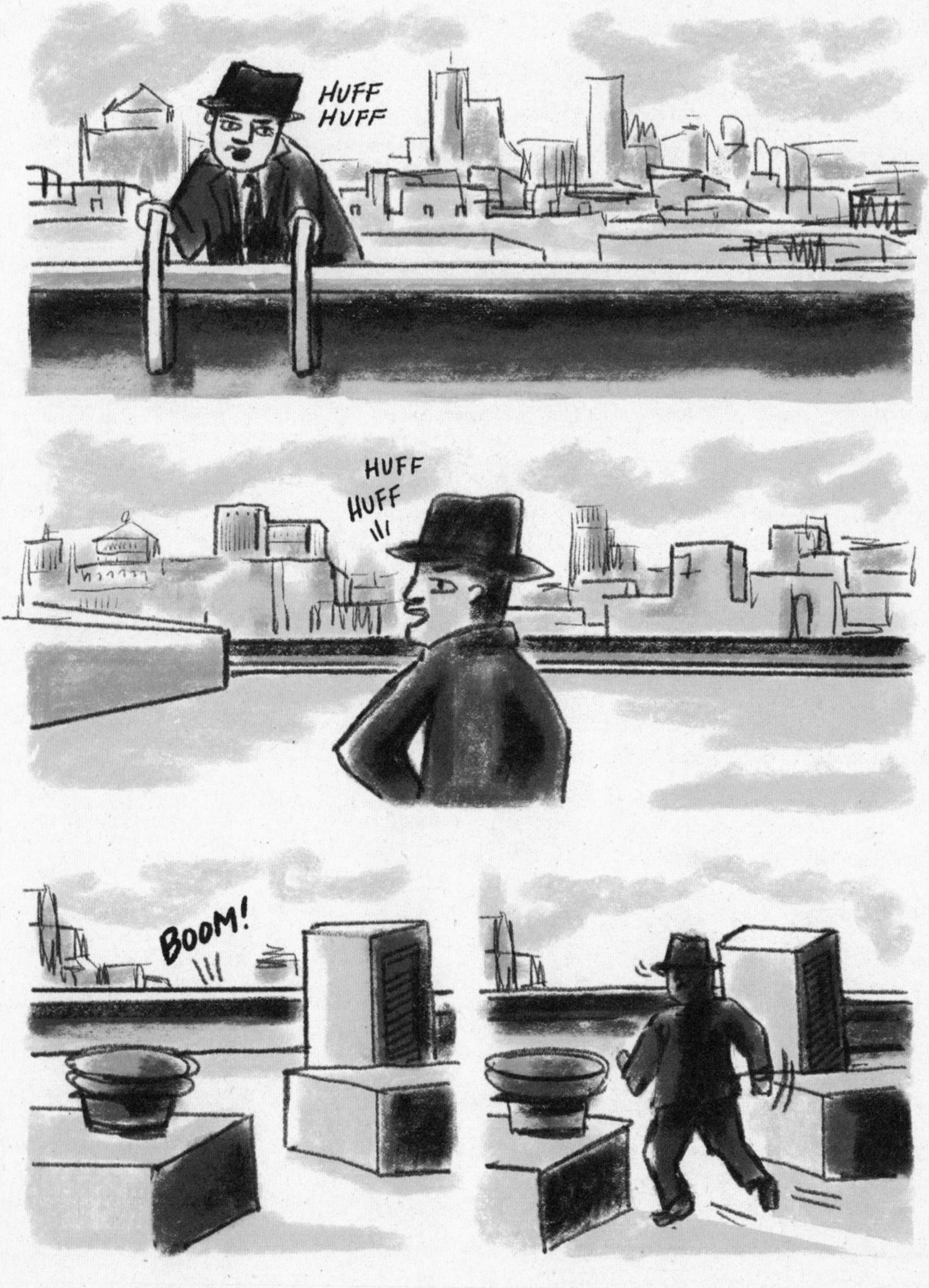
HUFF
HUFF
HUFF
HUFF
BOOM!

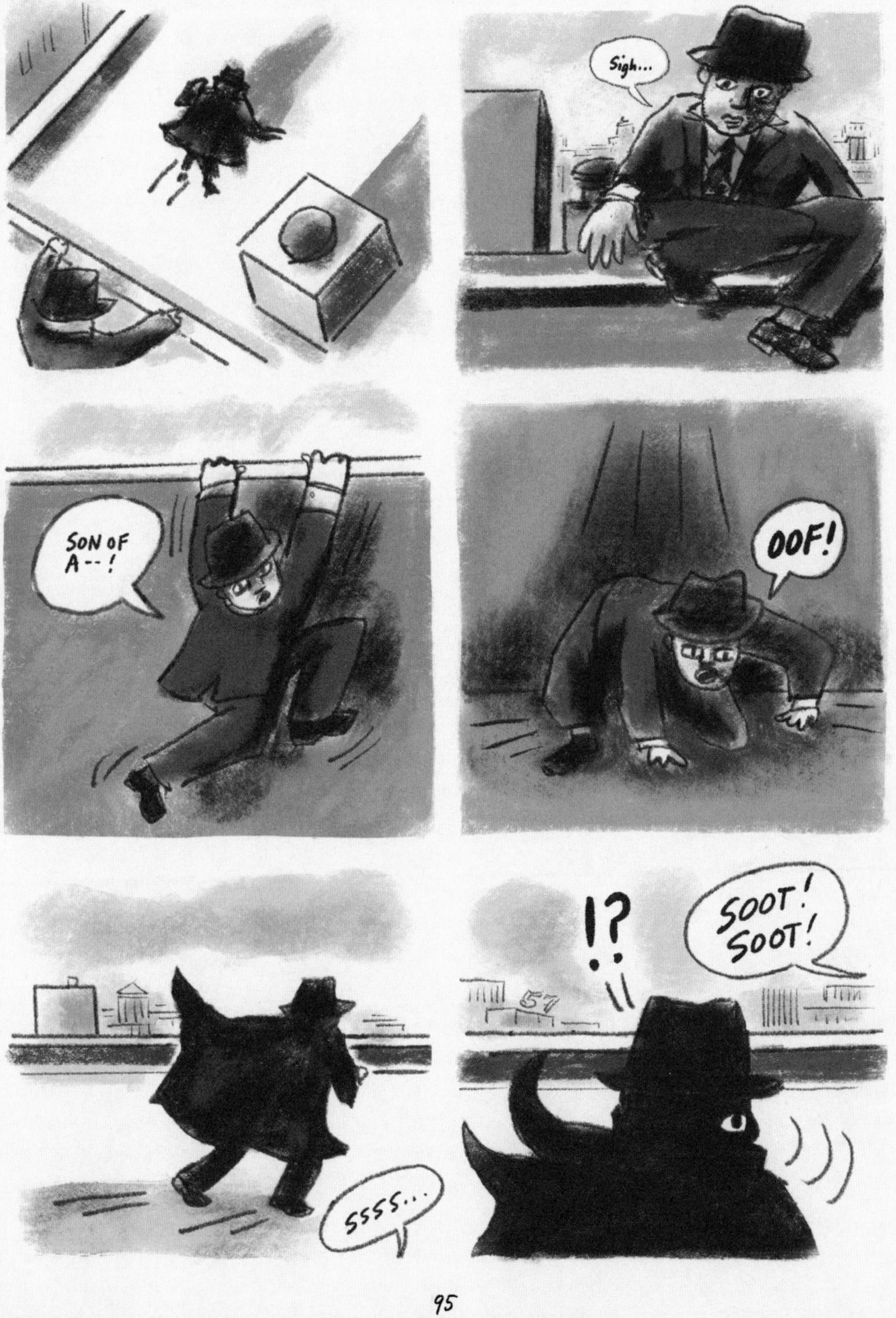
Sigh...
SON OF A--!
OOF!
SSSS...
!?
SOOT! SOOT!

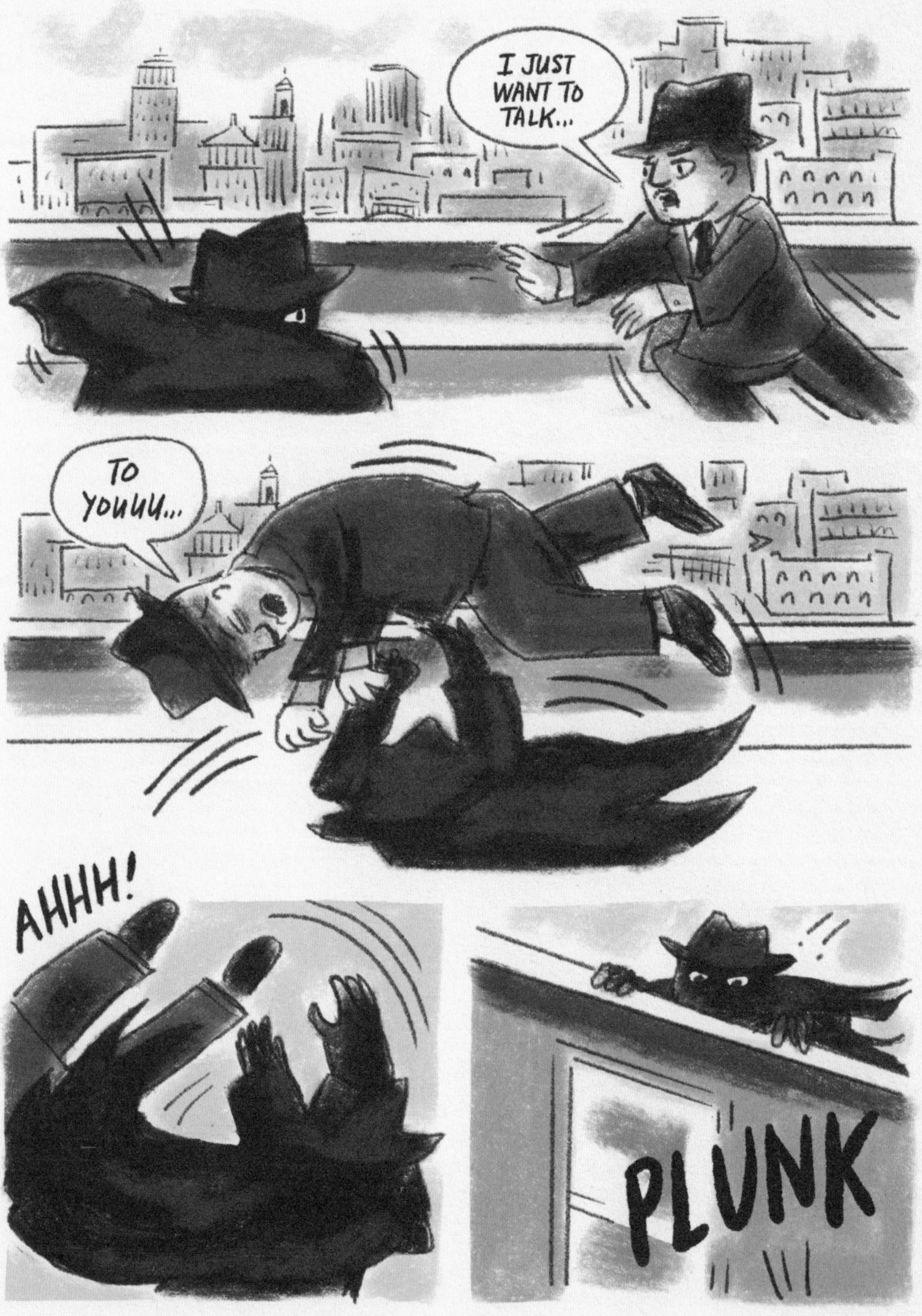
I JUST WANT TO TALK...
TO YOUUU...
AHHH!
PLUNK

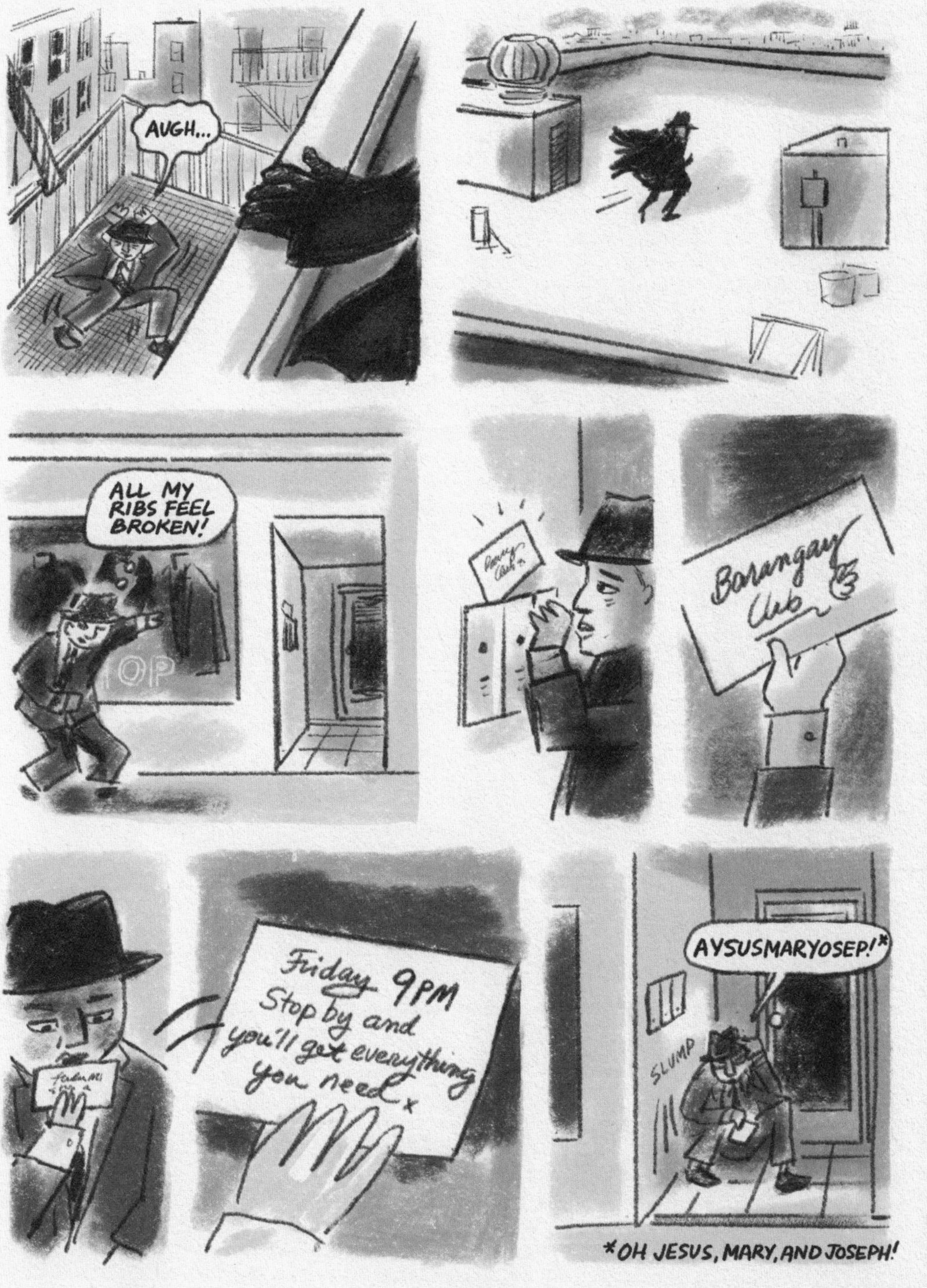
AUGH...
ALL MY RIBS FEEL BROKEN!
Barangay Club
Friday 9PM
Stop by and you'll get everything you need.
SLUMP
AYSUSMARYOSEP!*
*OH JESUS, MARY, AND JOSEPH!

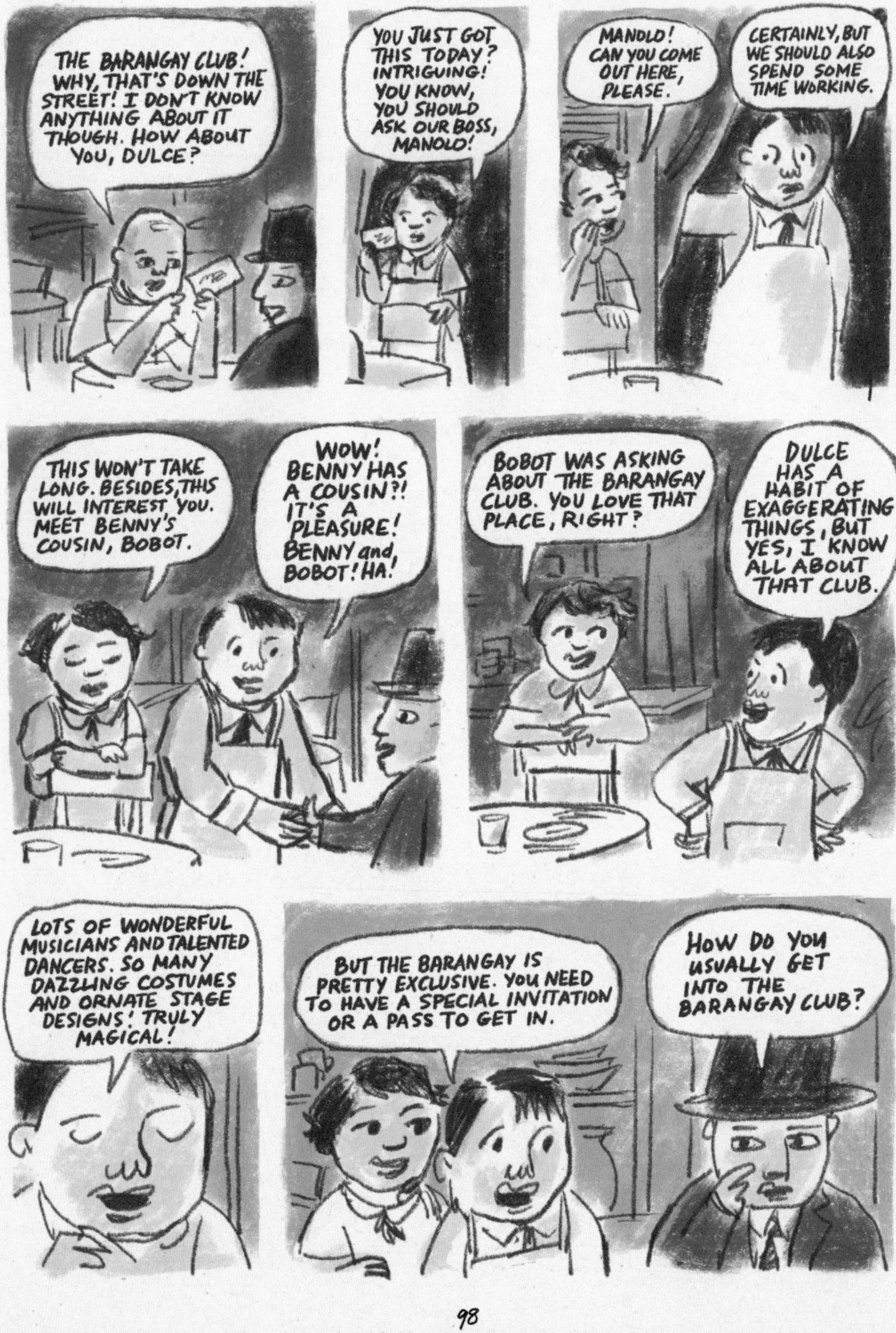
THE BARANGAY CLUB! WHY, THAT'S DOWN THE STREET! I DON'T KNOW ANYTHING ABOUT IT THOUGH. HOW ABOUT YOU, DULCE?
YOU JUST GOT THIS TODAY? INTRIGUING! YOU KNOW, YOU SHOULD ASK OUR BOSS, MANOLO!
MANOLO! CAN YOU COME OUT HERE, PLEASE.
CERTAINLY, BUT WE SHOULD ALSO SPEND SOME TIME WORKING.
THIS WON'T TAKE LONG. BESIDES, THIS WILL INTEREST YOU. MEET BENNY'S COUSIN, BOBOT.
WOW! BENNY HAS A COUSIN?! IT'S A PLEASURE! BENNY and BOBOT! HA!
BOBOT WAS ASKING ABOUT THE BARANGAY CLUB. YOU LOVE THAT PLACE, RIGHT?
DULCE HAS A HABIT OF EXAGGERATING THINGS, BUT YES, I KNOW ALL ABOUT THAT CLUB.
LOTS OF WONDERFUL MUSICIANS AND TALENTED DANCERS. SO MANY DAZZLING COSTUMES AND ORNATE STAGE DESIGNS! TRULY MAGICAL!
BUT THE BARANGAY IS PRETTY EXCLUSIVE. YOU NEED TO HAVE A SPECIAL INVITATION OR A PASS TO GET IN.
HOW DO YOU USUALLY GET INTO THE BARANGAY CLUB?

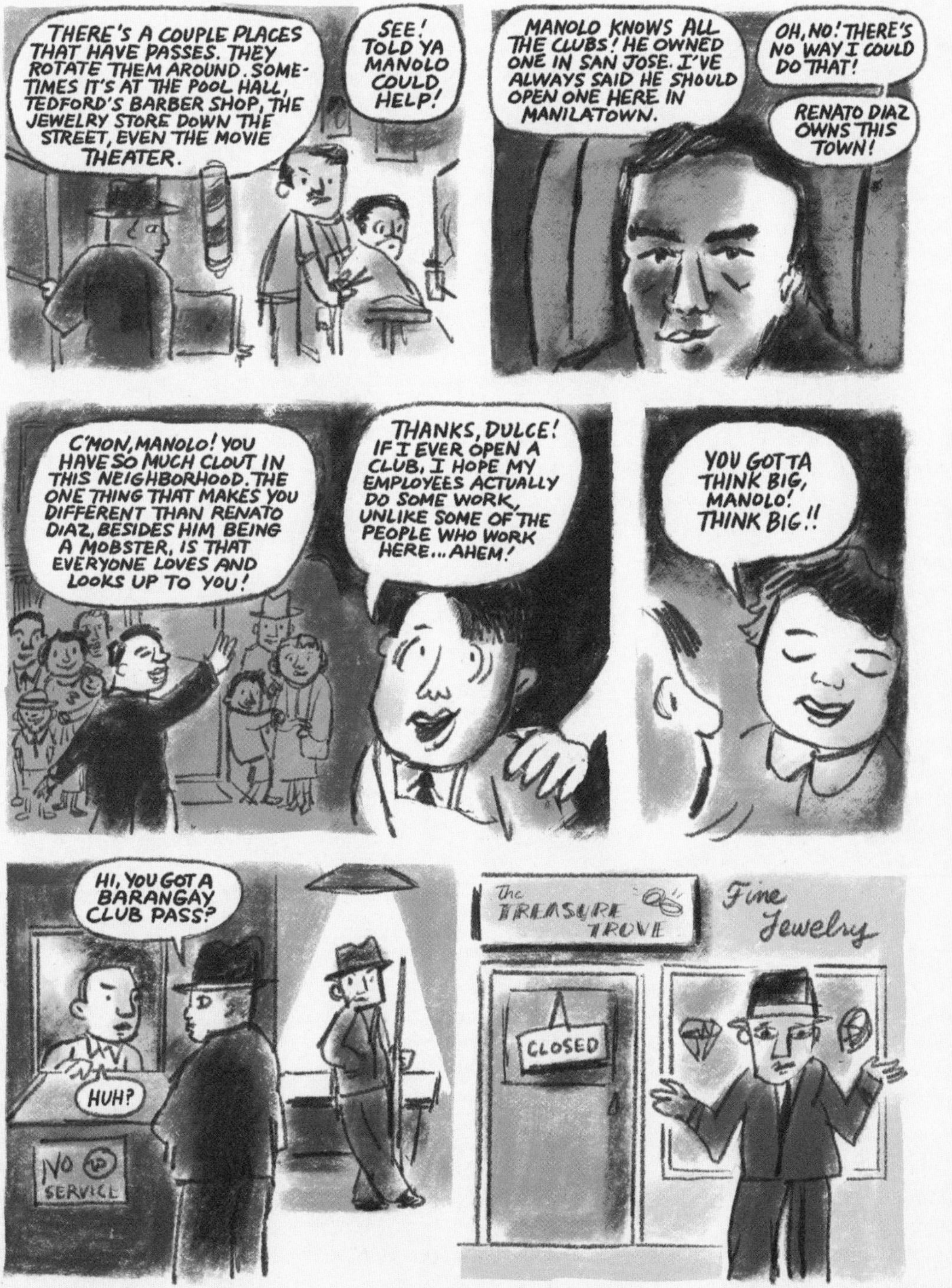
THERE'S A COUPLE PLACES THAT HAVE PASSES. THEY ROTATE THEM AROUND. SOMETIMES IT'S AT THE POOL HALL, TEDFORD'S BARBER SHOP, THE JEWELRY STORE DOWN THE STREET, EVEN THE MOVIE THEATER.
SEE! TOLD YA MANOLO COULD HELP!
MANOLO KNOWS ALL THE CLUBS! HE OWNED ONE IN SAN JOSE. I'VE ALWAYS SAID HE SHOULD OPEN ONE HERE IN MANILATOWN.
OH, NO! THERE'S NO WAY I COULD DO THAT!
RENATO DIAZ OWNS THIS TOWN!
C'MON, MANOLO! YOU HAVE SO MUCH CLOUT IN THIS NEIGHBORHOOD. THE ONE THING THAT MAKES YOU DIFFERENT THAN RENATO DIAZ, BESIDES HIM BEING A MOBSTER, IS THAT EVERYONE LOVES AND LOOKS UP TO YOU!
THANKS, DULCE! IF I EVER OPEN A CLUB, I HOPE MY EMPLOYEES ACTUALLY DO SOME WORK, UNLIKE SOME OF THE PEOPLE WHO WORK HERE... AHEM!
YOU GOTTA THINK BIG, MANOLO! THINK BIG!!
HI, YOU GOT A BARANGAY CLUB PASS?
HUH?
NO SERVICE
The TREASURE TROVE
Fine Jewelry
CLOSED

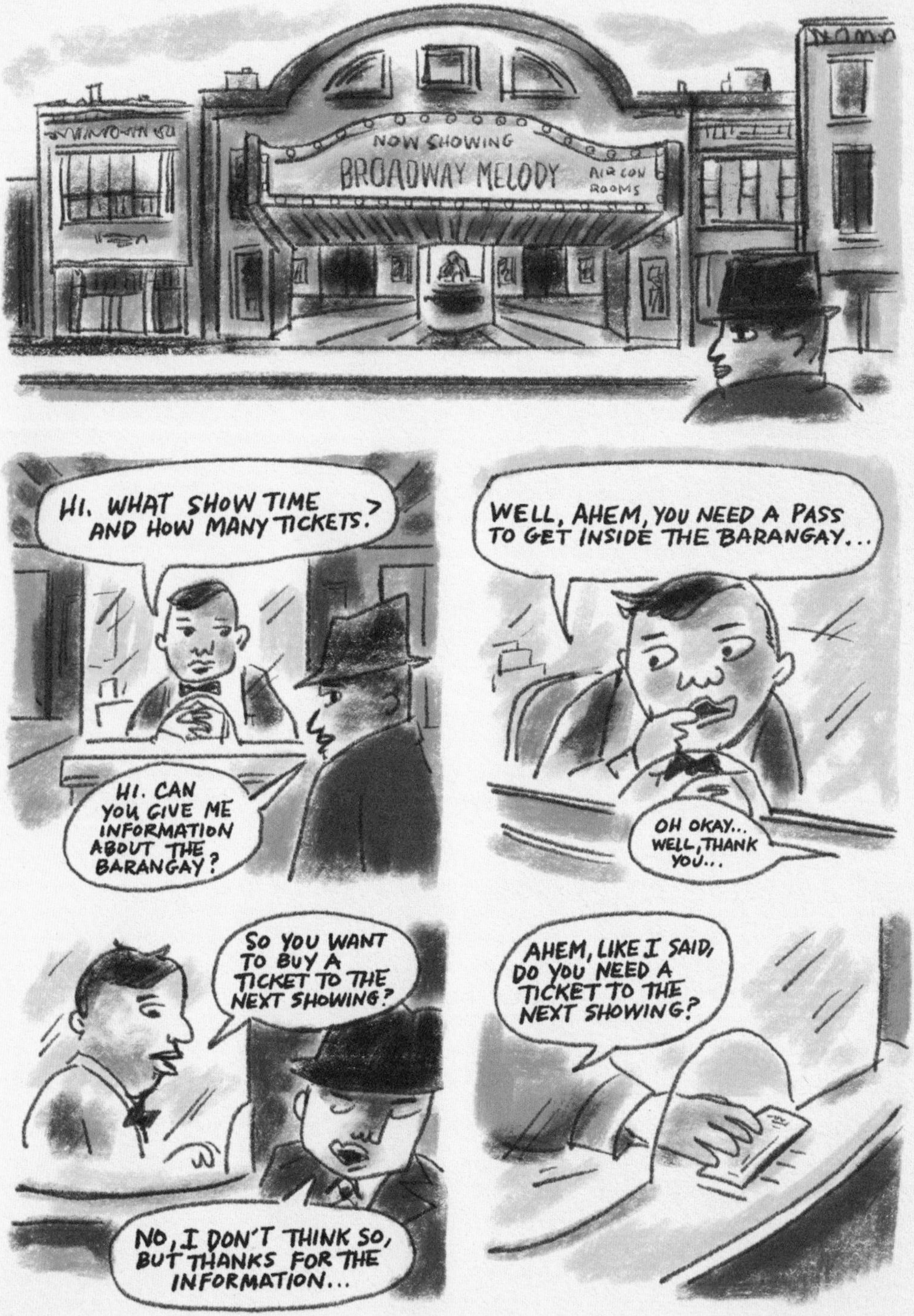

NOW SHOWING
BROADWAY MELODY
AIR CON ROOMS
HI. WHAT SHOW TIME AND HOW MANY TICKETS?
HI. CAN YOU GIVE ME INFORMATION ABOUT THE BARANGAY?
WELL, AHEM, YOU NEED A PASS TO GET INSIDE THE BARANGAY...
OH OKAY... WELL, THANK YOU...
SO YOU WANT TO BUY A TICKET TO THE NEXT SHOWING?
NO, I DON'T THINK SO, BUT THANKS FOR THE INFORMATION...
AHEM, LIKE I SAID, DO YOU NEED A TICKET TO THE NEXT SHOWING?

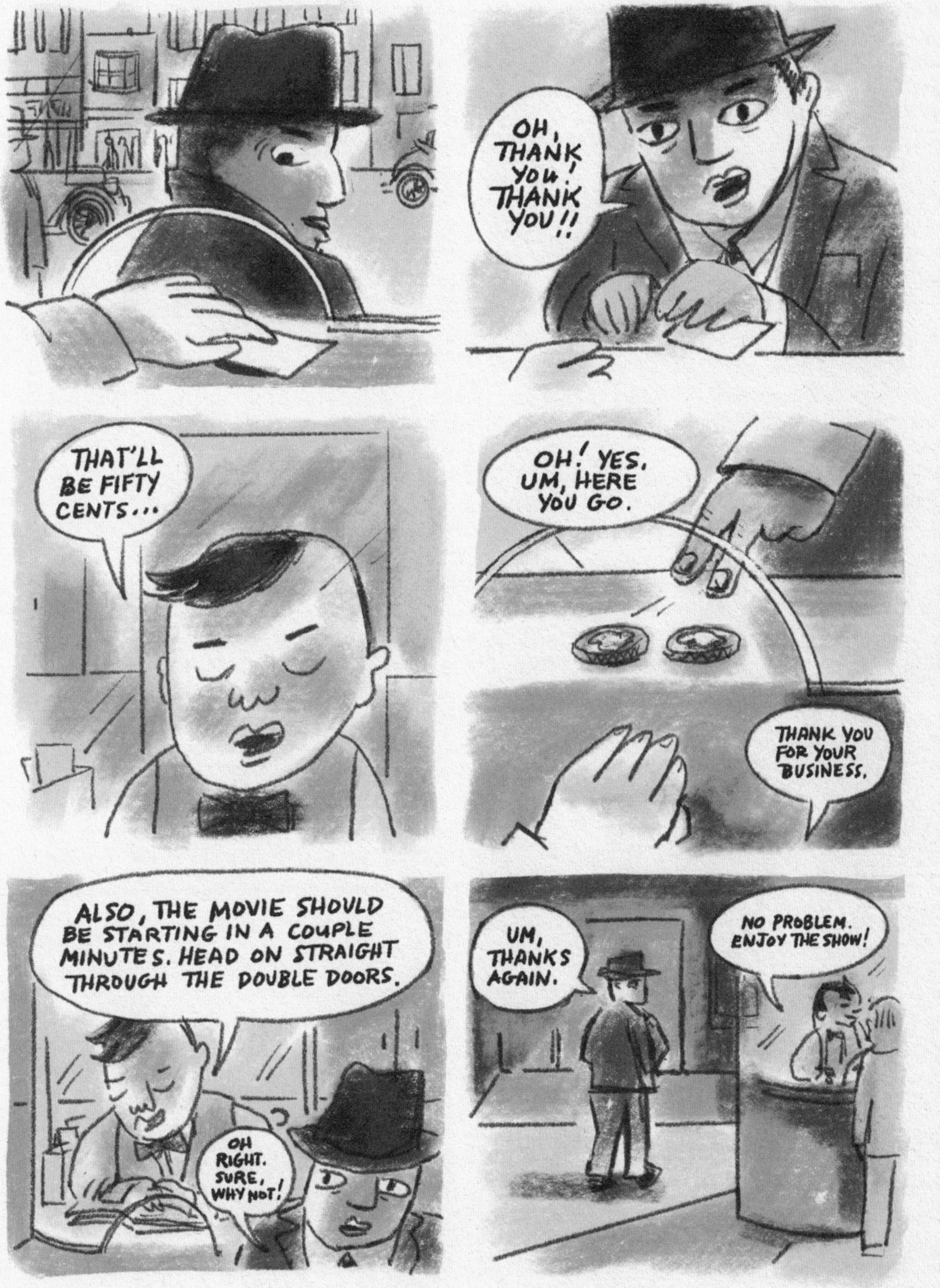
OH, THANK YOU! THANK YOU!!
THAT'LL BE FIFTY CENTS...
OH! YES. UM, HERE YOU GO.
THANK YOU FOR YOUR BUSINESS.
ALSO, THE MOVIE SHOULD BE STARTING IN A COUPLE MINUTES. HEAD ON STRAIGHT THROUGH THE DOUBLE DOORS.
OH RIGHT. SURE, WHY NOT!
UM, THANKS AGAIN.
NO PROBLEM. ENJOY THE SHOW!

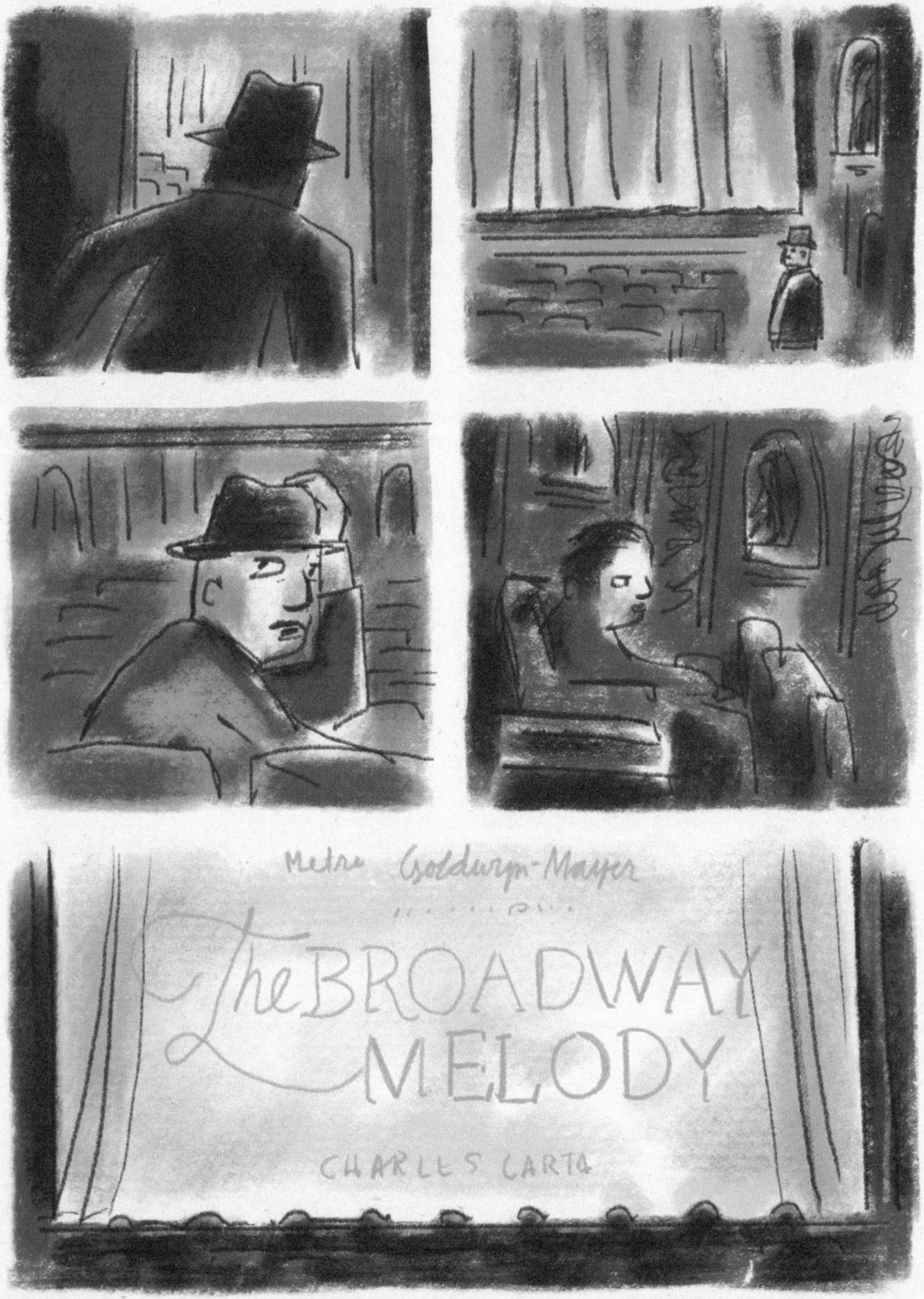
Metro Goldwyn-Mayer
The BROADWAY MELODY
CHARLES CARTA

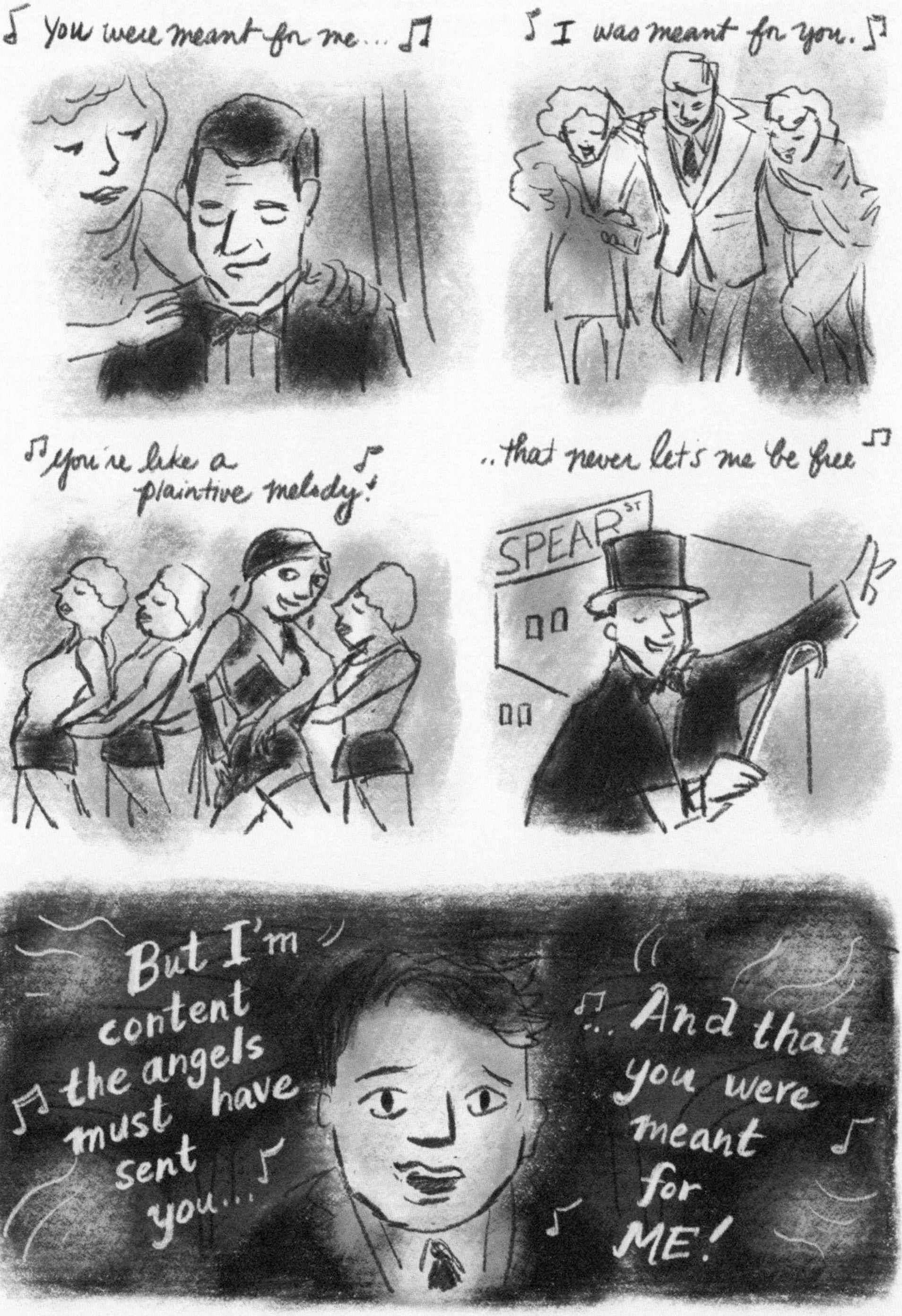
♪ You were meant for me... ♫
♪ I was meant for you. ♫
♫ You're like a plaintive melody! ♪
..that never let's me be free ♫
SPEAR ST
But I'm content the angels must have sent you...
♫.. And that you were meant for ME!

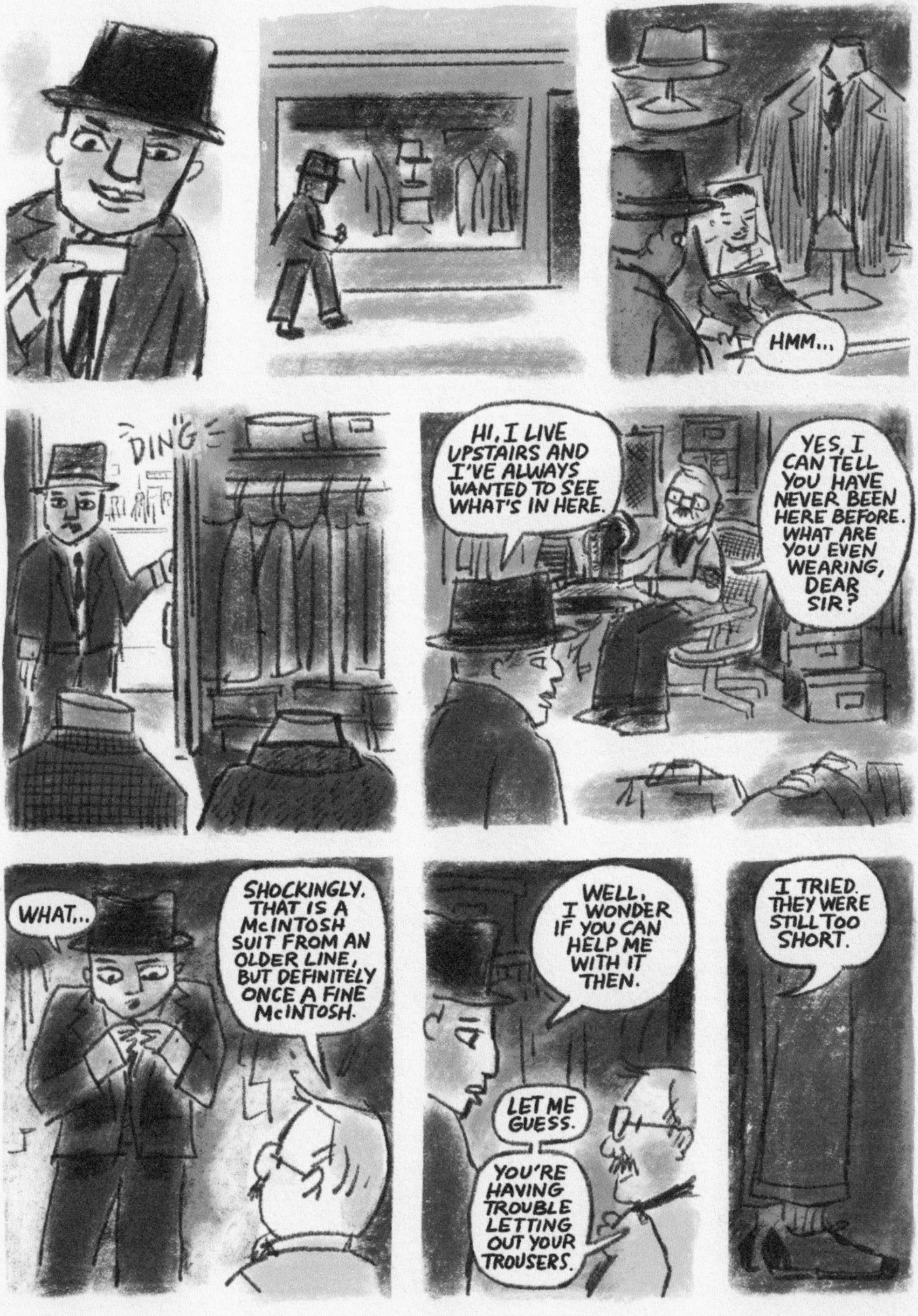
HMM...
DING
HI, I LIVE UPSTAIRS AND I'VE ALWAYS WANTED TO SEE WHAT'S IN HERE.
YES, I CAN TELL YOU HAVE NEVER BEEN HERE BEFORE. WHAT ARE YOU EVEN WEARING, DEAR SIR?
WHAT...
SHOCKINGLY. THAT IS A McINTOSH SUIT FROM AN OLDER LINE, BUT DEFINITELY ONCE A FINE McINTOSH.
WELL, I WONDER IF YOU CAN HELP ME WITH IT THEN.
LET ME GUESS.
YOU'RE HAVING TROUBLE LETTING OUT YOUR TROUSERS.
I TRIED. THEY WERE STILL TOO SHORT.

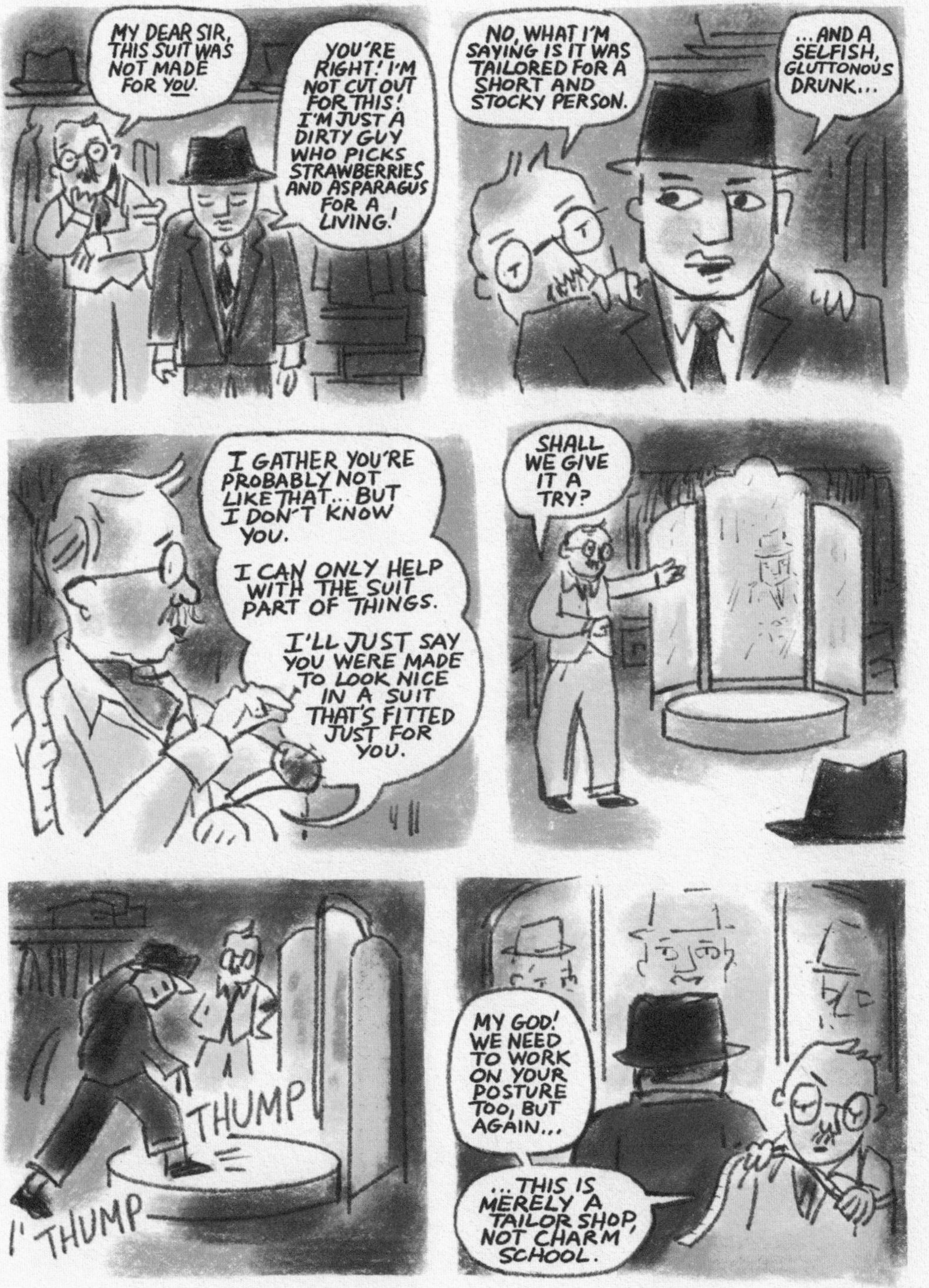
MY DEAR SIR, THIS SUIT WAS NOT MADE FOR YOU.
YOU'RE RIGHT! I'M NOT CUT OUT FOR THIS! I'M JUST A DIRTY GUY WHO PICKS STRAWBERRIES AND ASPARAGUS FOR A LIVING!
NO, WHAT I'M SAYING IS IT WAS TAILORED FOR A SHORT AND STOCKY PERSON.
...AND A SELFISH, GLUTTONOUS DRUNK...
I GATHER YOU'RE PROBABLY NOT LIKE THAT... BUT I DON'T KNOW YOU.
I CAN ONLY HELP WITH THE SUIT PART OF THINGS.
I'LL JUST SAY YOU WERE MADE TO LOOK NICE IN A SUIT THAT'S FITTED JUST FOR YOU.
SHALL WE GIVE IT A TRY?
THUMP
THUMP
MY GOD! WE NEED TO WORK ON YOUR POSTURE TOO, BUT AGAIN...
...THIS IS MERELY A TAILOR SHOP, NOT CHARM SCHOOL.

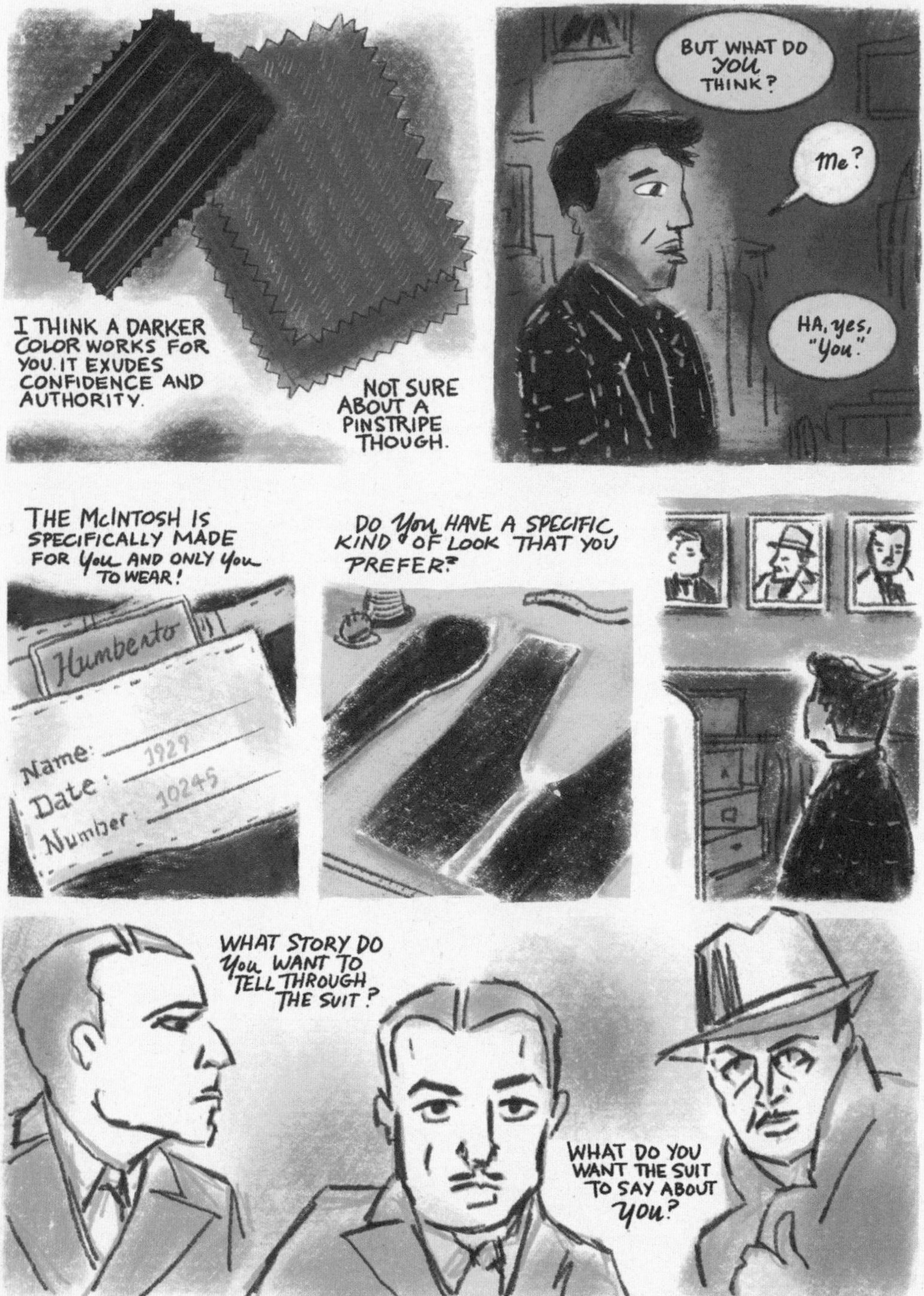
I THINK A DARKER COLOR WORKS FOR YOU. IT EXUDES CONFIDENCE AND AUTHORITY.
NOT SURE ABOUT A PINSTRIPE THOUGH.
BUT WHAT DO YOU THINK?
Me?
HA, yes, "You."
THE McINTOSH IS SPECIFICALLY MADE FOR You AND ONLY You TO WEAR!
Humberto
Name: 1929
Date: 10245
Number
DO You HAVE A SPECIFIC KIND OF LOOK THAT YOU PREFER?
WHAT STORY DO You WANT TO TELL THROUGH THE SUIT?
WHAT DO YOU WANT THE SUIT TO SAY ABOUT You?

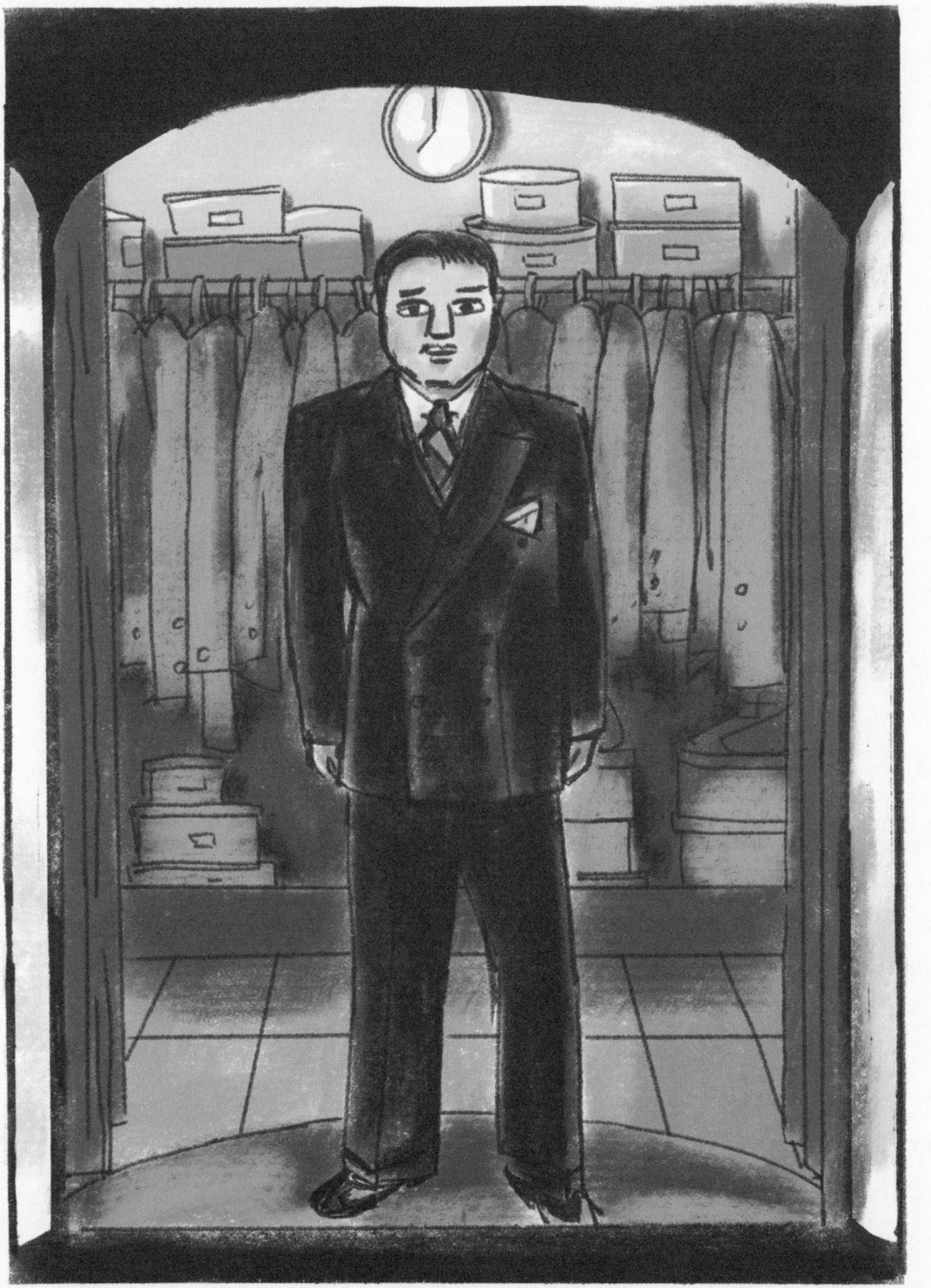

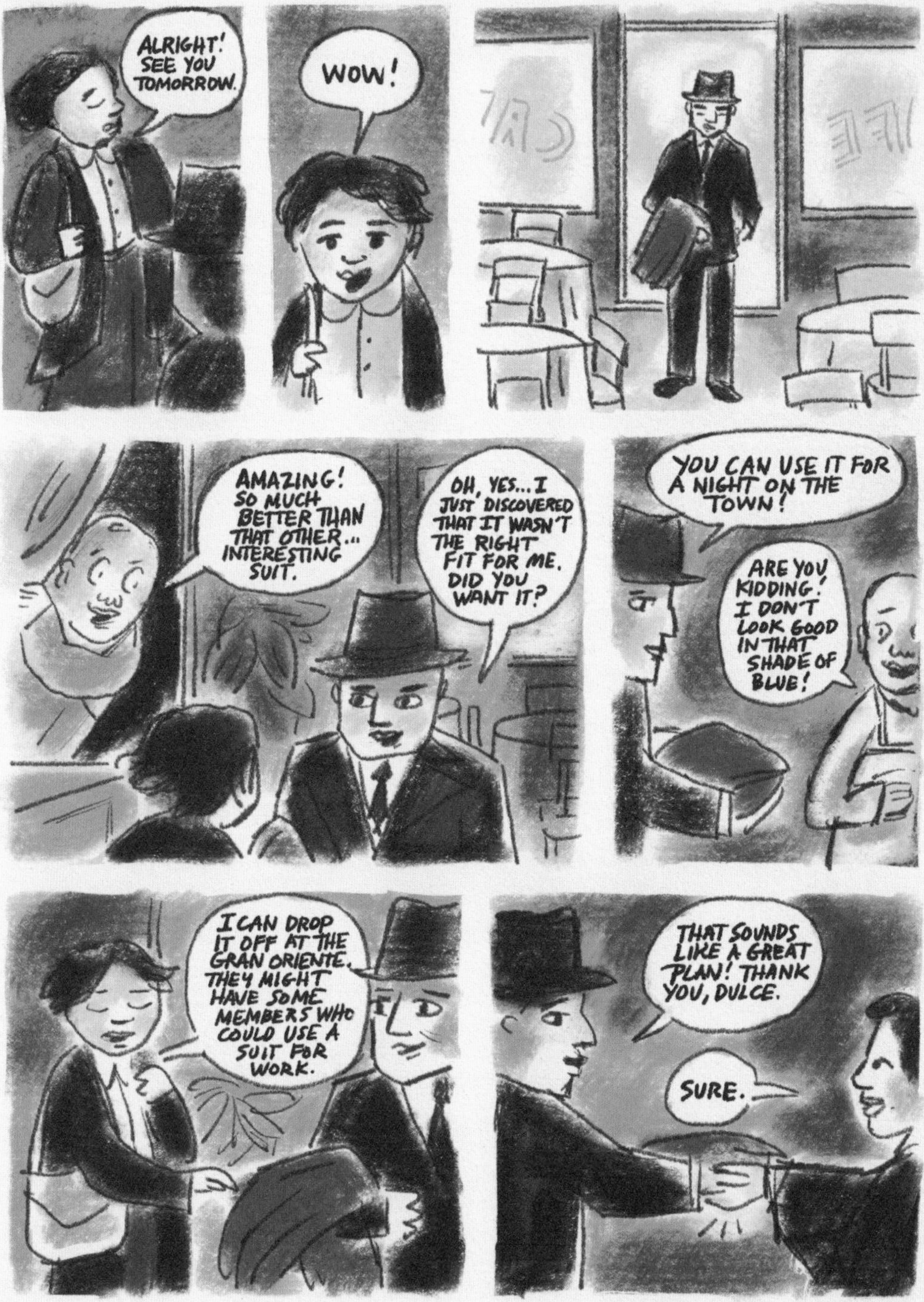
ALRIGHT! SEE YOU TOMORROW.
WOW!
AMAZING! SO MUCH BETTER THAN THAT OTHER... INTERESTING SUIT.
OH, YES... I JUST DISCOVERED THAT IT WASN'T THE RIGHT FIT FOR ME. DID YOU WANT IT?
YOU CAN USE IT FOR A NIGHT ON THE TOWN!
ARE YOU KIDDING! I DON'T LOOK GOOD IN THAT SHADE OF BLUE!
I CAN DROP IT OFF AT THE GRAN ORIENTE. THEY MIGHT HAVE SOME MEMBERS WHO COULD USE A SUIT FOR WORK.
THAT SOUNDS LIKE A GREAT PLAN! THANK YOU, DULCE.
SURE.

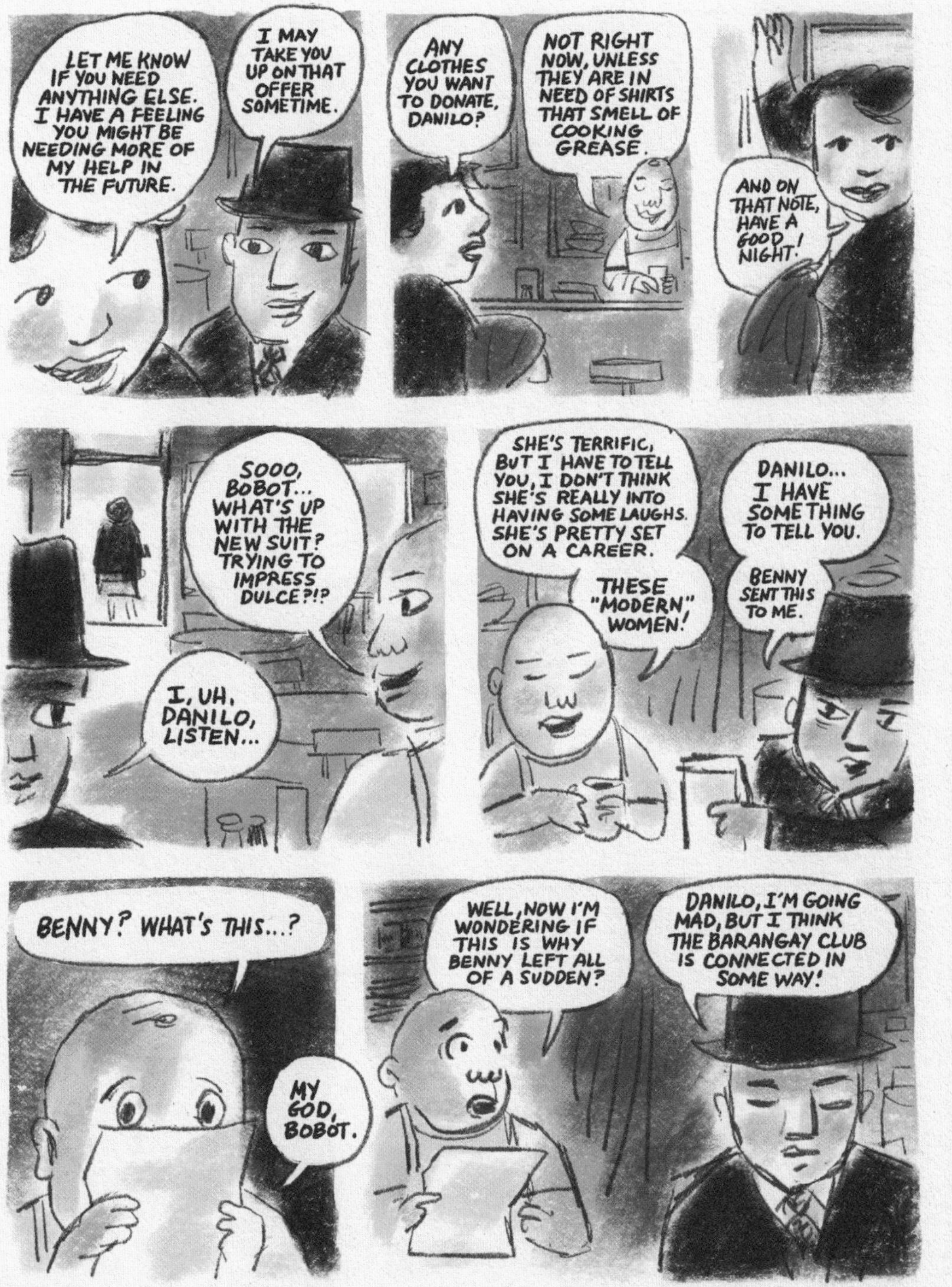
LET ME KNOW IF YOU NEED ANYTHING ELSE. I HAVE A FEELING YOU MIGHT BE NEEDING MORE OF MY HELP IN THE FUTURE.
I MAY TAKE YOU UP ON THAT OFFER SOMETIME.
ANY CLOTHES YOU WANT TO DONATE, DANILO?
NOT RIGHT NOW, UNLESS THEY ARE IN NEED OF SHIRTS THAT SMELL OF COOKING GREASE.
AND ON THAT NOTE, HAVE A GOOD NIGHT!
SOOO, BOBOT... WHAT'S UP WITH THE NEW SUIT? TRYING TO IMPRESS DULCE?!?
I, UH, DANILO, LISTEN...
SHE'S TERRIFIC, BUT I HAVE TO TELL YOU, I DON'T THINK SHE'S REALLY INTO HAVING SOME LAUGHS. SHE'S PRETTY SET ON A CAREER.
THESE "MODERN" WOMEN!
DANILO... I HAVE SOMETHING TO TELL YOU.
BENNY SENT THIS TO ME.
BENNY? WHAT'S THIS...?
MY GOD, BOBOT.
WELL, NOW I'M WONDERING IF THIS IS WHY BENNY LEFT ALL OF A SUDDEN?
DANILO, I'M GOING MAD, BUT I THINK THE BARANGAY CLUB IS CONNECTED IN SOME WAY!

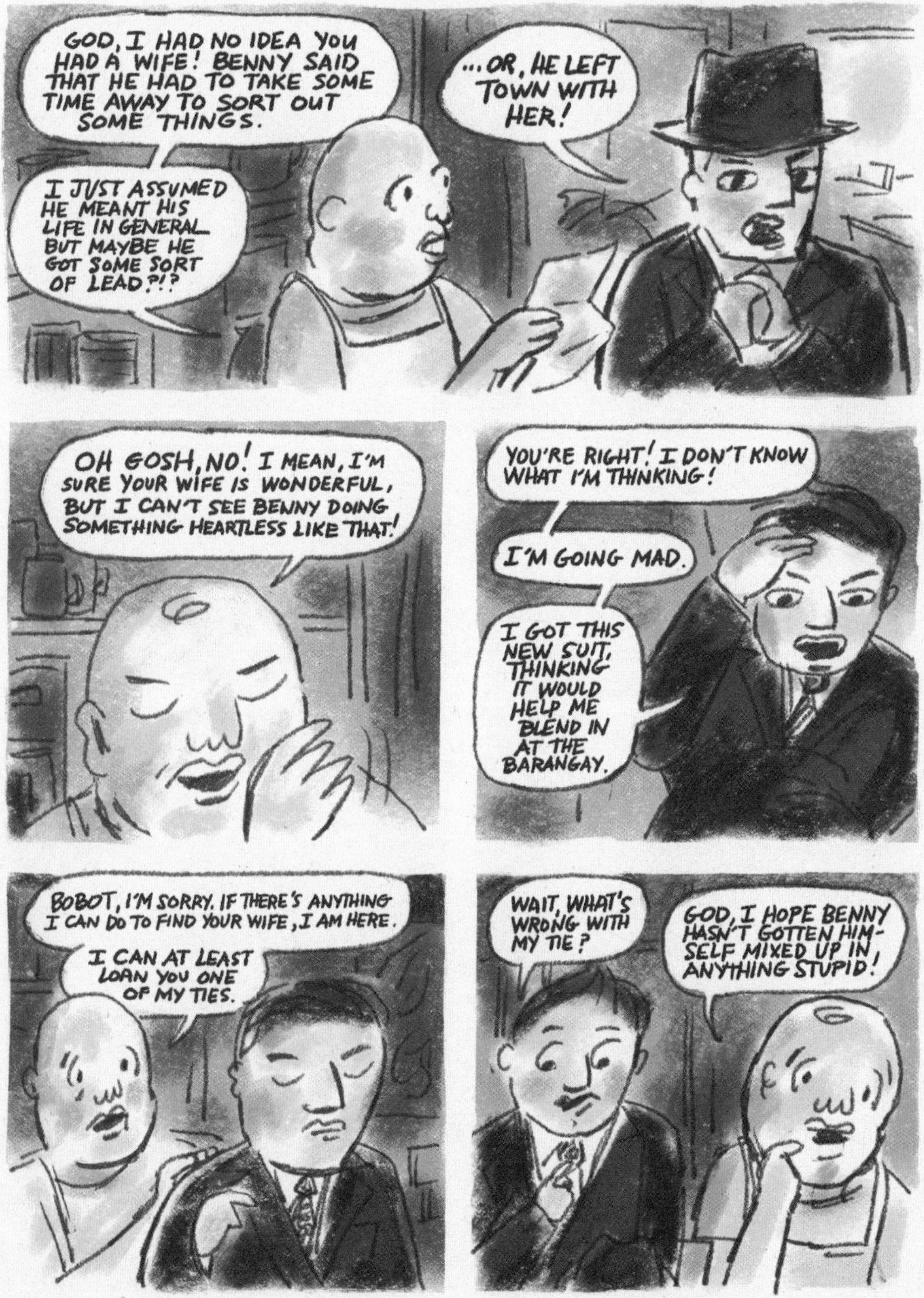
GOD, I HAD NO IDEA YOU HAD A WIFE! BENNY SAID THAT HE HAD TO TAKE SOME TIME AWAY TO SORT OUT SOME THINGS.
I JUST ASSUMED HE MEANT HIS LIFE IN GENERAL BUT MAYBE HE GOT SOME SORT OF LEAD?!?
...OR, HE LEFT TOWN WITH HER!
OH GOSH, NO! I MEAN, I'M SURE YOUR WIFE IS WONDERFUL, BUT I CAN'T SEE BENNY DOING SOMETHING HEARTLESS LIKE THAT!
YOU'RE RIGHT! I DON'T KNOW WHAT I'M THINKING!
I'M GOING MAD.
I GOT THIS NEW SUIT, THINKING IT WOULD HELP ME BLEND IN AT THE BARANGAY.
BOBOT, I'M SORRY. IF THERE'S ANYTHING I CAN DO TO FIND YOUR WIFE, I AM HERE.
I CAN AT LEAST LOAN YOU ONE OF MY TIES.
WAIT, WHAT'S WRONG WITH MY TIE?
GOD, I HOPE BENNY HASN'T GOTTEN HIMSELF MIXED UP IN ANYTHING STUPID!

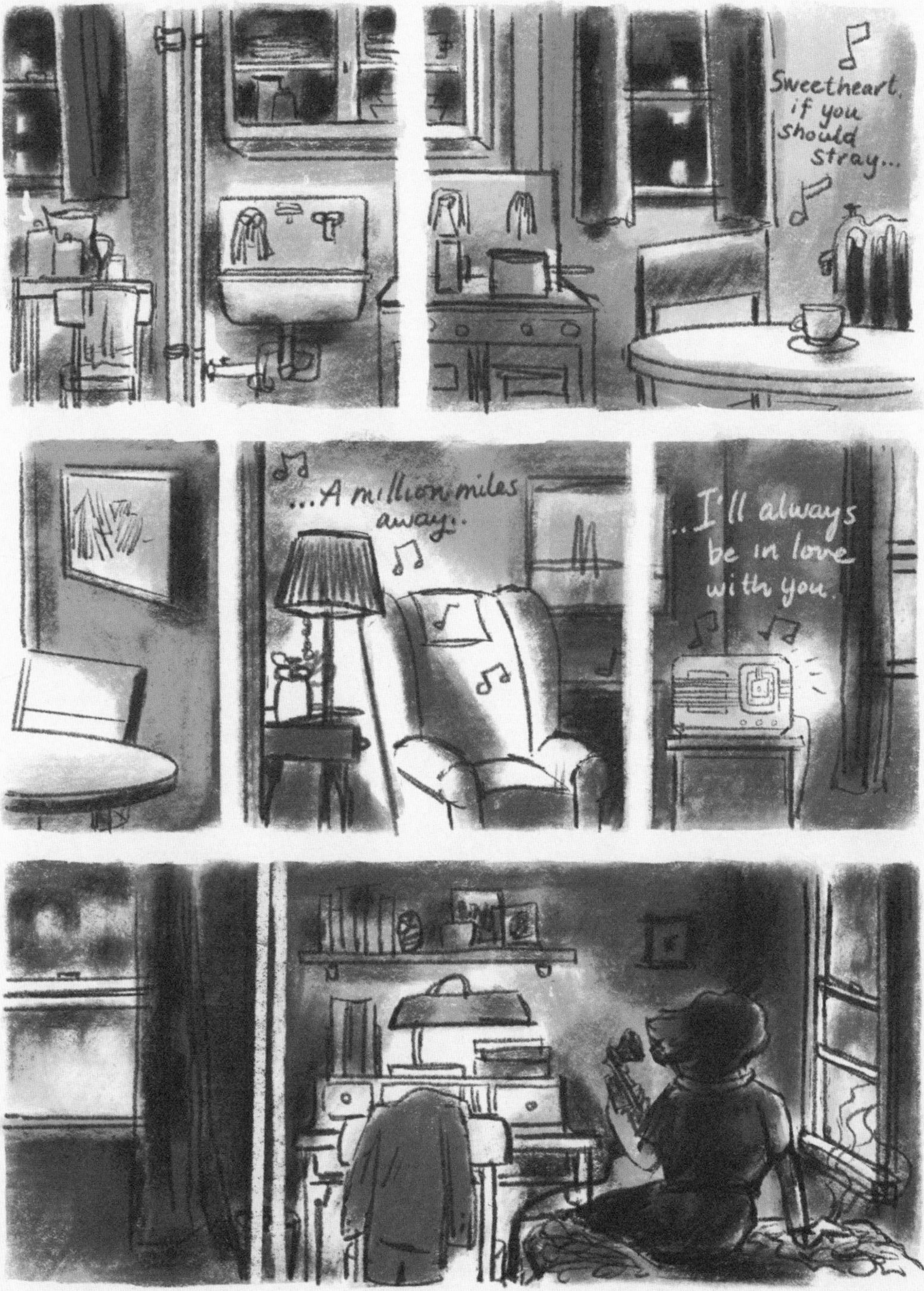
Sweetheart, if you should stray...
...A million miles away...
...I'll always be in love with you.

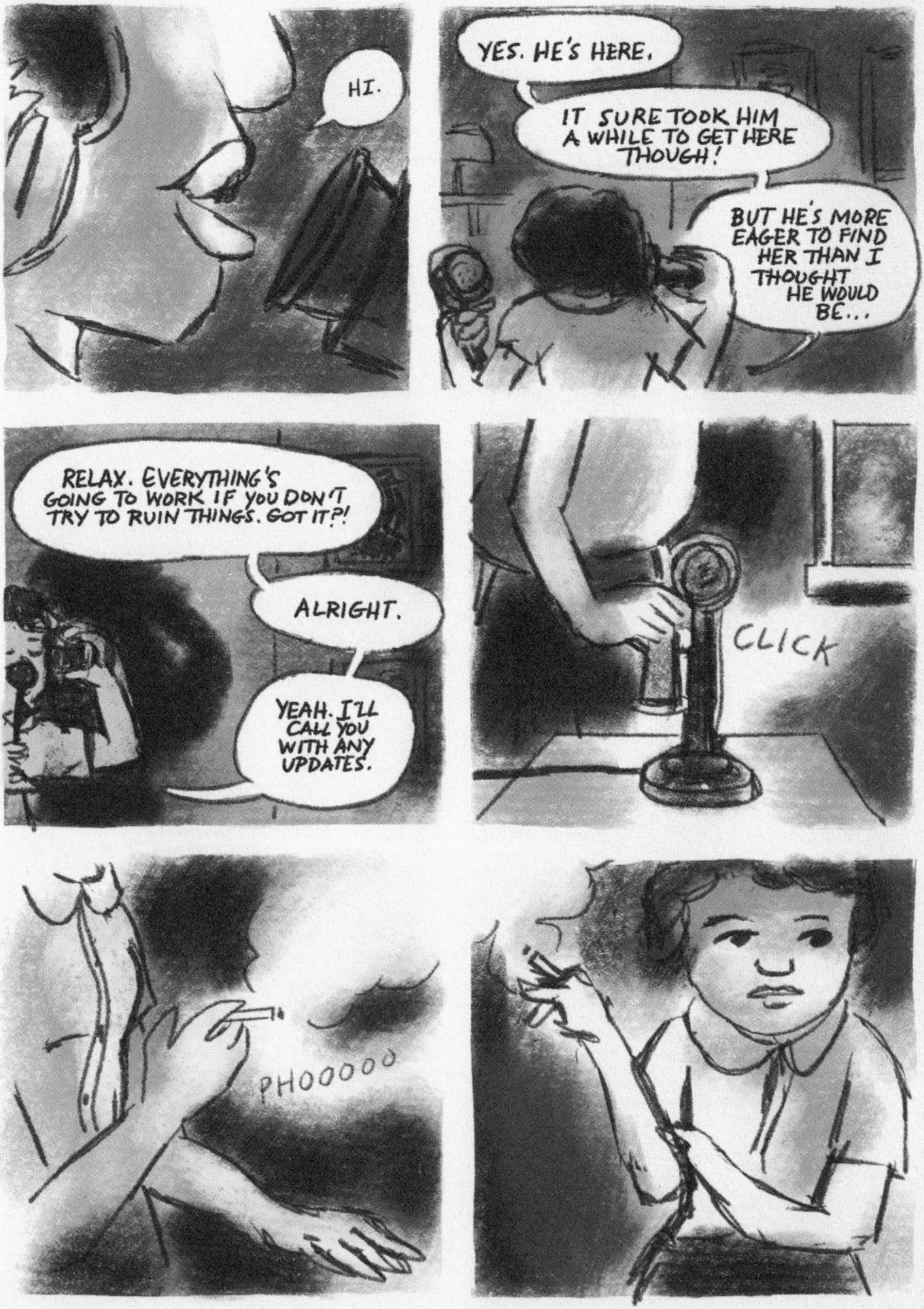
HI.
YES. HE'S HERE.
IT SURE TOOK HIM A WHILE TO GET HERE THOUGH!
BUT HE'S MORE EAGER TO FIND HER THAN I THOUGHT HE WOULD BE...
RELAX. EVERYTHING'S GOING TO WORK IF YOU DON'T TRY TO RUIN THINGS. GOT IT?!
ALRIGHT.
YEAH. I'LL CALL YOU WITH ANY UPDATES.
CLICK
PHOOOOO

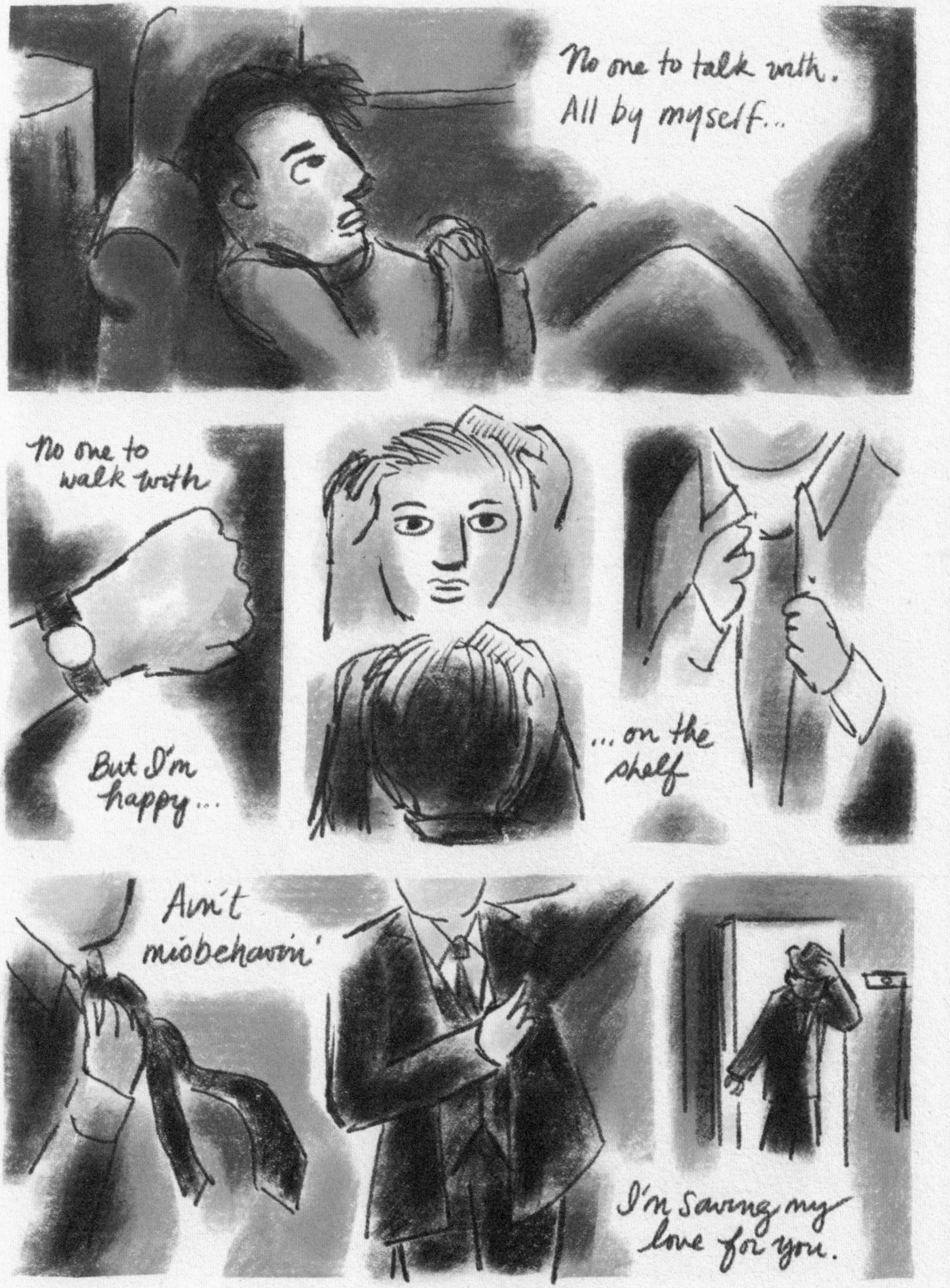
No one to talk with.
All by myself...
No one to walk with
But I'm happy...
...on the shelf
Ain't misbehavin'
I'm saving my love for you.

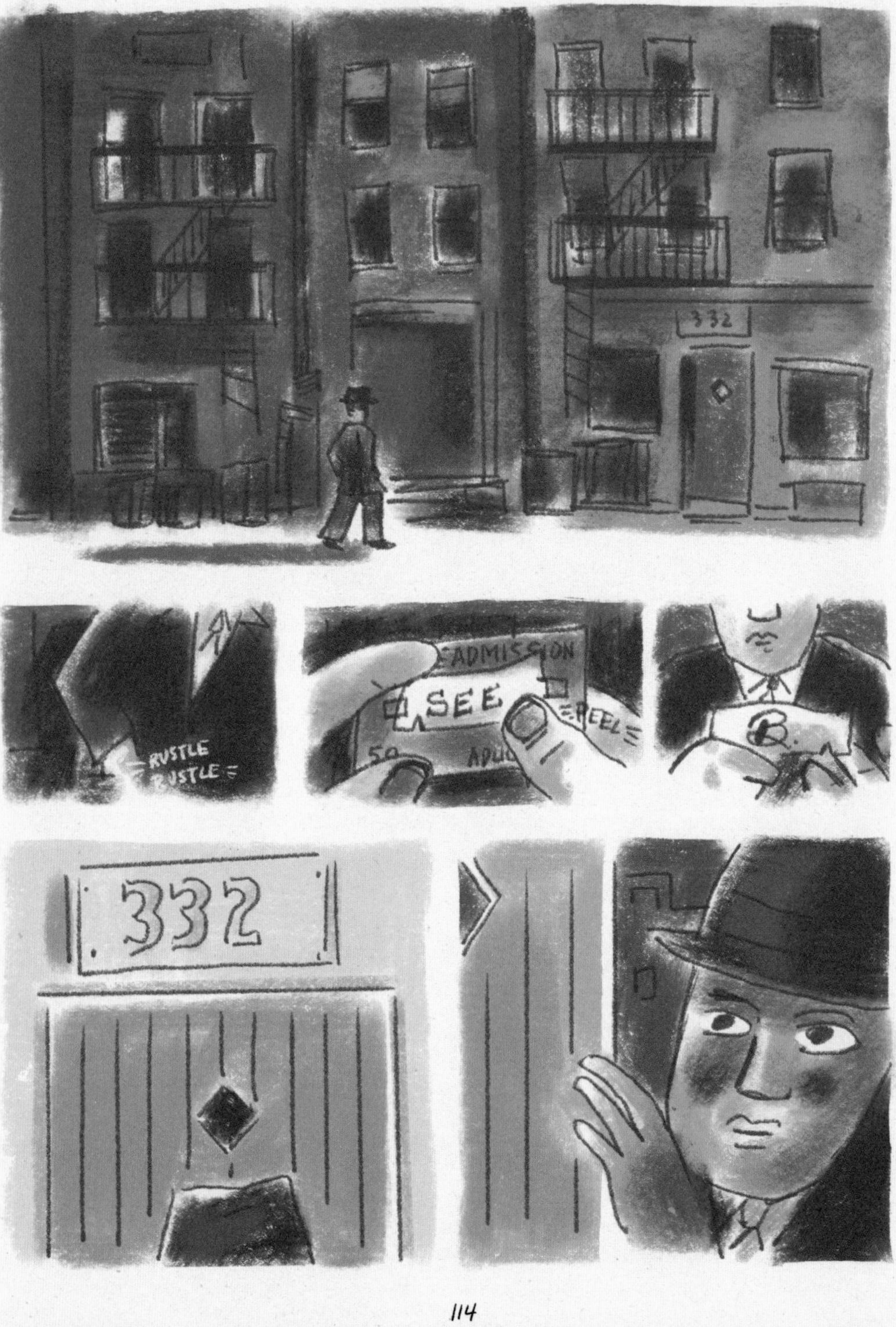
332
RUSTLE
RUSTLE
ADMISSION
SEE
PEEL
332

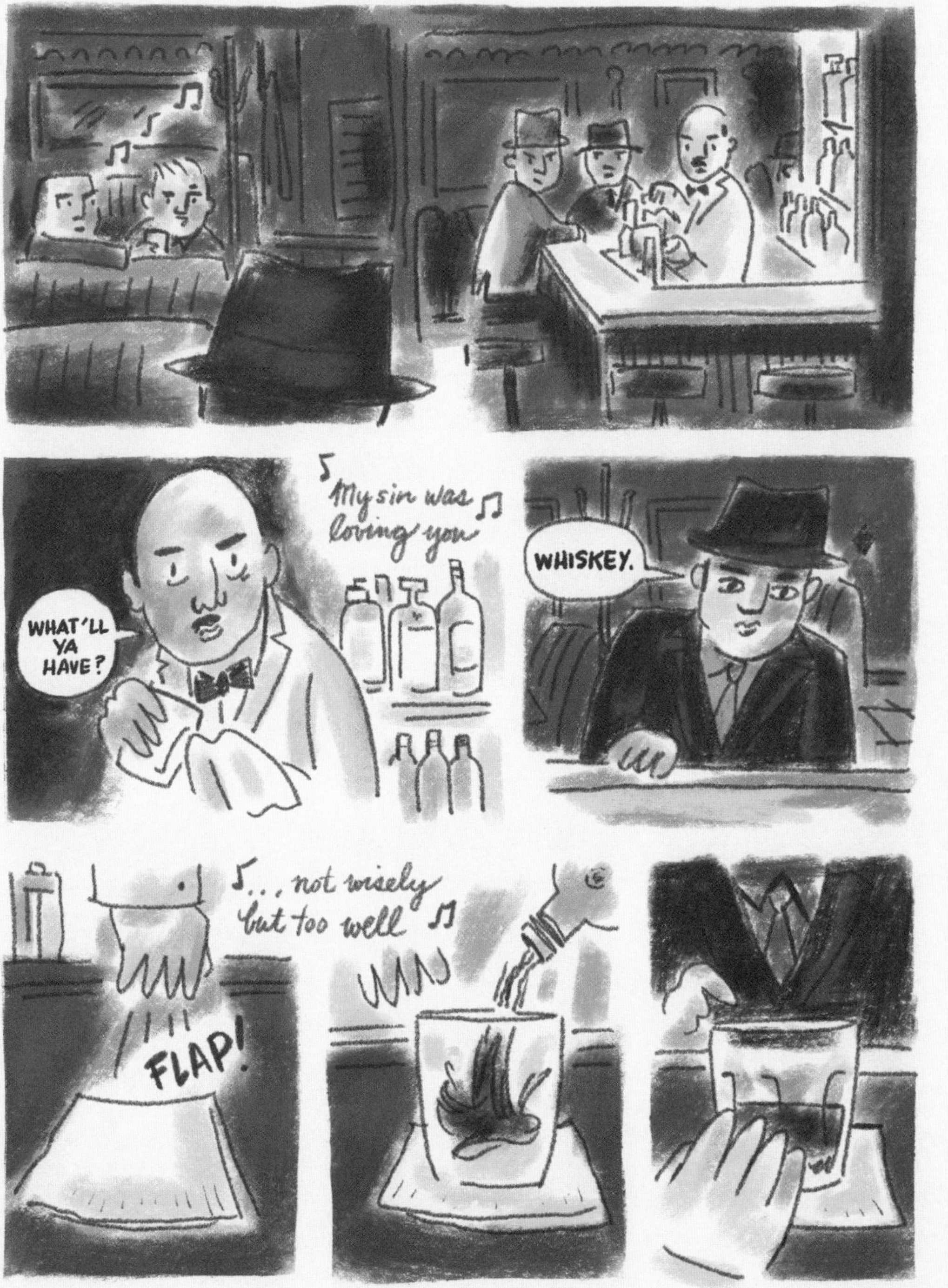
My sin was loving you
WHAT'LL YA HAVE?
WHISKEY.
... not wisely but too well
FLAP!

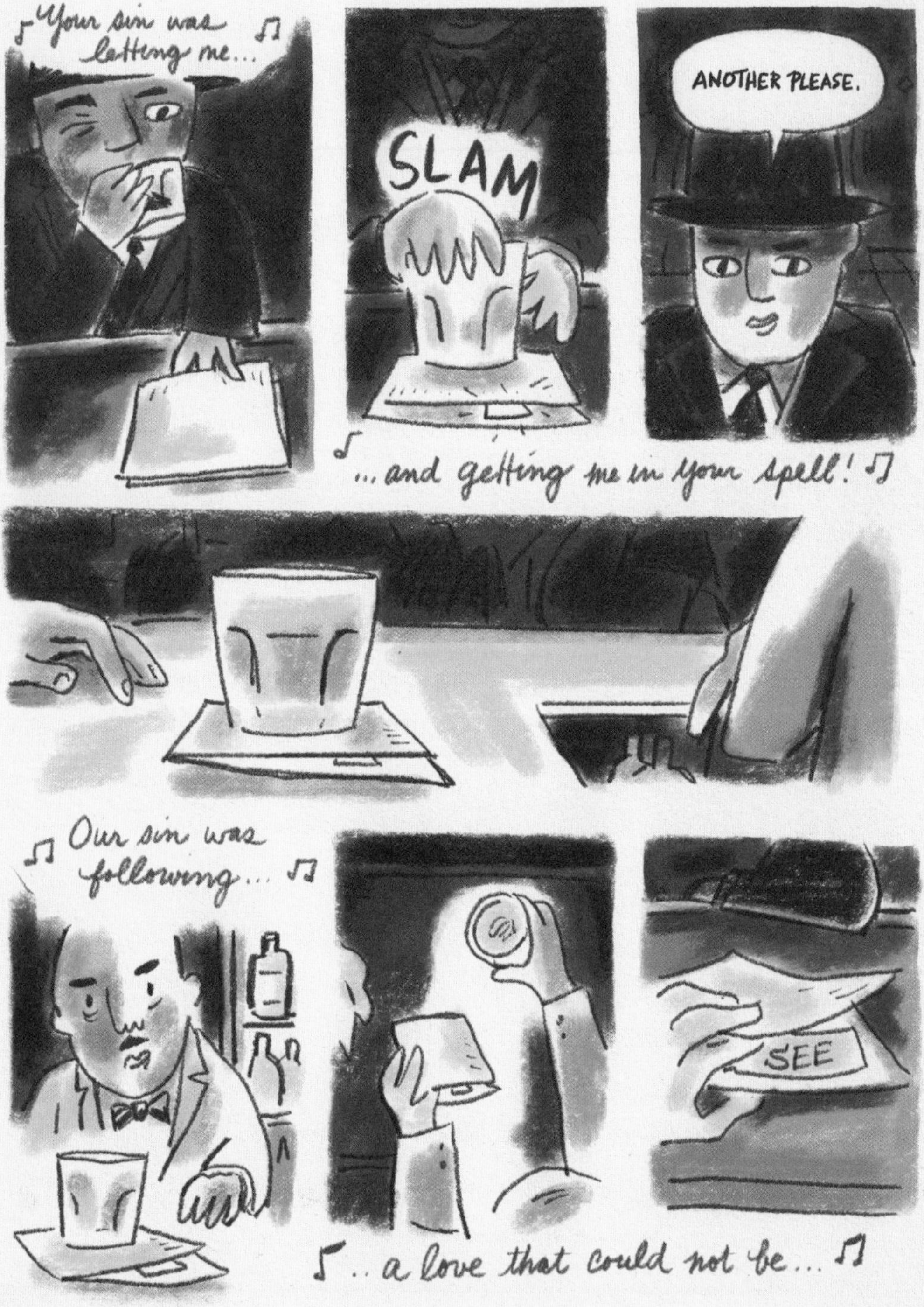
♪ Your sin was letting me... ♫
SLAM
ANOTHER PLEASE.
♪ ...and getting me in your spell! ♫
♫ Our sin was following... ♫
SEE
♪ .. a love that could not be... ♫

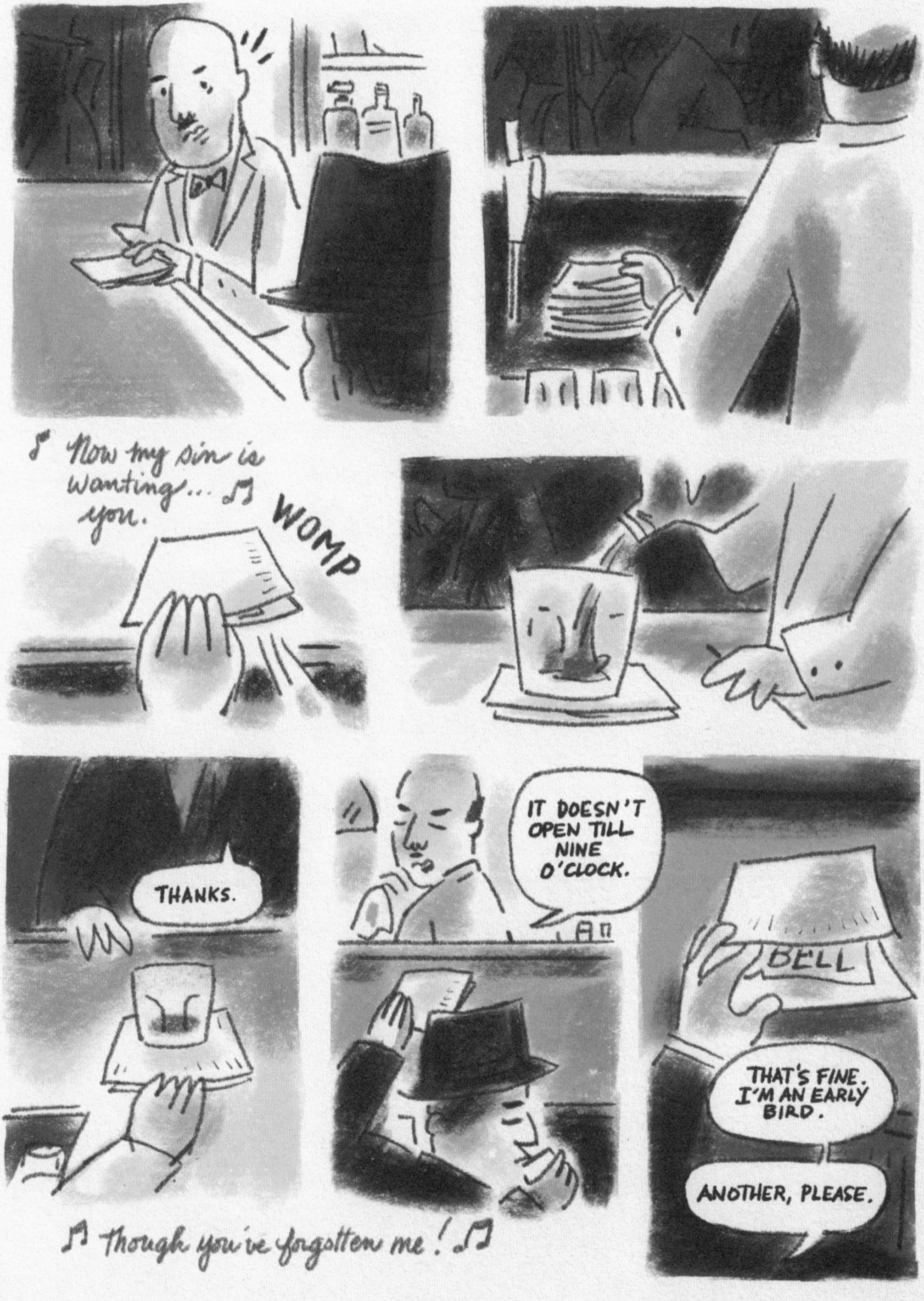
Now my sin is wanting... you.
WOMP
THANKS.
IT DOESN'T OPEN TILL NINE O'CLOCK.
BELL
THAT'S FINE. I'M AN EARLY BIRD.
ANOTHER, PLEASE.
Though you've forgotten me!

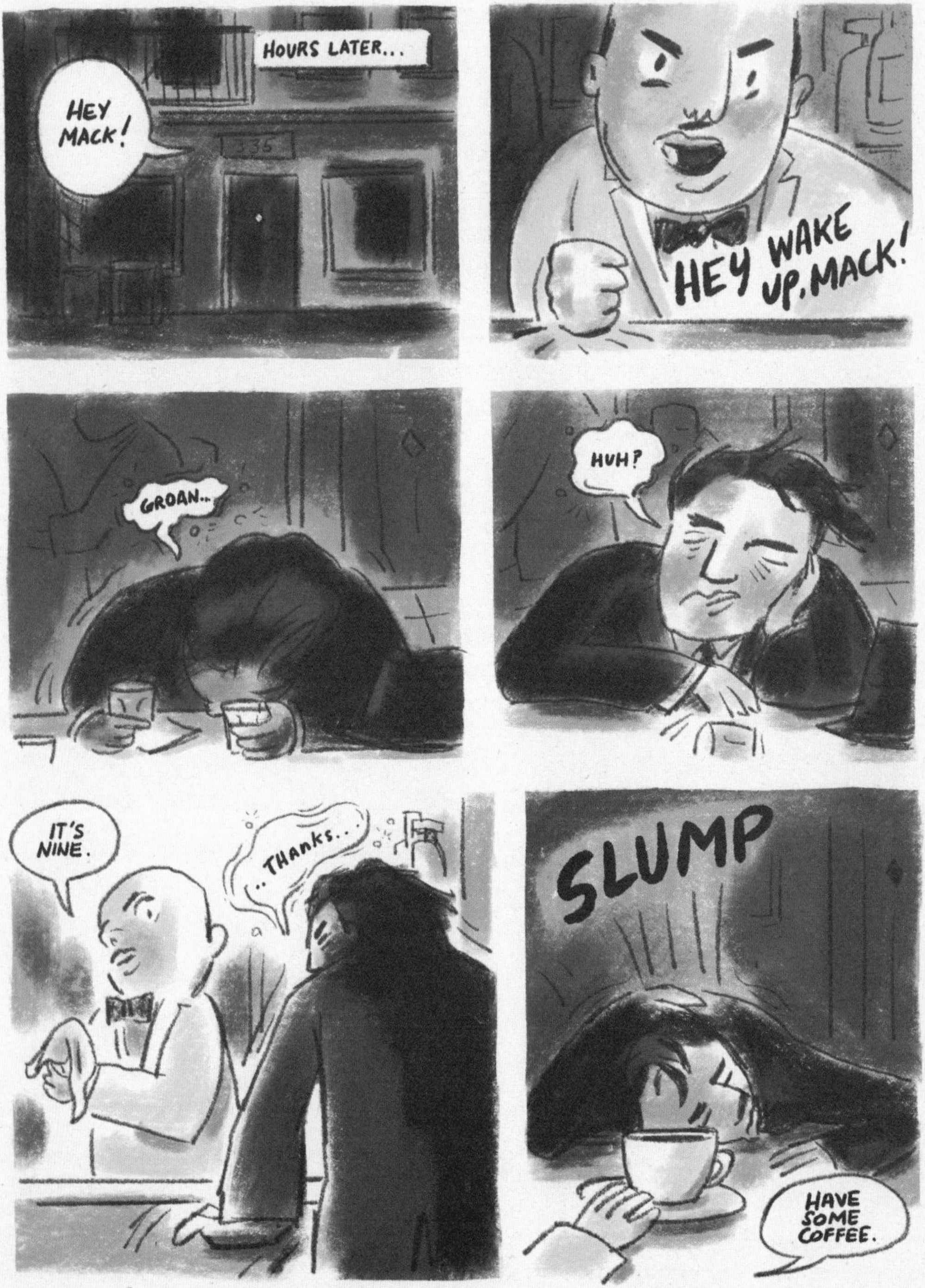
HOURS LATER...
HEY MACK!
HEY WAKE UP, MACK!
GROAN..
HUH?
IT'S NINE.
..THANKS...
SLUMP
HAVE SOME COFFEE.

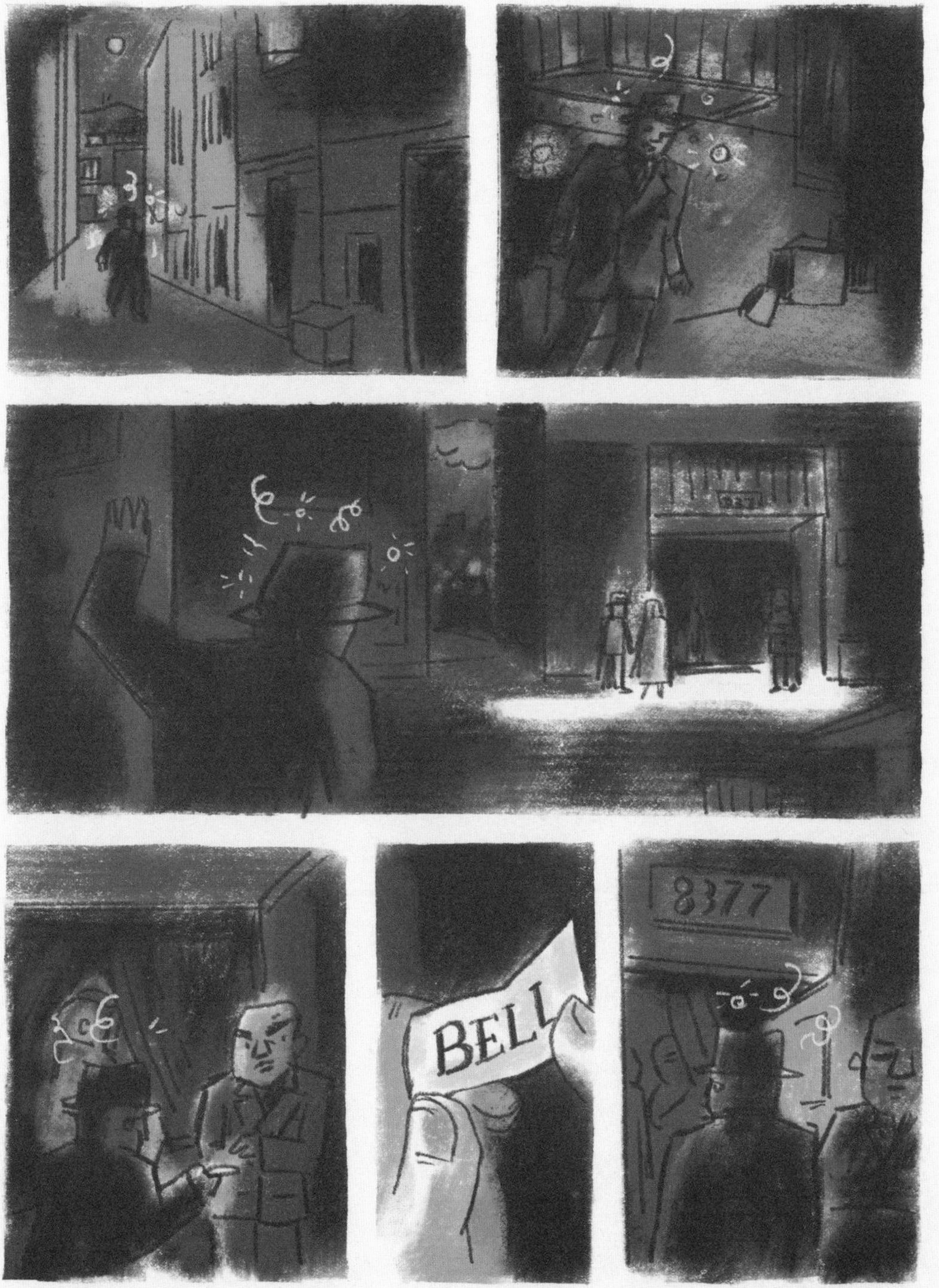
BELL
8377

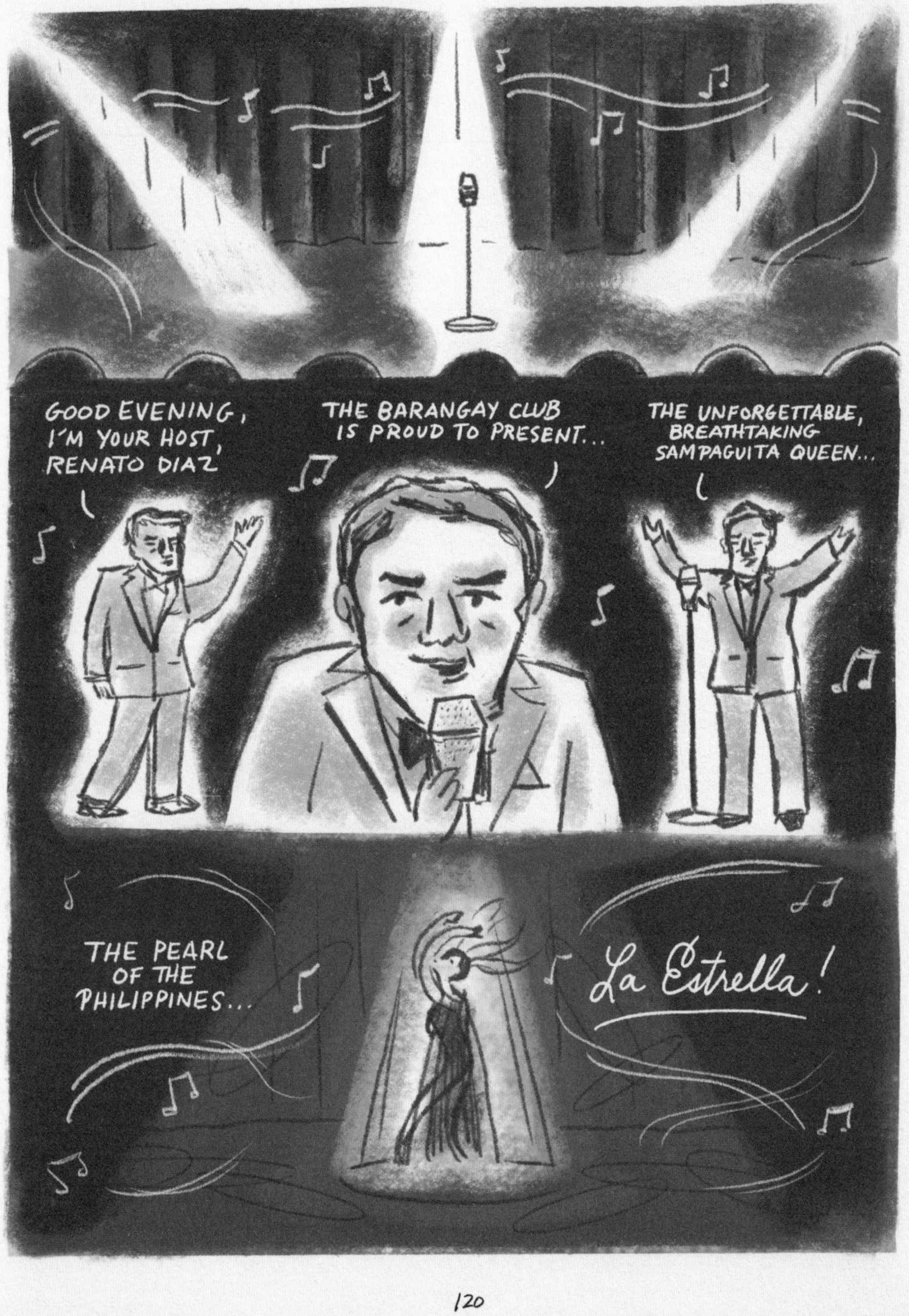
GOOD EVENING, I'M YOUR HOST, RENATO DIAZ
THE BARANGAY CLUB IS PROUD TO PRESENT...
THE UNFORGETTABLE, BREATHTAKING SAMPAGUITA QUEEN...
THE PEARL OF THE PHILIPPINES...
La Estrella!

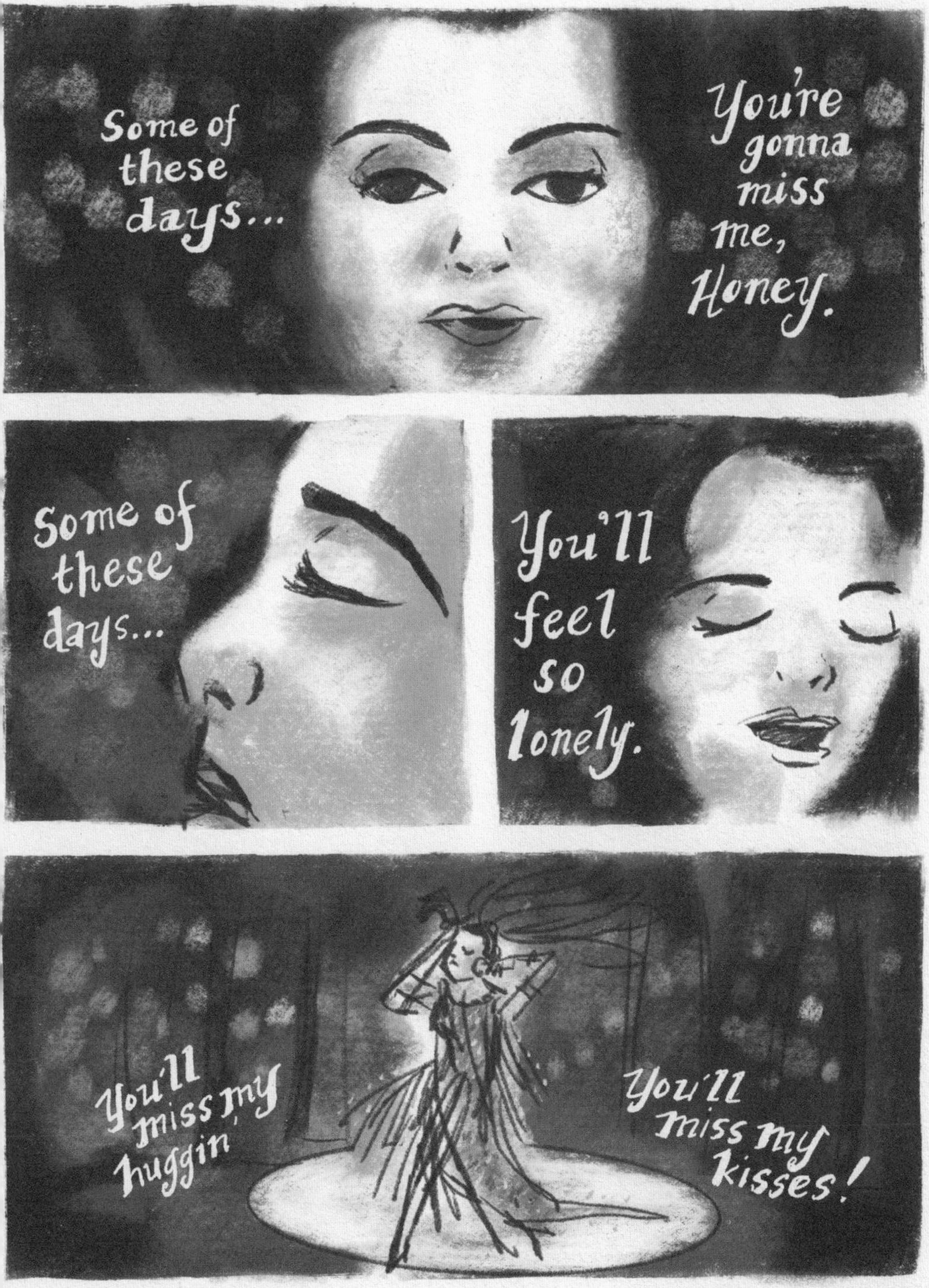
Some of these days...
You're gonna miss me, Honey.
Some of these days...
You'll feel so lonely.
You'll miss my huggin'
You'll miss my kisses!

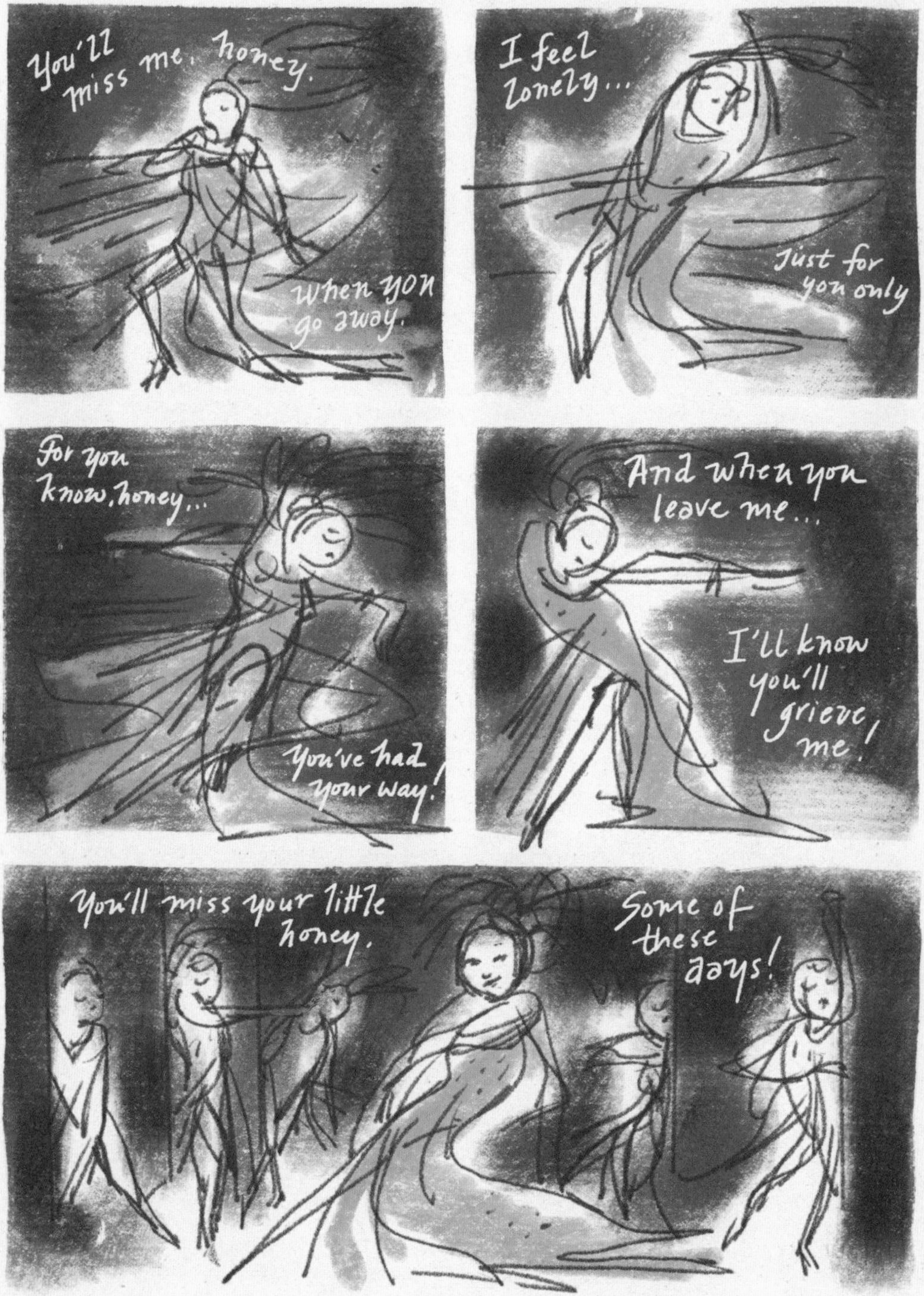
You'll miss me, honey.
When you go away.
I feel lonely...
Just for you only
For you know, honey...
You've had your way!
And when you leave me...
I'll know you'll grieve, me!
You'll miss your little honey.
Some of these days!

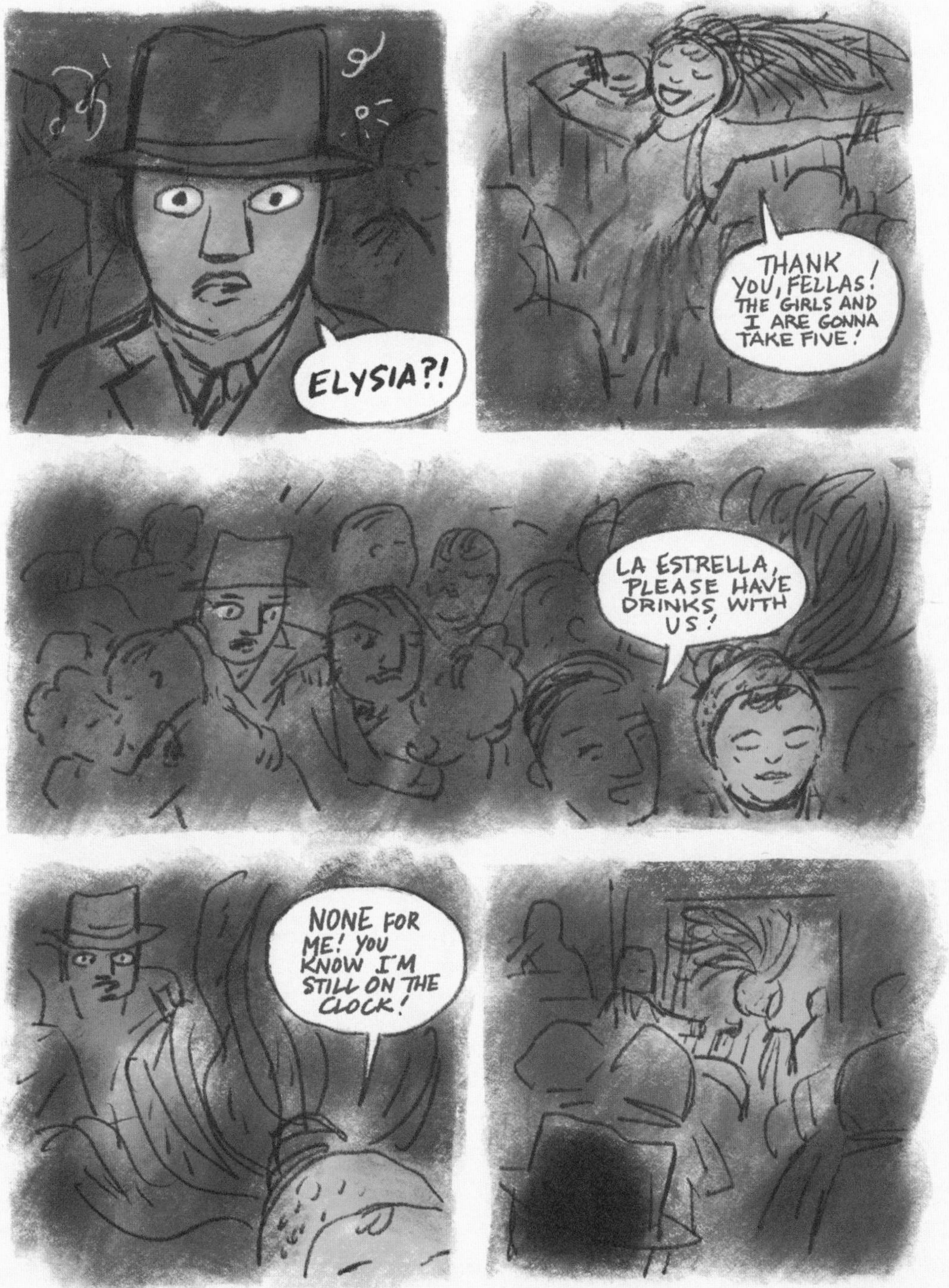
ELYSIA?!
THANK YOU, FELLAS! THE GIRLS AND I ARE GONNA TAKE FIVE!
LA ESTRELLA, PLEASE HAVE DRINKS WITH US!
NONE FOR ME! YOU KNOW I'M STILL ON THE CLOCK!

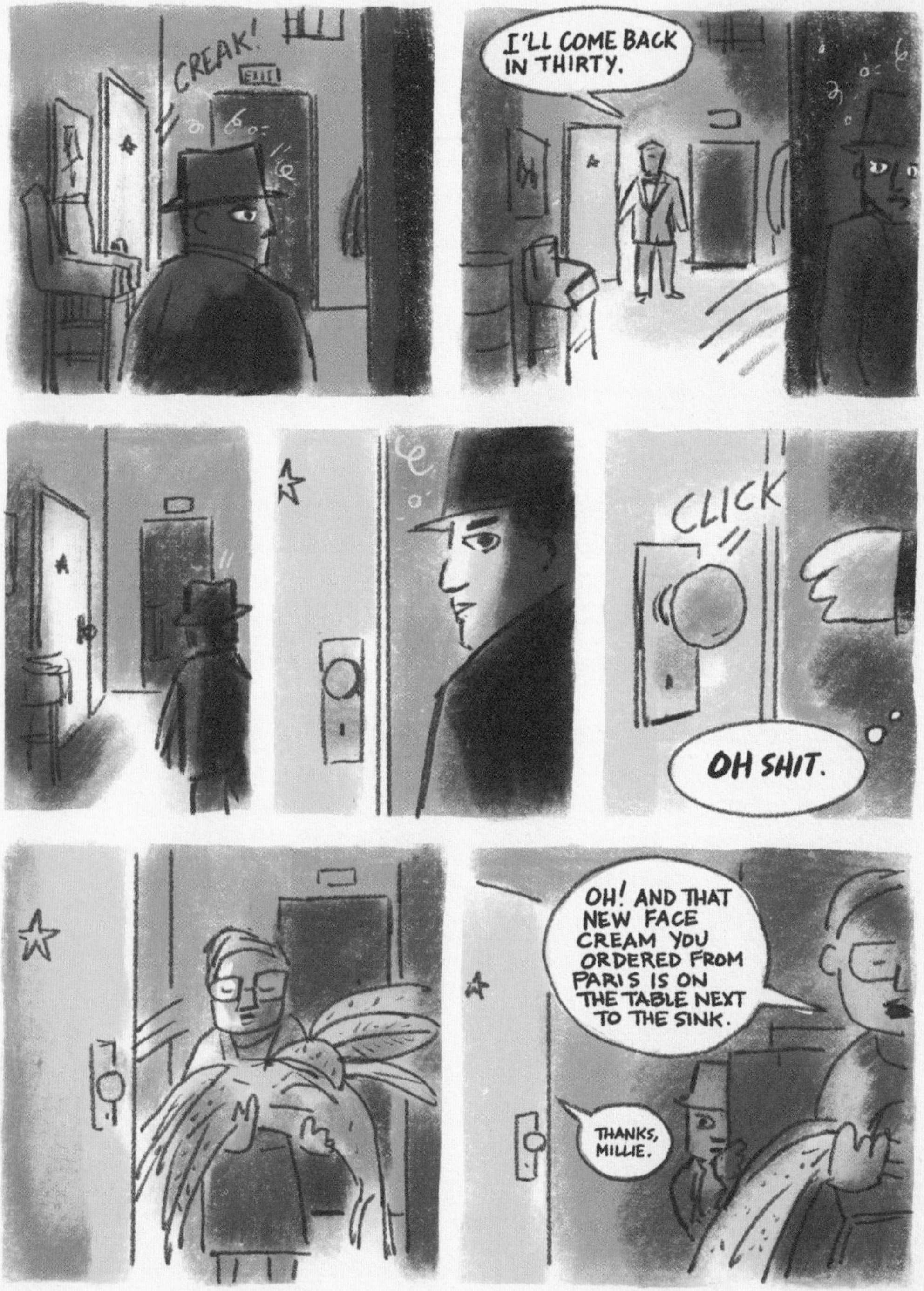
CREAK!
I'LL COME BACK IN THIRTY.
CLICK
OH SHIT.
OH! AND THAT NEW FACE CREAM YOU ORDERED FROM PARIS IS ON THE TABLE NEXT TO THE SINK.
THANKS, MILLIE.

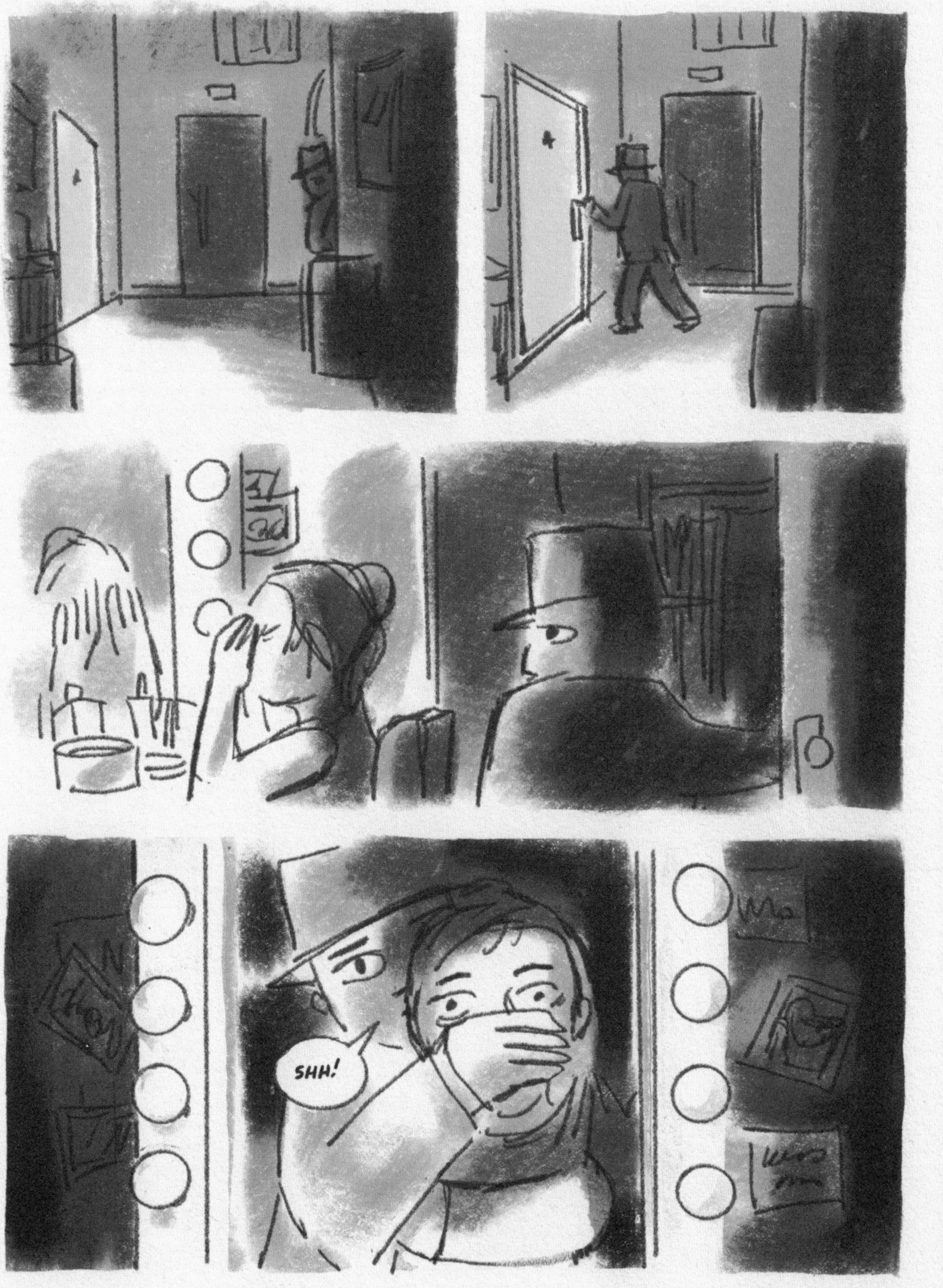
SHH!

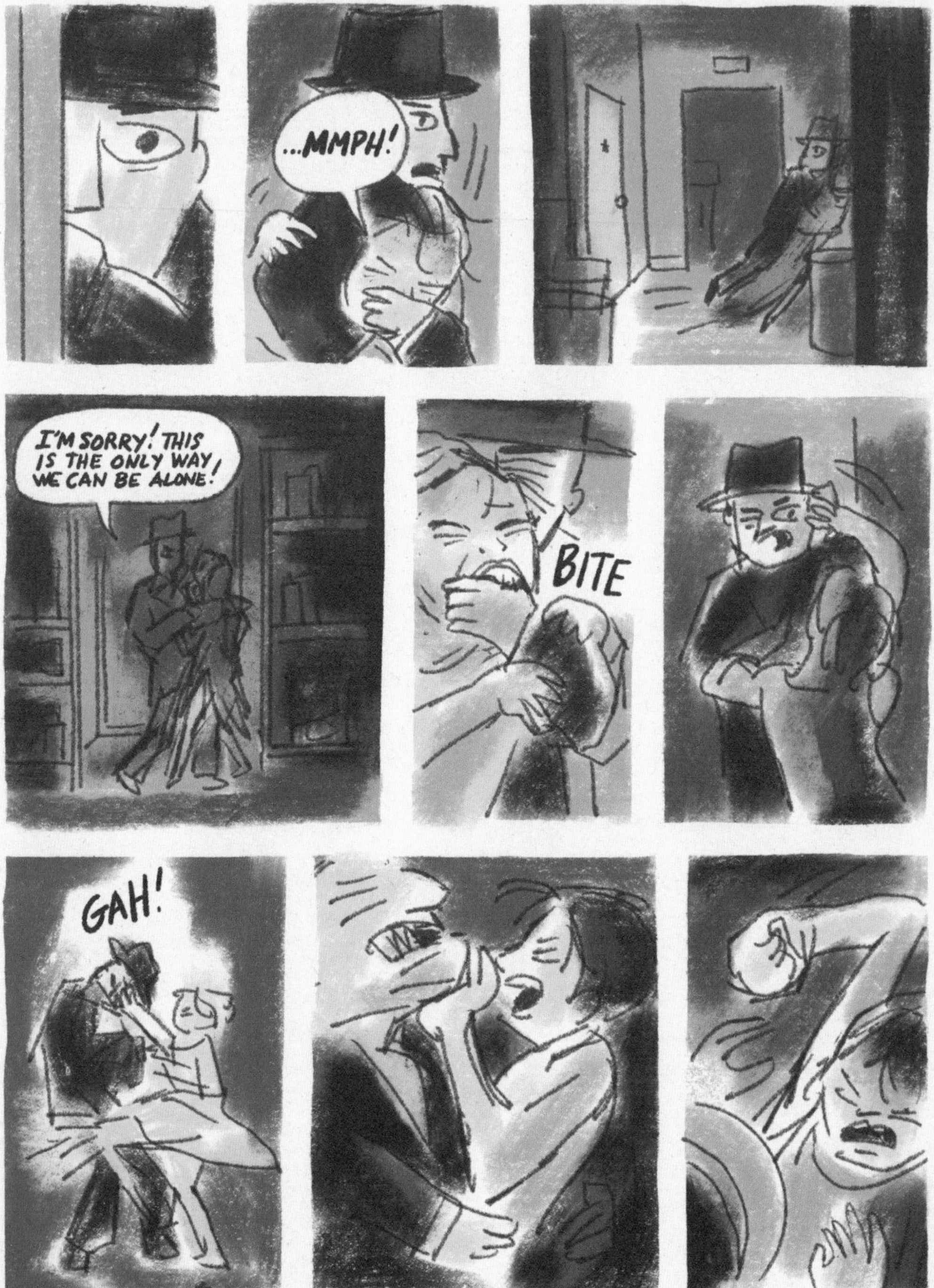
...MMPH!
I'M SORRY! THIS IS THE ONLY WAY! WE CAN BE ALONE!
BITE
GAH!

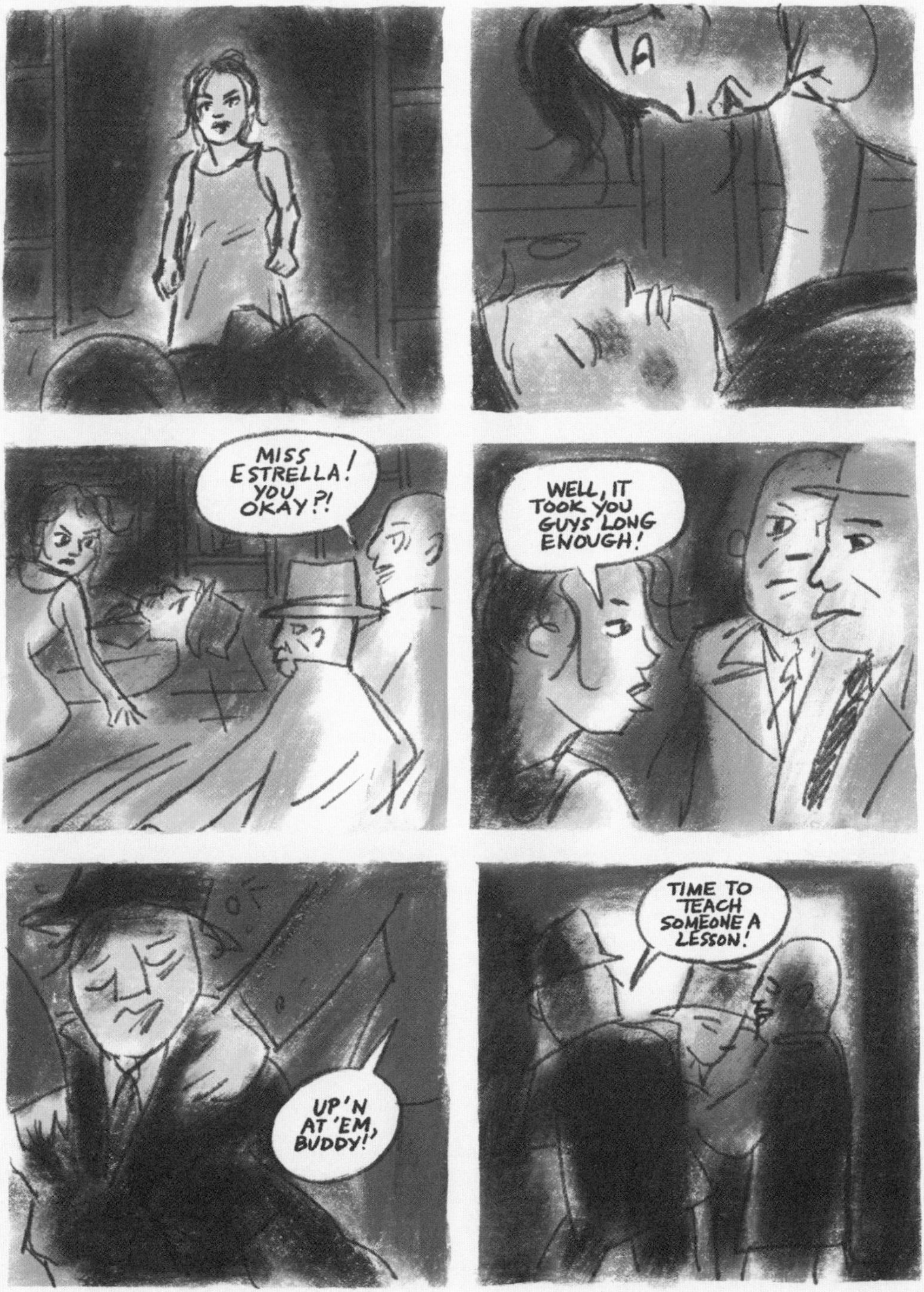
MISS ESTRELLA! YOU OKAY?!
WELL, IT TOOK YOU GUYS LONG ENOUGH!
UP'N AT 'EM, BUDDY!
TIME TO TEACH SOMEONE A LESSON!

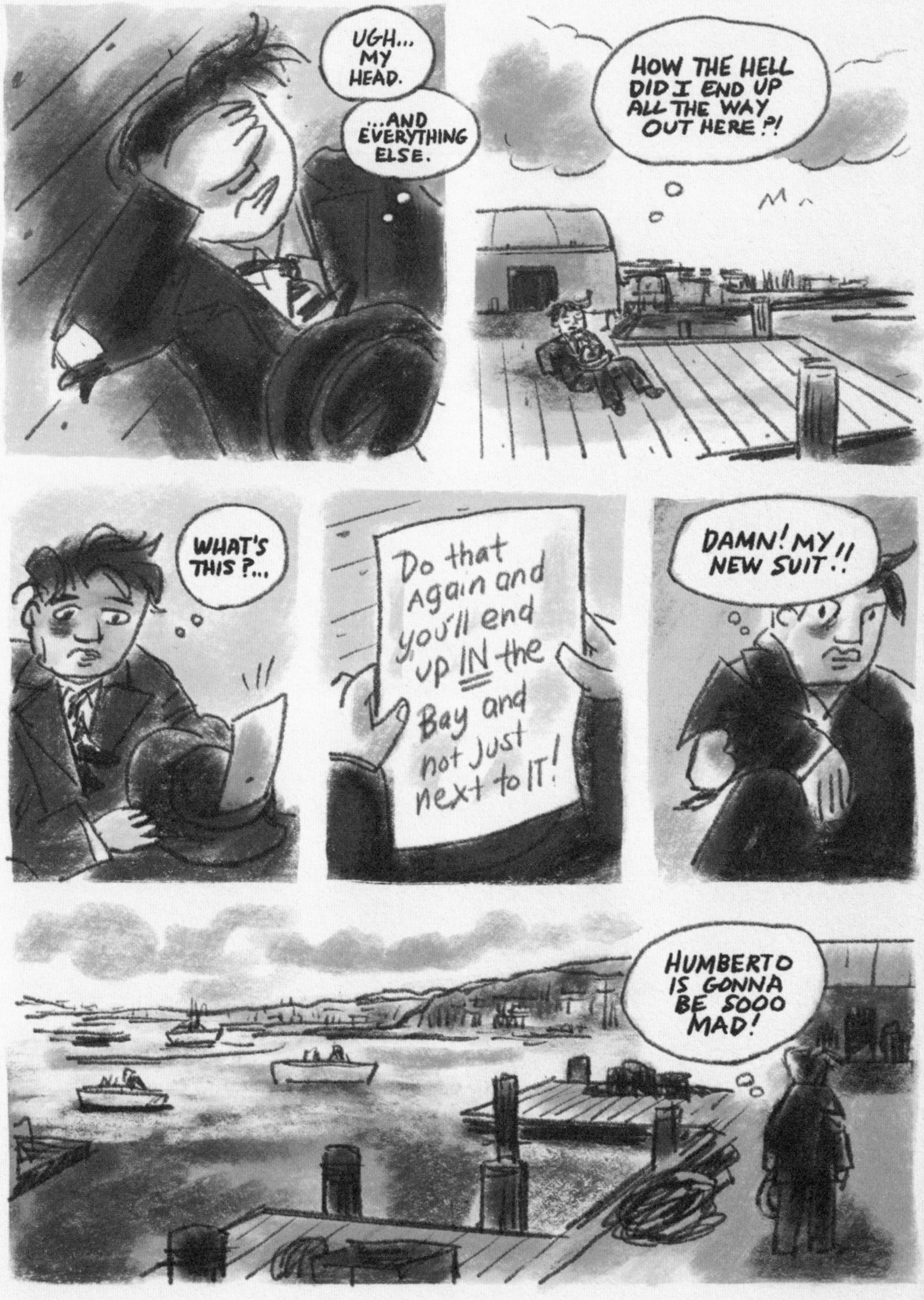
UGH... MY HEAD.
...AND EVERYTHING ELSE.
HOW THE HELL DID I END UP ALL THE WAY OUT HERE?!
WHAT'S THIS?...
Do that again and you'll end up IN the Bay and not just next to IT!
DAMN! MY NEW SUIT!!
HUMBERTO IS GONNA BE SOOO MAD!

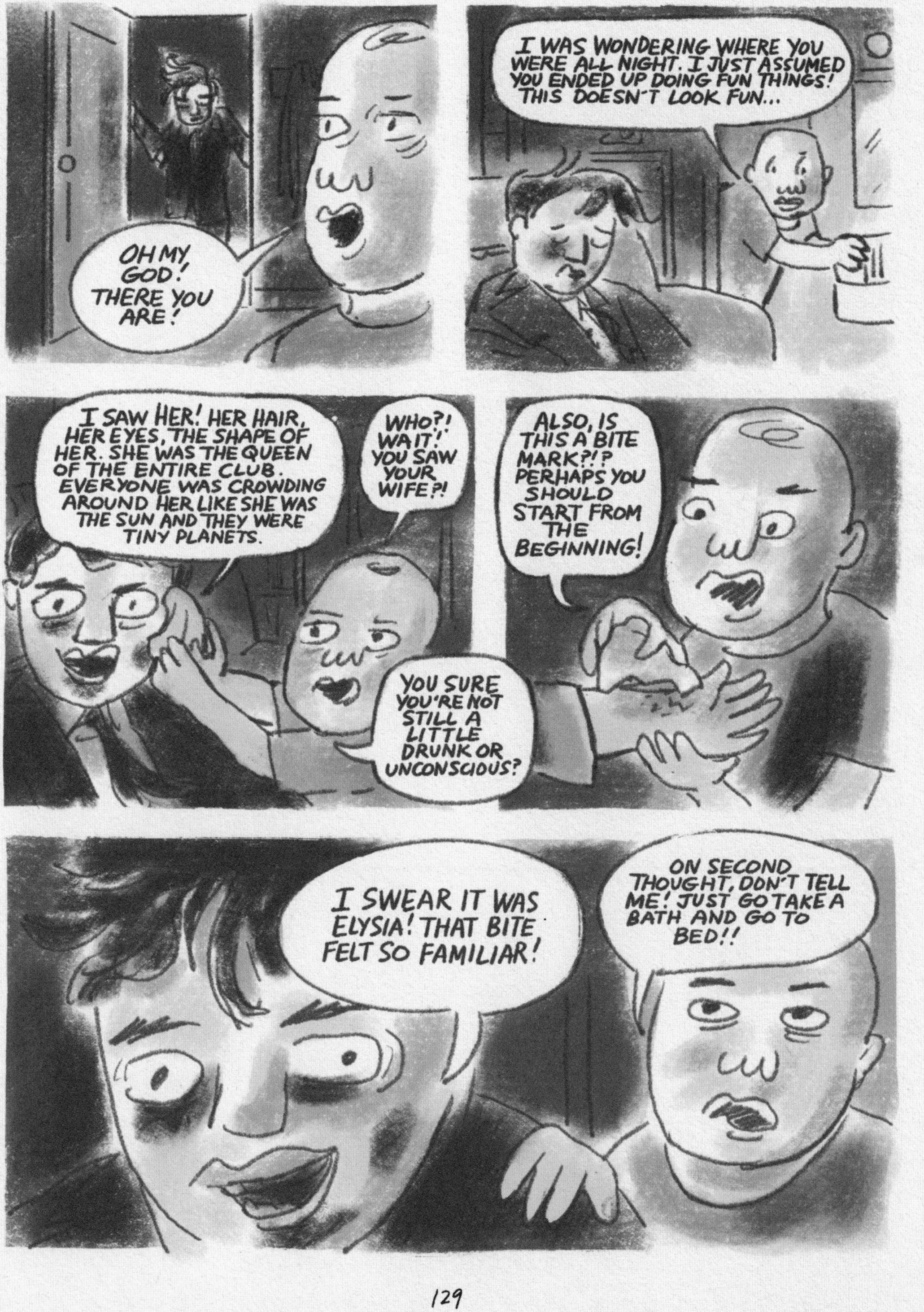

OH MY, GOD! THERE YOU ARE!
I WAS WONDERING WHERE YOU WERE ALL NIGHT. I JUST ASSUMED YOU ENDED UP DOING FUN THINGS! THIS DOESN'T LOOK FUN...
I SAW HER! HER HAIR, HER EYES, THE SHAPE OF HER. SHE WAS THE QUEEN OF THE ENTIRE CLUB. EVERYONE WAS CROWDING AROUND HER LIKE SHE WAS THE SUN AND THEY WERE TINY PLANETS.
WHO?! WAIT! YOU SAW YOUR WIFE?!
YOU SURE YOU'RE NOT STILL A LITTLE DRUNK OR UNCONSCIOUS?
ALSO, IS THIS A BITE MARK?!? PERHAPS YOU SHOULD START FROM THE BEGINNING!
I SWEAR IT WAS ELYSIA! THAT BITE FELT SO FAMILIAR!
ON SECOND THOUGHT, DON'T TELL ME! JUST GO TAKE A BATH AND GO TO BED!!

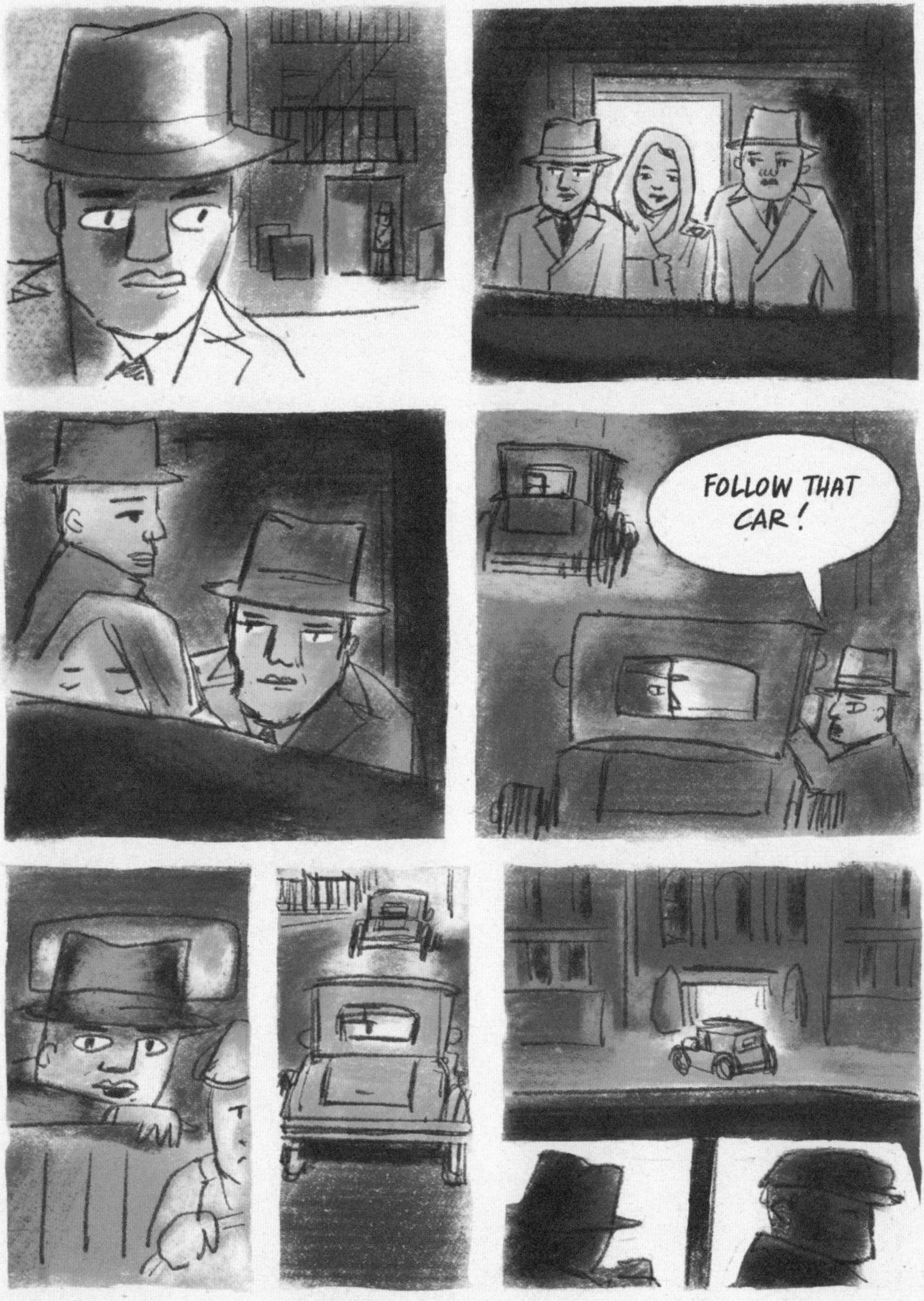
FOLLOW THAT CAR!

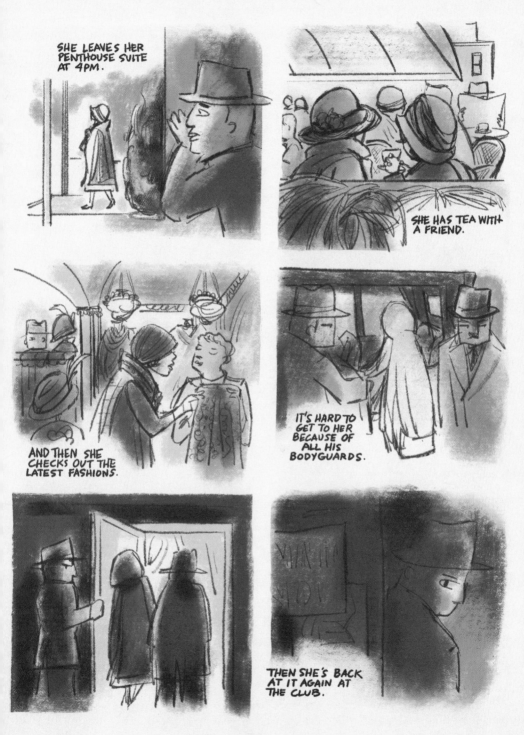

SHE LEAVES HER PENTHOUSE SUITE AT 4PM.

SHE HAS TEA WITH A FRIEND.

AND THEN SHE CHECKS OUT THE LATEST FASHIONS.

IT'S HARD TO GET TO HER BECAUSE OF ALL HIS BODYGUARDS.

THEN SHE'S BACK AT IT AGAIN AT THE CLUB.

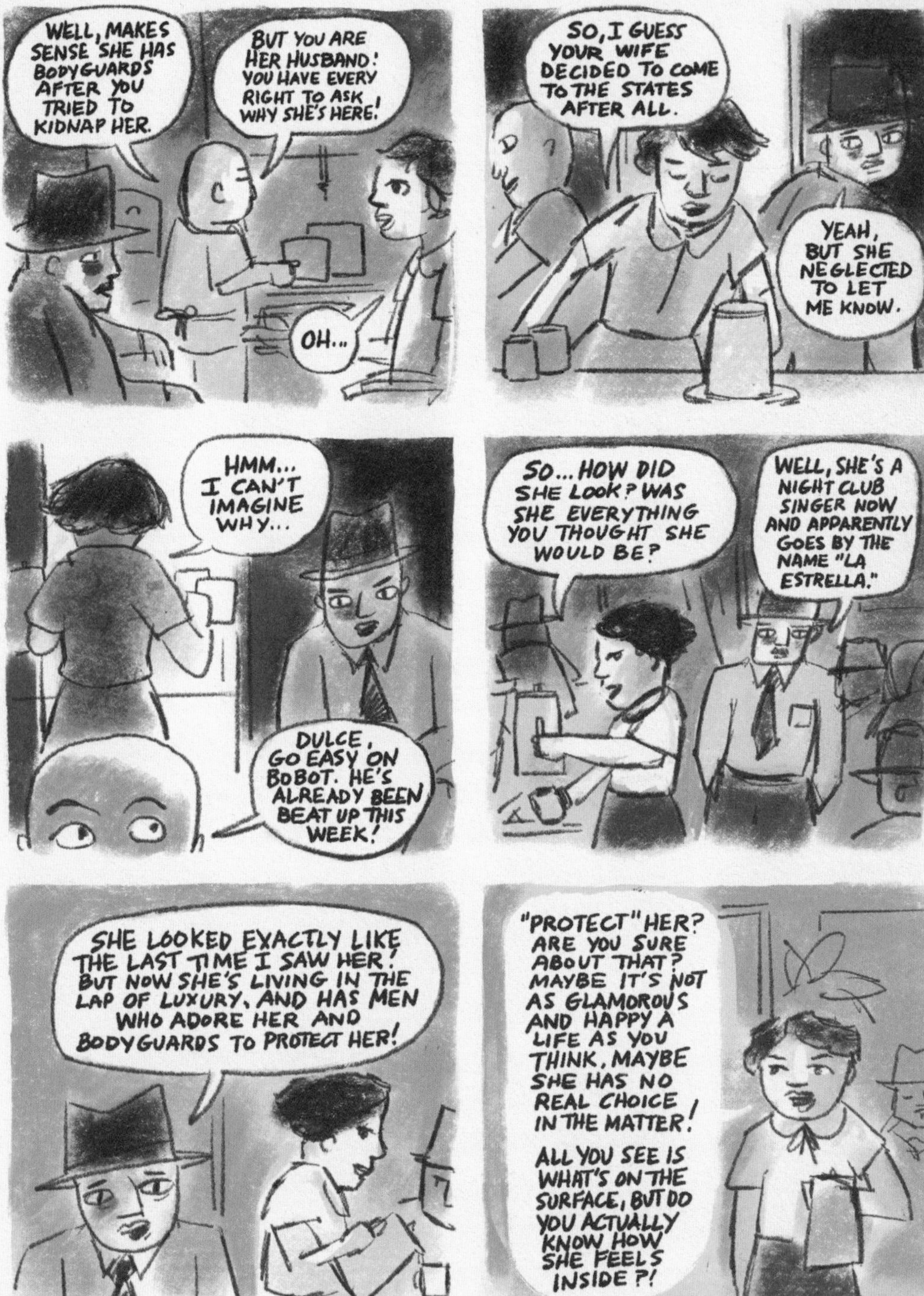
WELL, MAKES SENSE SHE HAS BODYGUARDS AFTER YOU TRIED TO KIDNAP HER.
BUT YOU ARE HER HUSBAND! YOU HAVE EVERY RIGHT TO ASK WHY SHE'S HERE!
OH...
SO, I GUESS YOUR WIFE DECIDED TO COME TO THE STATES AFTER ALL.
YEAH, BUT SHE NEGLECTED TO LET ME KNOW.
HMM... I CAN'T IMAGINE WHY...
DULCE, GO EASY ON BOBOT. HE'S ALREADY BEEN BEAT UP THIS WEEK!
SO... HOW DID SHE LOOK? WAS SHE EVERYTHING YOU THOUGHT SHE WOULD BE?
WELL, SHE'S A NIGHT CLUB SINGER NOW AND APPARENTLY GOES BY THE NAME "LA ESTRELLA."
SHE LOOKED EXACTLY LIKE THE LAST TIME I SAW HER! BUT NOW SHE'S LIVING IN THE LAP OF LUXURY, AND HAS MEN WHO ADORE HER AND BODYGUARDS TO PROTECT HER!
"PROTECT" HER? ARE YOU SURE ABOUT THAT? MAYBE IT'S NOT AS GLAMOROUS AND HAPPY A LIFE AS YOU THINK. MAYBE SHE HAS NO REAL CHOICE IN THE MATTER!
ALL YOU SEE IS WHAT'S ON THE SURFACE, BUT DO YOU ACTUALLY KNOW HOW SHE FEELS INSIDE?!

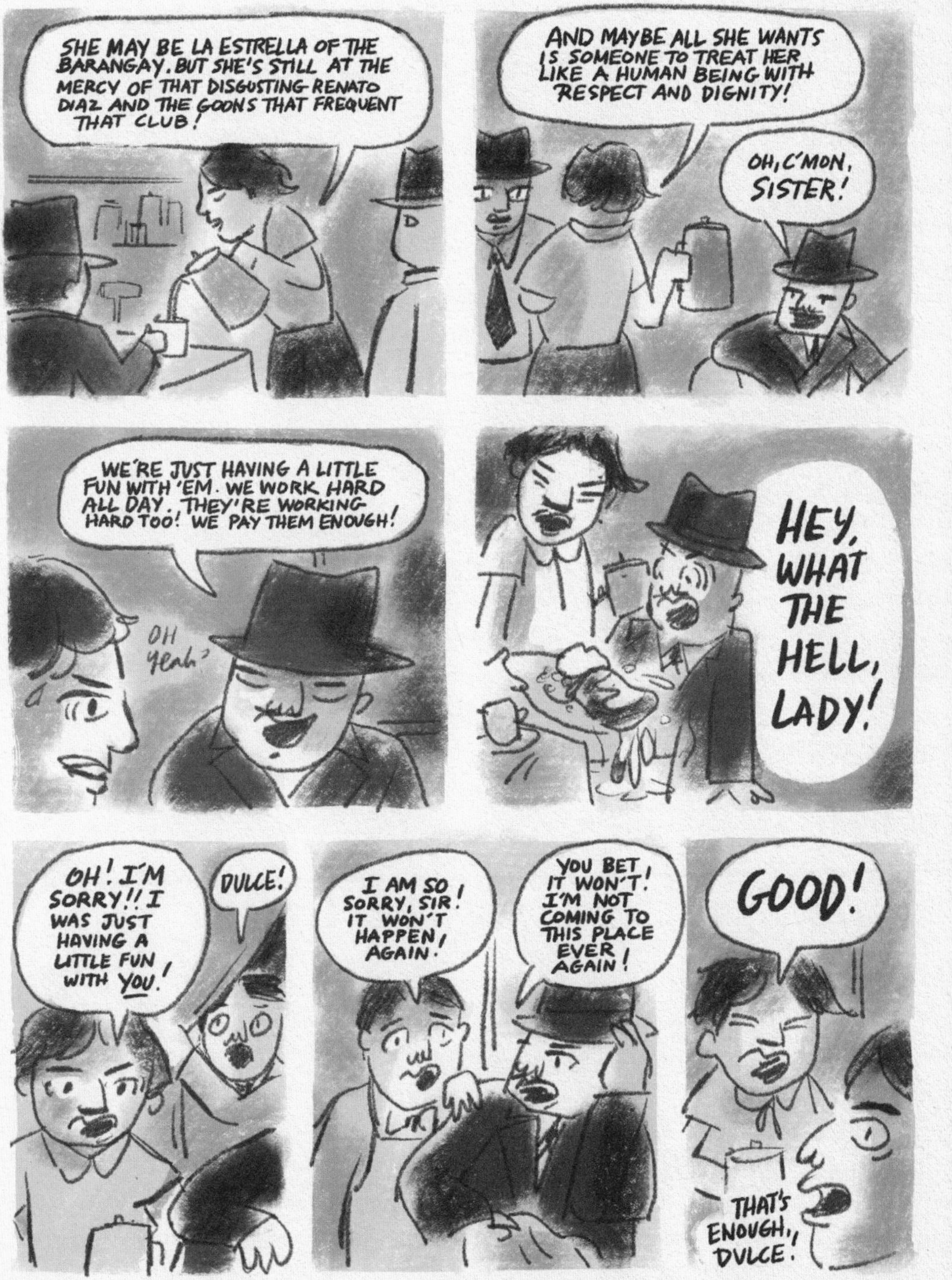
SHE MAY BE LA ESTRELLA OF THE BARANGAY. BUT SHE'S STILL AT THE MERCY OF THAT DISGUSTING RENATO DIAZ AND THE GOONS THAT FREQUENT THAT CLUB!
AND MAYBE ALL SHE WANTS IS SOMEONE TO TREAT HER LIKE A HUMAN BEING WITH RESPECT AND DIGNITY!
OH, C'MON, SISTER!
WE'RE JUST HAVING A LITTLE FUN WITH 'EM. WE WORK HARD ALL DAY. THEY'RE WORKING HARD TOO! WE PAY THEM ENOUGH!
OH yeah?
HEY, WHAT THE HELL, LADY!
OH! I'M SORRY!! I WAS JUST HAVING A LITTLE FUN WITH YOU!
DULCE!
I AM SO SORRY, SIR! IT WON'T HAPPEN AGAIN!
YOU BET IT WON'T! I'M NOT COMING TO THIS PLACE EVER AGAIN!
GOOD!
THAT'S ENOUGH, DULCE!

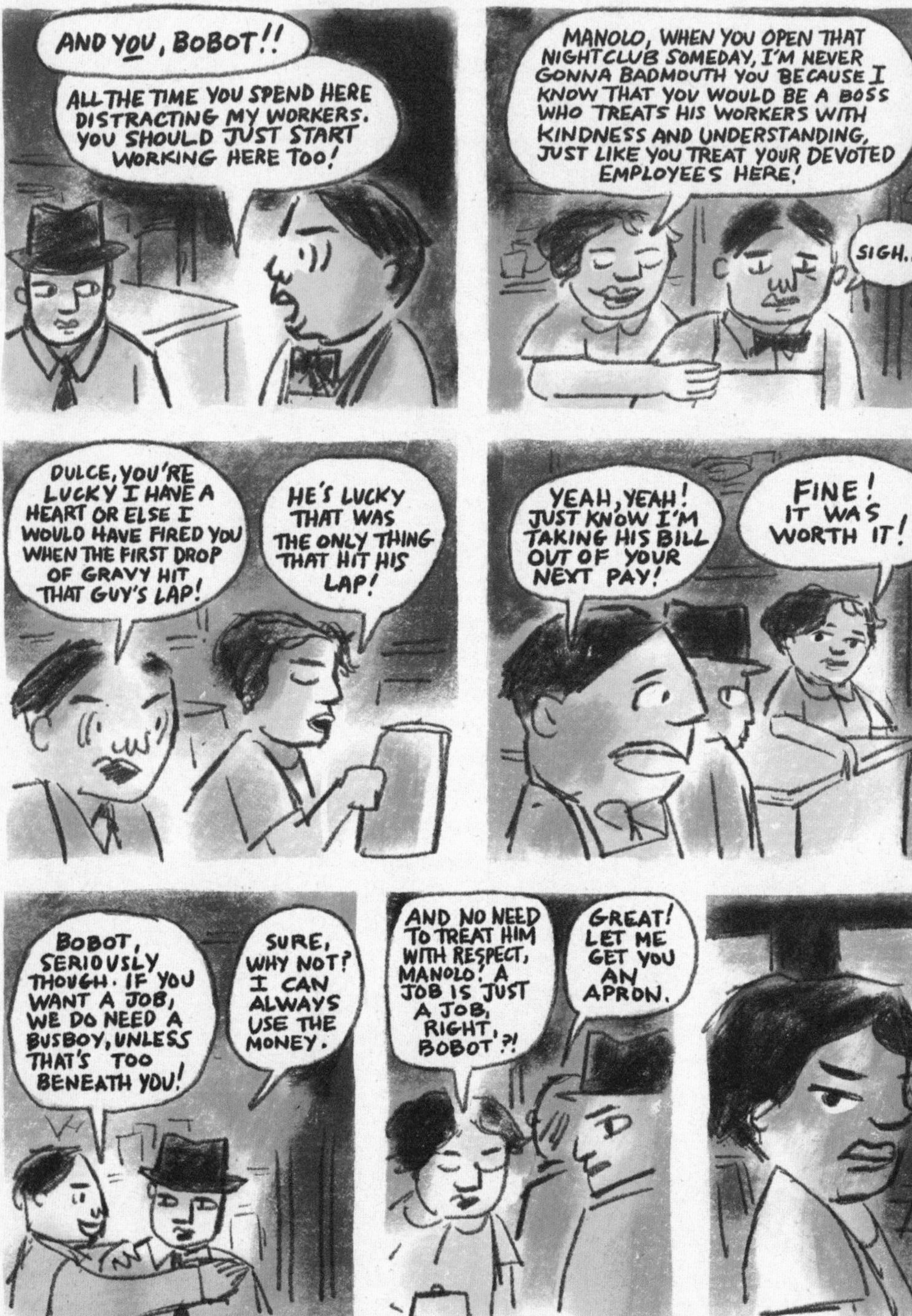
AND YOU, BOBOT!!
ALL THE TIME YOU SPEND HERE DISTRACTING MY WORKERS. YOU SHOULD JUST START WORKING HERE TOO!
MANOLO, WHEN YOU OPEN THAT NIGHTCLUB SOMEDAY, I'M NEVER GONNA BADMOUTH YOU BECAUSE I KNOW THAT YOU WOULD BE A BOSS WHO TREATS HIS WORKERS WITH KINDNESS AND UNDERSTANDING, JUST LIKE YOU TREAT YOUR DEVOTED EMPLOYEES HERE!
SIGH...
DULCE, YOU'RE LUCKY I HAVE A HEART OR ELSE I WOULD HAVE FIRED YOU WHEN THE FIRST DROP OF GRAVY HIT THAT GUY'S LAP!
HE'S LUCKY THAT WAS THE ONLY THING THAT HIT HIS LAP!
YEAH, YEAH! JUST KNOW I'M TAKING HIS BILL OUT OF YOUR NEXT PAY!
FINE! IT WAS WORTH IT!
BOBOT, SERIOUSLY THOUGH. IF YOU WANT A JOB, WE DO NEED A BUSBOY, UNLESS THAT'S TOO BENEATH YOU!
SURE, WHY NOT? I CAN ALWAYS USE THE MONEY.
AND NO NEED TO TREAT HIM WITH RESPECT, MANOLO! A JOB IS JUST A JOB, RIGHT, BOBOT?!
GREAT! LET ME GET YOU AN APRON.

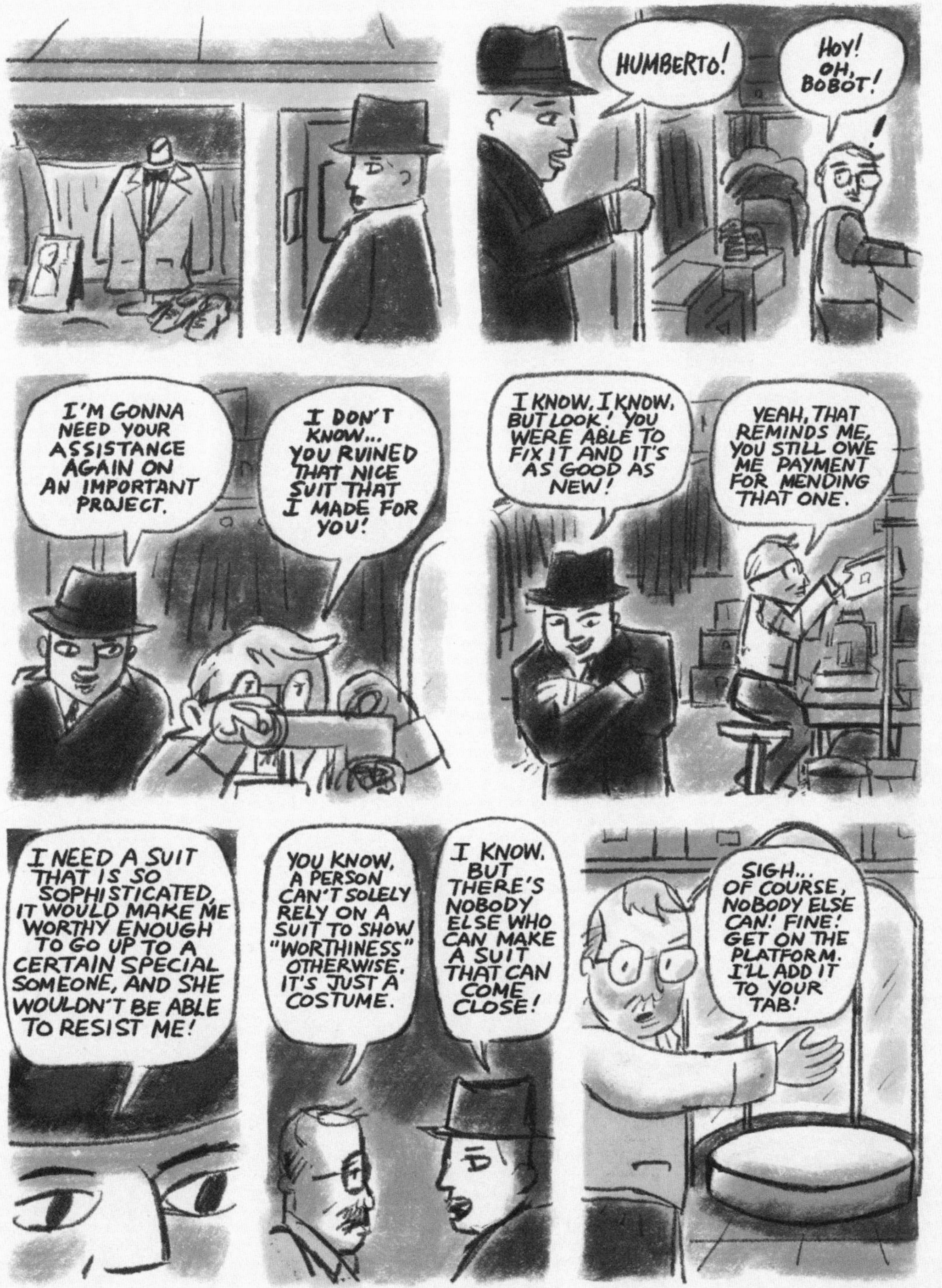
HUMBERTO!
HOY! OH, BOBOT!
I'M GONNA NEED YOUR ASSISTANCE AGAIN ON AN IMPORTANT PROJECT.
I DON'T KNOW... YOU RUINED THAT NICE SUIT THAT I MADE FOR YOU!
I KNOW, I KNOW, BUT LOOK! YOU WERE ABLE TO FIX IT AND IT'S AS GOOD AS NEW!
YEAH, THAT REMINDS ME, YOU STILL OWE ME PAYMENT FOR MENDING THAT ONE.
I NEED A SUIT THAT IS SO SOPHISTICATED, IT WOULD MAKE ME WORTHY ENOUGH TO GO UP TO A CERTAIN SPECIAL SOMEONE, AND SHE WOULDN'T BE ABLE TO RESIST ME!
YOU KNOW, A PERSON CAN'T SOLELY RELY ON A SUIT TO SHOW "WORTHINESS" OTHERWISE, IT'S JUST A COSTUME.
I KNOW. BUT THERE'S NOBODY ELSE WHO CAN MAKE A SUIT THAT CAN COME CLOSE!
SIGH... OF COURSE, NOBODY ELSE CAN! FINE! GET ON THE PLATFORM. I'LL ADD IT TO YOUR TAB!

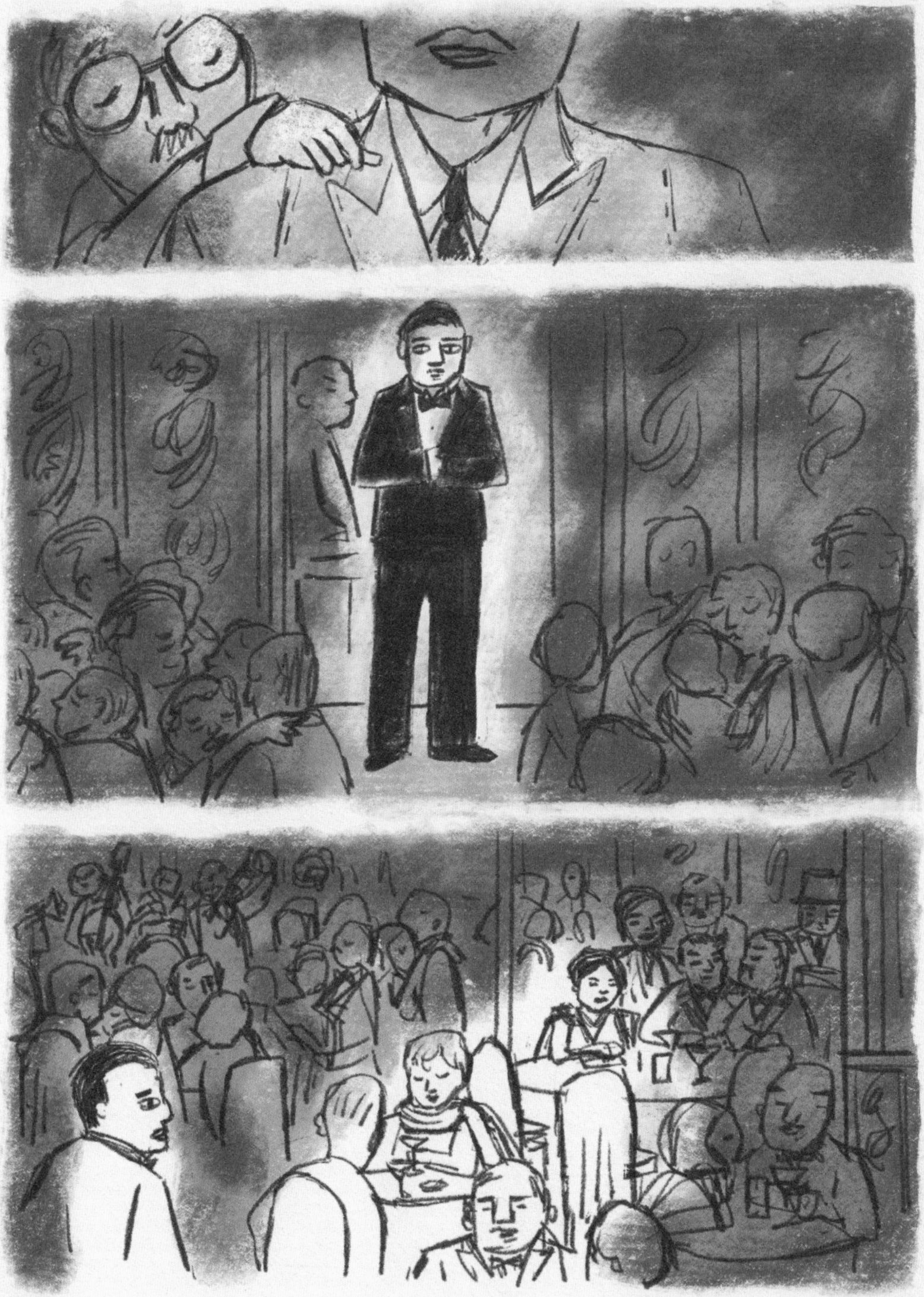

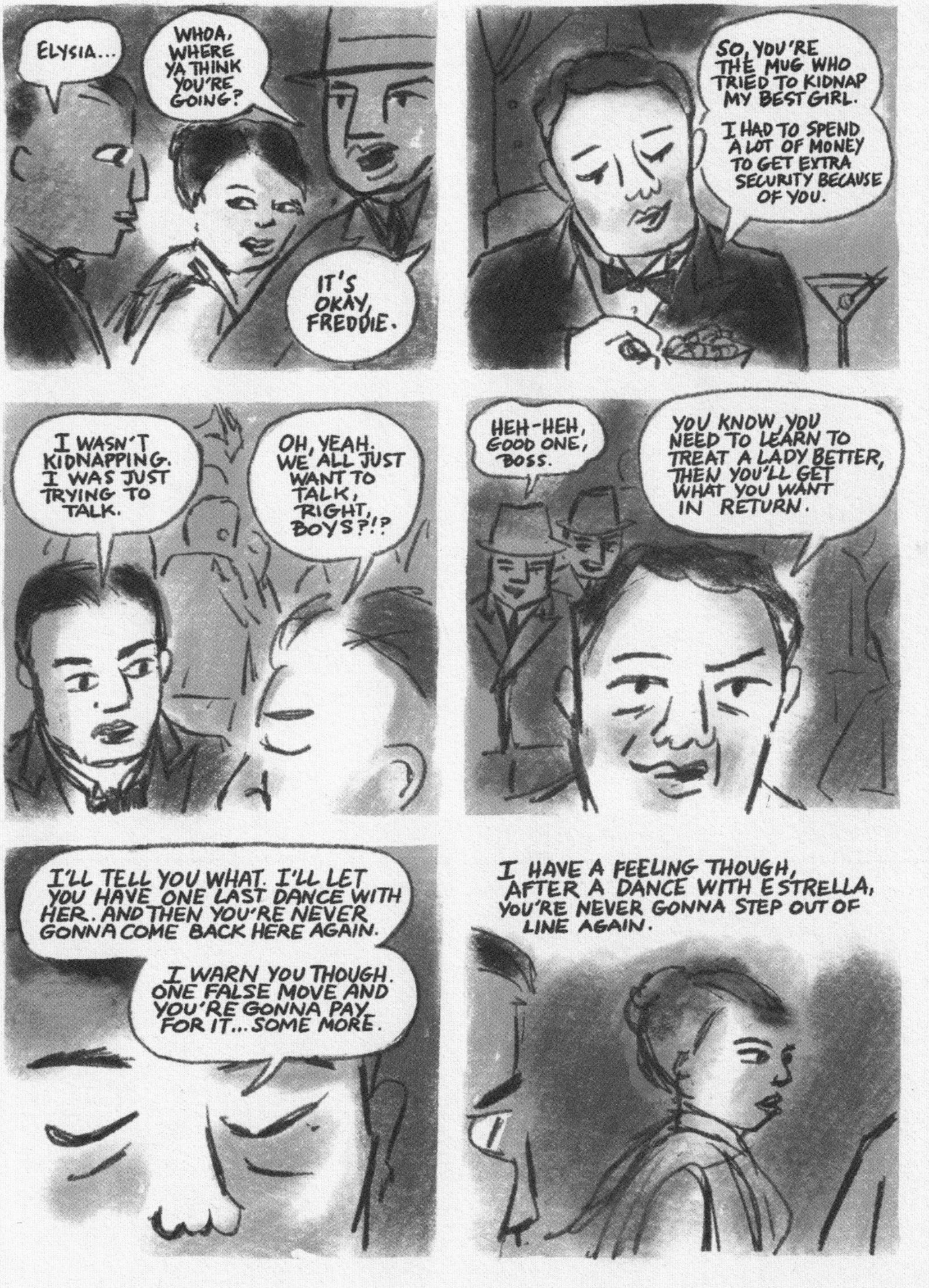
ELYSIA...
WHOA, WHERE YA THINK YOU'RE GOING?
IT'S OKAY, FREDDIE.
SO, YOU'RE THE MUG WHO TRIED TO KIDNAP MY BEST GIRL.
I HAD TO SPEND A LOT OF MONEY TO GET EXTRA SECURITY BECAUSE OF YOU.
I WASN'T KIDNAPPING. I WAS JUST TRYING TO TALK.
OH, YEAH. WE ALL JUST WANT TO TALK, RIGHT, BOYS?!?
HEH-HEH, GOOD ONE, BOSS.
YOU KNOW, YOU NEED TO LEARN TO TREAT A LADY BETTER, THEN YOU'LL GET WHAT YOU WANT IN RETURN.
I'LL TELL YOU WHAT. I'LL LET YOU HAVE ONE LAST DANCE WITH HER.. AND THEN YOU'RE NEVER GONNA COME BACK HERE AGAIN.
I WARN YOU THOUGH. ONE FALSE MOVE AND YOU'RE GONNA PAY FOR IT... SOME MORE.
I HAVE A FEELING THOUGH, AFTER A DANCE WITH ESTRELLA, YOU'RE NEVER GONNA STEP OUT OF LINE AGAIN.

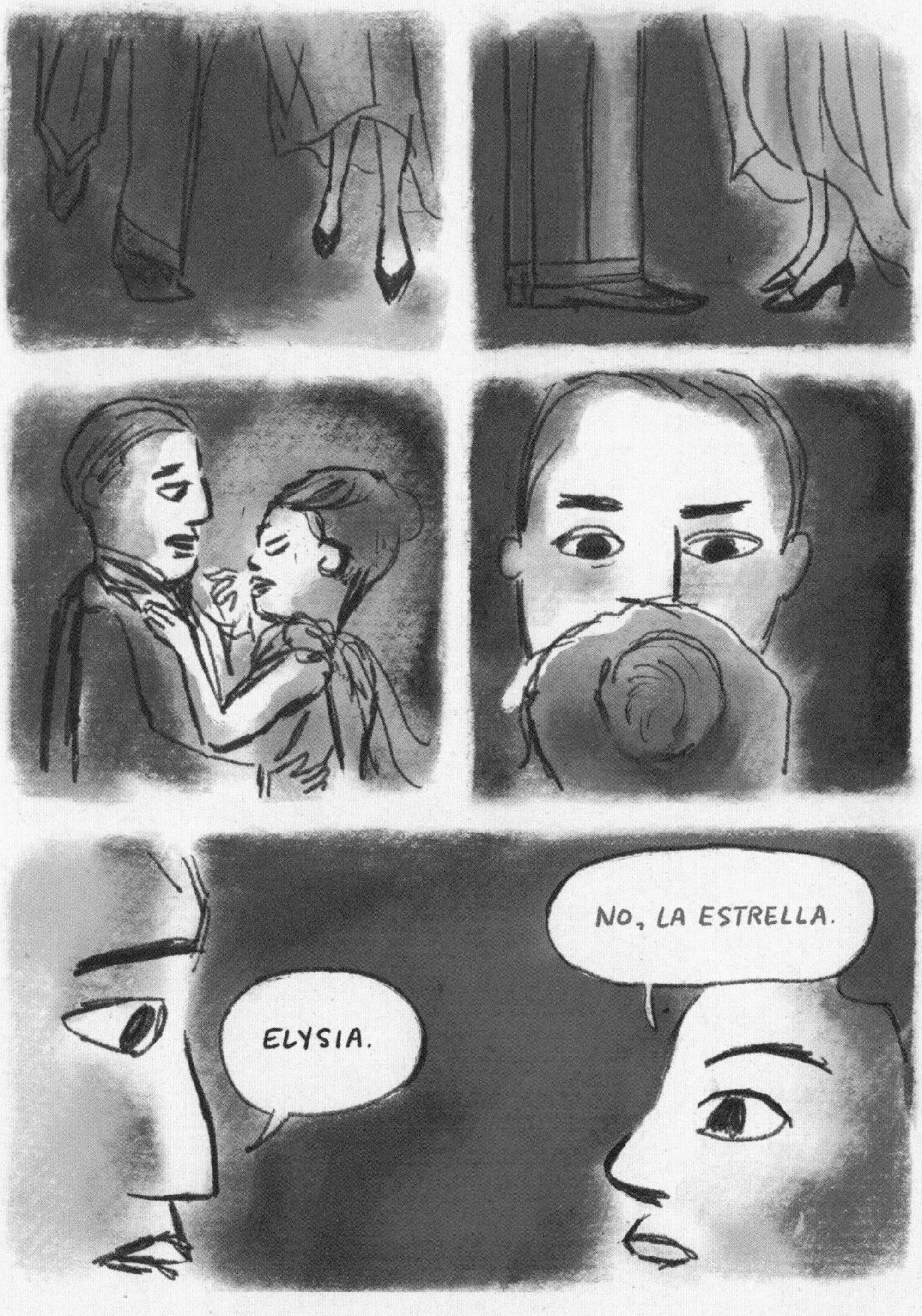
NO, LA ESTRELLA.
ELYSIA.

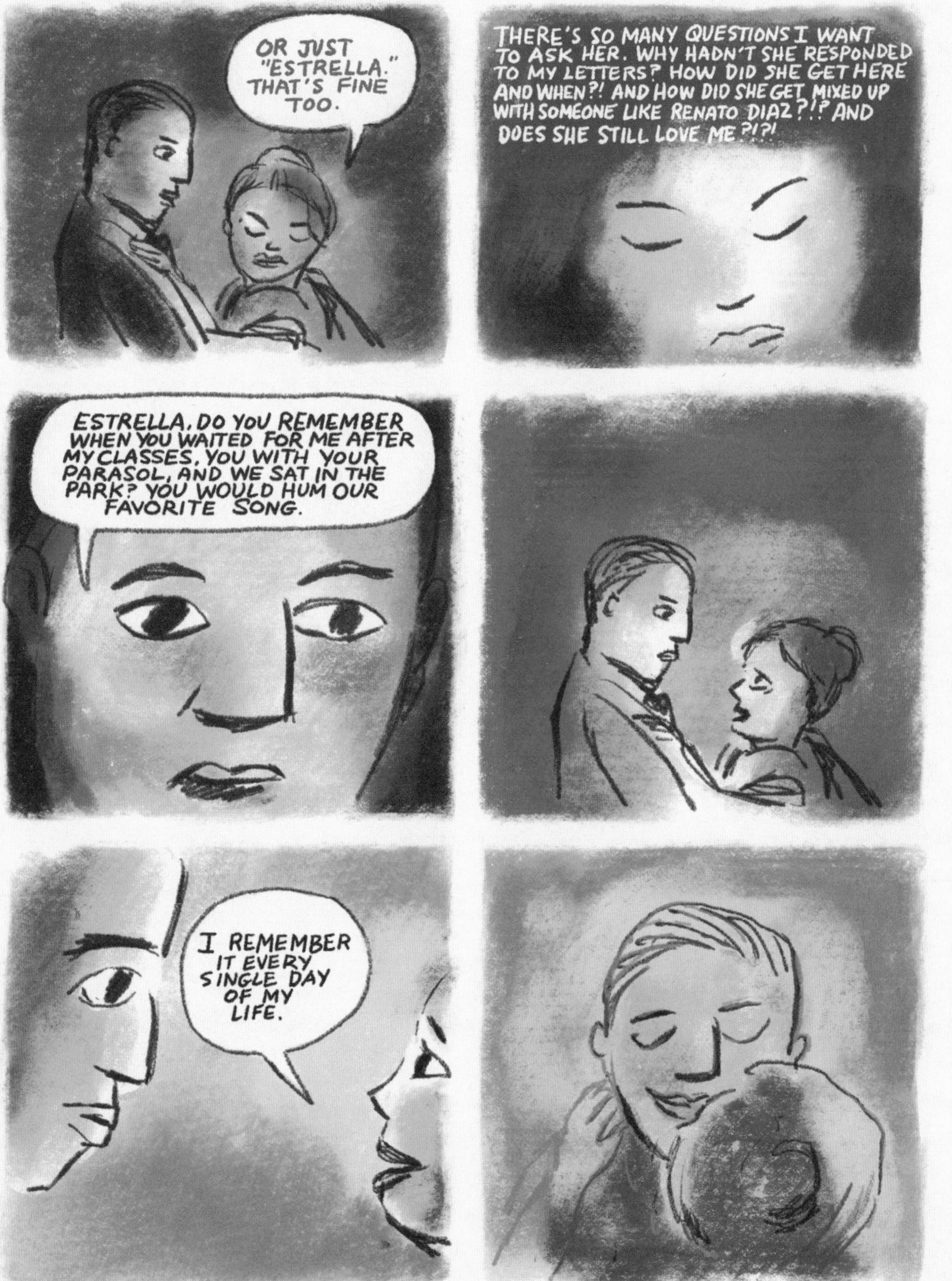
OR JUST "ESTRELLA." THAT'S FINE TOO.
THERE'S SO MANY QUESTIONS I WANT TO ASK HER. WHY HADN'T SHE RESPONDED TO MY LETTERS? HOW DID SHE GET HERE AND WHEN?! AND HOW DID SHE GET MIXED UP WITH SOMEONE LIKE RENATO DIAZ?!? AND DOES SHE STILL LOVE ME?!?!
ESTRELLA, DO YOU REMEMBER WHEN YOU WAITED FOR ME AFTER MY CLASSES, YOU WITH YOUR PARASOL, AND WE SAT IN THE PARK? YOU WOULD HUM OUR FAVORITE SONG.
I REMEMBER IT EVERY SINGLE DAY OF MY LIFE.

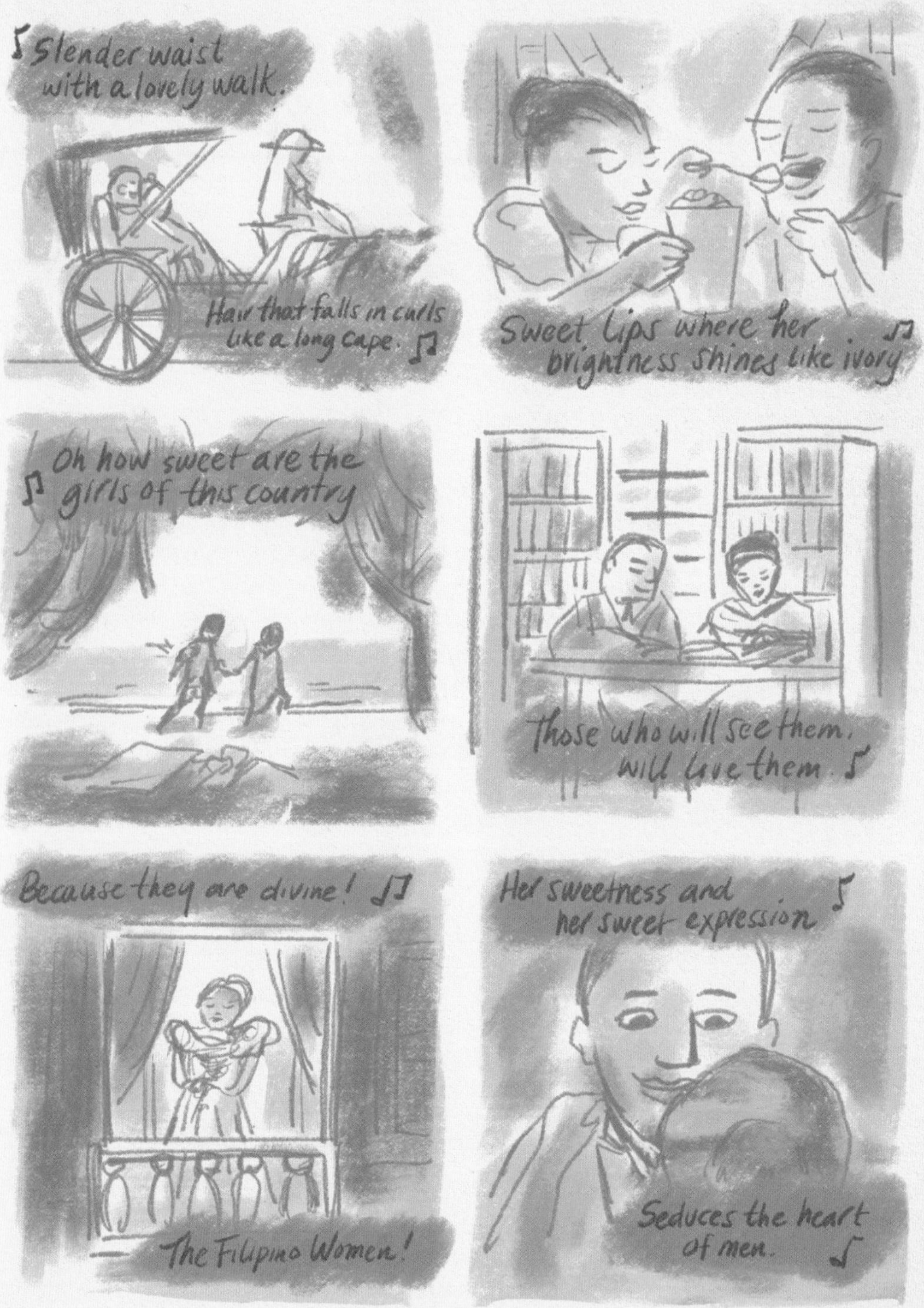
Slender waist with a lovely walk.
Hair that falls in curls like a long cape.
Sweet lips where her brightness shines like ivory
Oh how sweet are the girls of this country
Those who will see them, will love them.
Because they are divine!
The Filipino Women!
Her sweetness and her sweet expression
Seduces the heart of men.

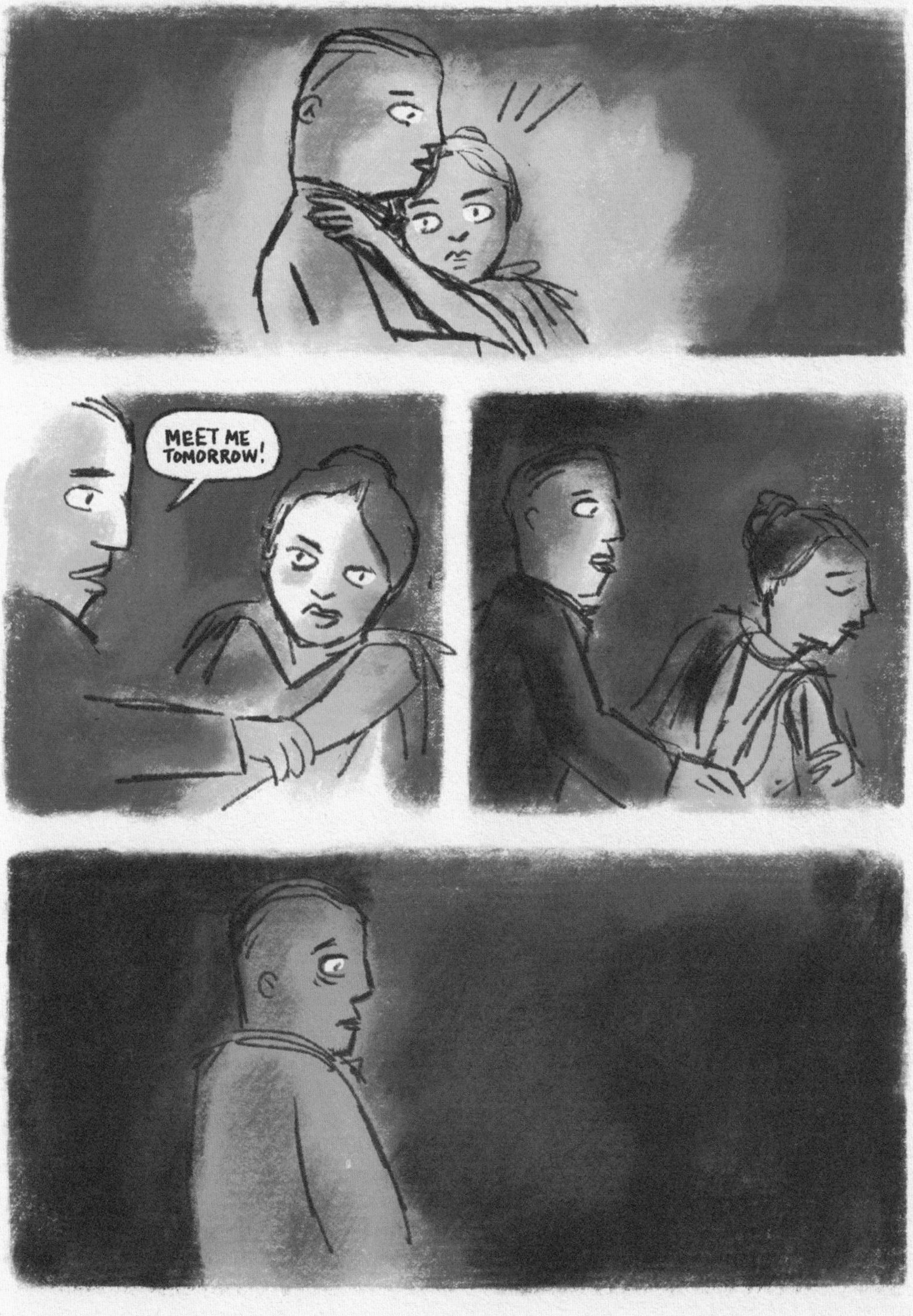
MEET ME TOMORROW!

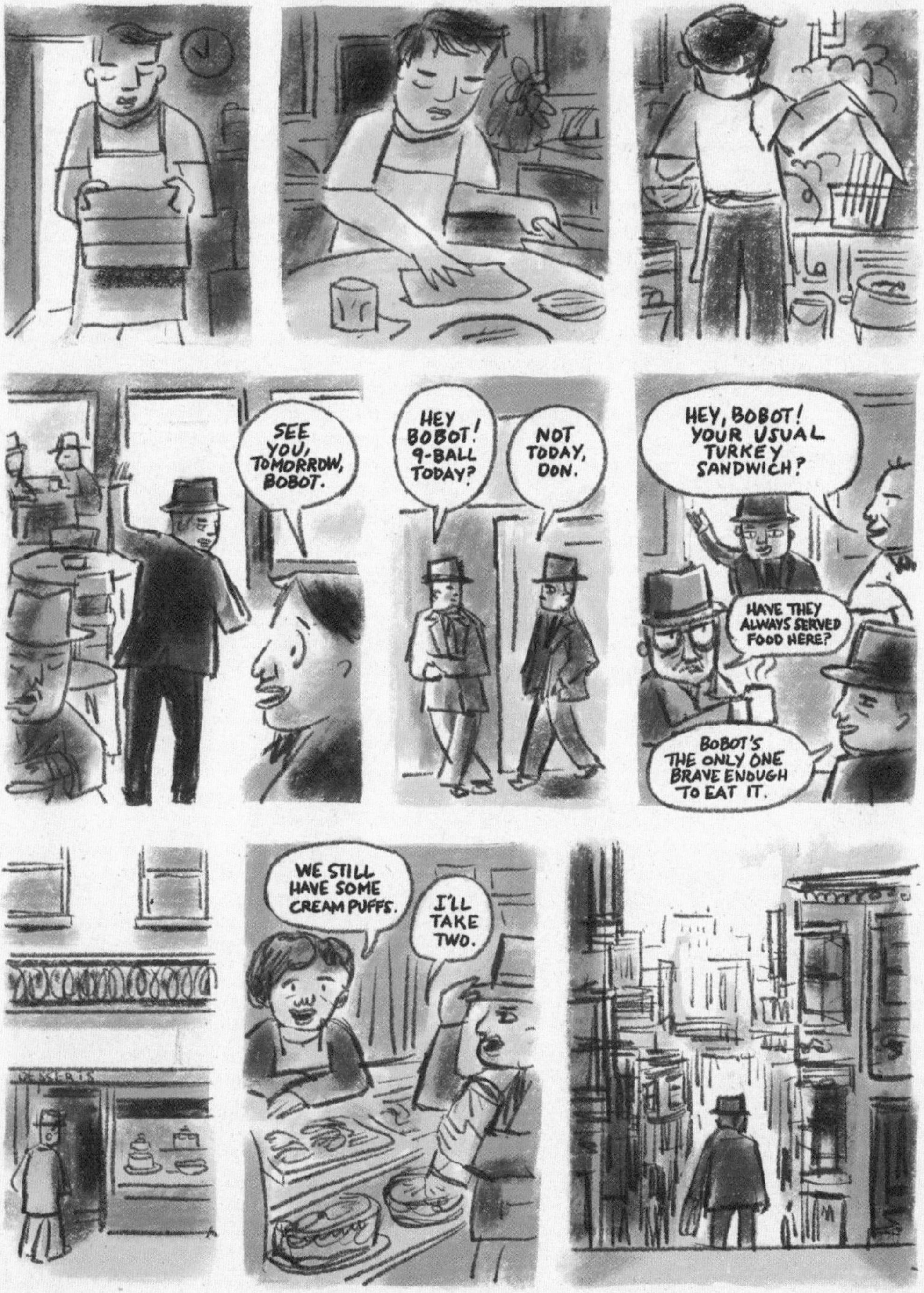
SEE YOU, TOMORROW, BOBOT.
HEY BOBOT! 9-BALL TODAY?
NOT TODAY, DON.
HEY, BOBOT! YOUR USUAL TURKEY SANDWICH?
HAVE THEY ALWAYS SERVED FOOD HERE?
BOBOT'S THE ONLY ONE BRAVE ENOUGH TO EAT IT.
WE STILL HAVE SOME CREAM PUFFS.
I'LL TAKE TWO.

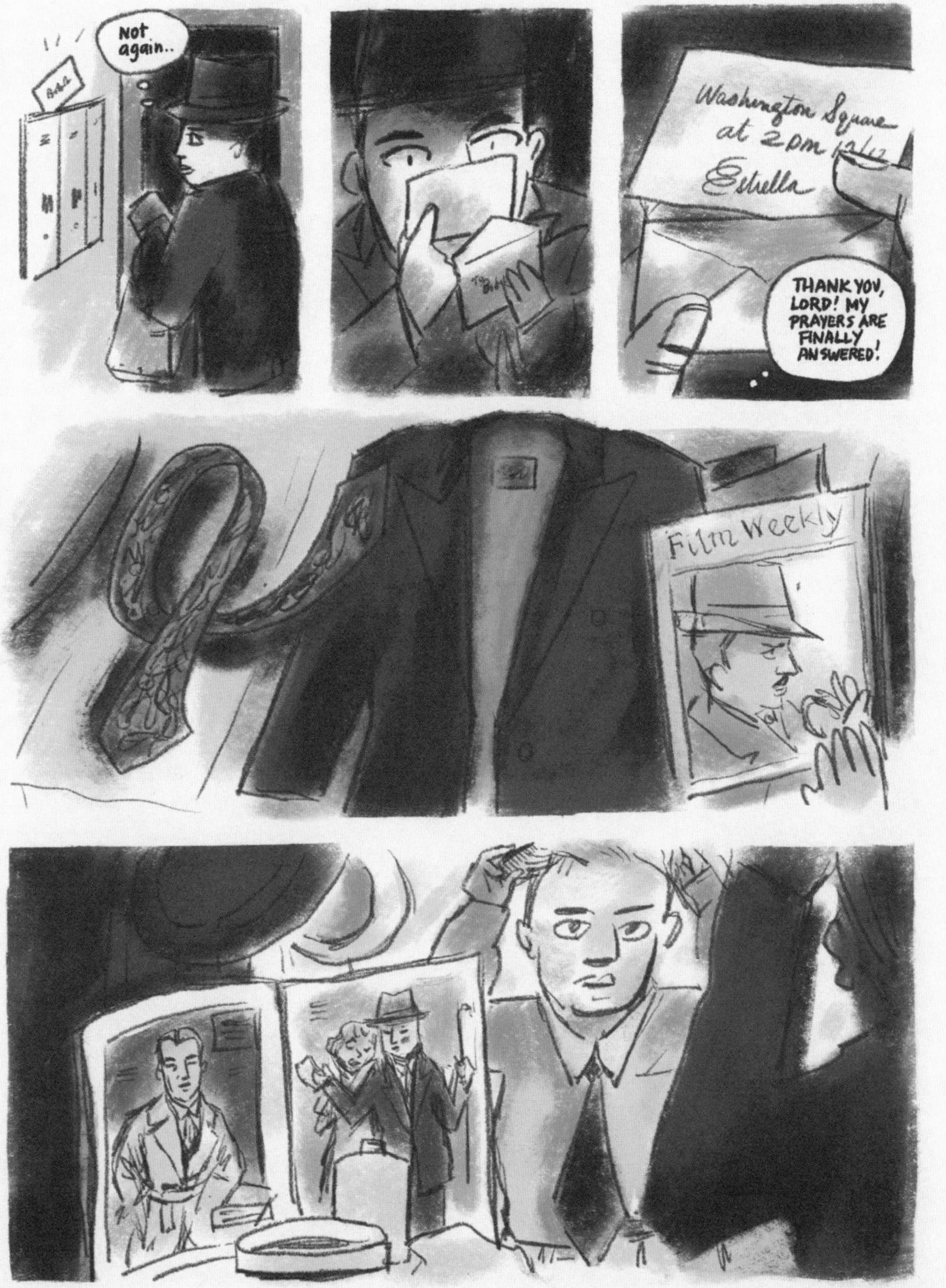
Not again..
Washington Square at 2pm 12/12
Estrella
THANK YOU, LORD! MY PRAYERS ARE FINALLY ANSWERED!
Film Weekly

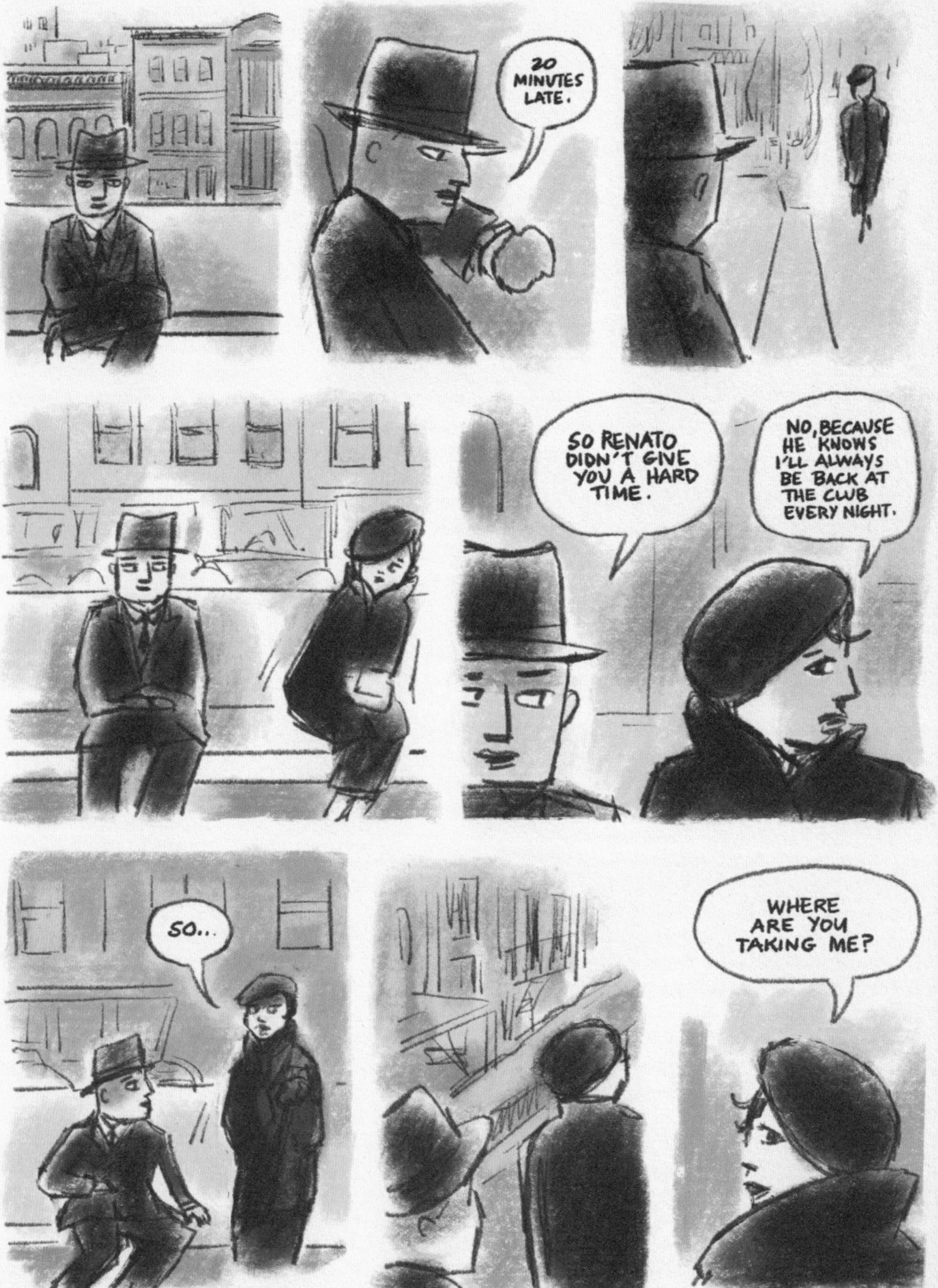
20 MINUTES LATE.
SO RENATO DIDN'T GIVE YOU A HARD TIME.
NO, BECAUSE HE KNOWS I'LL ALWAYS BE BACK AT THE CLUB EVERY NIGHT.
SO...
WHERE ARE YOU TAKING ME?

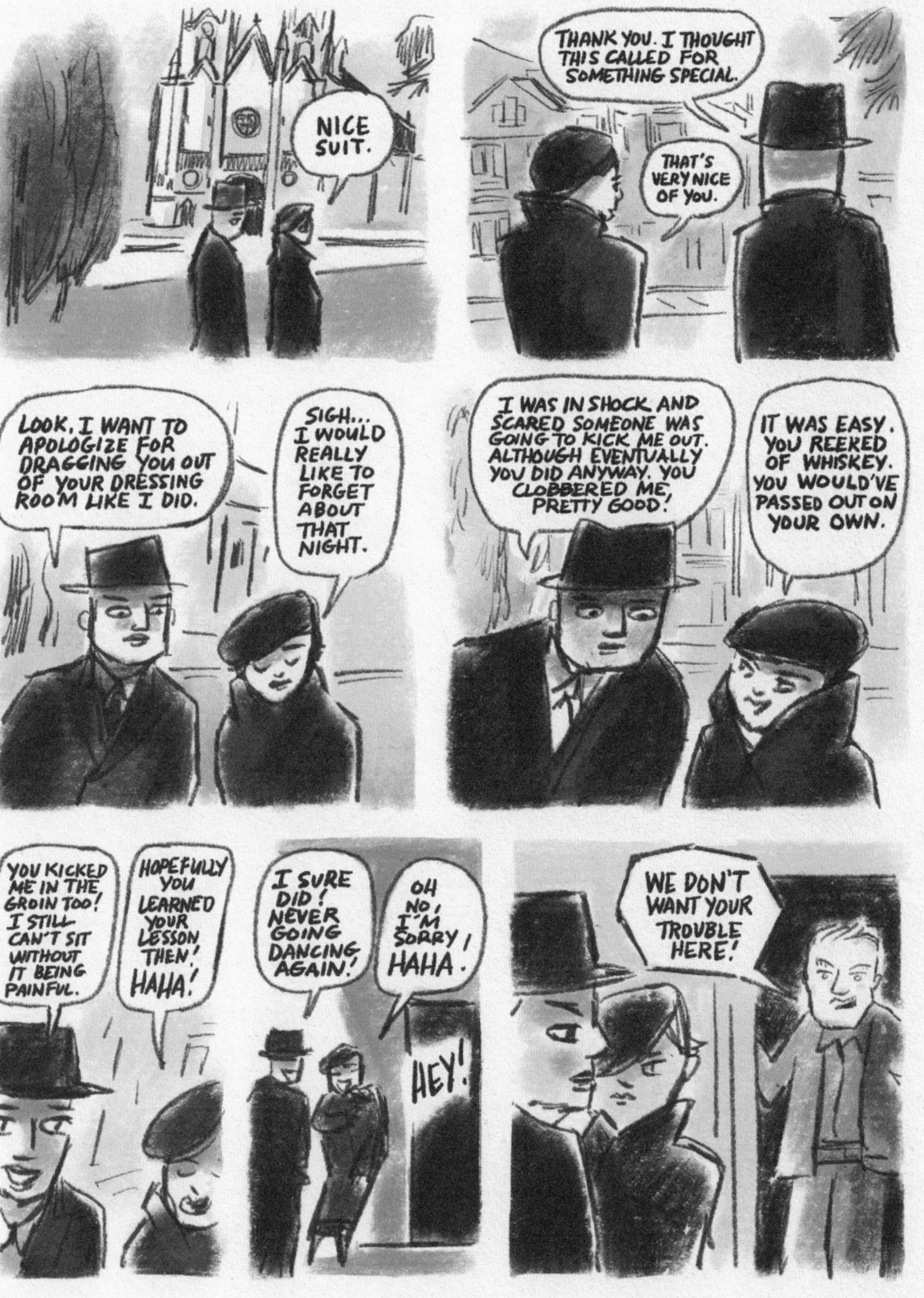
NICE SUIT.
THANK YOU. I THOUGHT THIS CALLED FOR SOMETHING SPECIAL.
THAT'S VERY NICE OF YOU.
LOOK, I WANT TO APOLOGIZE FOR DRAGGING YOU OUT OF YOUR DRESSING ROOM LIKE I DID.
SIGH... I WOULD REALLY LIKE TO FORGET ABOUT THAT NIGHT.
I WAS IN SHOCK AND SCARED SOMEONE WAS GOING TO KICK ME OUT. ALTHOUGH EVENTUALLY YOU DID ANYWAY. YOU CLOBBERED ME, PRETTY GOOD!
IT WAS EASY. YOU REEKED OF WHISKEY. YOU WOULD'VE PASSED OUT ON YOUR OWN.
YOU KICKED ME IN THE GROIN TOO! I STILL CAN'T SIT WITHOUT IT BEING PAINFUL.
HOPEFULLY YOU LEARNED YOUR LESSON THEN! HAHA!
I SURE DID! NEVER GOING DANCING AGAIN!
OH NO, I'M SORRY! HAHA.
HEY!
WE DON'T WANT YOUR TROUBLE HERE!

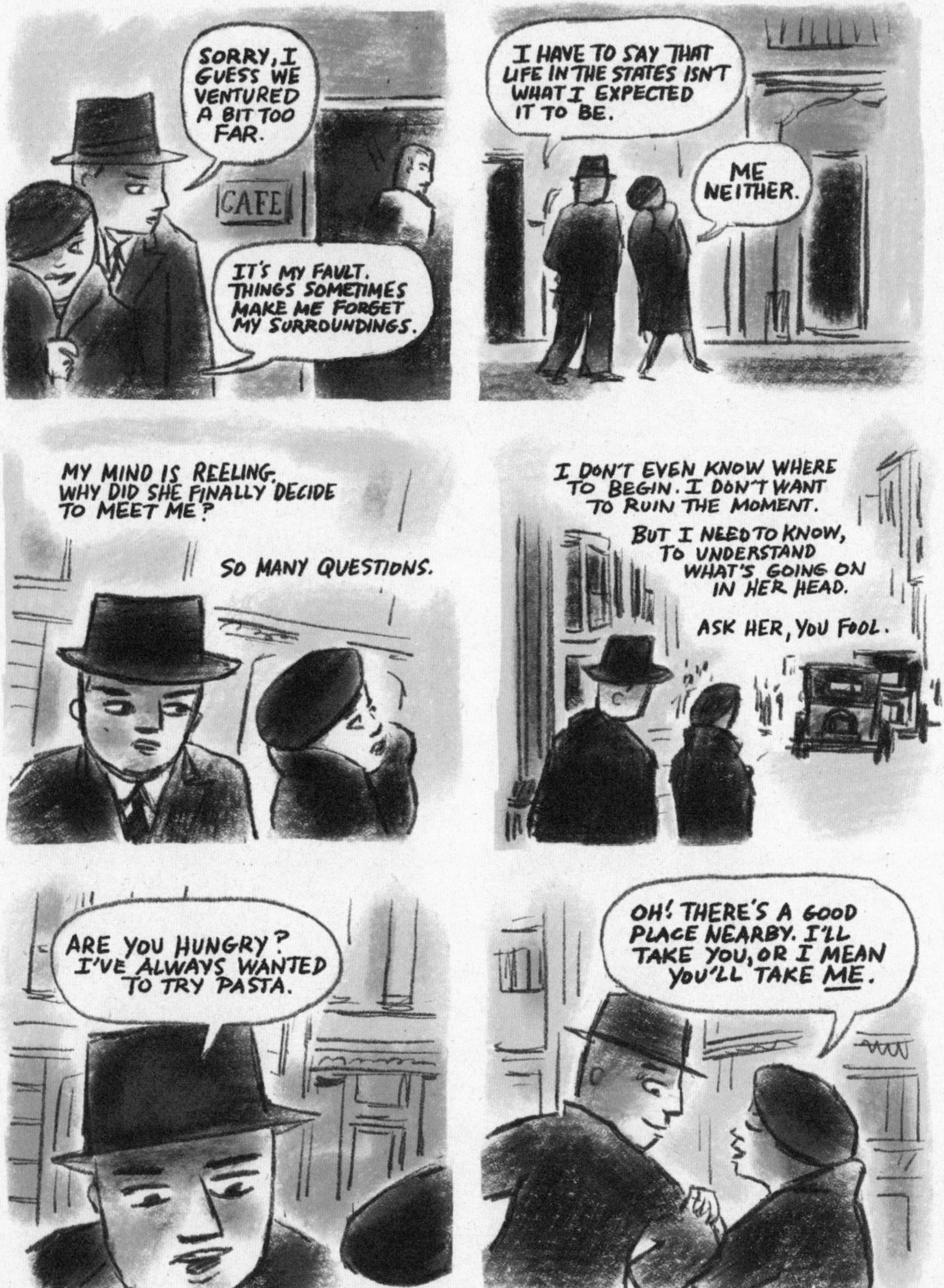

SORRY, I GUESS WE VENTURED A BIT TOO FAR.
CAFE
IT'S MY FAULT. THINGS SOMETIMES MAKE ME FORGET MY SURROUNDINGS.
I HAVE TO SAY THAT LIFE IN THE STATES ISN'T WHAT I EXPECTED IT TO BE.
ME NEITHER.
MY MIND IS REELING. WHY DID SHE FINALLY DECIDE TO MEET ME?
SO MANY QUESTIONS.
I DON'T EVEN KNOW WHERE TO BEGIN. I DON'T WANT TO RUIN THE MOMENT.
BUT I NEED TO KNOW, TO UNDERSTAND WHAT'S GOING ON IN HER HEAD.
ASK HER, YOU FOOL.
ARE YOU HUNGRY? I'VE ALWAYS WANTED TO TRY PASTA.
OH! THERE'S A GOOD PLACE NEARBY. I'LL TAKE YOU, OR I MEAN YOU'LL TAKE ME.

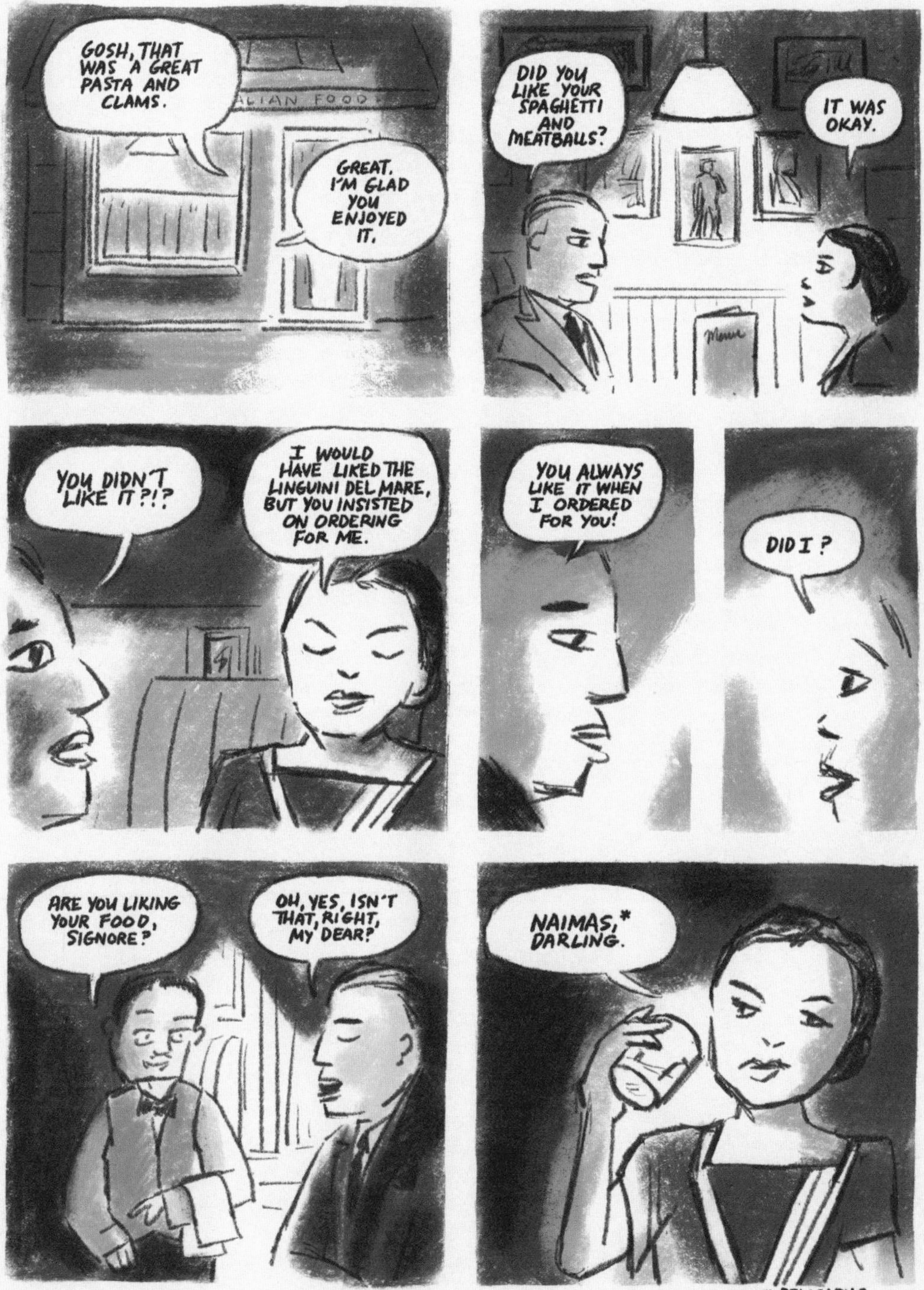
GOSH, THAT WAS A GREAT PASTA AND CLAMS.
GREAT. I'M GLAD YOU ENJOYED IT.
DID YOU LIKE YOUR SPAGHETTI AND MEATBALLS?
IT WAS OKAY.
YOU DIDN'T LIKE IT?!?
I WOULD HAVE LIKED THE LINGUINI DEL MARE, BUT YOU INSISTED ON ORDERING FOR ME.
YOU ALWAYS LIKE IT WHEN I ORDERED FOR YOU!
DID I?
ARE YOU LIKING YOUR FOOD, SIGNORE?
OH, YES, ISN'T THAT, RIGHT, MY DEAR?
NAIMAS,* DARLING.
* DELICIOUS

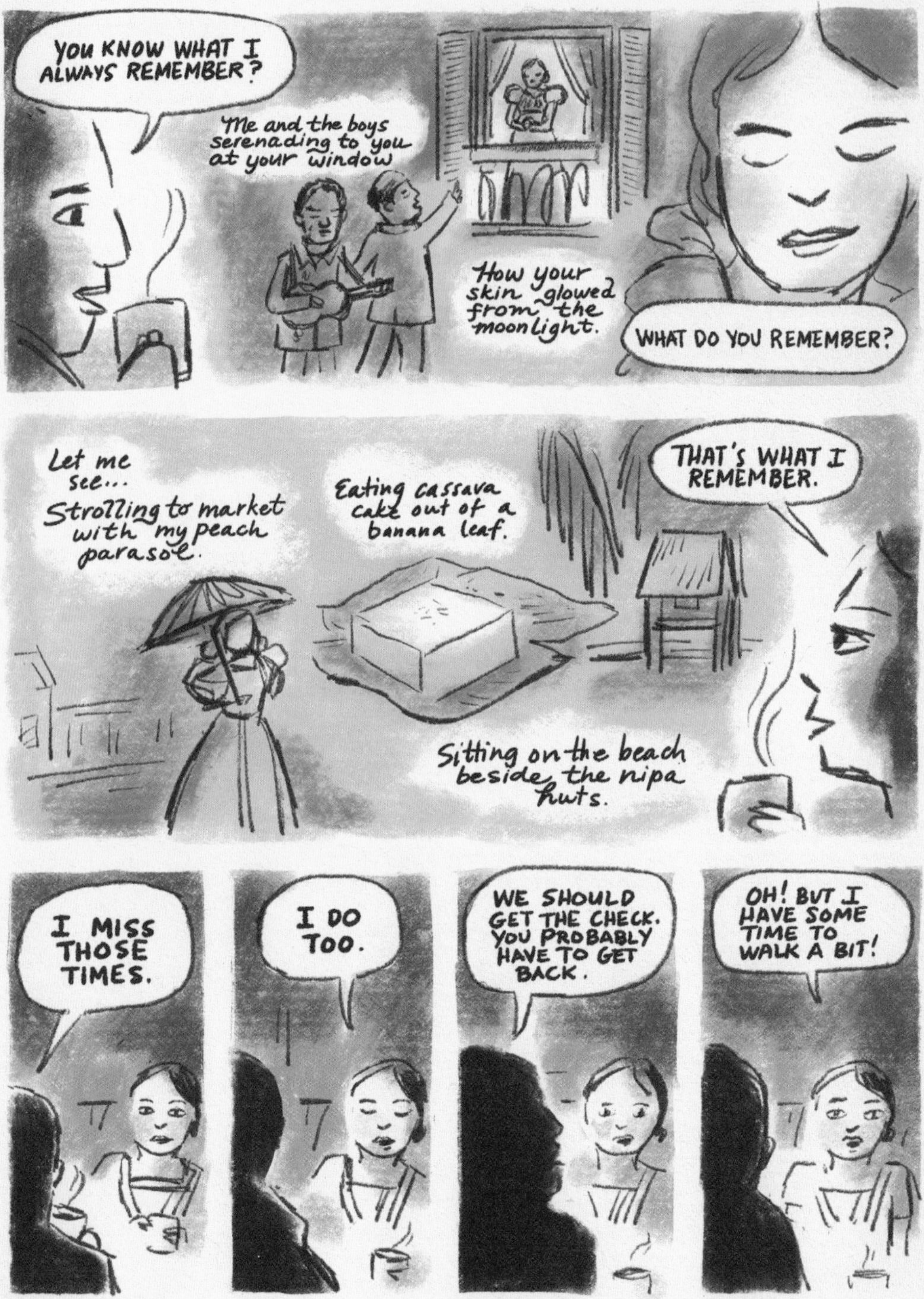
YOU KNOW WHAT I ALWAYS REMEMBER?
Me and the boys serenading to you at your window
How your skin glowed from the moonlight.
WHAT DO YOU REMEMBER?
Let me see... Strolling to market with my peach parasol.
Eating cassava cake out of a banana leaf.
THAT'S WHAT I REMEMBER.
Sitting on the beach beside the nipa huts.
I MISS THOSE TIMES.
I DO TOO.
WE SHOULD GET THE CHECK. YOU PROBABLY HAVE TO GET BACK.
OH! BUT I HAVE SOME TIME TO WALK A BIT!

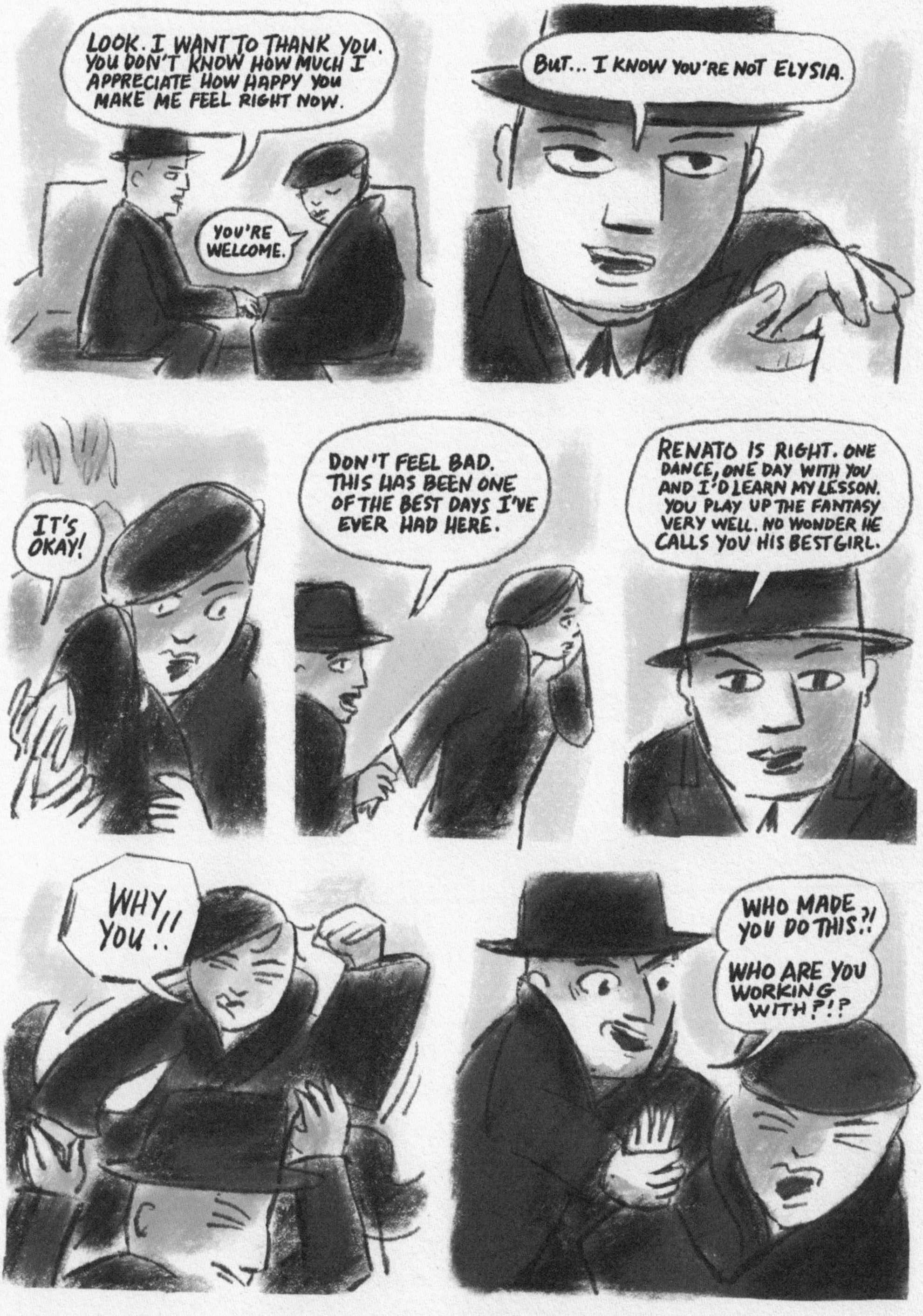
LOOK. I WANT TO THANK YOU. YOU DON'T KNOW HOW MUCH I APPRECIATE HOW HAPPY YOU MAKE ME FEEL RIGHT NOW.
YOU'RE WELCOME.
BUT... I KNOW YOU'RE NOT ELYSIA.
IT'S OKAY!
DON'T FEEL BAD. THIS HAS BEEN ONE OF THE BEST DAYS I'VE EVER HAD HERE.
RENATO IS RIGHT. ONE DANCE, ONE DAY WITH YOU AND I'D LEARN MY LESSON. YOU PLAY UP THE FANTASY VERY WELL. NO WONDER HE CALLS YOU HIS BEST GIRL.
WHY YOU..!!
WHO MADE YOU DO THIS?!
WHO ARE YOU WORKING WITH?!?

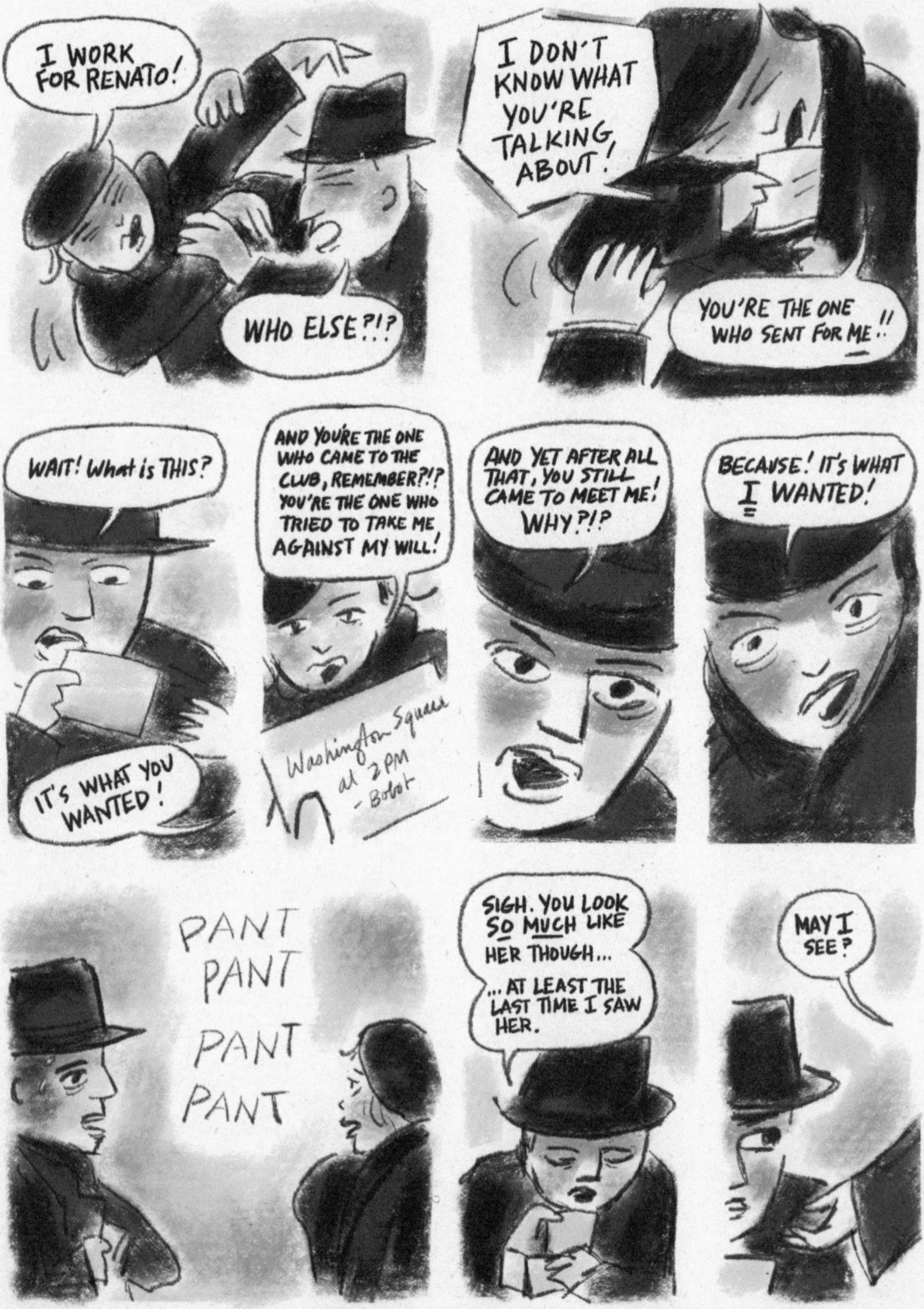
I WORK FOR RENATO!
WHO ELSE?!?
I DON'T KNOW WHAT YOU'RE TALKING ABOUT!
YOU'RE THE ONE WHO SENT FOR ME!!
WAIT! What is THIS?
IT'S WHAT YOU WANTED!
AND YOU'RE THE ONE WHO CAME TO THE CLUB, REMEMBER?!? YOU'RE THE ONE WHO TRIED TO TAKE ME AGAINST MY WILL!
Washington Square at 2PM - Bobot
AND YET AFTER ALL THAT, YOU STILL CAME TO MEET ME! WHY?!?
BECAUSE! IT'S WHAT I WANTED!
PANT PANT PANT PANT
SIGH. YOU LOOK SO MUCH LIKE HER THOUGH...
...AT LEAST THE LAST TIME I SAW HER.
MAY I SEE?

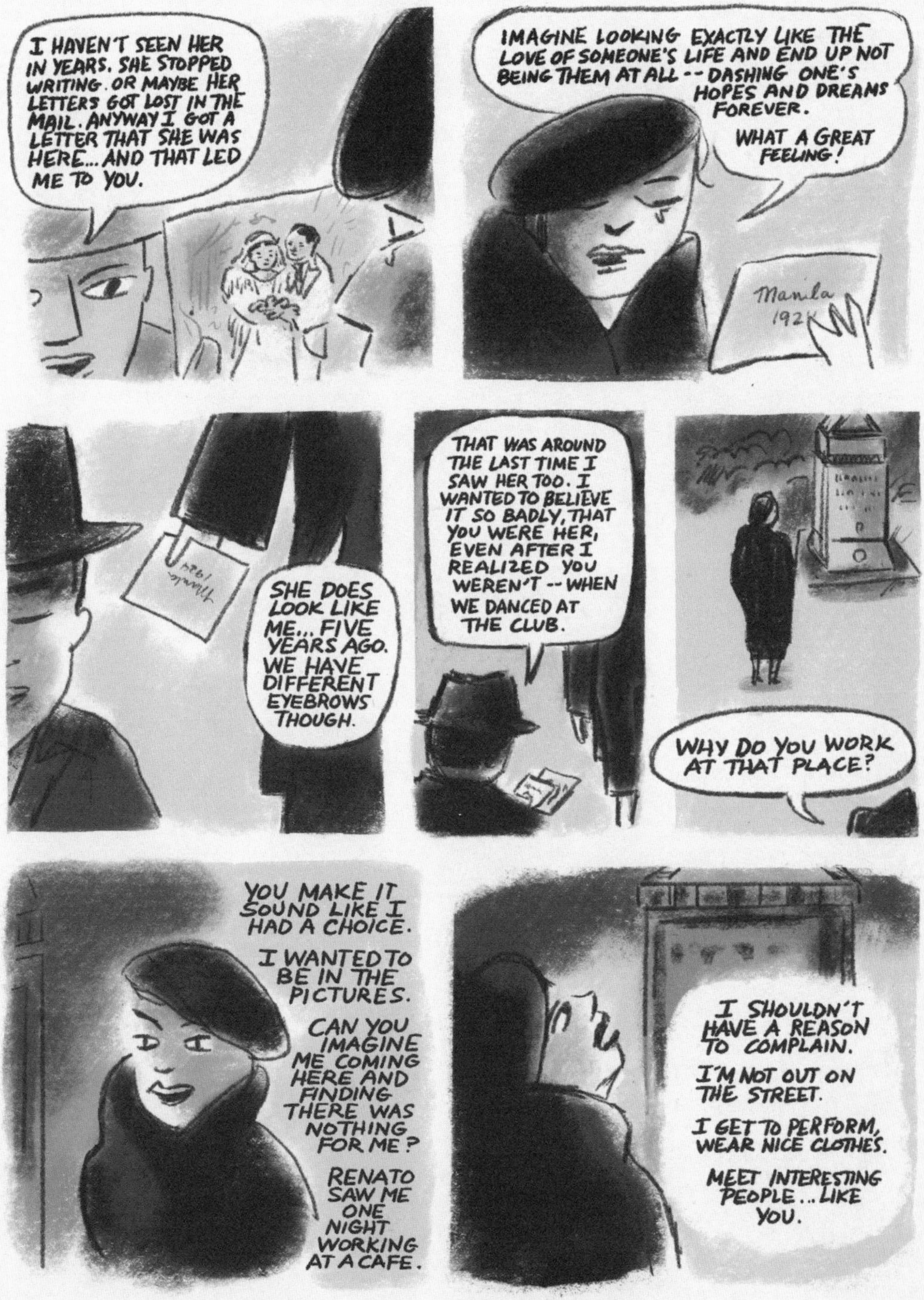
I HAVEN'T SEEN HER IN YEARS. SHE STOPPED WRITING. OR MAYBE HER LETTERS GOT LOST IN THE MAIL. ANYWAY I GOT A LETTER THAT SHE WAS HERE... AND THAT LED ME TO YOU.
IMAGINE LOOKING EXACTLY LIKE THE LOVE OF SOMEONE'S LIFE AND END UP NOT BEING THEM AT ALL -- DASHING ONE'S HOPES AND DREAMS FOREVER.
WHAT A GREAT FEELING!
Manila 1924
SHE DOES LOOK LIKE ME... FIVE YEARS AGO. WE HAVE DIFFERENT EYEBROWS THOUGH.
THAT WAS AROUND THE LAST TIME I SAW HER TOO. I WANTED TO BELIEVE IT SO BADLY, THAT YOU WERE HER, EVEN AFTER I REALIZED YOU WEREN'T -- WHEN WE DANCED AT THE CLUB.
WHY DO YOU WORK AT THAT PLACE?
YOU MAKE IT SOUND LIKE I HAD A CHOICE.
I WANTED TO BE IN THE PICTURES.
CAN YOU IMAGINE ME COMING HERE AND FINDING THERE WAS NOTHING FOR ME?
RENATO SAW ME ONE NIGHT WORKING AT A CAFE.
I SHOULDN'T HAVE A REASON TO COMPLAIN.
I'M NOT OUT ON THE STREET.
I GET TO PERFORM, WEAR NICE CLOTHES.
MEET INTERESTING PEOPLE... LIKE YOU.

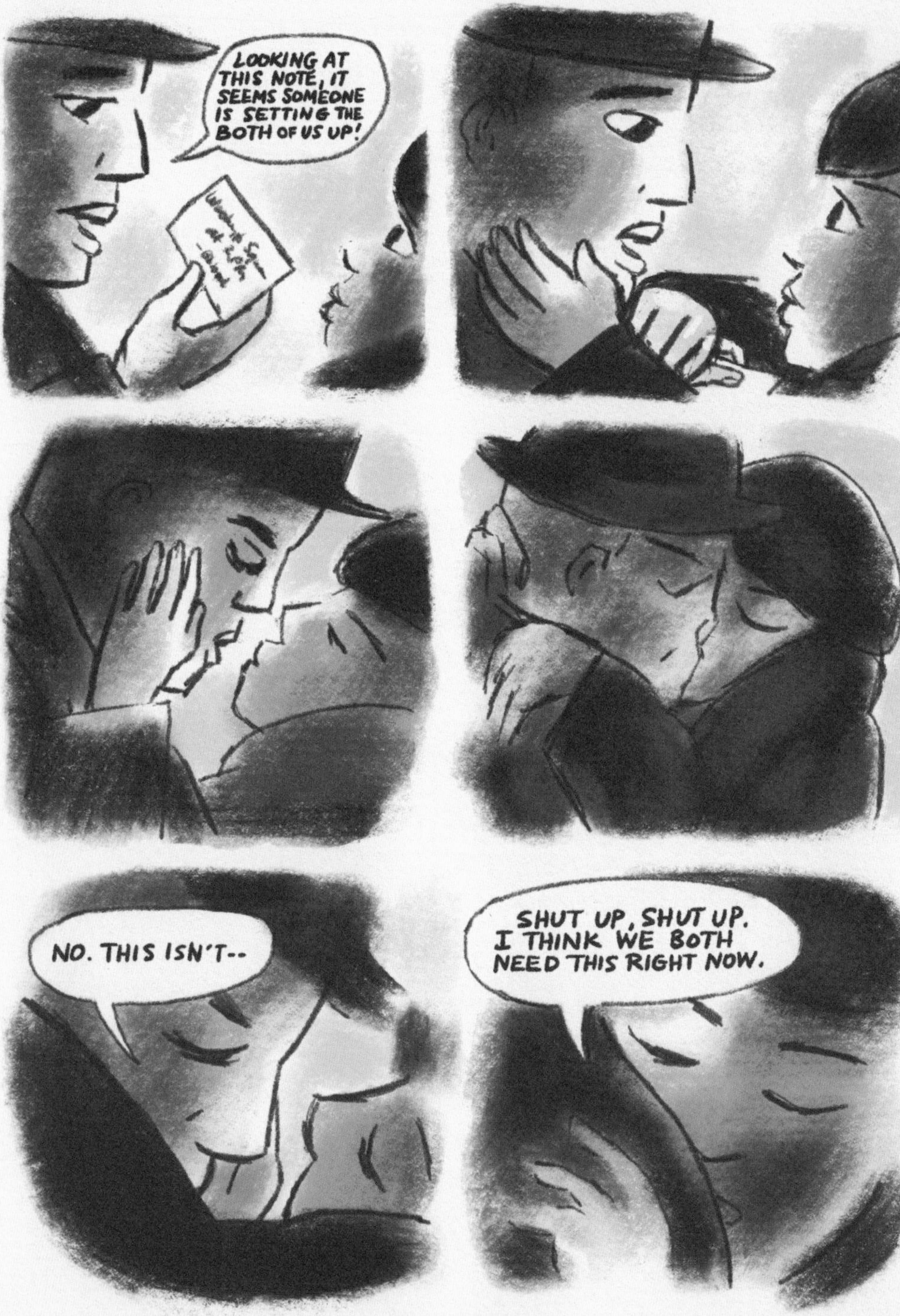
LOOKING AT THIS NOTE, IT SEEMS SOMEONE IS SETTING THE BOTH OF US UP!
NO. THIS ISN'T--
SHUT UP, SHUT UP. I THINK WE BOTH NEED THIS RIGHT NOW.

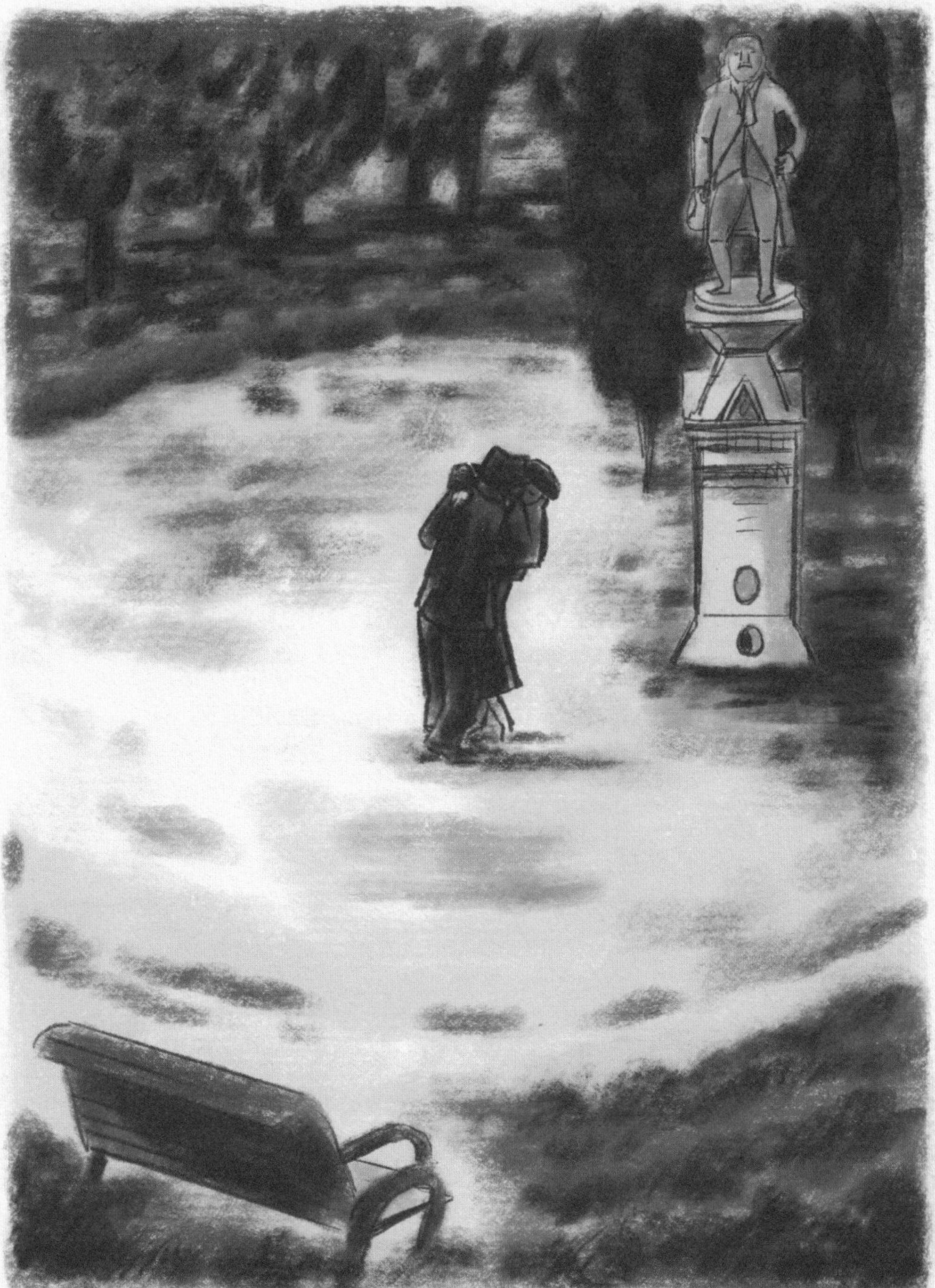

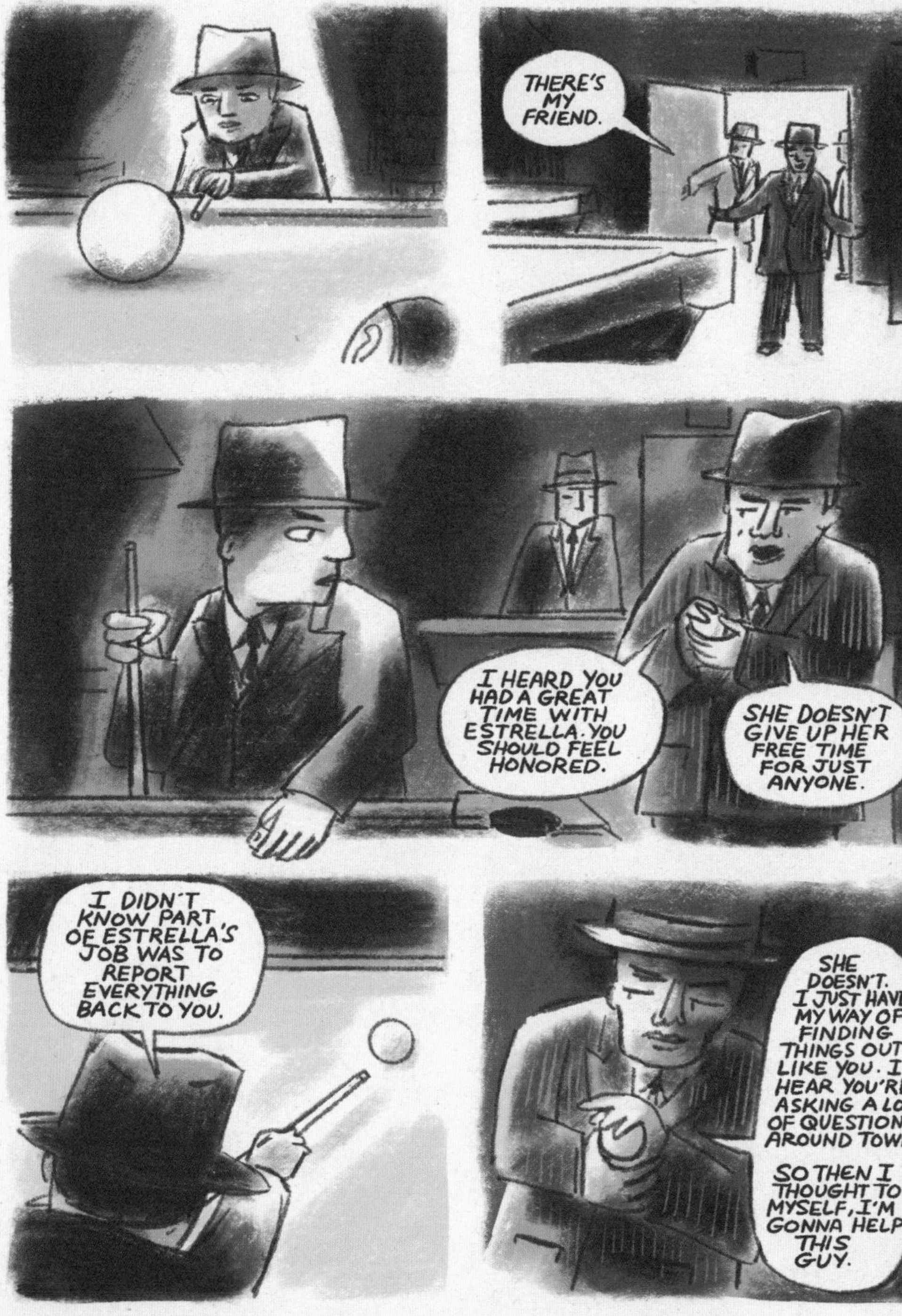
THERE'S MY FRIEND.
I HEARD YOU HAD A GREAT TIME WITH ESTRELLA. YOU SHOULD FEEL HONORED.
SHE DOESN'T GIVE UP HER FREE TIME FOR JUST ANYONE.
I DIDN'T KNOW PART OF ESTRELLA'S JOB WAS TO REPORT EVERYTHING BACK TO YOU.
SHE DOESN'T. I JUST HAVE MY WAY OF FINDING THINGS OUT. LIKE YOU. I HEAR YOU'RE ASKING A LOT OF QUESTIONS AROUND TOWN.
SO THEN I THOUGHT TO MYSELF, I'M GONNA HELP THIS GUY.

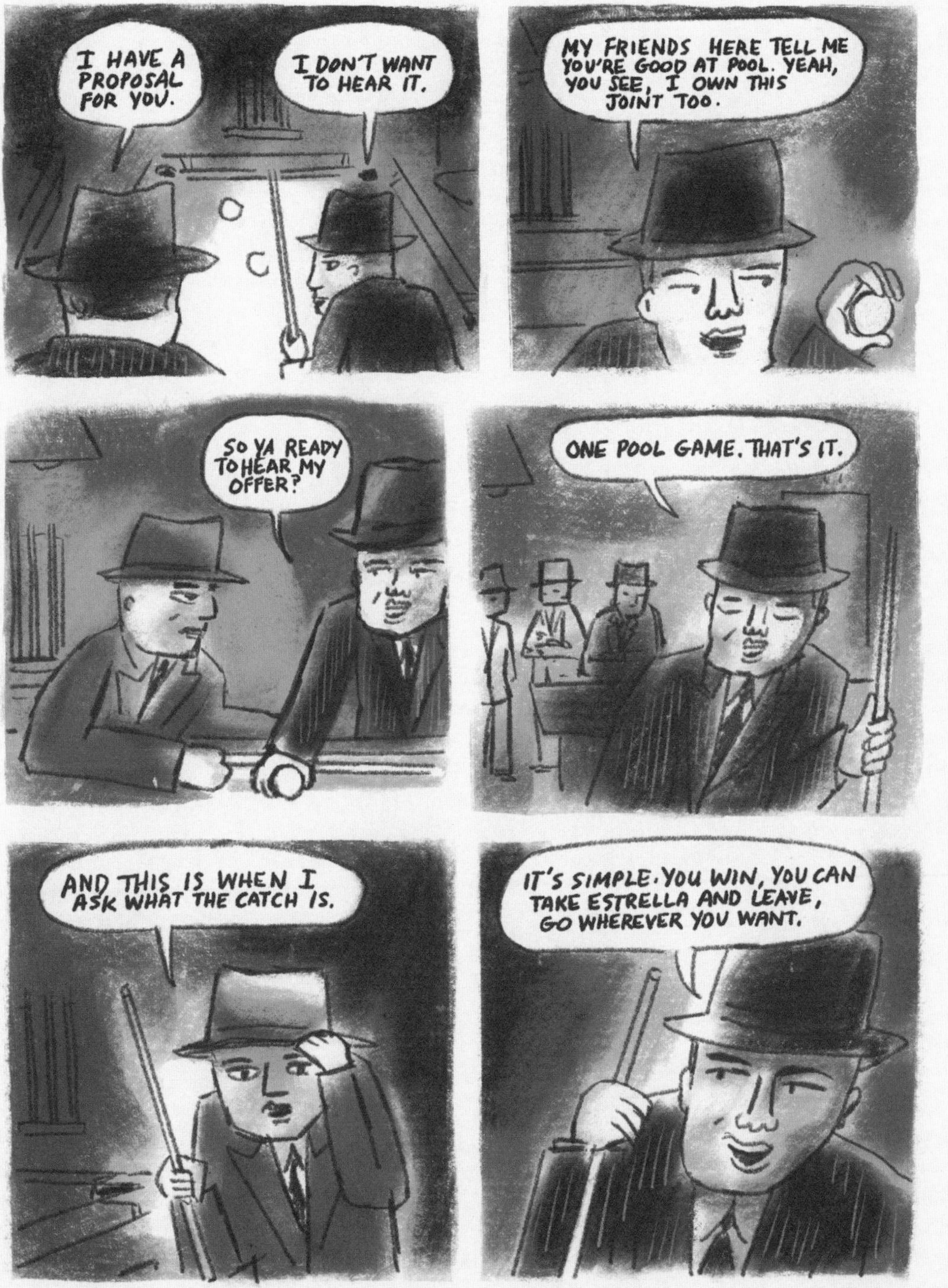
I HAVE A PROPOSAL FOR YOU.
I DON'T WANT TO HEAR IT.
MY FRIENDS HERE TELL ME YOU'RE GOOD AT POOL. YEAH, YOU SEE, I OWN THIS JOINT TOO.
SO YA READY TO HEAR MY OFFER?
ONE POOL GAME. THAT'S IT.
AND THIS IS WHEN I ASK WHAT THE CATCH IS.
IT'S SIMPLE. YOU WIN, YOU CAN TAKE ESTRELLA AND LEAVE, GO WHEREVER YOU WANT.

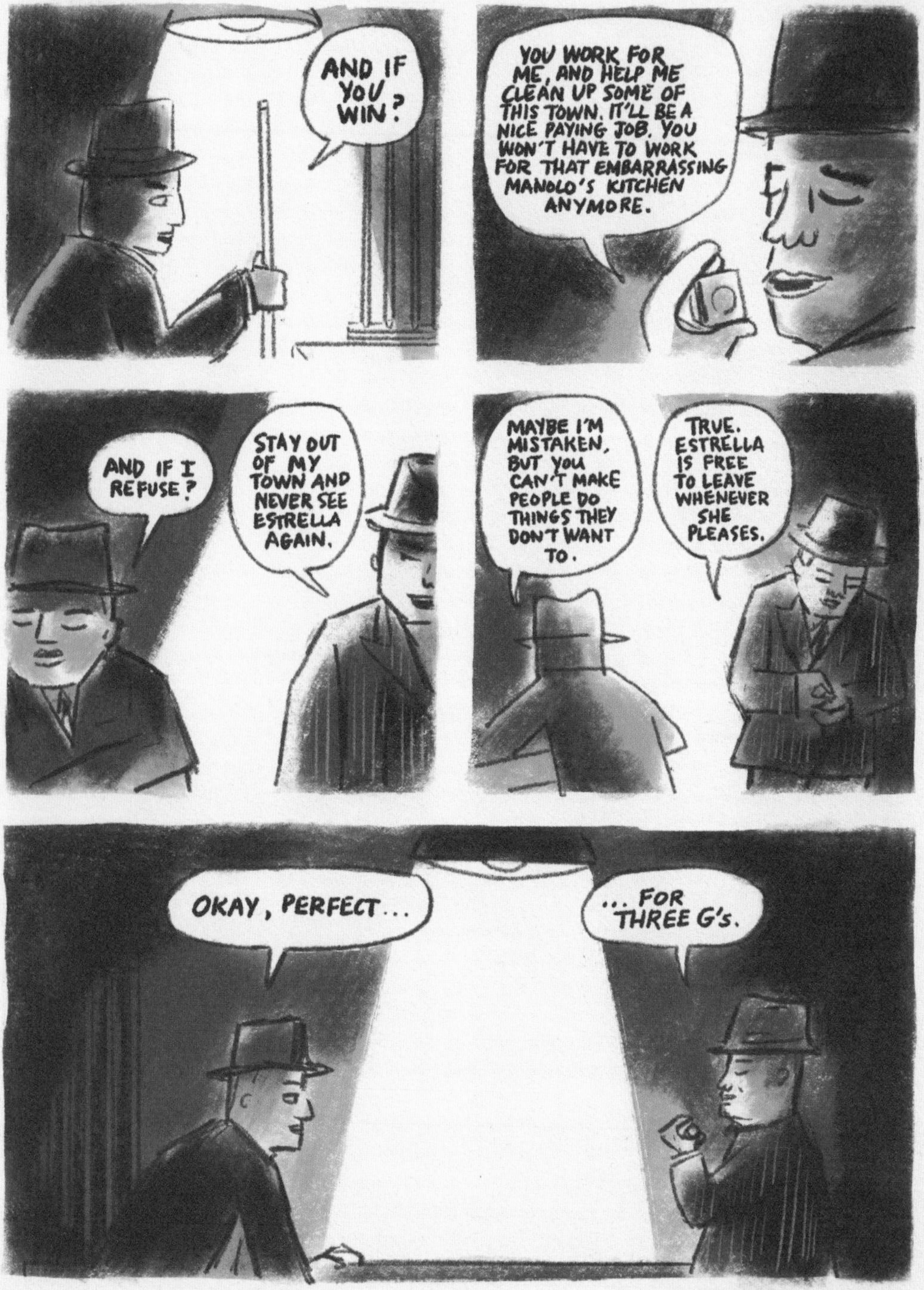
AND IF YOU WIN?
YOU WORK FOR ME, AND HELP ME CLEAN UP SOME OF THIS TOWN. IT'LL BE A NICE PAYING JOB. YOU WON'T HAVE TO WORK FOR THAT EMBARRASSING MANOLO'S KITCHEN ANYMORE.
AND IF I REFUSE?
STAY OUT OF MY TOWN AND NEVER SEE ESTRELLA AGAIN.
MAYBE I'M MISTAKEN, BUT YOU CAN'T MAKE PEOPLE DO THINGS THEY DON'T WANT TO.
TRUE. ESTRELLA IS FREE TO LEAVE WHENEVER SHE PLEASES.
OKAY, PERFECT...
...FOR THREE G's.

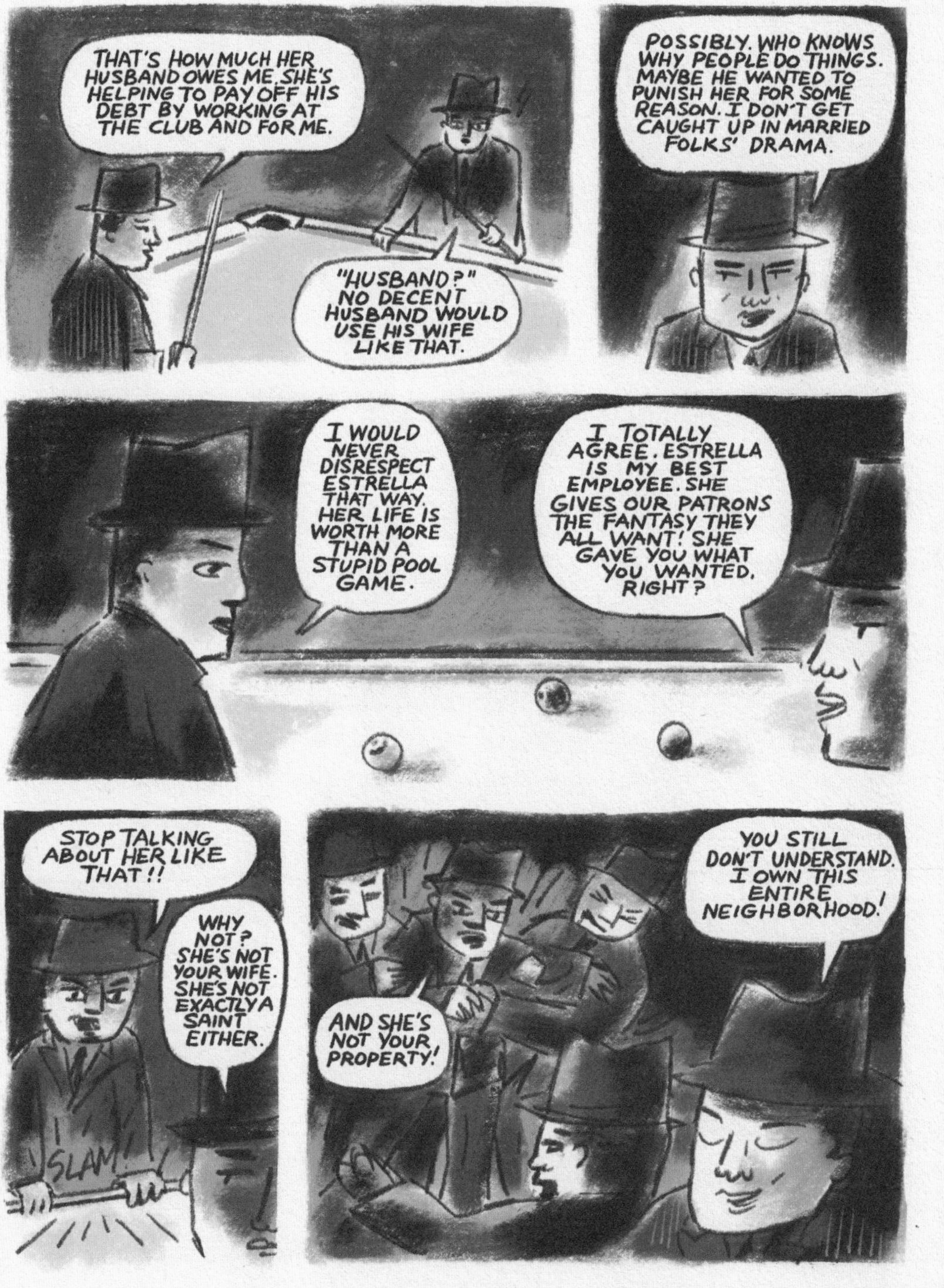
THAT'S HOW MUCH HER HUSBAND OWES ME. SHE'S HELPING TO PAY OFF HIS DEBT BY WORKING AT THE CLUB AND FOR ME.
"HUSBAND?" NO DECENT HUSBAND WOULD USE HIS WIFE LIKE THAT.
POSSIBLY. WHO KNOWS WHY PEOPLE DO THINGS. MAYBE HE WANTED TO PUNISH HER FOR SOME REASON. I DON'T GET CAUGHT UP IN MARRIED FOLKS' DRAMA.
I WOULD NEVER DISRESPECT ESTRELLA THAT WAY. HER LIFE IS WORTH MORE THAN A STUPID POOL GAME.
I TOTALLY AGREE. ESTRELLA IS MY BEST EMPLOYEE. SHE GIVES OUR PATRONS THE FANTASY THEY ALL WANT! SHE GAVE YOU WHAT YOU WANTED, RIGHT?
STOP TALKING ABOUT HER LIKE THAT!!
WHY NOT? SHE'S NOT YOUR WIFE. SHE'S NOT EXACTLY A SAINT EITHER.
SLAM
AND SHE'S NOT YOUR PROPERTY!
YOU STILL DON'T UNDERSTAND. I OWN THIS ENTIRE NEIGHBORHOOD!

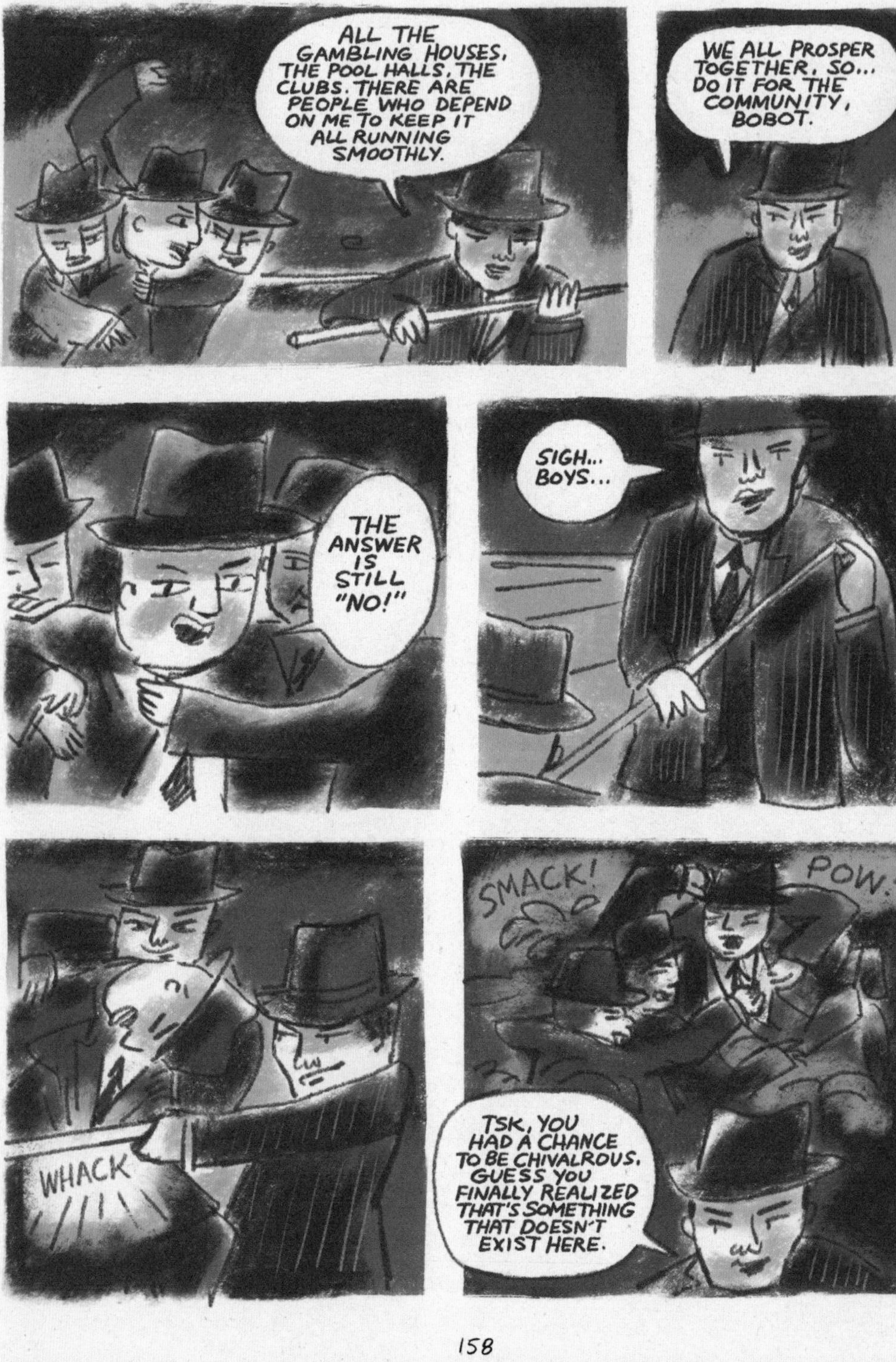
ALL THE GAMBLING HOUSES, THE POOL HALLS, THE CLUBS. THERE ARE PEOPLE WHO DEPEND ON ME TO KEEP IT ALL RUNNING SMOOTHLY.
WE ALL PROSPER TOGETHER, SO... DO IT FOR THE COMMUNITY, BOBOT.
THE ANSWER IS STILL "NO!"
SIGH... BOYS...
WHACK
SMACK!
POW!
TSK, YOU HAD A CHANCE TO BE CHIVALROUS. GUESS YOU FINALLY REALIZED THAT'S SOMETHING THAT DOESN'T EXIST HERE.

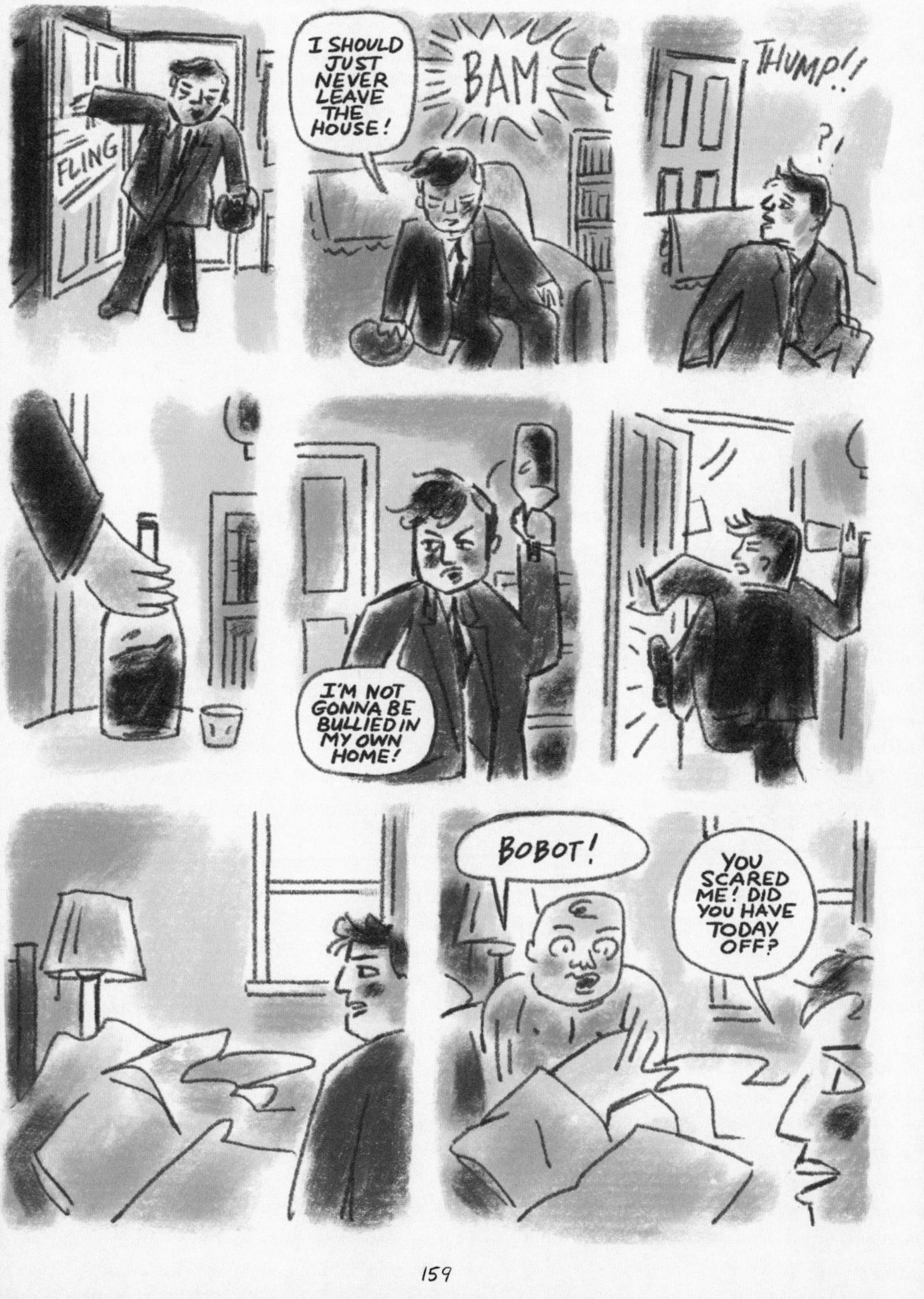
FLING
I SHOULD JUST NEVER LEAVE THE HOUSE!
BAM
THUMP!!
?!
I'M NOT GONNA BE BULLIED IN MY OWN HOME!
BOBOT!
YOU SCARED ME! DID YOU HAVE TODAY OFF?

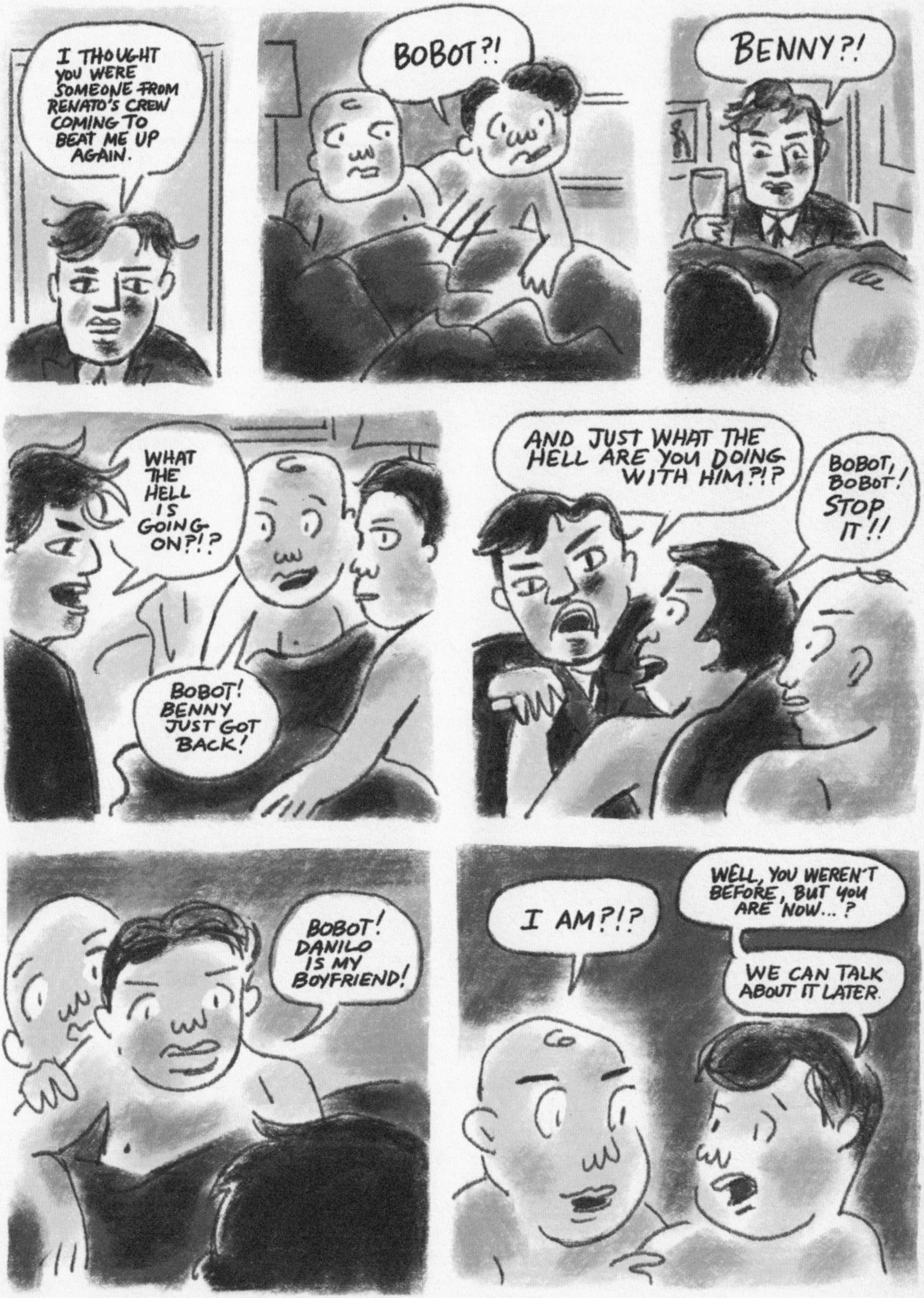
I THOUGHT YOU WERE SOMEONE FROM RENATO'S CREW COMING TO BEAT ME UP AGAIN.
BOBOT?!
BENNY?!
WHAT THE HELL IS GOING ON?!?
BOBOT! BENNY JUST GOT BACK!
AND JUST WHAT THE HELL ARE YOU DOING WITH HIM?!?
BOBOT, BOBOT! STOP IT!!
BOBOT! DANILO IS MY BOYFRIEND!
I AM?!?
WELL, YOU WEREN'T BEFORE, BUT YOU ARE NOW...?
WE CAN TALK ABOUT IT LATER.

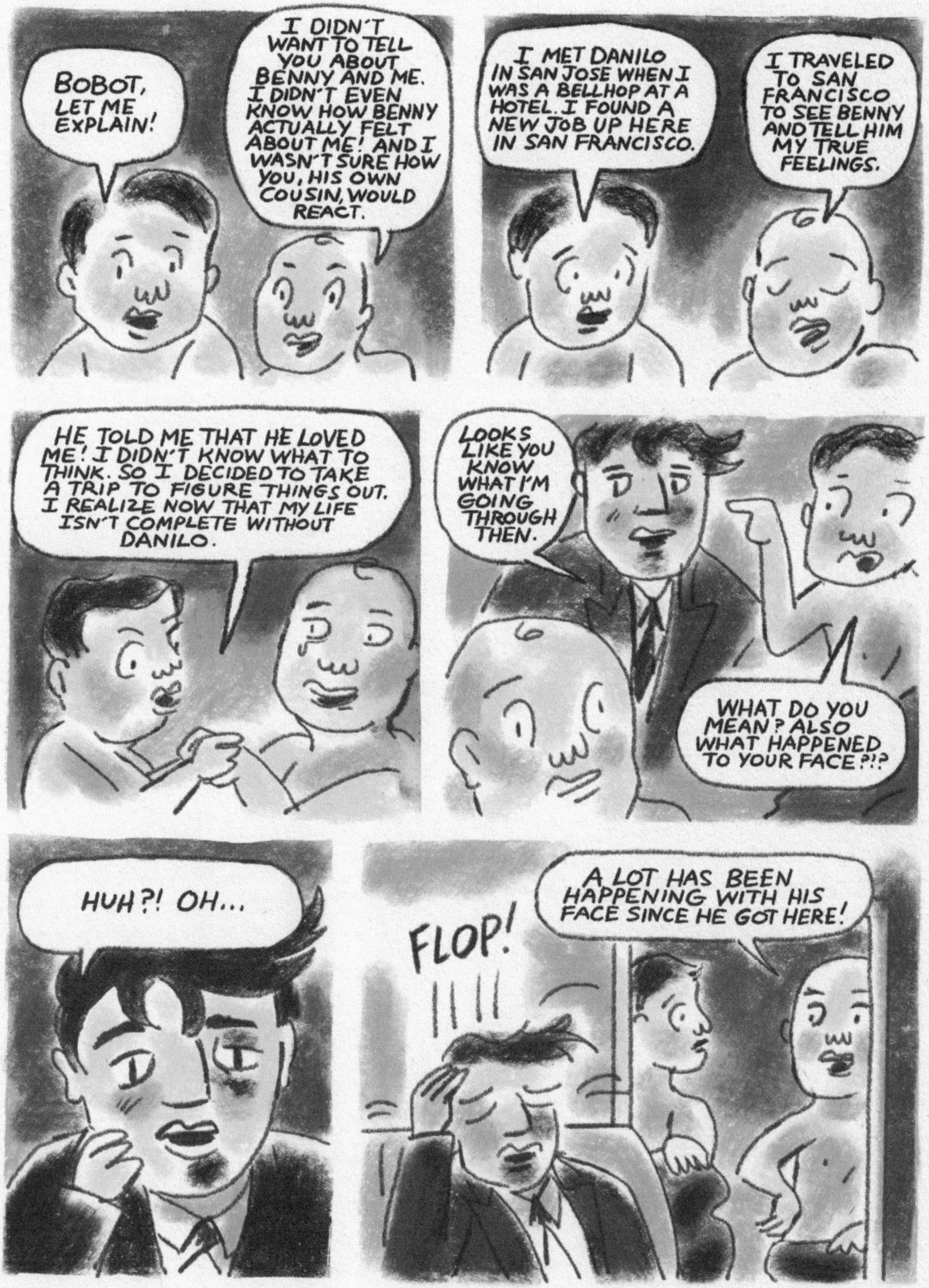
BOBOT, LET ME EXPLAIN!
I DIDN'T WANT TO TELL YOU ABOUT BENNY AND ME. I DIDN'T EVEN KNOW HOW BENNY ACTUALLY FELT ABOUT ME! AND I WASN'T SURE HOW YOU, HIS OWN COUSIN, WOULD REACT.
I MET DANILO IN SAN JOSE WHEN I WAS A BELLHOP AT A HOTEL. I FOUND A NEW JOB UP HERE IN SAN FRANCISCO.
I TRAVELED TO SAN FRANCISCO TO SEE BENNY AND TELL HIM MY TRUE FEELINGS.
HE TOLD ME THAT HE LOVED ME! I DIDN'T KNOW WHAT TO THINK. SO I DECIDED TO TAKE A TRIP TO FIGURE THINGS OUT. I REALIZE NOW THAT MY LIFE ISN'T COMPLETE WITHOUT DANILO.
LOOKS LIKE YOU KNOW WHAT I'M GOING THROUGH THEN.
WHAT DO YOU MEAN? ALSO WHAT HAPPENED TO YOUR FACE?!?
HUH?! OH...
FLOP!
A LOT HAS BEEN HAPPENING WITH HIS FACE SINCE HE GOT HERE!

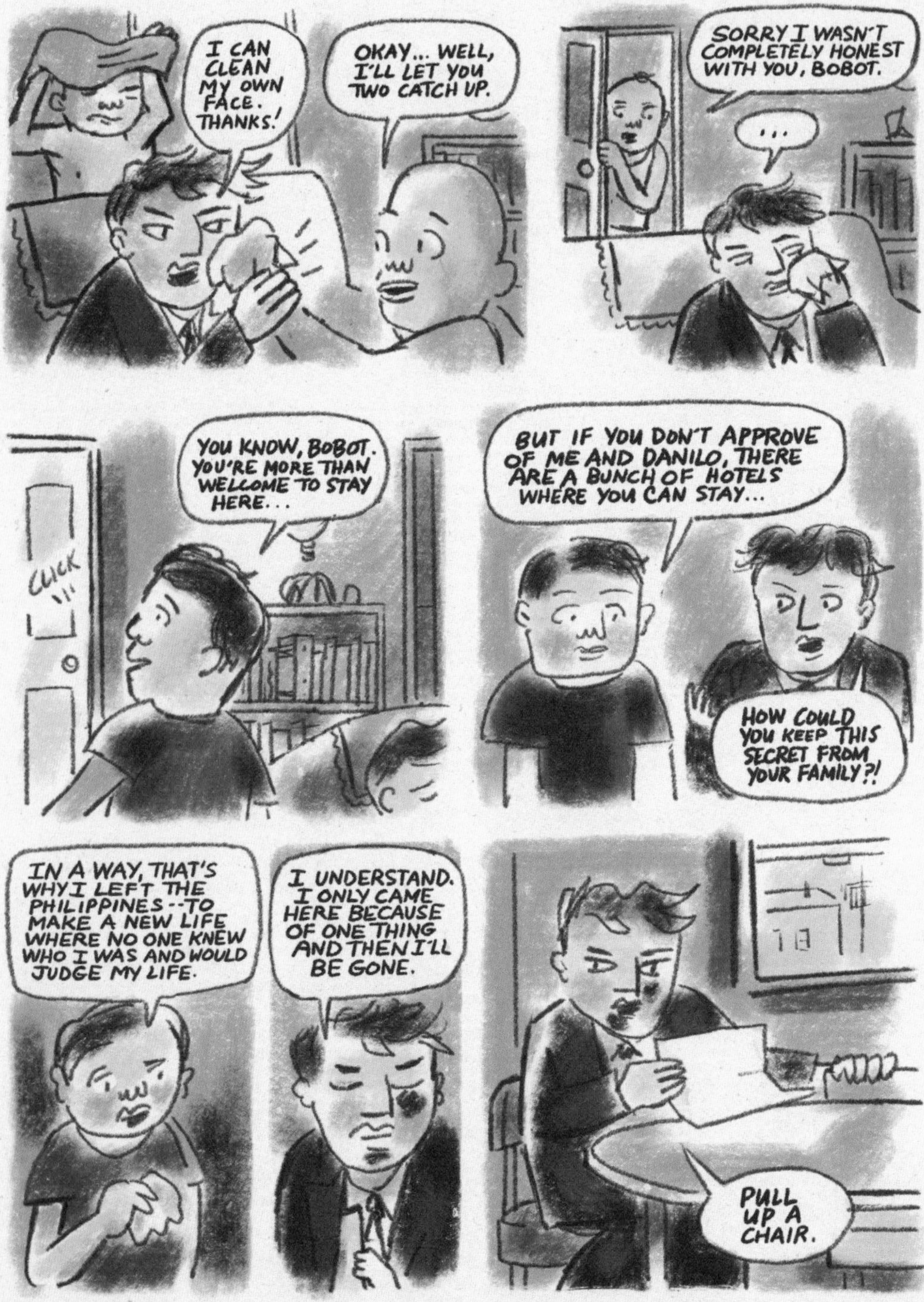

I CAN CLEAN MY OWN FACE. THANKS!
OKAY... WELL, I'LL LET YOU TWO CATCH UP.
SORRY I WASN'T COMPLETELY HONEST WITH YOU, BOBOT.
...
YOU KNOW, BOBOT. YOU'RE MORE THAN WELCOME TO STAY HERE...
CLICK
BUT IF YOU DON'T APPROVE OF ME AND DANILO, THERE ARE A BUNCH OF HOTELS WHERE YOU CAN STAY...
HOW COULD YOU KEEP THIS SECRET FROM YOUR FAMILY?!
IN A WAY, THAT'S WHY I LEFT THE PHILIPPINES--TO MAKE A NEW LIFE WHERE NO ONE KNEW WHO I WAS AND WOULD JUDGE MY LIFE.
I UNDERSTAND. I ONLY CAME HERE BECAUSE OF ONE THING AND THEN I'LL BE GONE.
PULL UP A CHAIR.

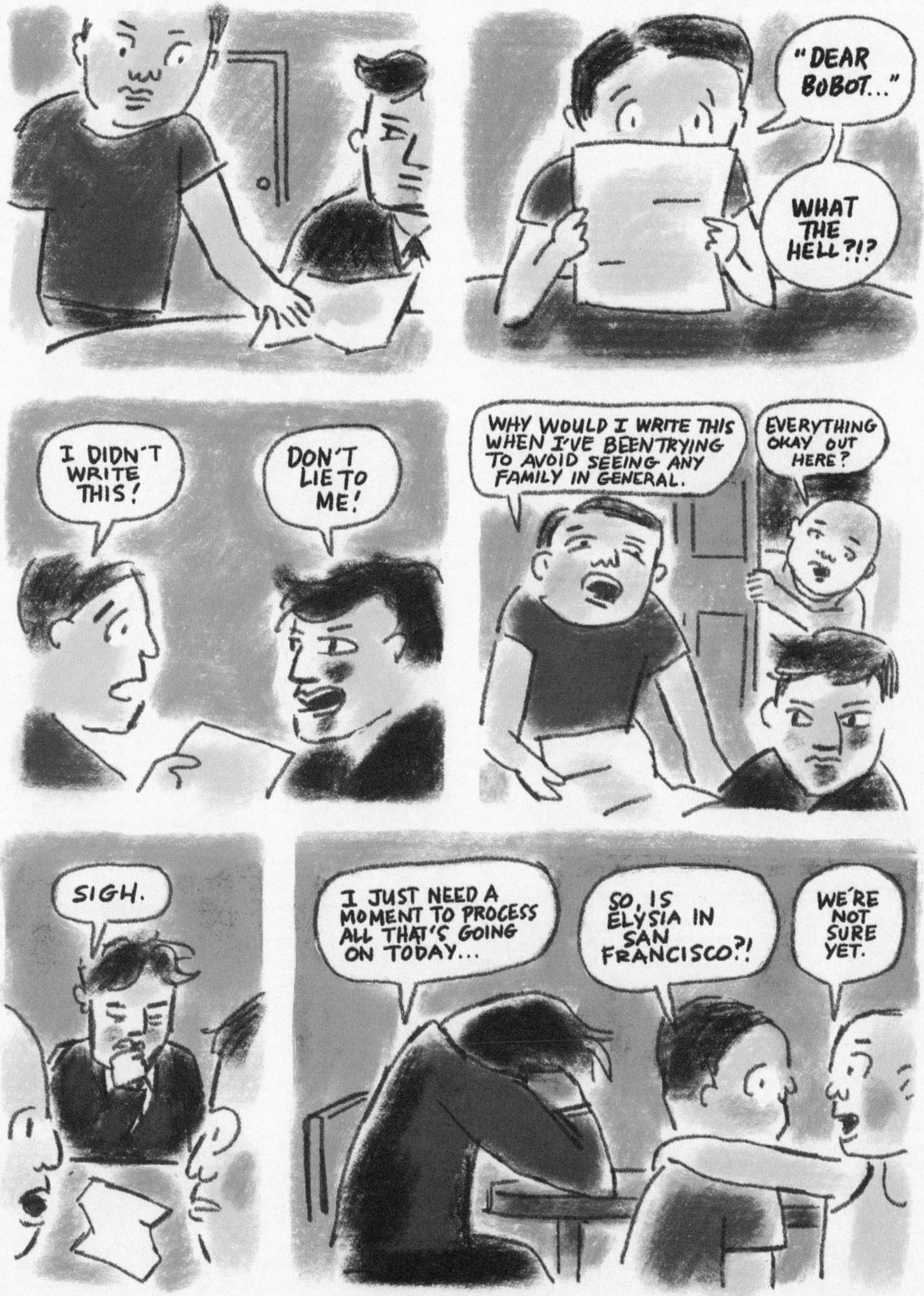
"DEAR BOBOT..."
WHAT THE HELL?!?
I DIDN'T WRITE THIS!
DON'T LIE TO ME!
WHY WOULD I WRITE THIS WHEN I'VE BEEN TRYING TO AVOID SEEING ANY FAMILY IN GENERAL.
EVERYTHING OKAY OUT HERE?
SIGH.
I JUST NEED A MOMENT TO PROCESS ALL THAT'S GOING ON TODAY...
SO, IS ELYSIA IN SAN FRANCISCO?!
WE'RE NOT SURE YET.

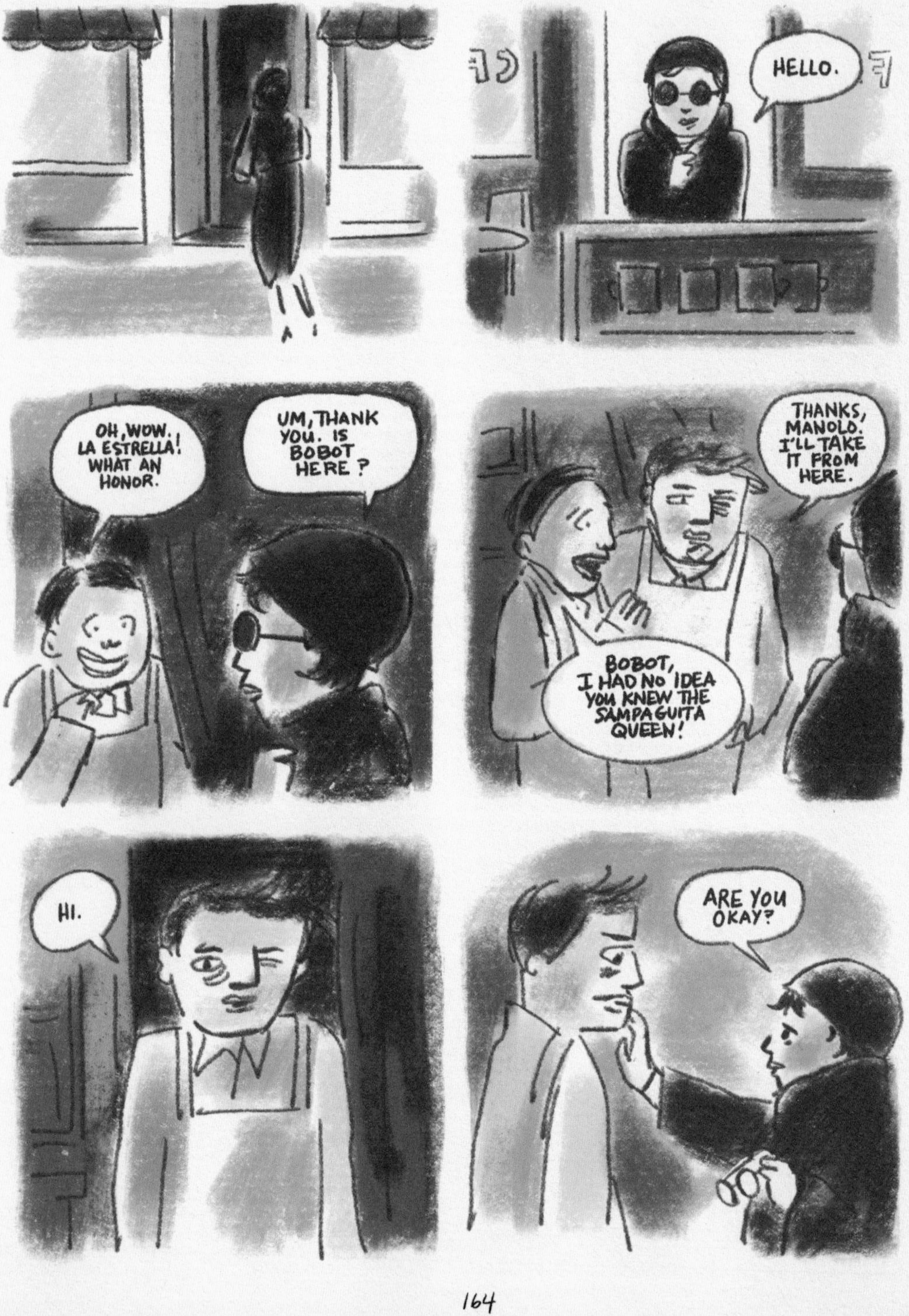
HELLO.
OH, WOW. LA ESTRELLA! WHAT AN HONOR.
UM, THANK YOU. IS BOBOT HERE?
BOBOT, I HAD NO IDEA YOU KNEW THE SAMPAGUITA QUEEN!
THANKS, MANOLO. I'LL TAKE IT FROM HERE.
HI.
ARE YOU OKAY?

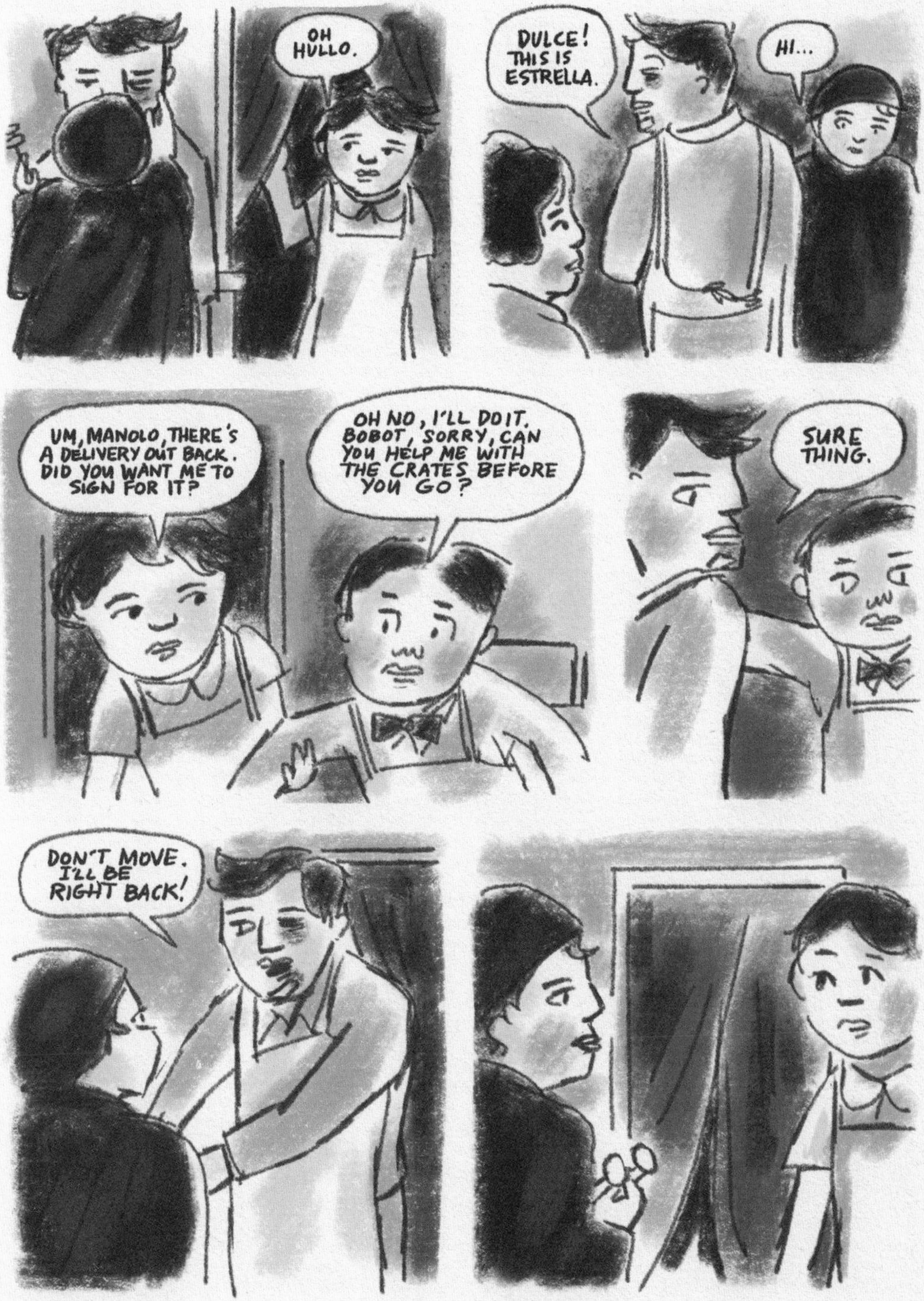
OH HULLO.
DULCE! THIS IS ESTRELLA.
HI...
UM, MANOLO, THERE'S A DELIVERY OUT BACK. DID YOU WANT ME TO SIGN FOR IT?
OH NO, I'LL DO IT. BOBOT, SORRY, CAN YOU HELP ME WITH THE CRATES BEFORE YOU GO?
SURE THING.
DON'T MOVE. I'LL BE RIGHT BACK!

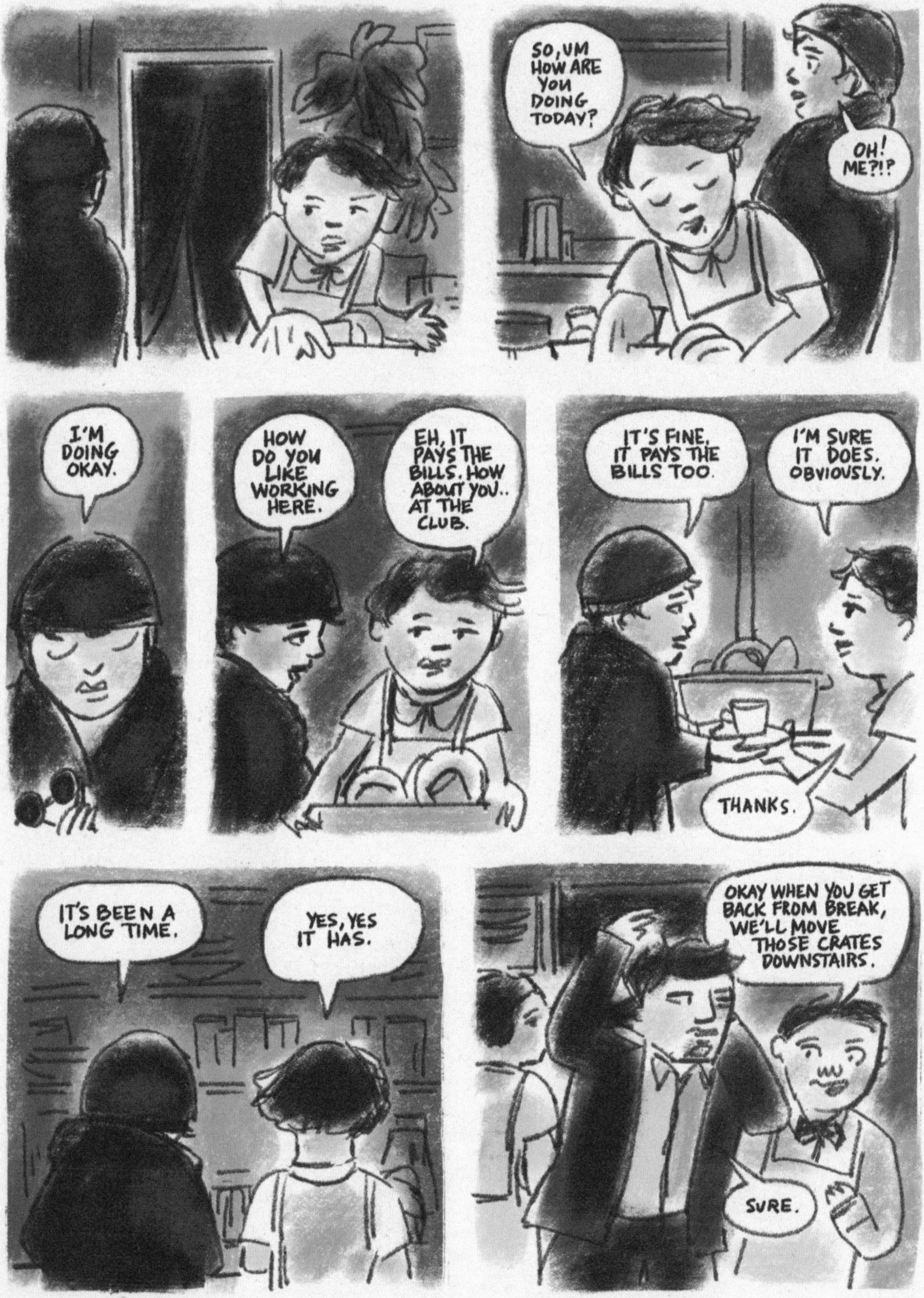
SO, UM HOW ARE YOU DOING TODAY?
OH! ME?!?
I'M DOING OKAY.
HOW DO YOU LIKE WORKING HERE.
EH, IT PAYS THE BILLS. HOW ABOUT YOU.. AT THE CLUB.
IT'S FINE, IT PAYS THE BILLS TOO.
I'M SURE IT DOES. OBVIOUSLY.
THANKS.
IT'S BEEN A LONG TIME.
YES, YES IT HAS.
OKAY WHEN YOU GET BACK FROM BREAK, WE'LL MOVE THOSE CRATES DOWNSTAIRS.
SURE.

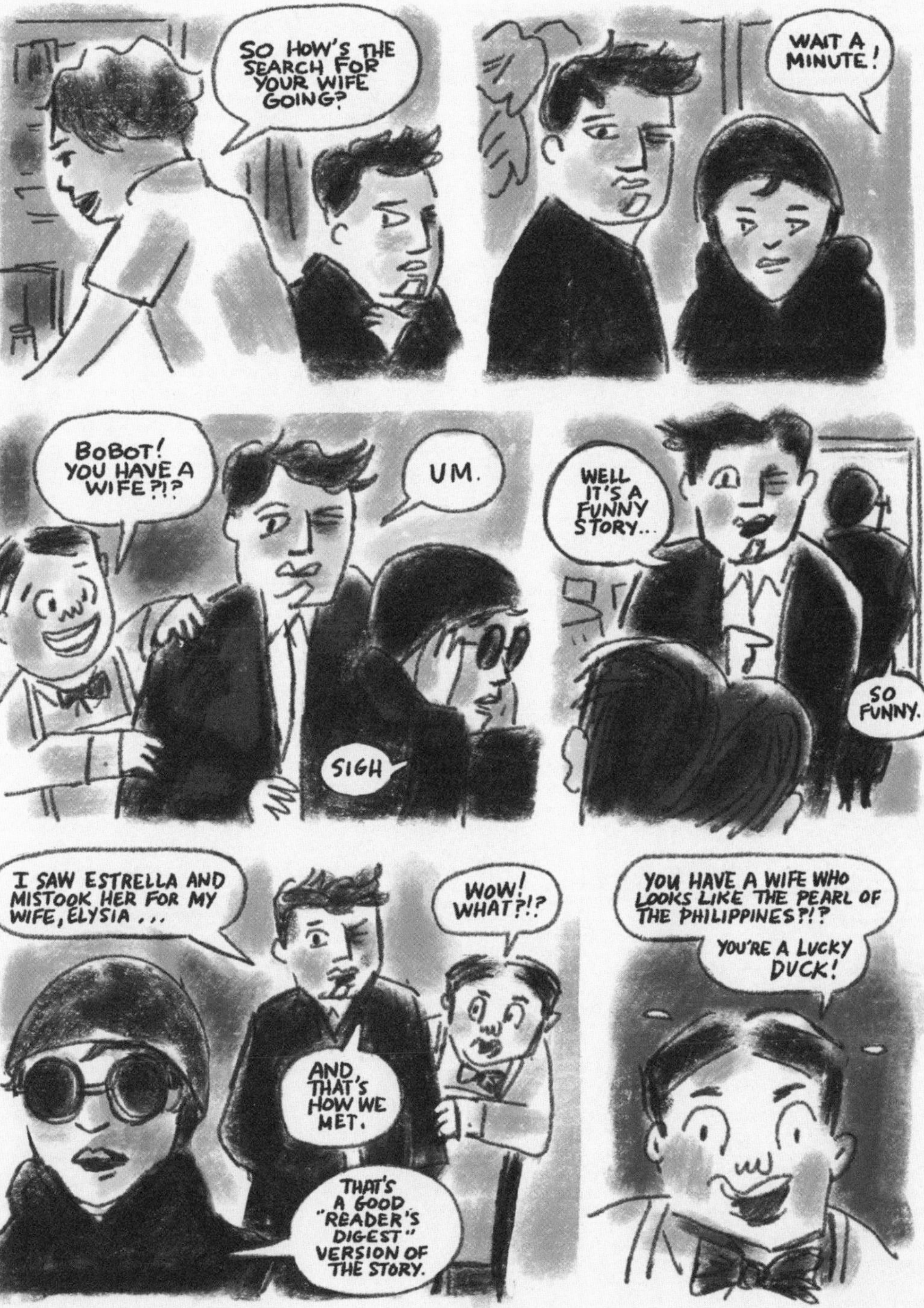
SO HOW'S THE SEARCH FOR YOUR WIFE GOING?
WAIT A MINUTE!
BOBOT! YOU HAVE A WIFE?!?
UM.
SIGH
WELL IT'S A FUNNY STORY...
SO FUNNY..
I SAW ESTRELLA AND MISTOOK HER FOR MY WIFE, ELYSIA ...
WOW! WHAT?!?
AND, THAT'S HOW WE MET.
THAT'S A GOOD "READER'S DIGEST" VERSION OF THE STORY.
YOU HAVE A WIFE WHO LOOKS LIKE THE PEARL OF THE PHILIPPINES?!?
YOU'RE A LUCKY DUCK!

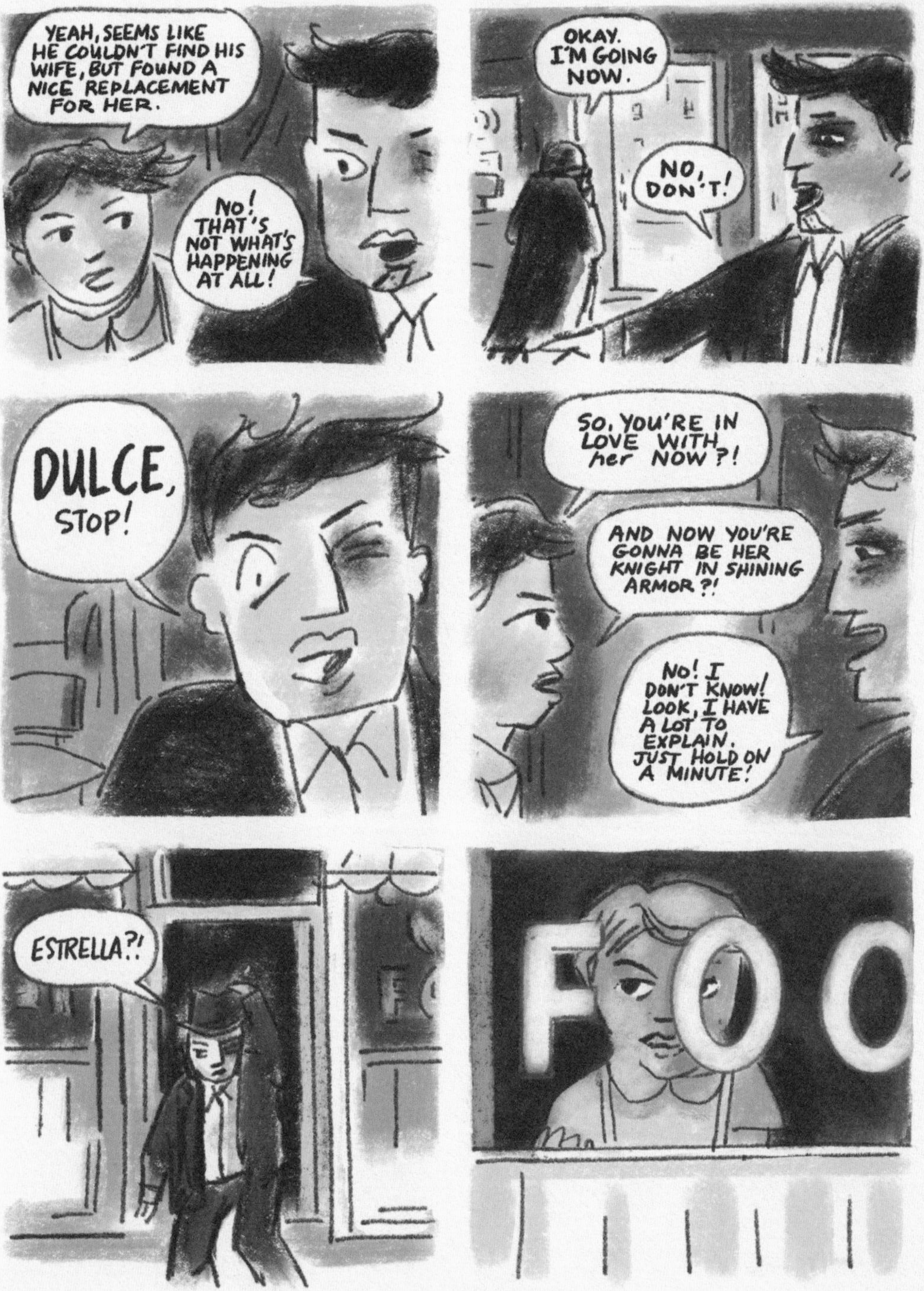
YEAH, SEEMS LIKE HE COULDN'T FIND HIS WIFE, BUT FOUND A NICE REPLACEMENT FOR HER.
NO! THAT'S NOT WHAT'S HAPPENING AT ALL!
OKAY. I'M GOING NOW.
NO, DON'T!
DULCE, STOP!
SO, YOU'RE IN LOVE WITH her NOW?!
AND NOW YOU'RE GONNA BE HER KNIGHT IN SHINING ARMOR?!
NO! I DON'T KNOW! LOOK, I HAVE A LOT TO EXPLAIN. JUST HOLD ON A MINUTE!
ESTRELLA?!

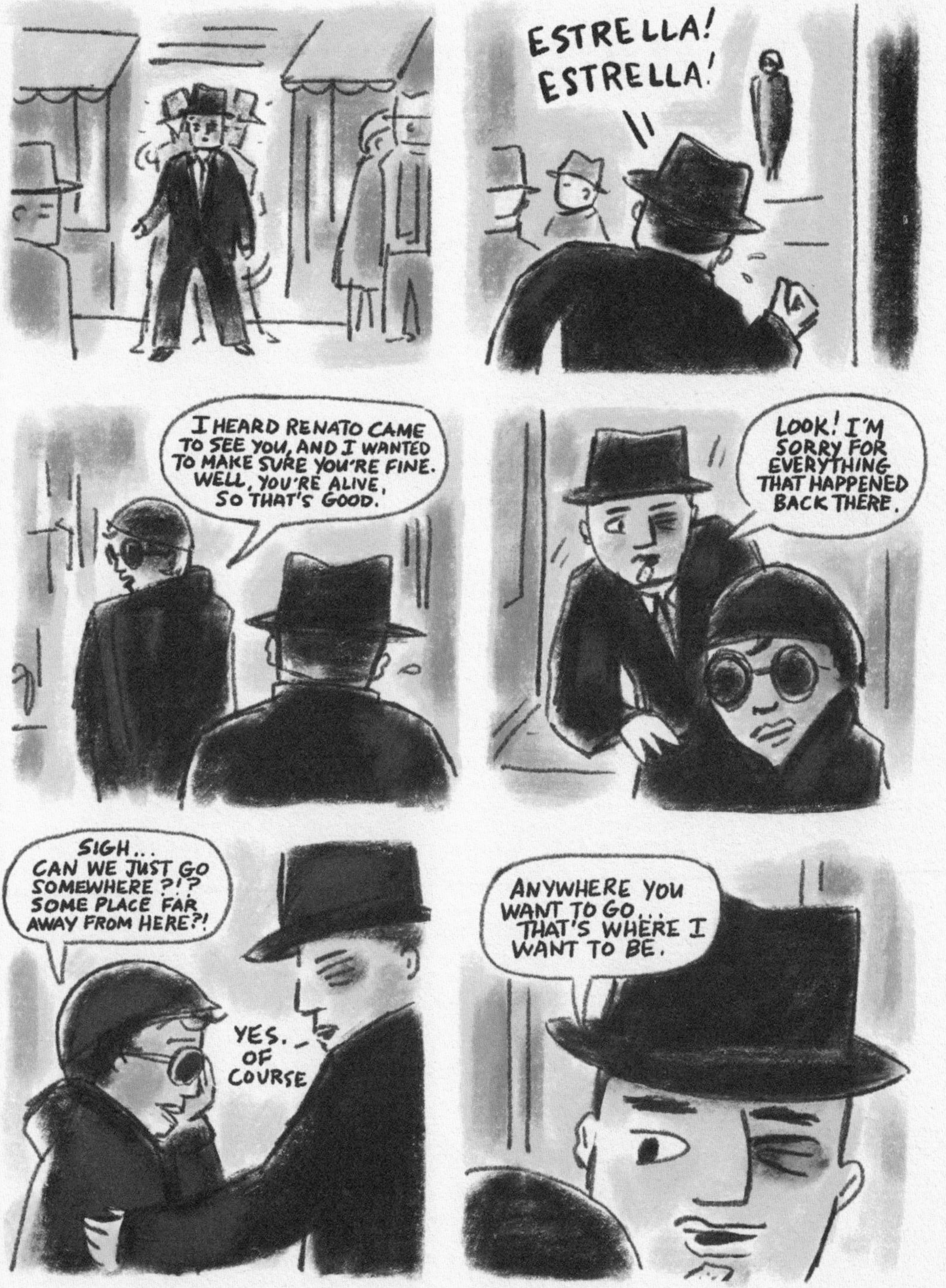
ESTRELLA! ESTRELLA!
I HEARD RENATO CAME TO SEE YOU, AND I WANTED TO MAKE SURE YOU'RE FINE. WELL, YOU'RE ALIVE, SO THAT'S GOOD.
LOOK! I'M SORRY FOR EVERYTHING THAT HAPPENED BACK THERE.
SIGH... CAN WE JUST GO SOMEWHERE?!? SOME PLACE FAR AWAY FROM HERE?!
YES. OF COURSE
ANYWHERE YOU WANT TO GO... THAT'S WHERE I WANT TO BE.

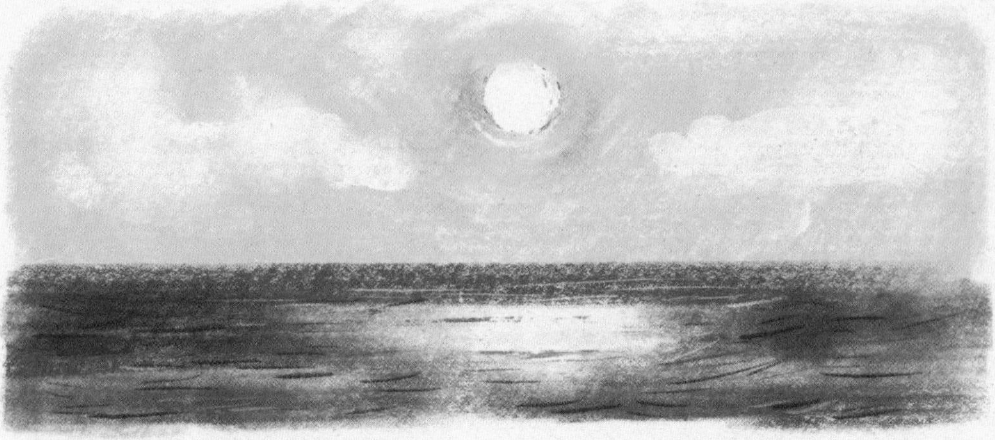

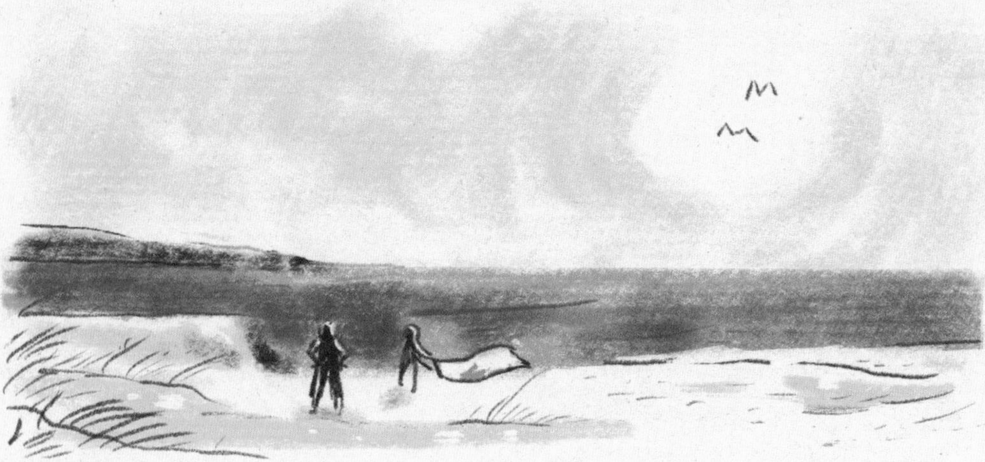

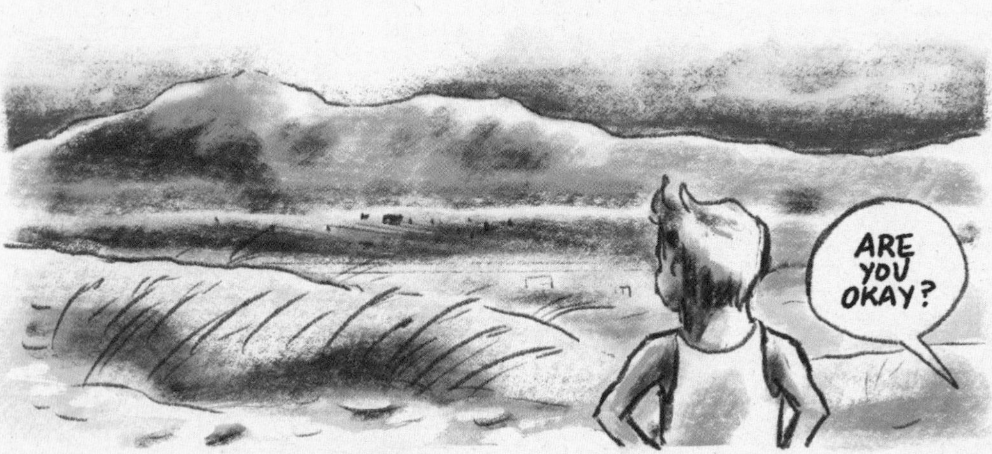
ARE YOU OKAY?

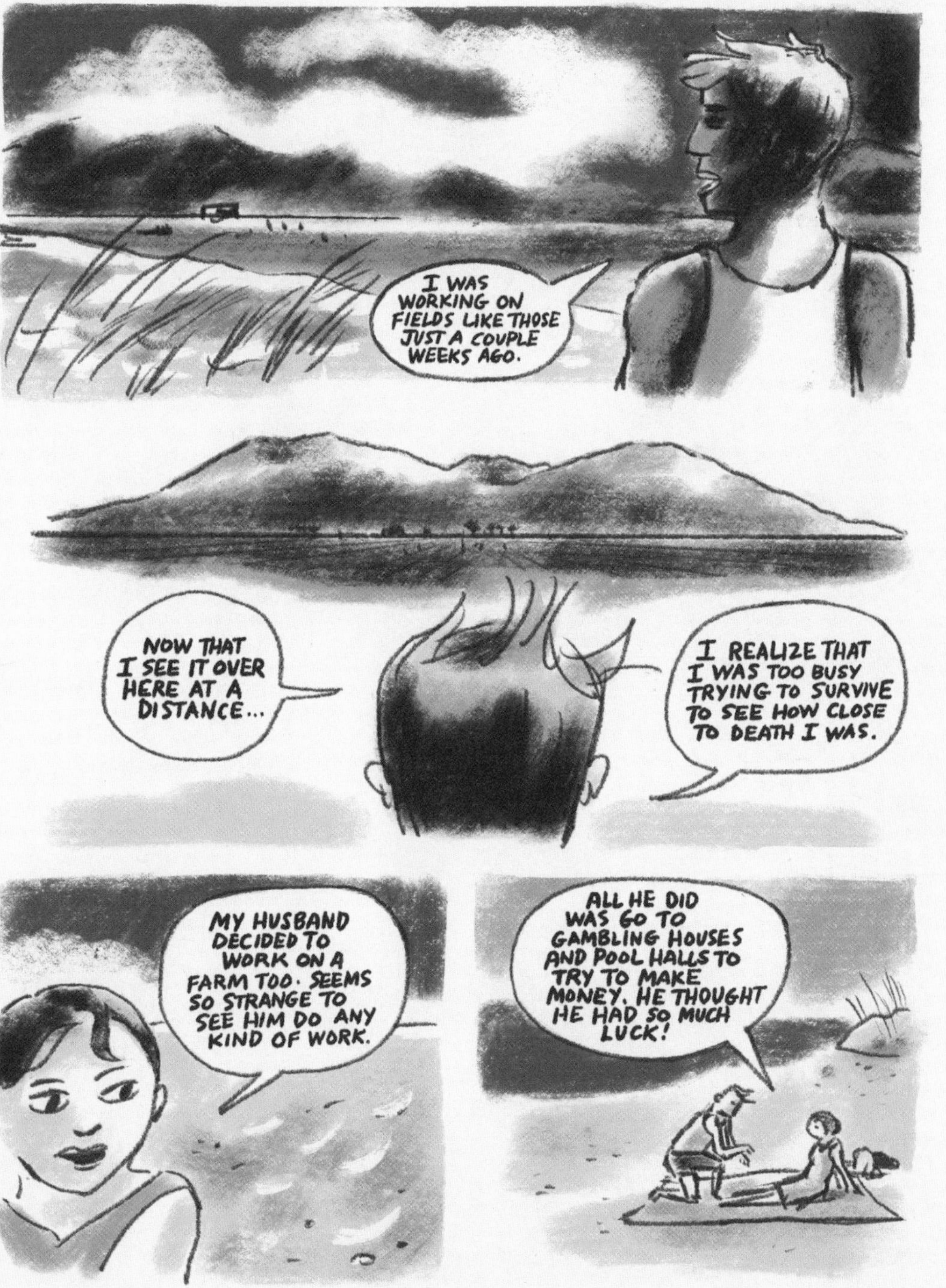
I WAS WORKING ON FIELDS LIKE THOSE JUST A COUPLE WEEKS AGO.
NOW THAT I SEE IT OVER HERE AT A DISTANCE...
I REALIZE THAT I WAS TOO BUSY TRYING TO SURVIVE TO SEE HOW CLOSE TO DEATH I WAS.
MY HUSBAND DECIDED TO WORK ON A FARM TOO. SEEMS SO STRANGE TO SEE HIM DO ANY KIND OF WORK.
ALL HE DID WAS GO TO GAMBLING HOUSES AND POOL HALLS TO TRY TO MAKE MONEY. HE THOUGHT HE HAD SO MUCH LUCK!

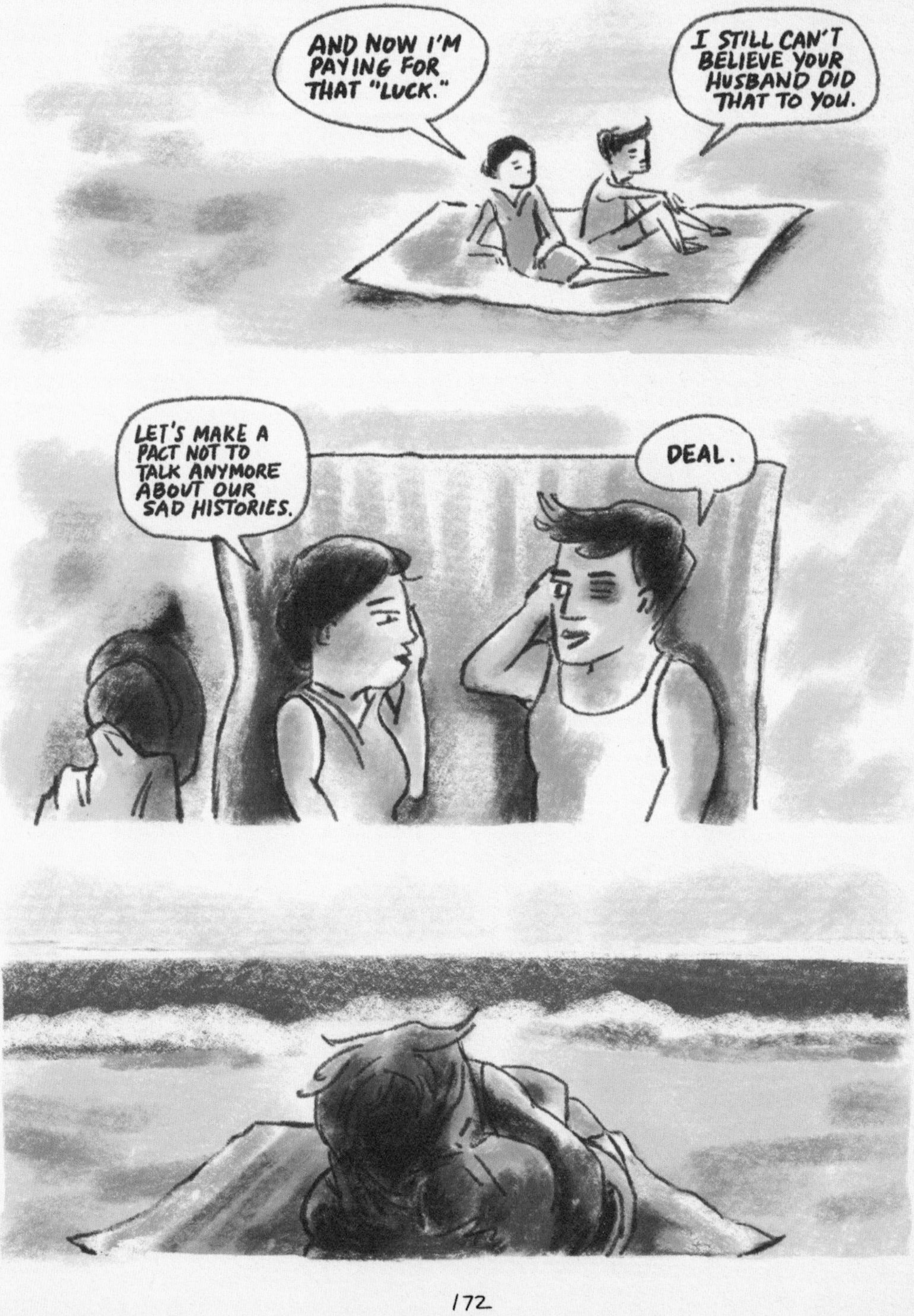
AND NOW I'M PAYING FOR THAT "LUCK."
I STILL CAN'T BELIEVE YOUR HUSBAND DID THAT TO YOU.
LET'S MAKE A PACT NOT TO TALK ANYMORE ABOUT OUR SAD HISTORIES.
DEAL.

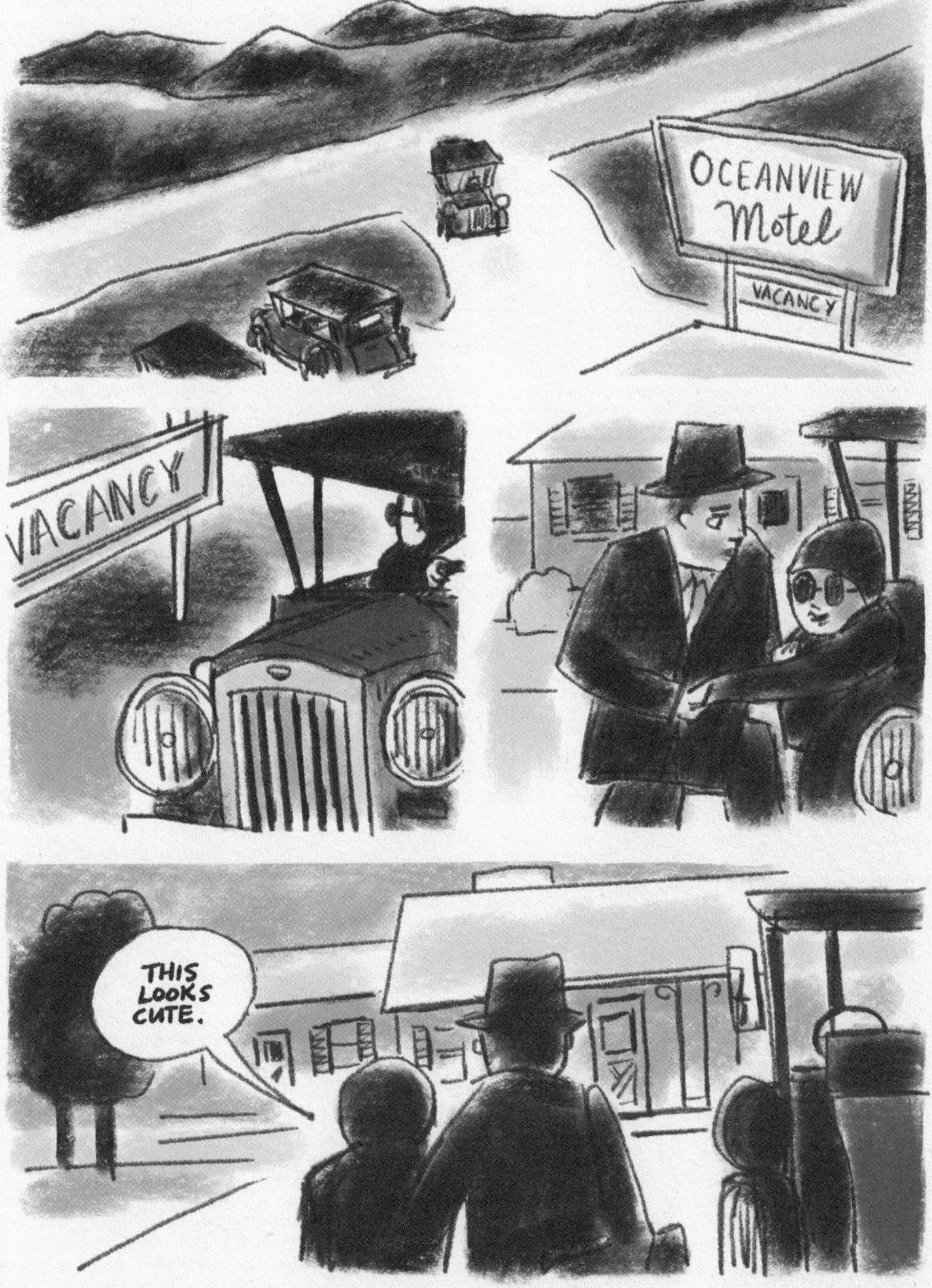
OCEANVIEW Motel
VACANCY
VACANCY
THIS LOOKS CUTE.

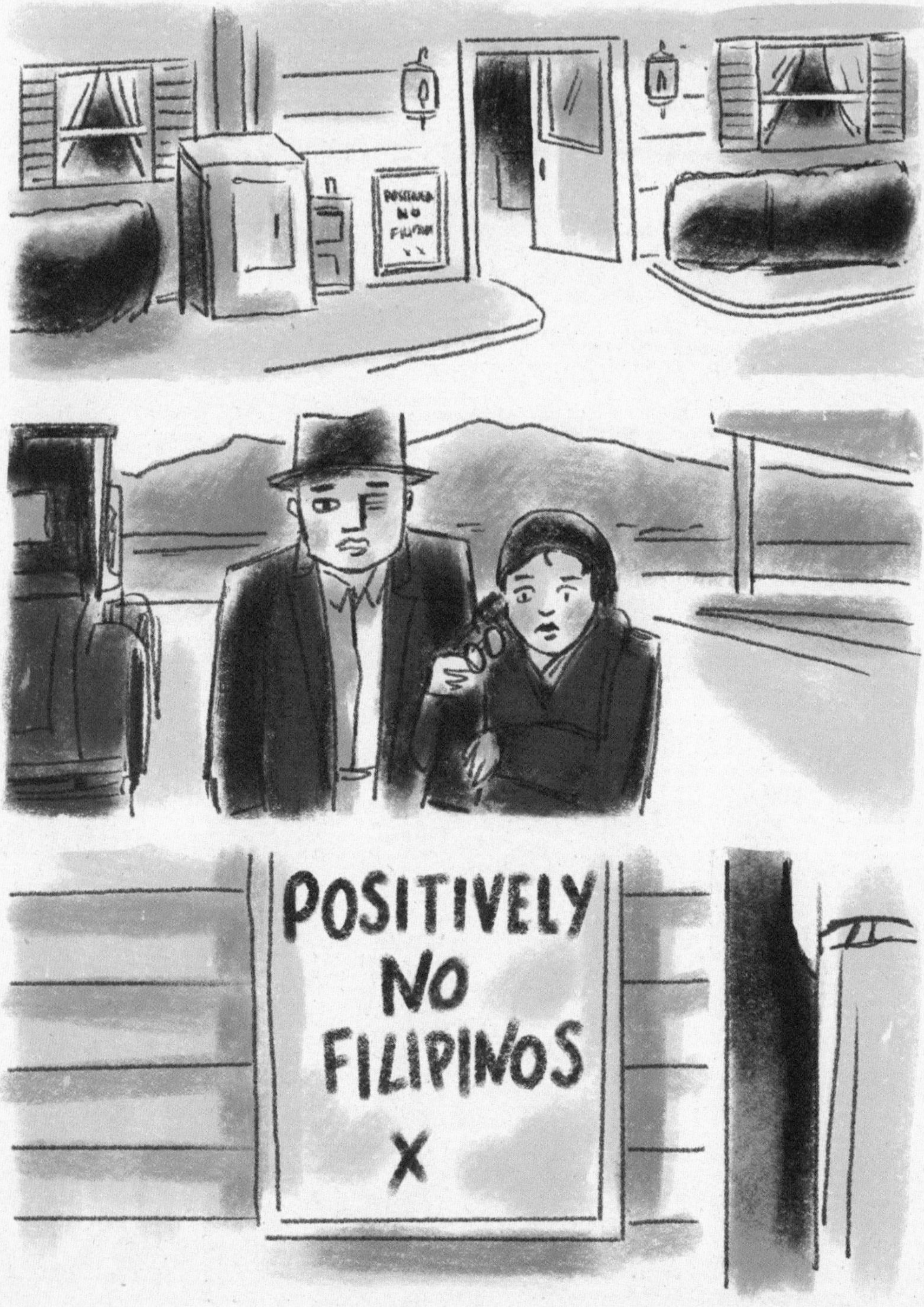
POSITIVELY
NO
FILIPINOS
X

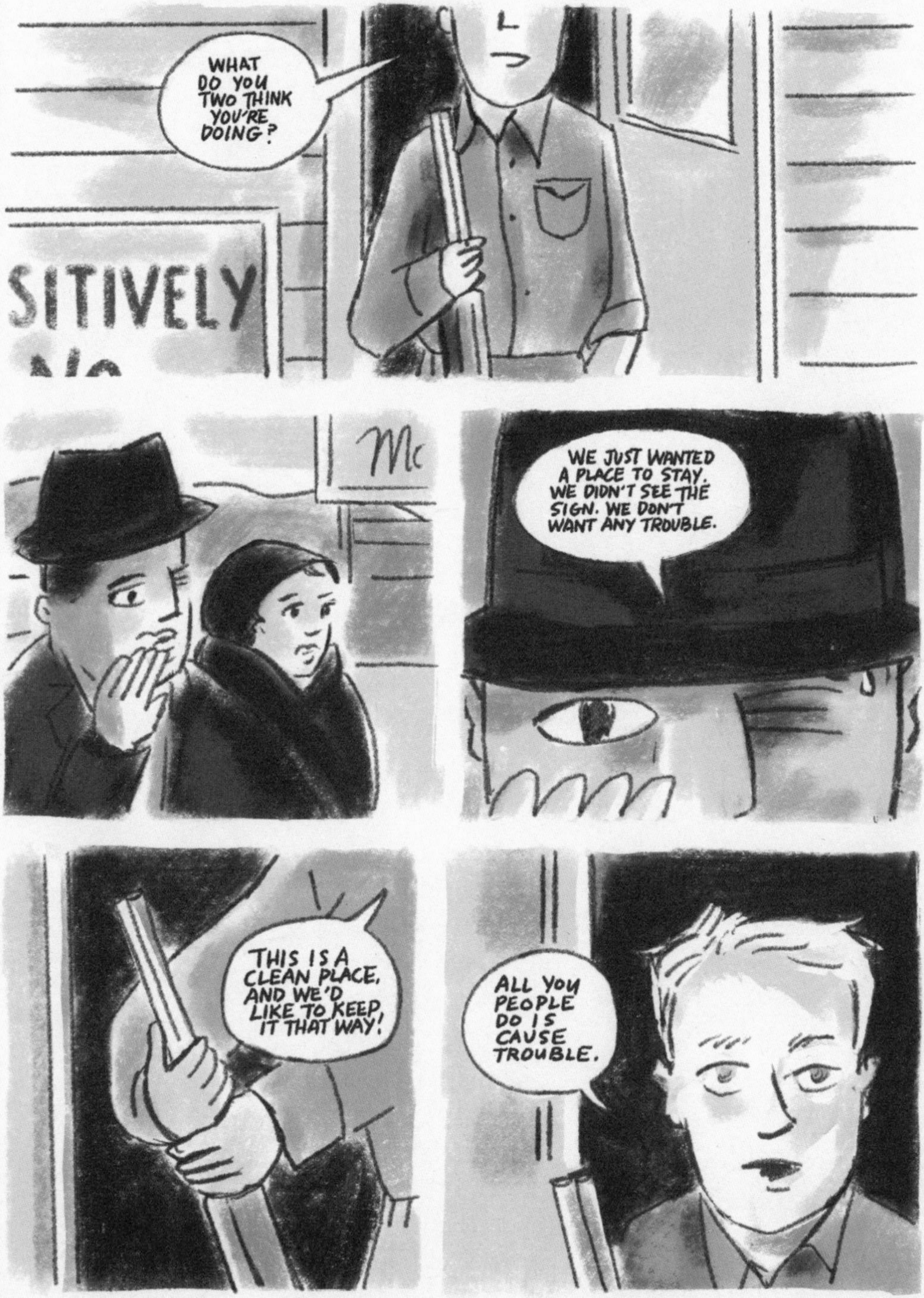
WHAT DO YOU TWO THINK YOU'RE DOING?
SITIVELY
Mc
WE JUST WANTED A PLACE TO STAY. WE DIDN'T SEE THE SIGN. WE DON'T WANT ANY TROUBLE.
THIS IS A CLEAN PLACE, AND WE'D LIKE TO KEEP IT THAT WAY!
ALL YOU PEOPLE DO IS CAUSE TROUBLE.

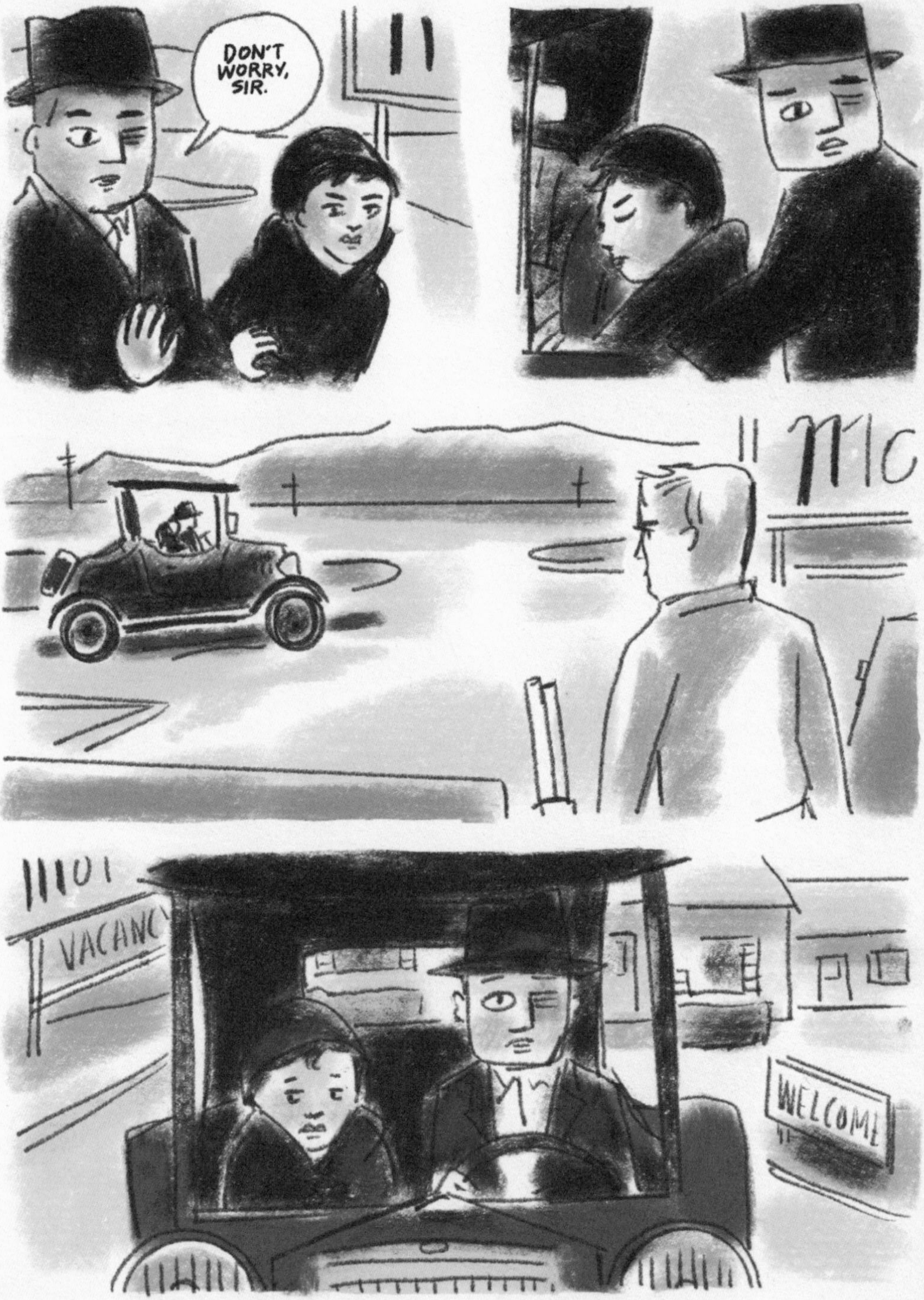
DON'T WORRY, SIR.
VACANC
WELCOME

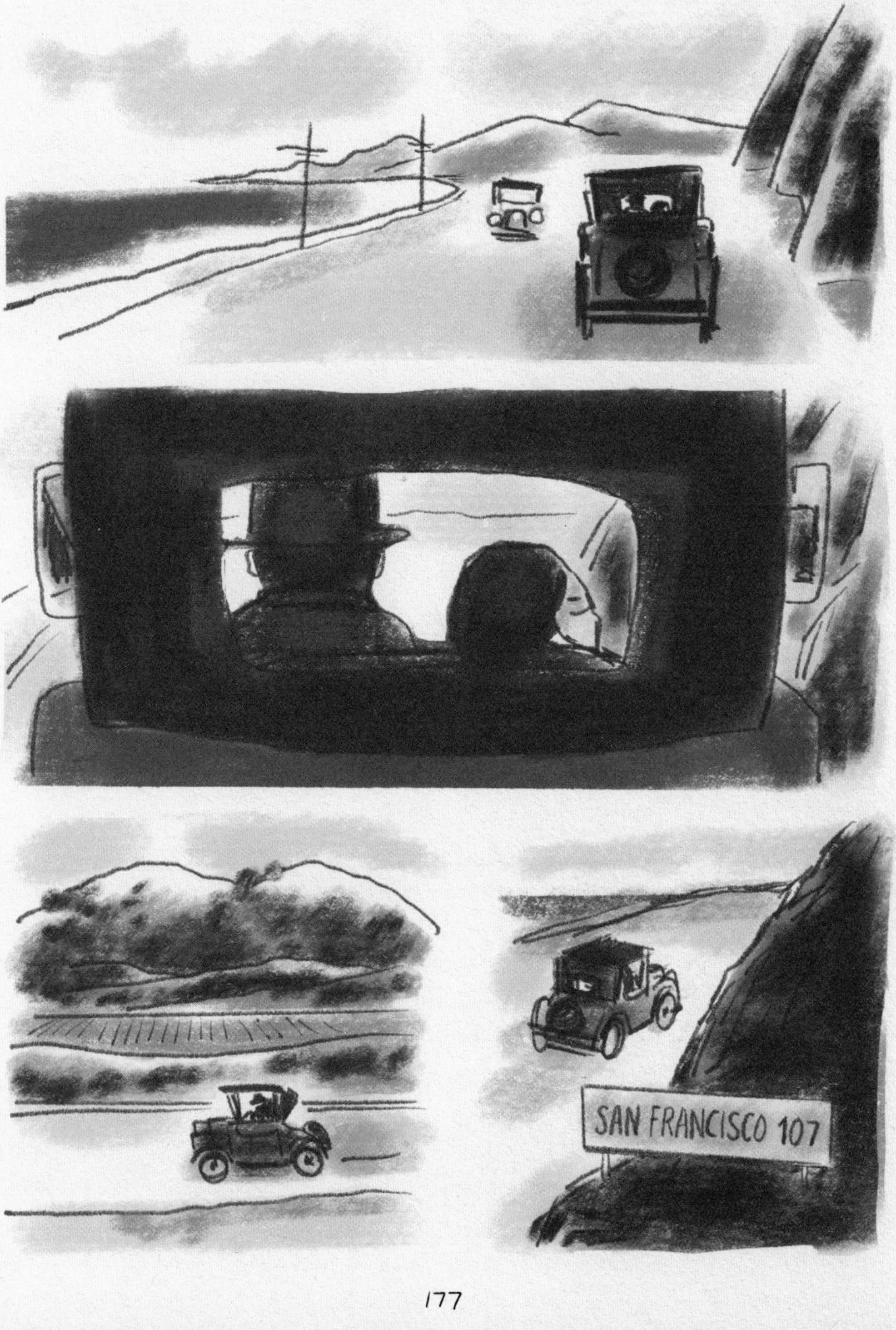
SAN FRANCISCO 107

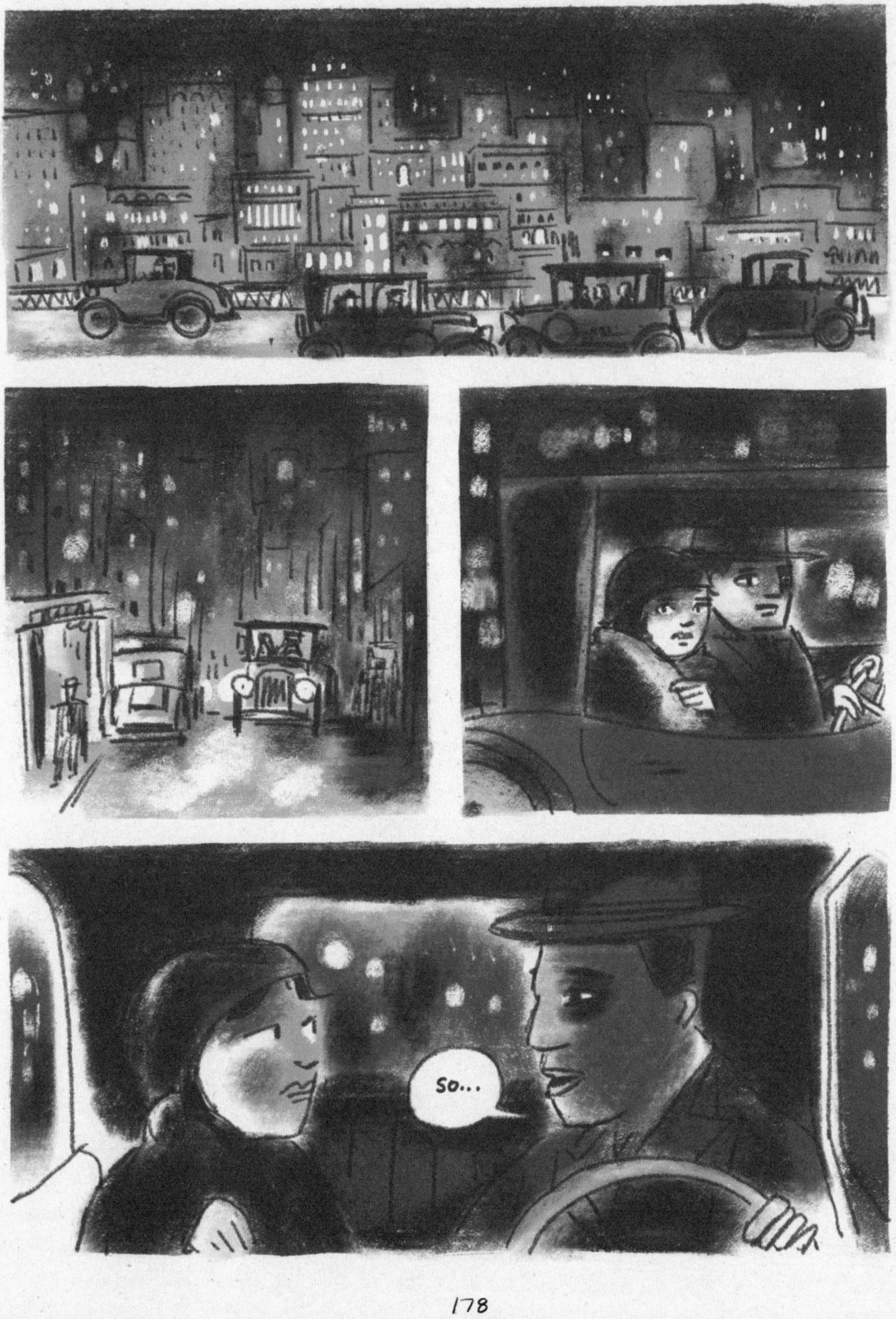
SO...

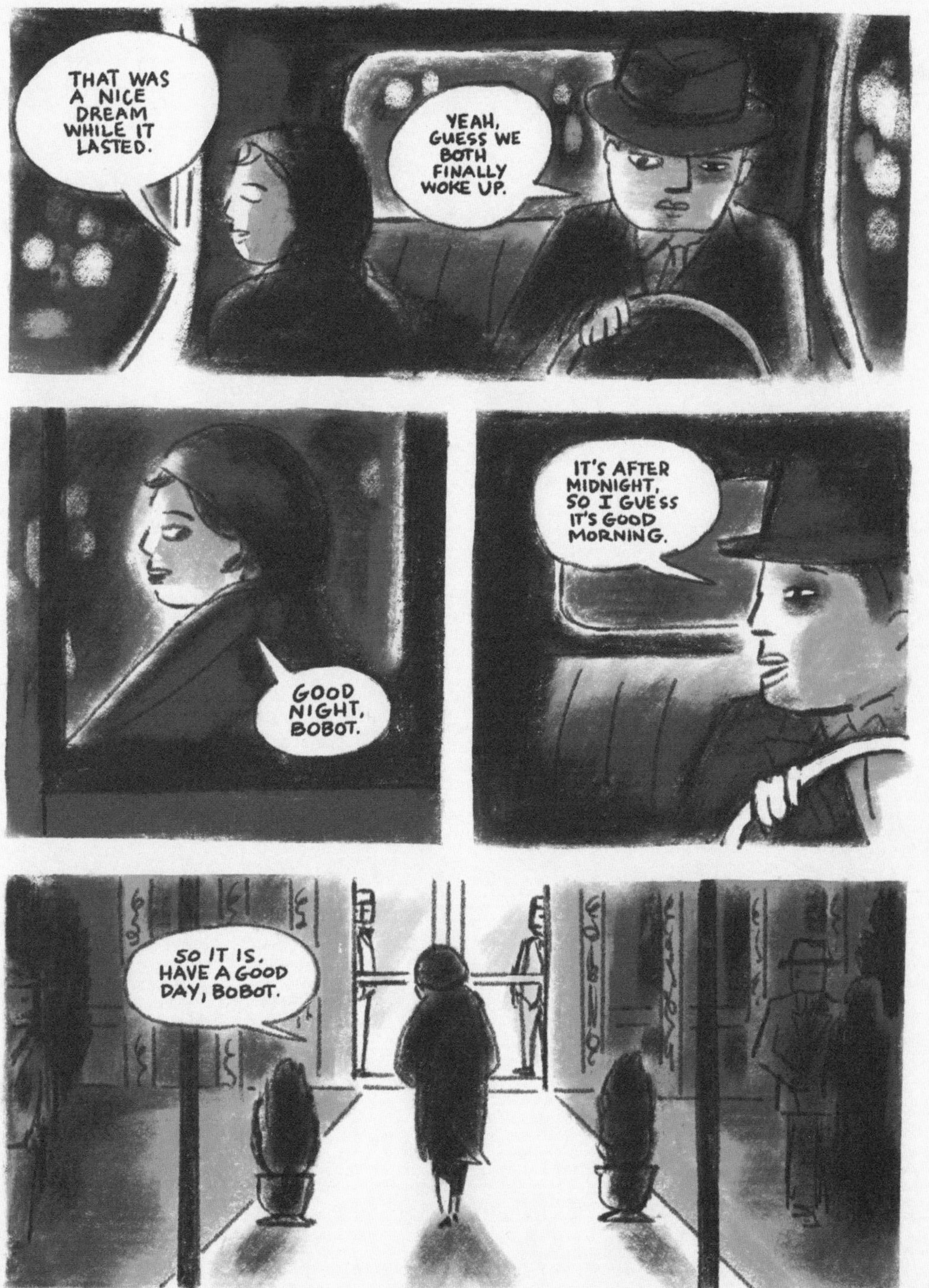
THAT WAS A NICE DREAM WHILE IT LASTED.
YEAH, GUESS WE BOTH FINALLY WOKE UP.
GOOD NIGHT, BOBOT.
IT'S AFTER MIDNIGHT, SO I GUESS IT'S GOOD MORNING.
SO IT IS. HAVE A GOOD DAY, BOBOT.

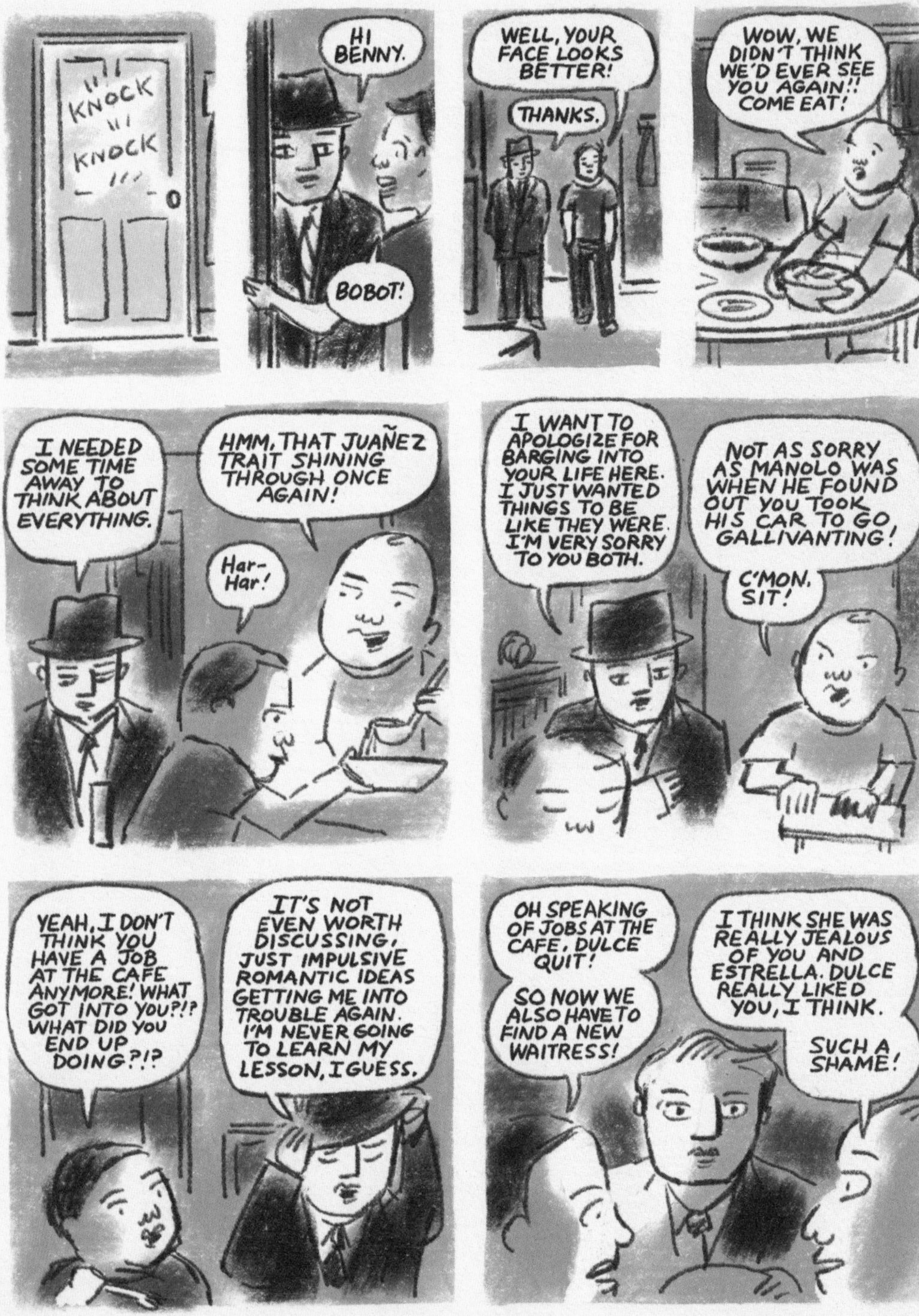
KNOCK
KNOCK
HI BENNY.
BOBOT!
WELL, YOUR FACE LOOKS BETTER!
THANKS.
WOW, WE DIDN'T THINK WE'D EVER SEE YOU AGAIN!! COME EAT!
I NEEDED SOME TIME AWAY TO THINK ABOUT EVERYTHING.
HMM, THAT JUAÑEZ TRAIT SHINING THROUGH ONCE AGAIN!
Har-Har!
I WANT TO APOLOGIZE FOR BARGING INTO YOUR LIFE HERE. I JUST WANTED THINGS TO BE LIKE THEY WERE. I'M VERY SORRY TO YOU BOTH.
NOT AS SORRY AS MANOLO WAS WHEN HE FOUND OUT YOU TOOK HIS CAR TO GO GALLIVANTING!
C'MON, SIT!
YEAH, I DON'T THINK YOU HAVE A JOB AT THE CAFE ANYMORE! WHAT GOT INTO YOU?!? WHAT DID YOU END UP DOING?!?
IT'S NOT EVEN WORTH DISCUSSING, JUST IMPULSIVE ROMANTIC IDEAS GETTING ME INTO TROUBLE AGAIN. I'M NEVER GOING TO LEARN MY LESSON, I GUESS.
OH SPEAKING OF JOBS AT THE CAFE, DULCE QUIT!
SO NOW WE ALSO HAVE TO FIND A NEW WAITRESS!
I THINK SHE WAS REALLY JEALOUS OF YOU AND ESTRELLA. DULCE REALLY LIKED YOU, I THINK.
SUCH A SHAME!

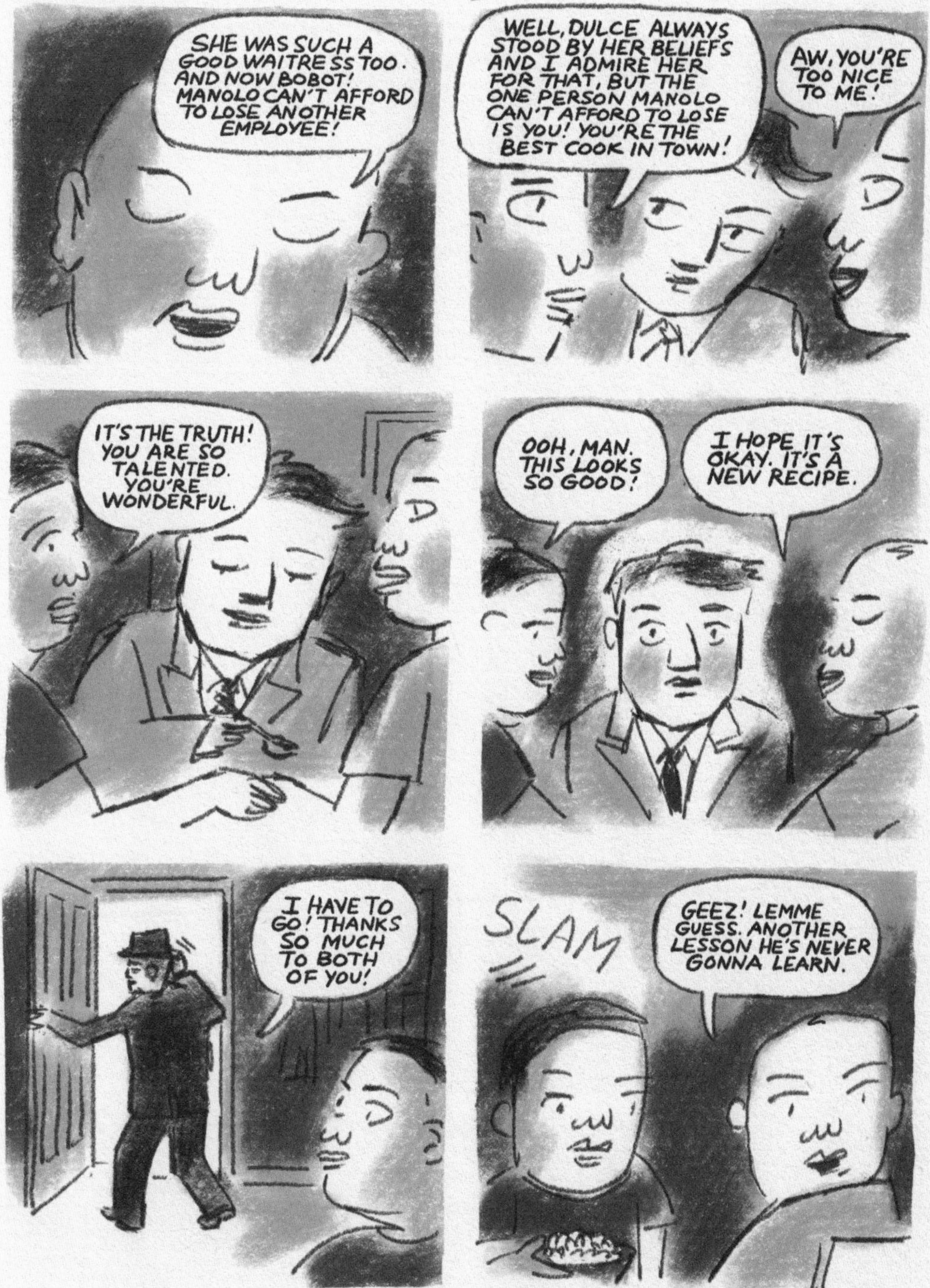
SHE WAS SUCH A GOOD WAITRESS TOO. AND NOW BOBOT! MANOLO CAN'T AFFORD TO LOSE ANOTHER EMPLOYEE!
WELL, DULCE ALWAYS STOOD BY HER BELIEFS AND I ADMIRE HER FOR THAT, BUT THE ONE PERSON MANOLO CAN'T AFFORD TO LOSE IS YOU! YOU'RE THE BEST COOK IN TOWN!
AW, YOU'RE TOO NICE TO ME!
IT'S THE TRUTH! YOU ARE SO TALENTED. YOU'RE WONDERFUL.
OOH, MAN. THIS LOOKS SO GOOD!
I HOPE IT'S OKAY. IT'S A NEW RECIPE.
I HAVE TO GO! THANKS SO MUCH TO BOTH OF YOU!
SLAM
GEEZ! LEMME GUESS. ANOTHER LESSON HE'S NEVER GONNA LEARN.

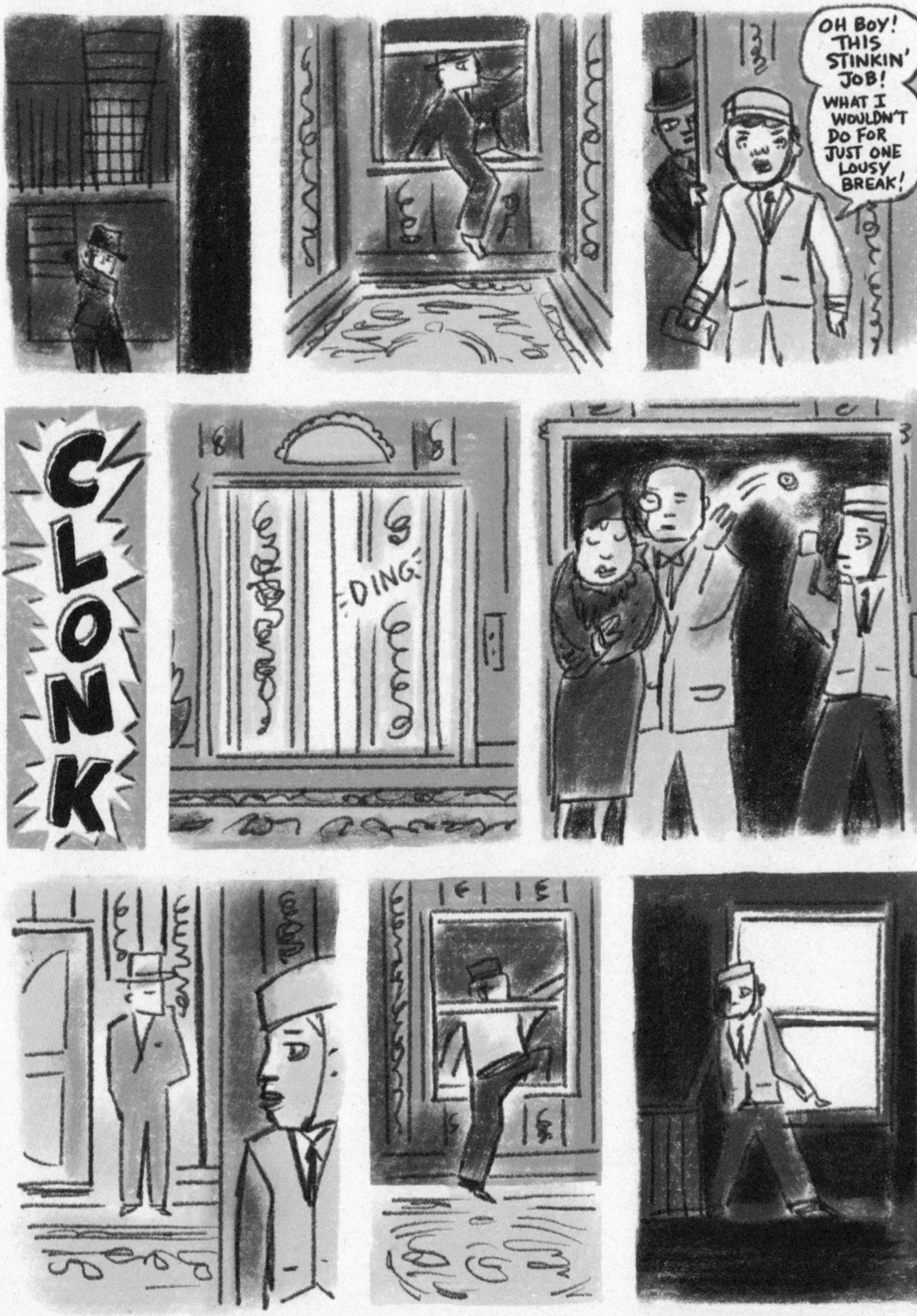
OH BOY! THIS STINKIN' JOB!
WHAT I WOULDN'T DO FOR JUST ONE LOUSY BREAK!
CLONK
DING

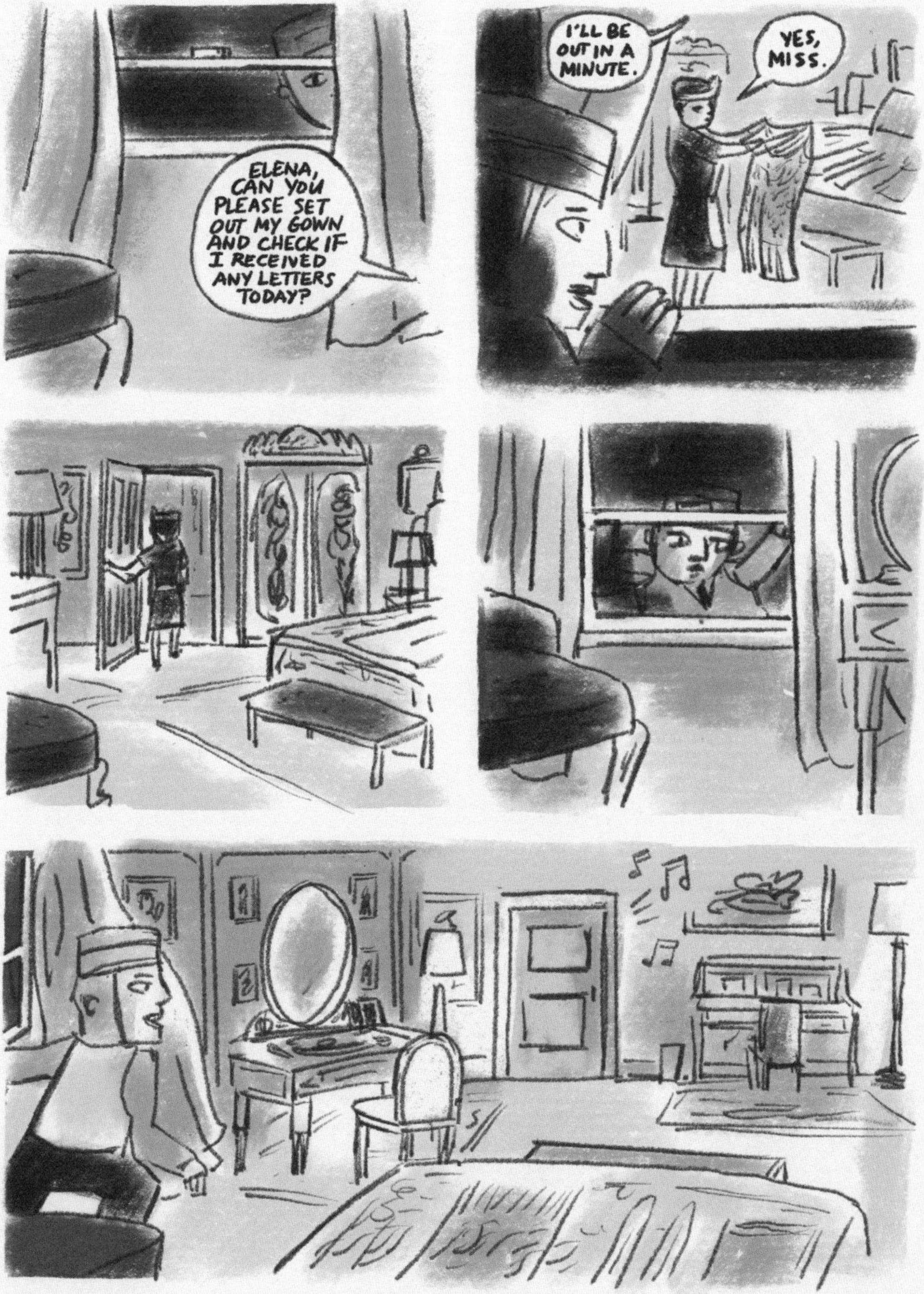
ELENA, CAN YOU PLEASE SET OUT MY GOWN AND CHECK IF I RECEIVED ANY LETTERS TODAY?
I'LL BE OUT IN A MINUTE.
YES, MISS.

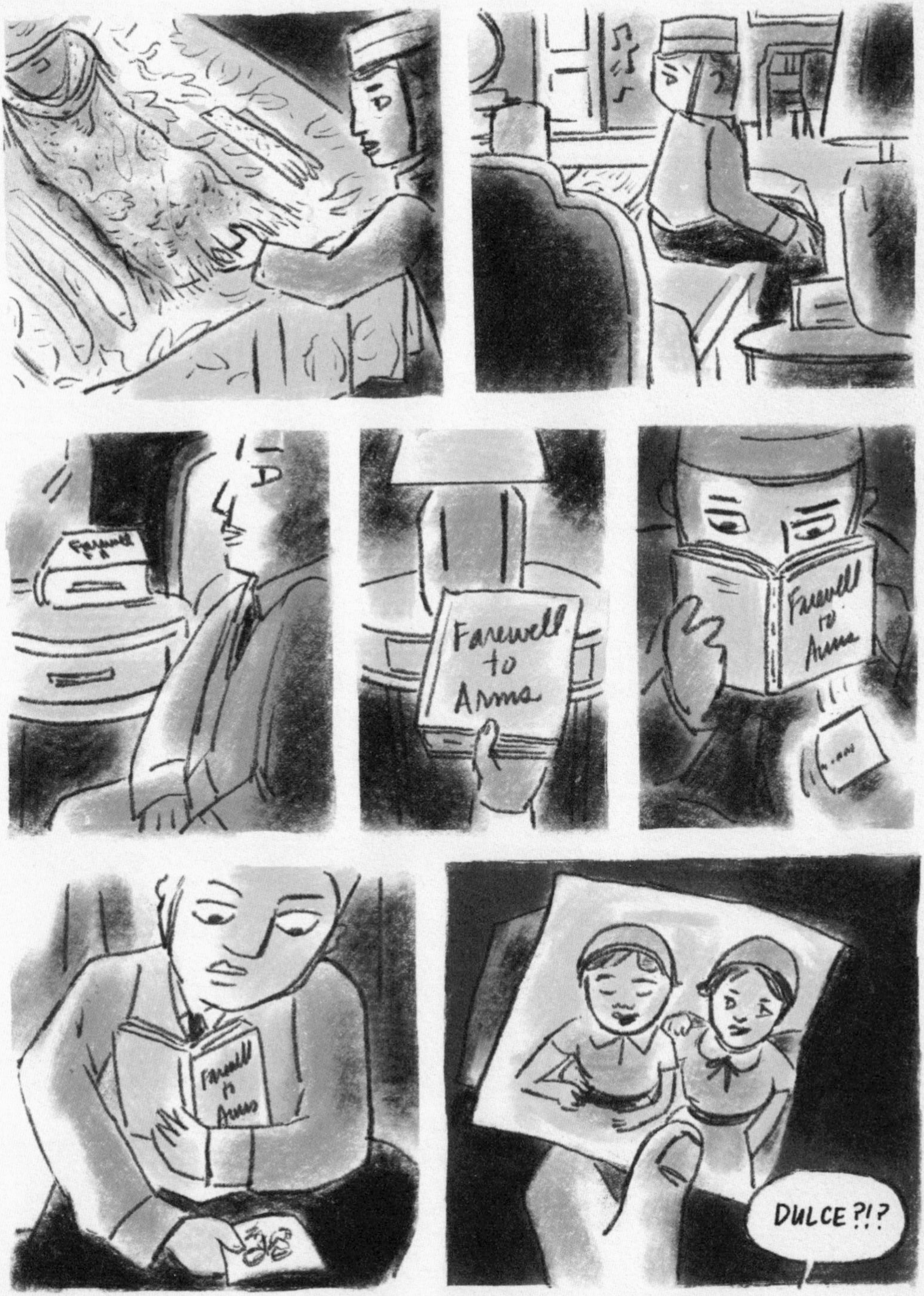
Farewell to Arms
Farewell to Arms
Farewell to Arms
DULCE?!?

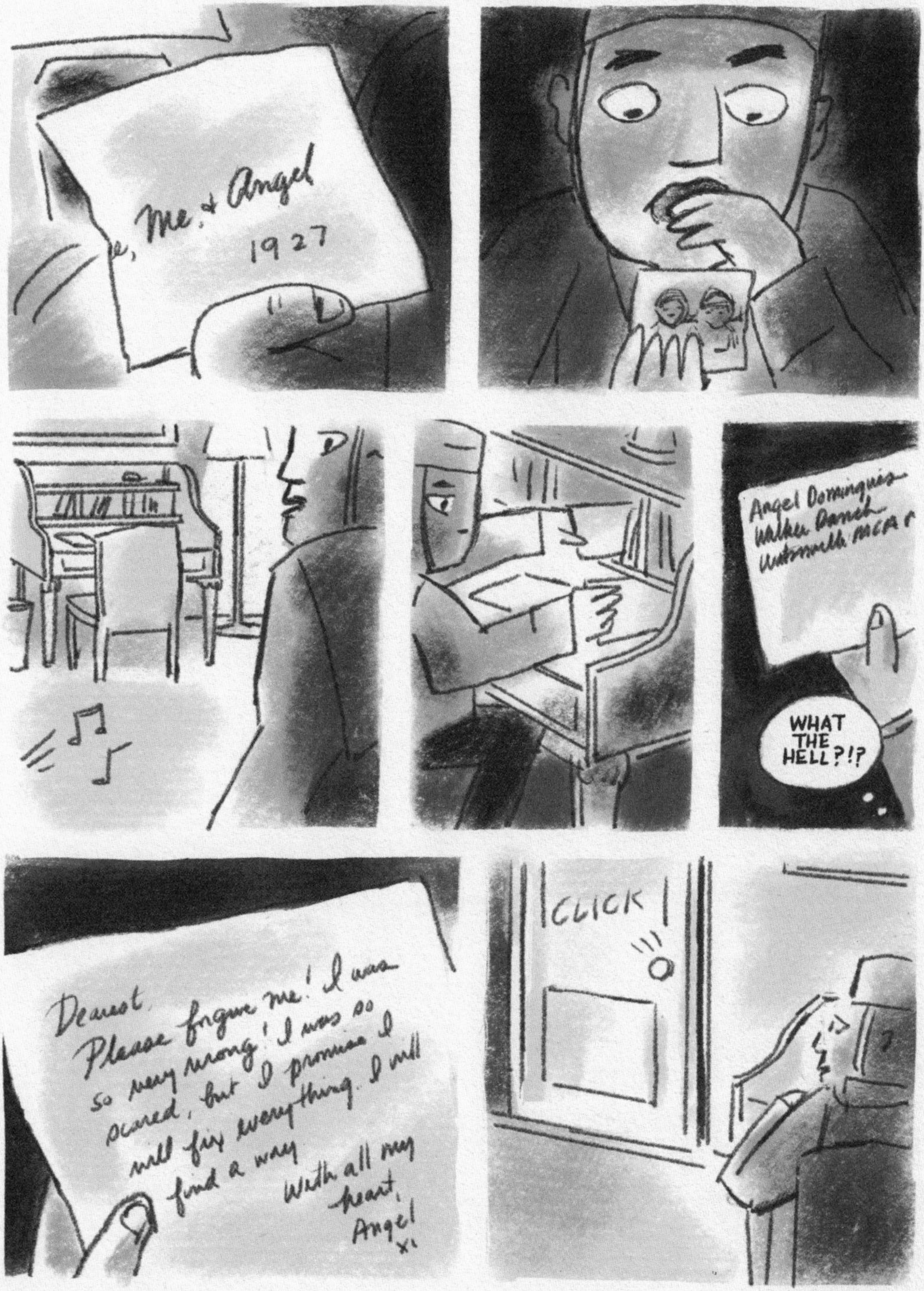
Me + Angel
1927
Angel Dominguez
WHAT THE HELL?!?
Dearest,
Please forgive me! I was so very wrong! I was so scared, but I promise I will fix everything. I will find a way.
With all my heart,
Angel
CLICK

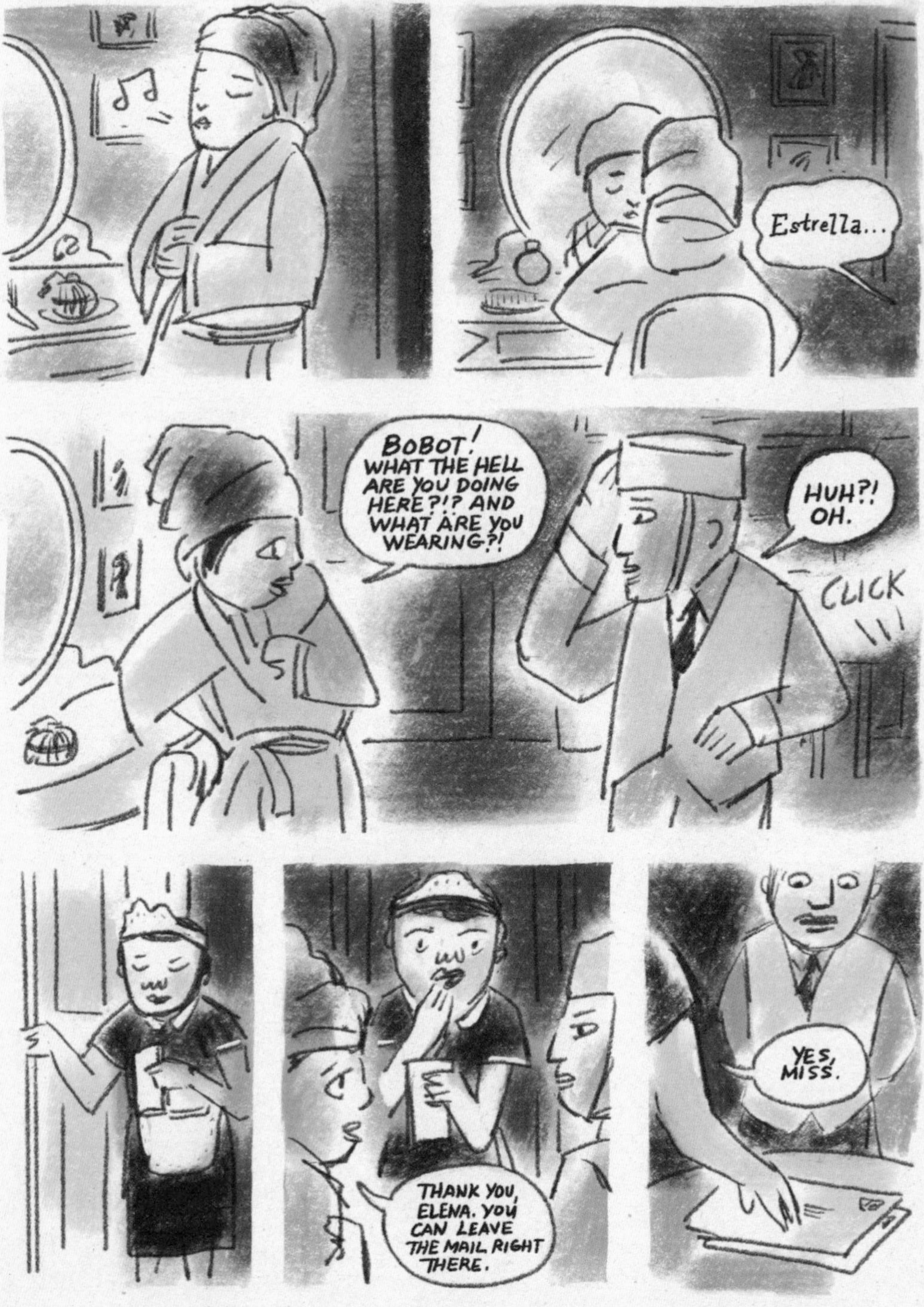
Estrella...
BOBOT! WHAT THE HELL ARE YOU DOING HERE?!? AND WHAT ARE YOU WEARING?!
HUH?! OH.
CLICK
THANK YOU, ELENA. YOU CAN LEAVE THE MAIL RIGHT THERE.
YES, MISS.

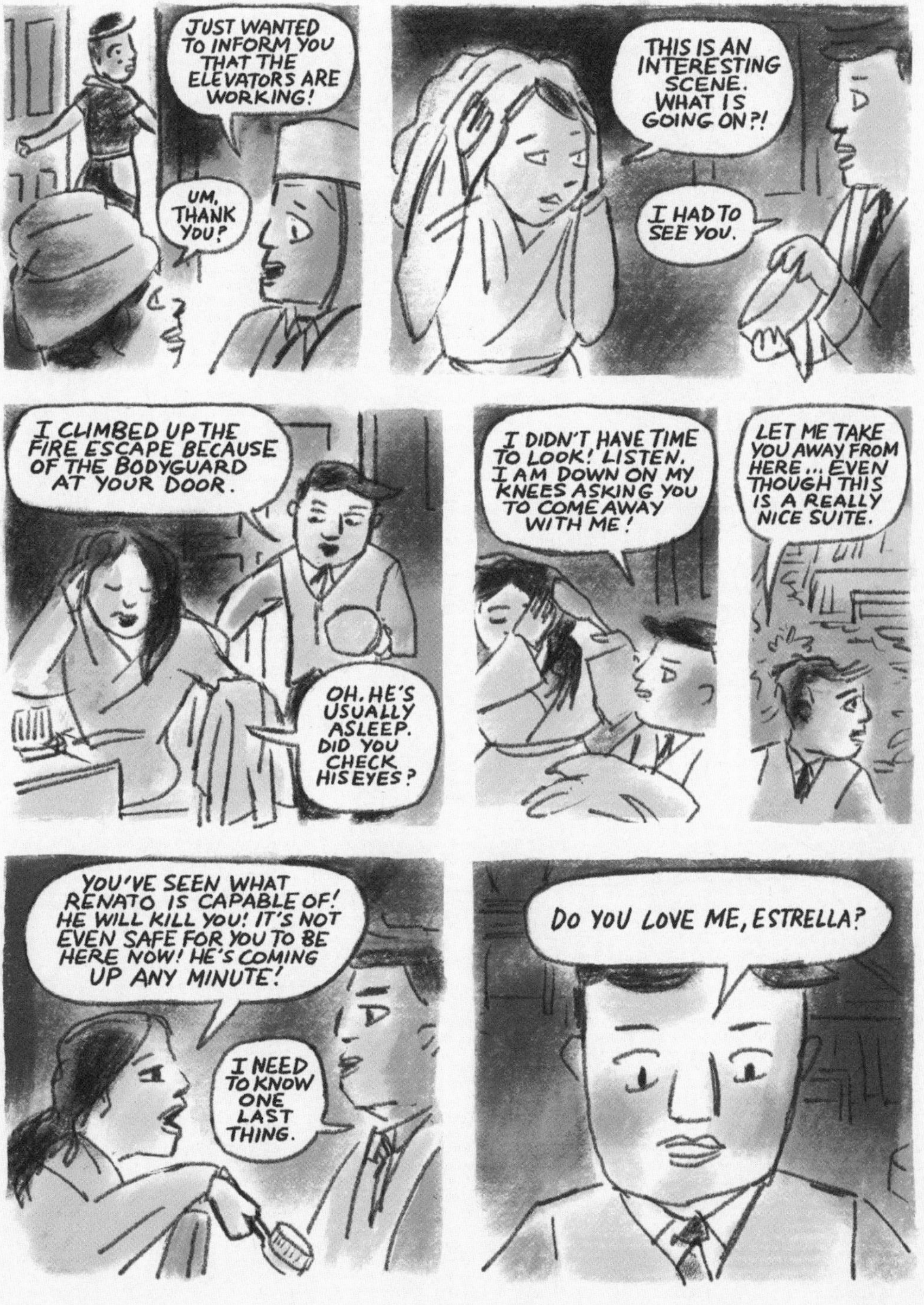
JUST WANTED TO INFORM YOU THAT THE ELEVATORS ARE WORKING!
UM, THANK YOU?
THIS IS AN INTERESTING SCENE. WHAT IS GOING ON?!
I HAD TO SEE YOU.
I CLIMBED UP THE FIRE ESCAPE BECAUSE OF THE BODYGUARD AT YOUR DOOR.
OH, HE'S USUALLY ASLEEP. DID YOU CHECK HIS EYES?
I DIDN'T HAVE TIME TO LOOK! LISTEN. I AM DOWN ON MY KNEES ASKING YOU TO COME AWAY WITH ME!
LET ME TAKE YOU AWAY FROM HERE... EVEN THOUGH THIS IS A REALLY NICE SUITE.
YOU'VE SEEN WHAT RENATO IS CAPABLE OF! HE WILL KILL YOU! IT'S NOT EVEN SAFE FOR YOU TO BE HERE NOW! HE'S COMING UP ANY MINUTE!
I NEED TO KNOW ONE LAST THING.
DO YOU LOVE ME, ESTRELLA?

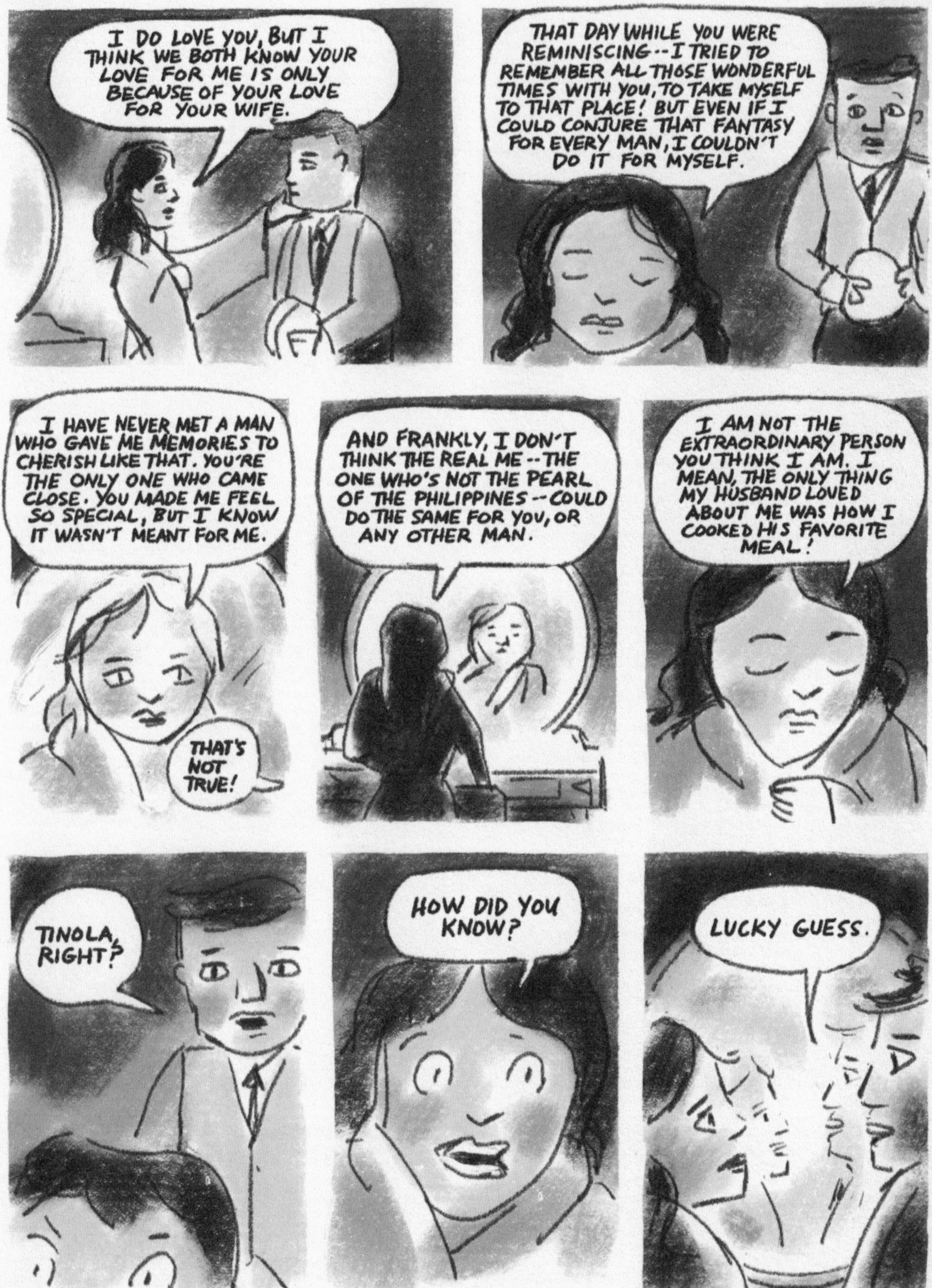
I DO LOVE YOU, BUT I THINK WE BOTH KNOW YOUR LOVE FOR ME IS ONLY BECAUSE OF YOUR LOVE FOR YOUR WIFE.
THAT DAY WHILE YOU WERE REMINISCING -- I TRIED TO REMEMBER ALL THOSE WONDERFUL TIMES WITH YOU, TO TAKE MYSELF TO THAT PLACE! BUT EVEN IF I COULD CONJURE THAT FANTASY FOR EVERY MAN, I COULDN'T DO IT FOR MYSELF.
I HAVE NEVER MET A MAN WHO GAVE ME MEMORIES TO CHERISH LIKE THAT. YOU'RE THE ONLY ONE WHO CAME CLOSE. YOU MADE ME FEEL SO SPECIAL, BUT I KNOW IT WASN'T MEANT FOR ME.
THAT'S NOT TRUE!
AND FRANKLY, I DON'T THINK THE REAL ME -- THE ONE WHO'S NOT THE PEARL OF THE PHILIPPINES -- COULD DO THE SAME FOR YOU, OR ANY OTHER MAN.
I AM NOT THE EXTRAORDINARY PERSON YOU THINK I AM. I MEAN, THE ONLY THING MY HUSBAND LOVED ABOUT ME WAS HOW I COOKED HIS FAVORITE MEAL!
TINOLA, RIGHT?
HOW DID YOU KNOW?
LUCKY GUESS.

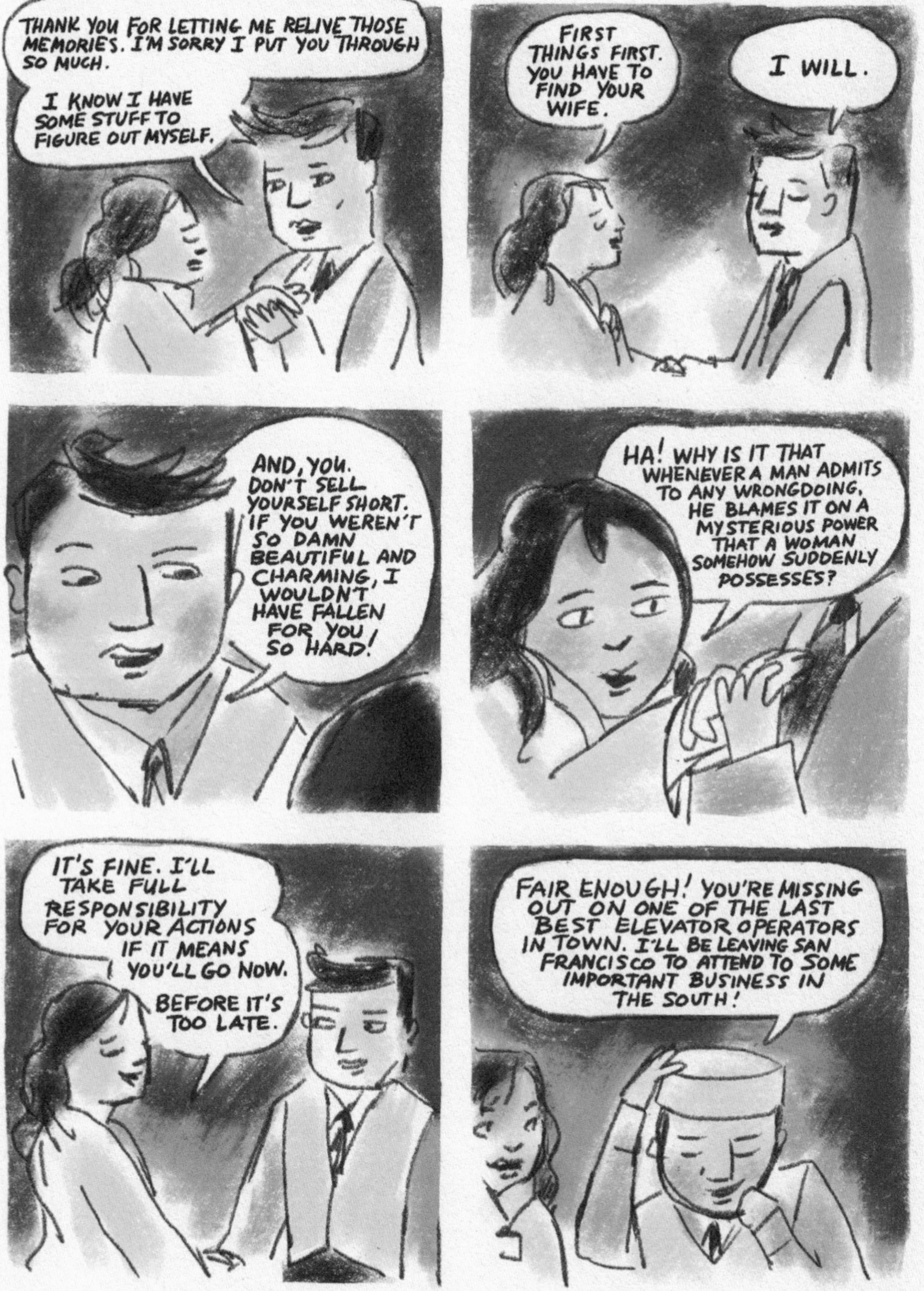

THANK YOU FOR LETTING ME RELIVE THOSE MEMORIES. I'M SORRY I PUT YOU THROUGH SO MUCH.
I KNOW I HAVE SOME STUFF TO FIGURE OUT MYSELF.
FIRST THINGS FIRST. YOU HAVE TO FIND YOUR WIFE.
I WILL.
AND, YOU. DON'T SELL YOURSELF SHORT. IF YOU WEREN'T SO DAMN BEAUTIFUL AND CHARMING, I WOULDN'T HAVE FALLEN FOR YOU SO HARD!
HA! WHY IS IT THAT WHENEVER A MAN ADMITS TO ANY WRONGDOING, HE BLAMES IT ON A MYSTERIOUS POWER THAT A WOMAN SOMEHOW SUDDENLY POSSESSES?
IT'S FINE. I'LL TAKE FULL RESPONSIBILITY FOR YOUR ACTIONS IF IT MEANS YOU'LL GO NOW.
BEFORE IT'S TOO LATE.
FAIR ENOUGH! YOU'RE MISSING OUT ON ONE OF THE LAST BEST ELEVATOR OPERATORS IN TOWN. I'LL BE LEAVING SAN FRANCISCO TO ATTEND TO SOME IMPORTANT BUSINESS IN THE SOUTH!

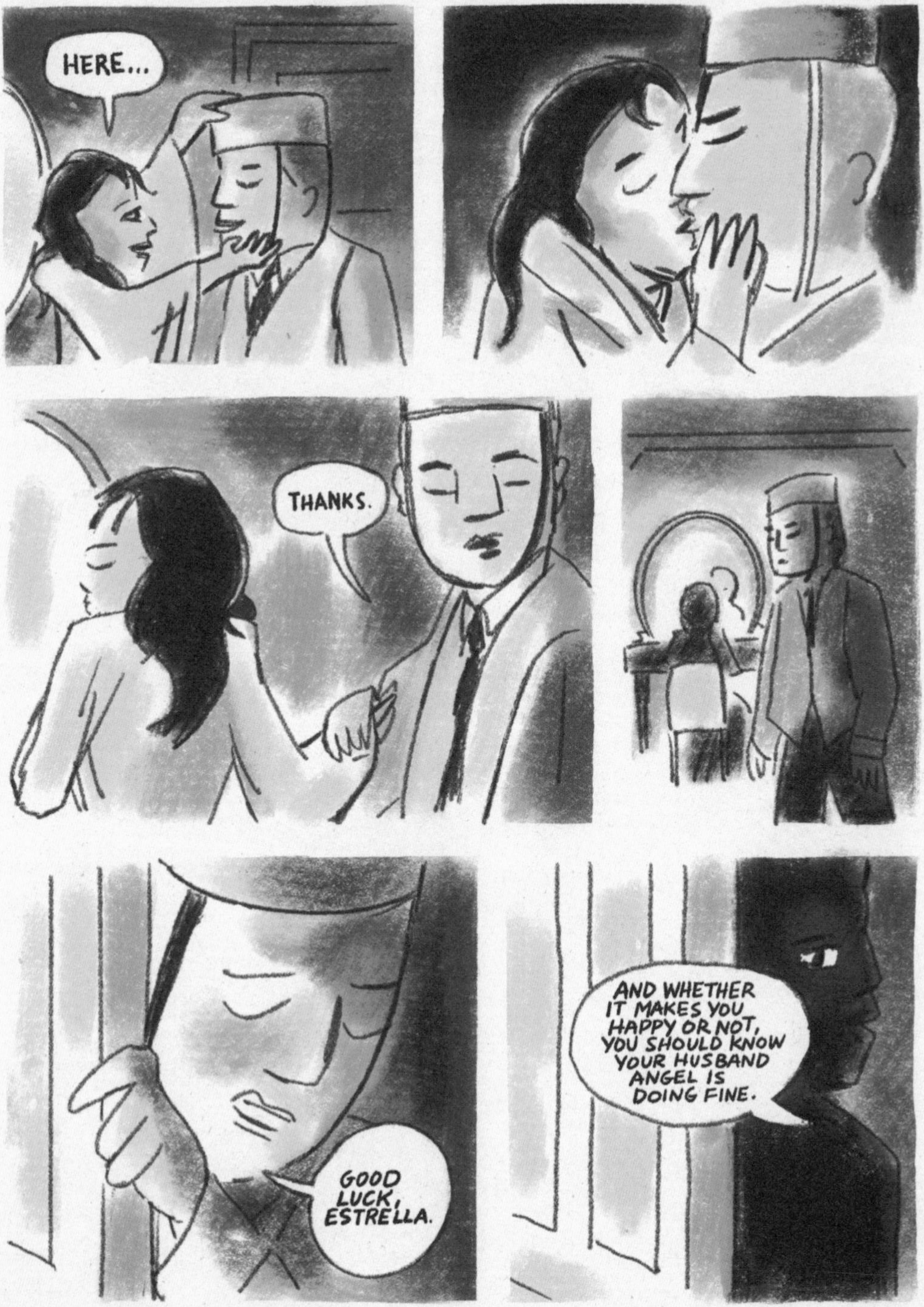
HERE...
THANKS.
GOOD LUCK, ESTRELLA.
AND WHETHER IT MAKES YOU HAPPY OR NOT, YOU SHOULD KNOW YOUR HUSBAND ANGEL IS DOING FINE.

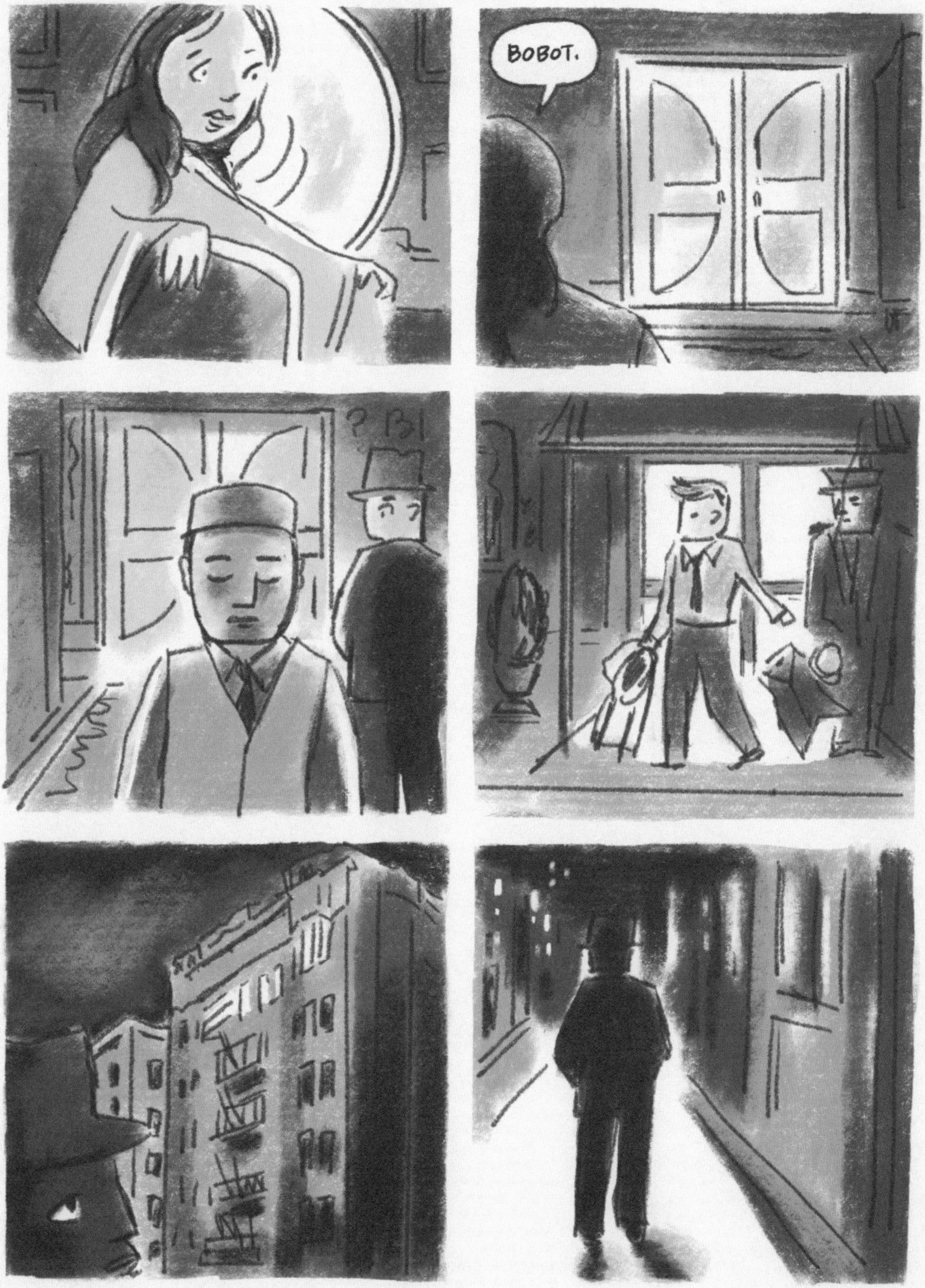
BOBOT.

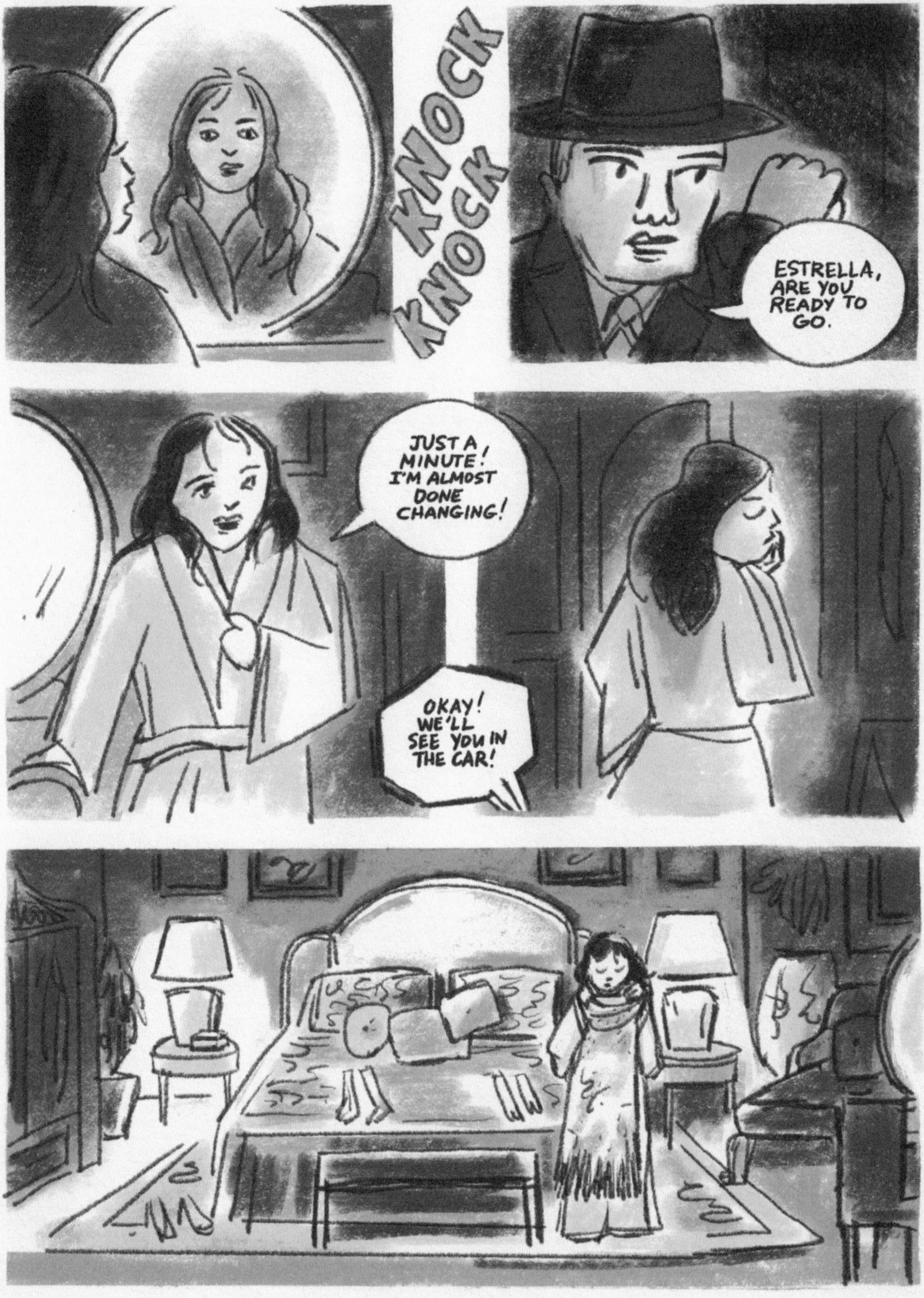
KNOCK KNOCK
ESTRELLA, ARE YOU READY TO GO.
JUST A MINUTE! I'M ALMOST DONE CHANGING!
OKAY! WE'LL SEE YOU IN THE CAR!

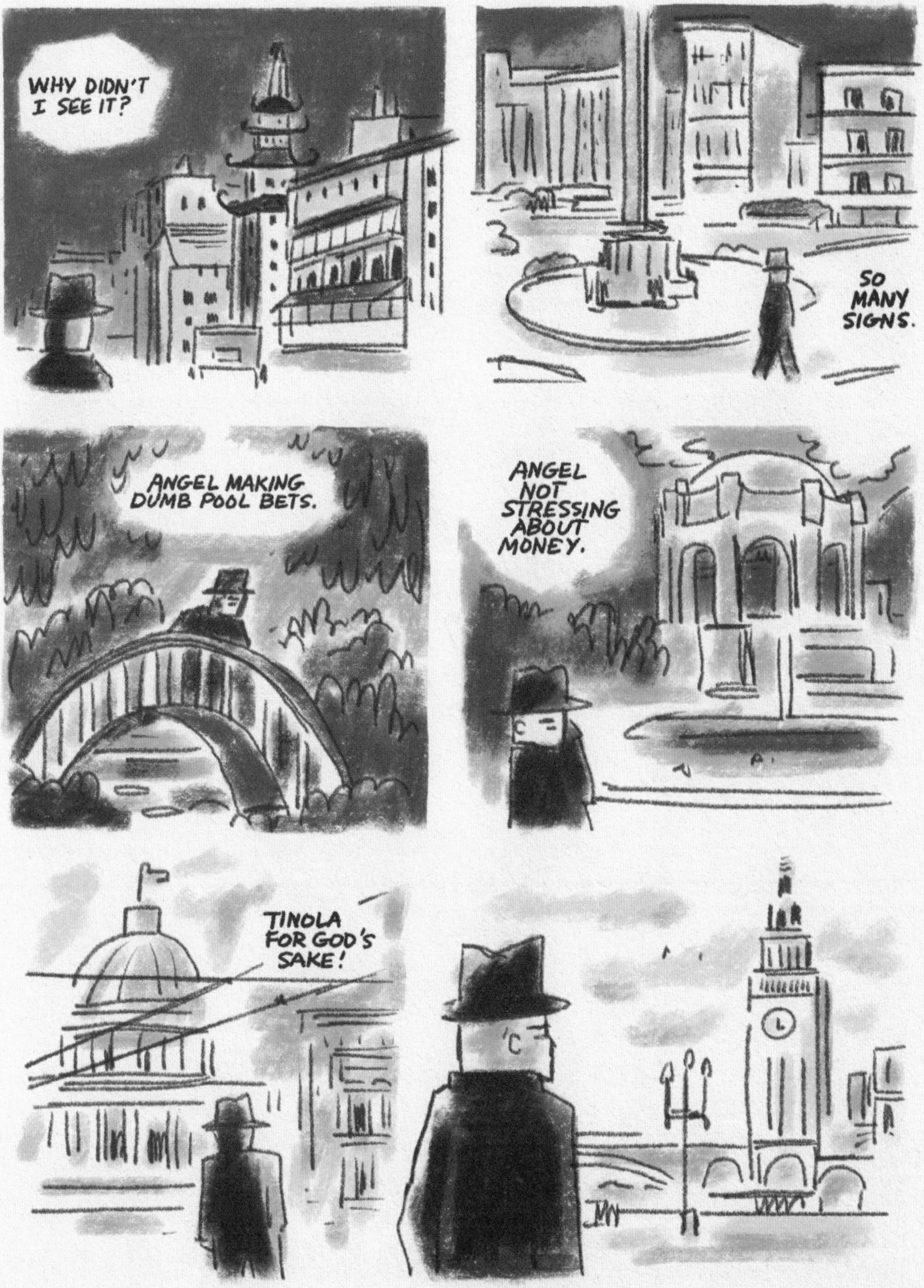
WHY DIDN'T I SEE IT?
SO MANY SIGNS.
ANGEL MAKING DUMB POOL BETS.
ANGEL NOT STRESSING ABOUT MONEY.
TINOLA FOR GOD'S SAKE!

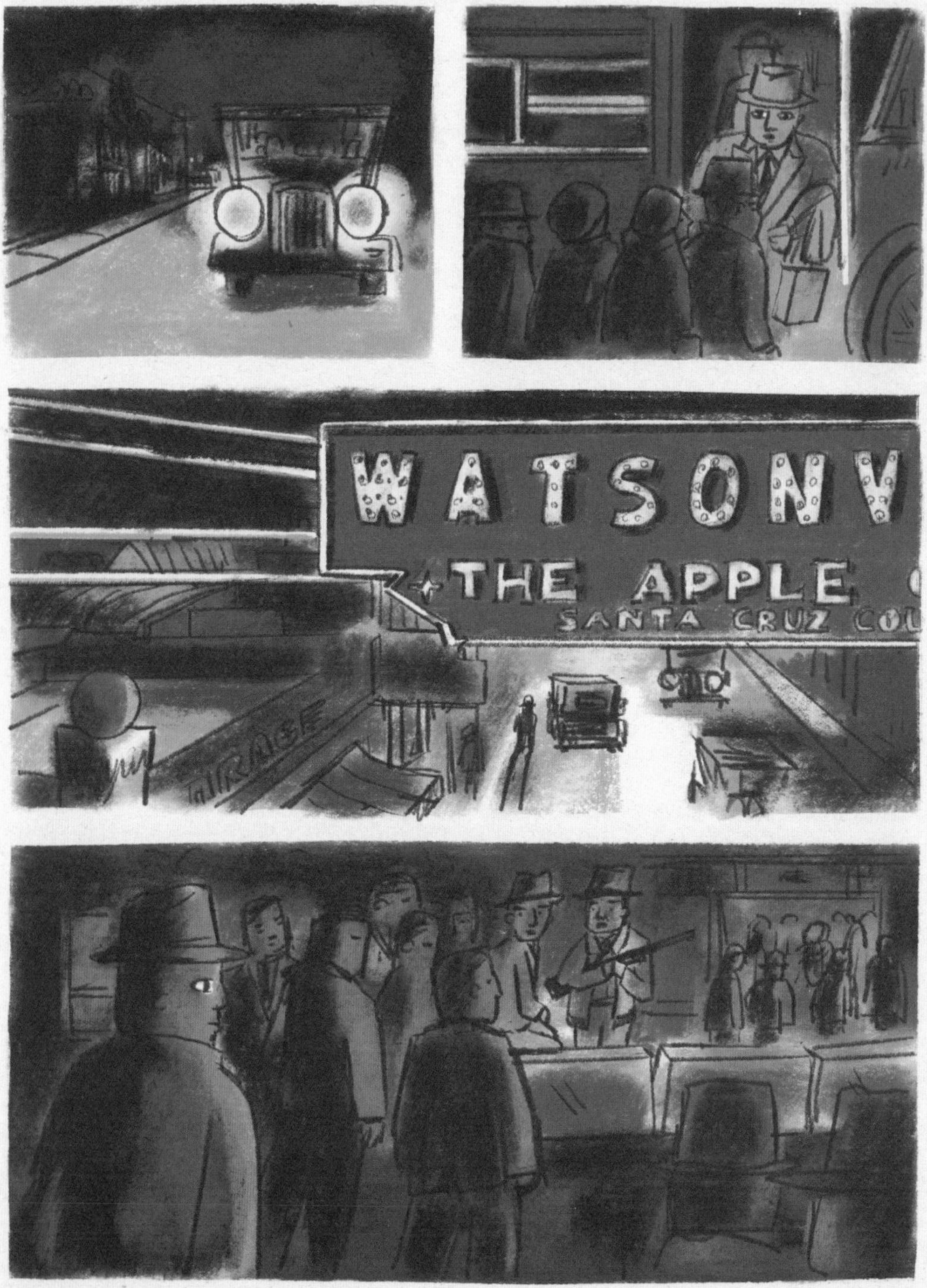
WATSONV
THE APPLE
SANTA CRUZ COU

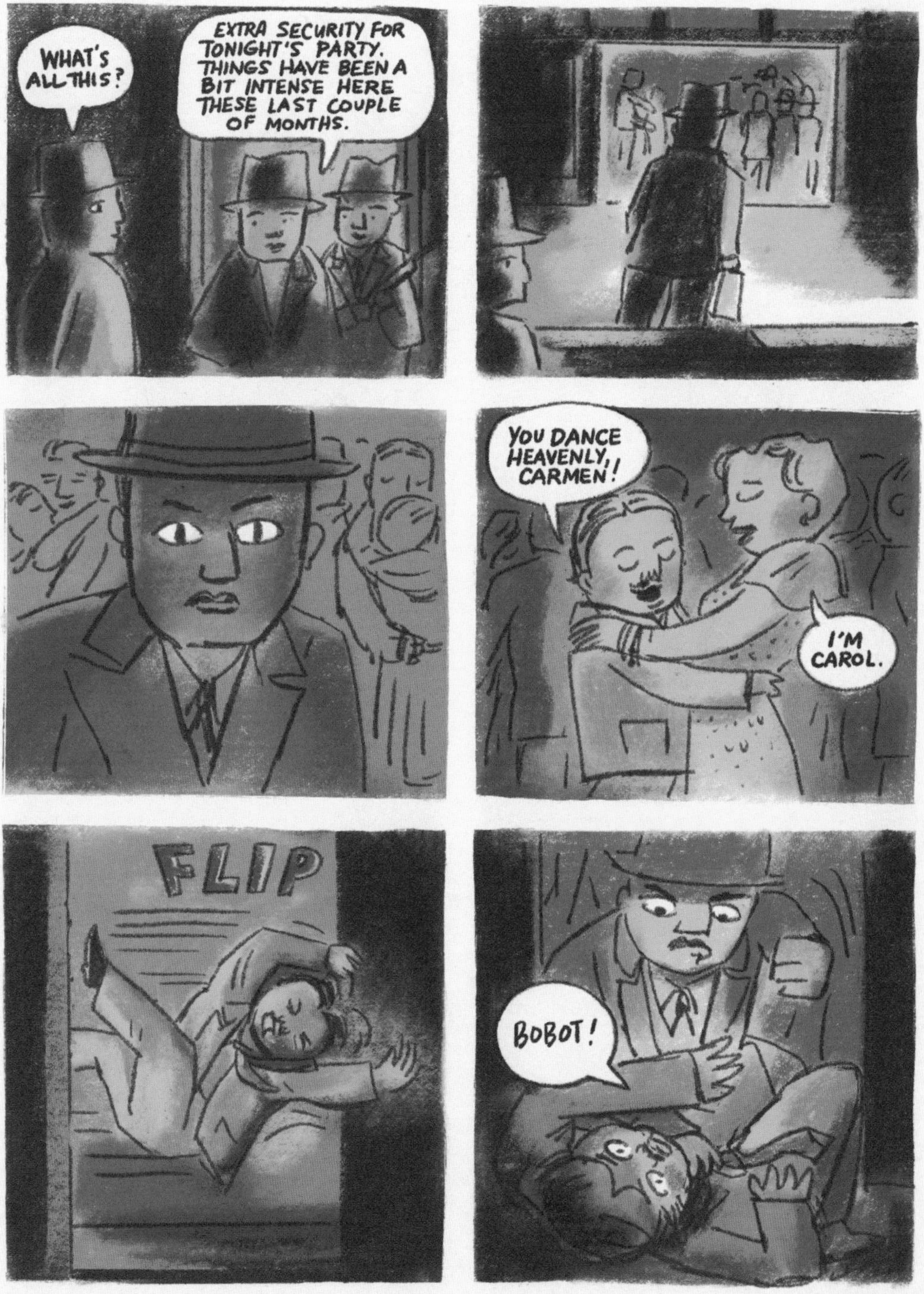
WHAT'S ALL THIS?
EXTRA SECURITY FOR TONIGHT'S PARTY. THINGS HAVE BEEN A BIT INTENSE HERE THESE LAST COUPLE OF MONTHS.
YOU DANCE HEAVENLY, CARMEN!
I'M CAROL.
FLIP
BOBOT!

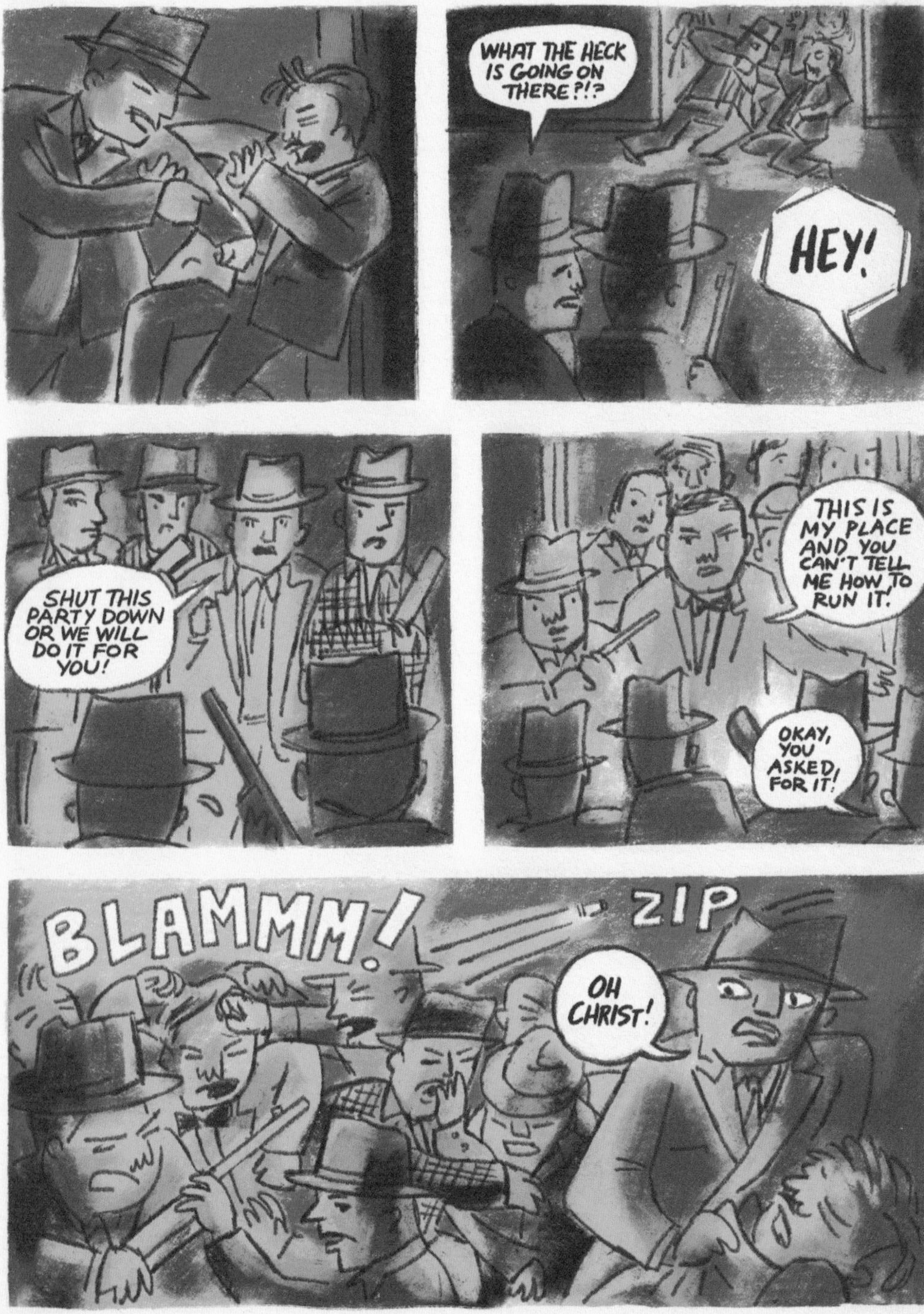
WHAT THE HECK IS GOING ON THERE?!?
HEY!
SHUT THIS PARTY DOWN OR WE WILL DO IT FOR YOU!
THIS IS MY PLACE AND YOU CAN'T TELL ME HOW TO RUN IT!
OKAY, YOU ASKED FOR IT!
BLAMMM!
ZIP
OH CHRIST!

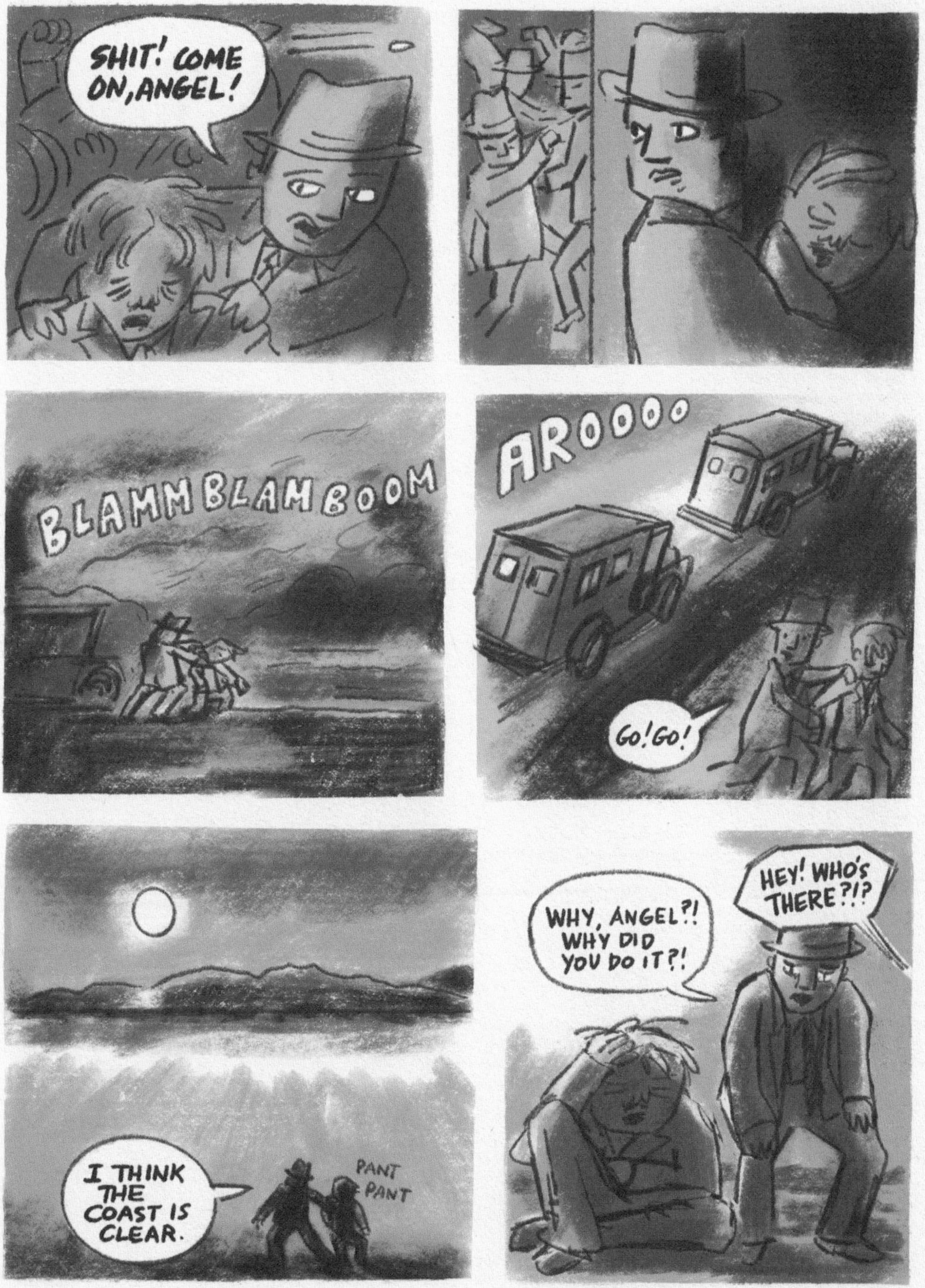

SHIT! COME ON, ANGEL!
BLAMM BLAM BOOM
AROOOO
GO! GO!
I THINK THE COAST IS CLEAR.
PANT PANT
WHY, ANGEL?! WHY DID YOU DO IT?!
HEY! WHO'S THERE?!?

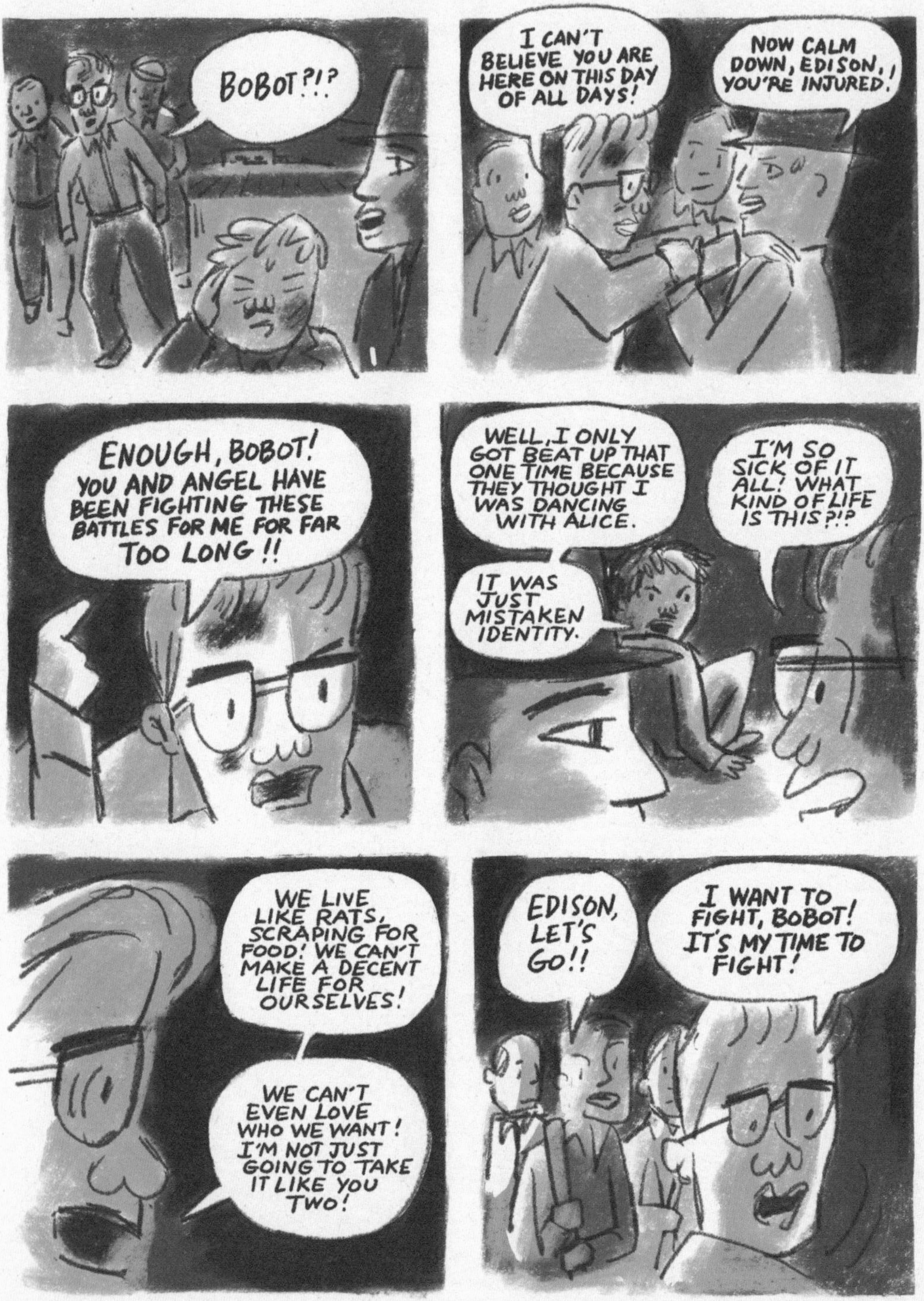
BOBOT?!?
I CAN'T BELIEVE YOU ARE HERE ON THIS DAY OF ALL DAYS!
NOW CALM DOWN, EDISON, YOU'RE INJURED!
ENOUGH, BOBOT! YOU AND ANGEL HAVE BEEN FIGHTING THESE BATTLES FOR ME FOR FAR TOO LONG!!
WELL, I ONLY GOT BEAT UP THAT ONE TIME BECAUSE THEY THOUGHT I WAS DANCING WITH ALICE.
IT WAS JUST MISTAKEN IDENTITY.
I'M SO SICK OF IT ALL! WHAT KIND OF LIFE IS THIS?!?
WE LIVE LIKE RATS, SCRAPING FOR FOOD! WE CAN'T MAKE A DECENT LIFE FOR OURSELVES!
WE CAN'T EVEN LOVE WHO WE WANT! I'M NOT JUST GOING TO TAKE IT LIKE YOU TWO!
EDISON, LET'S GO!!
I WANT TO FIGHT, BOBOT! IT'S MY TIME TO FIGHT!

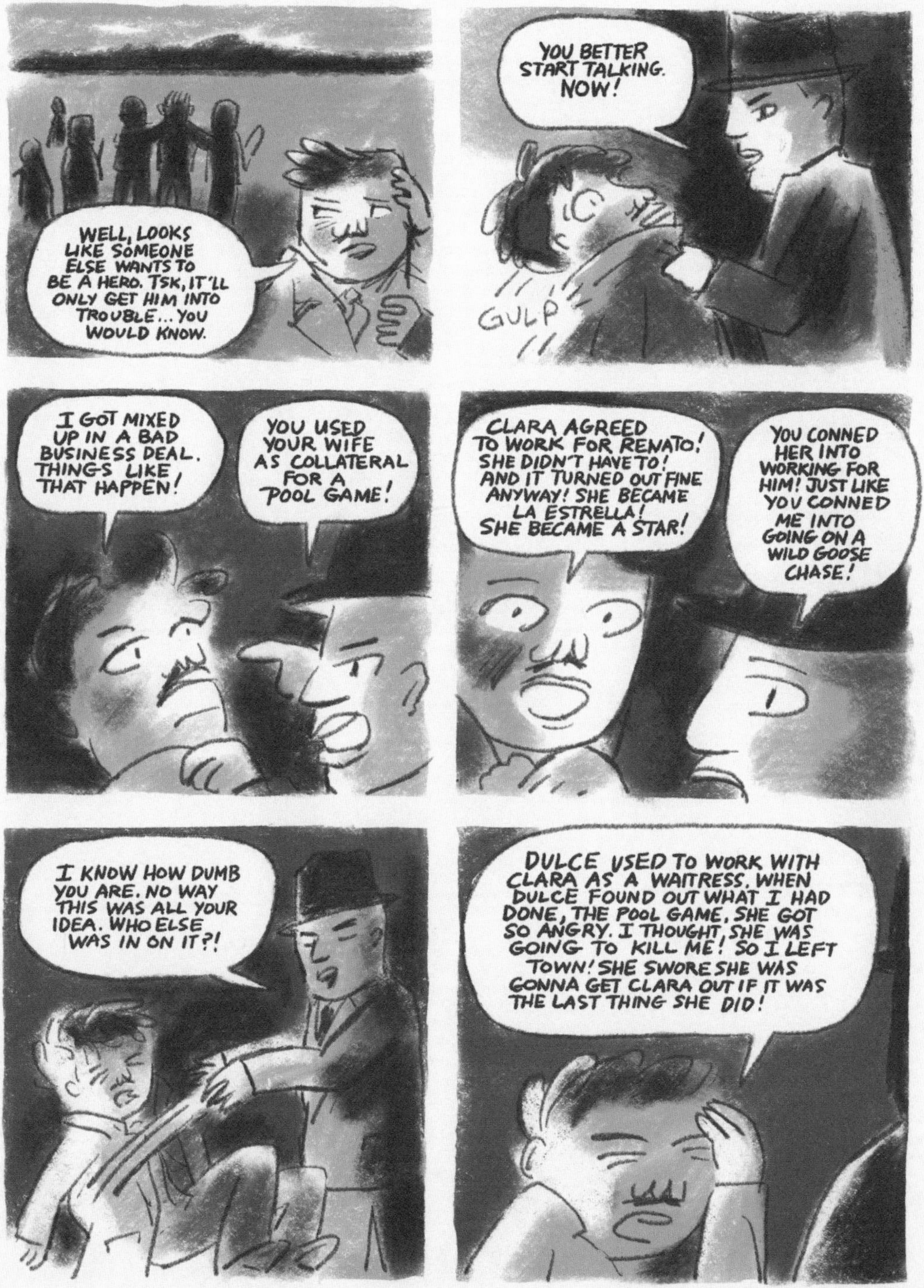
WELL, LOOKS LIKE SOMEONE ELSE WANTS TO BE A HERO. TSK, IT'LL ONLY GET HIM INTO TROUBLE... YOU WOULD KNOW.
YOU BETTER START TALKING. NOW!
GULP
I GOT MIXED UP IN A BAD BUSINESS DEAL. THINGS LIKE THAT HAPPEN!
YOU USED YOUR WIFE AS COLLATERAL FOR A POOL GAME!
CLARA AGREED TO WORK FOR RENATO! SHE DIDN'T HAVE TO! AND IT TURNED OUT FINE ANYWAY! SHE BECAME LA ESTRELLA! SHE BECAME A STAR!
YOU CONNED HER INTO WORKING FOR HIM! JUST LIKE YOU CONNED ME INTO GOING ON A WILD GOOSE CHASE!
I KNOW HOW DUMB YOU ARE. NO WAY THIS WAS ALL YOUR IDEA. WHO ELSE WAS IN ON IT?!
DULCE USED TO WORK WITH CLARA AS A WAITRESS. WHEN DULCE FOUND OUT WHAT I HAD DONE, THE POOL GAME, SHE GOT SO ANGRY. I THOUGHT SHE WAS GOING TO KILL ME! SO I LEFT TOWN! SHE SWORE SHE WAS GONNA GET CLARA OUT IF IT WAS THE LAST THING SHE DID!

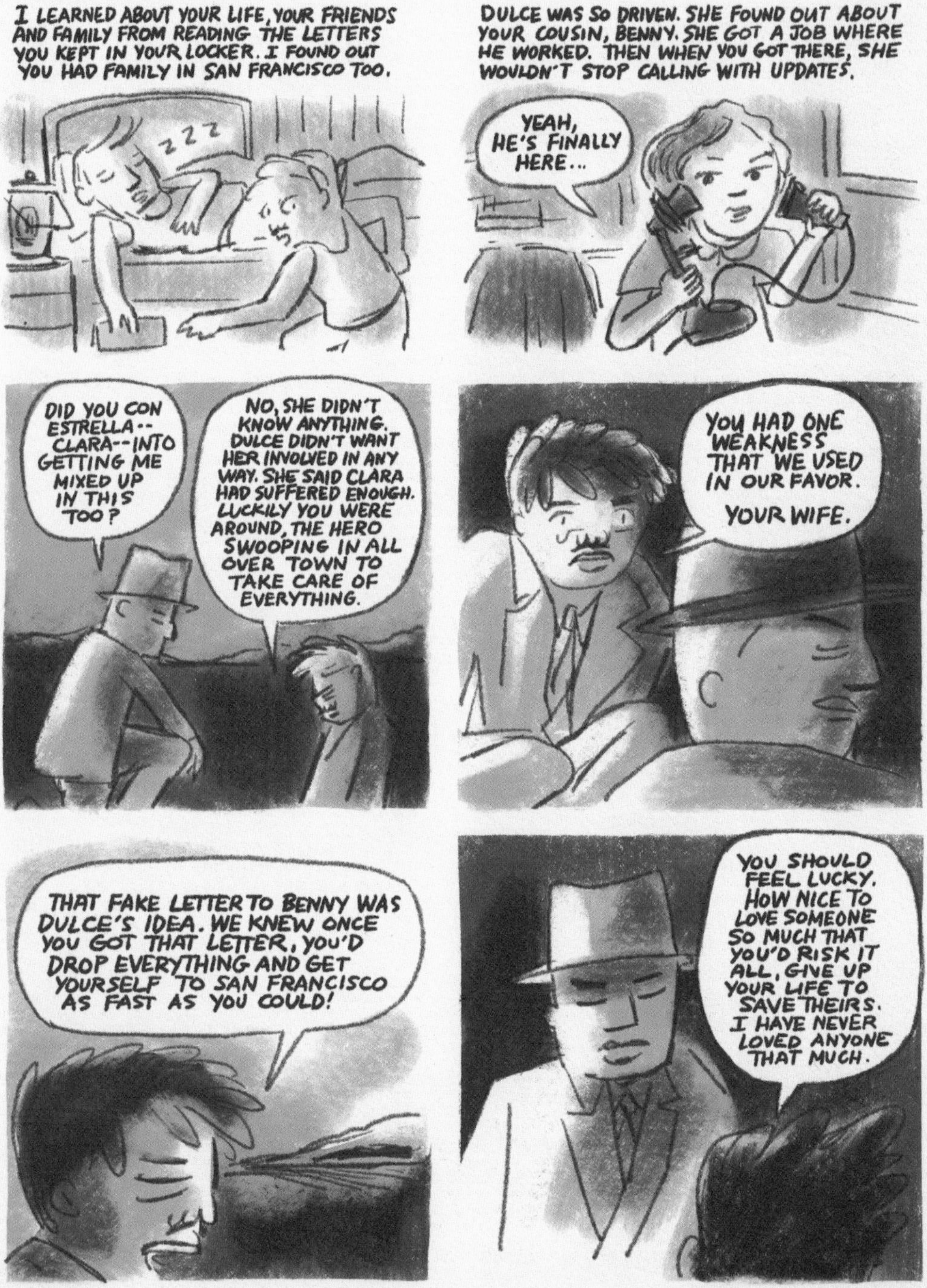
I LEARNED ABOUT YOUR LIFE, YOUR FRIENDS AND FAMILY FROM READING THE LETTERS YOU KEPT IN YOUR LOCKER. I FOUND OUT YOU HAD FAMILY IN SAN FRANCISCO TOO.
Z Z Z
DULCE WAS SO DRIVEN. SHE FOUND OUT ABOUT YOUR COUSIN, BENNY. SHE GOT A JOB WHERE HE WORKED. THEN WHEN YOU GOT THERE, SHE WOULDN'T STOP CALLING WITH UPDATES.
YEAH, HE'S FINALLY HERE...
DID YOU CON ESTRELLA-- CLARA--INTO GETTING ME MIXED UP IN THIS TOO?
NO, SHE DIDN'T KNOW ANYTHING. DULCE DIDN'T WANT HER INVOLVED IN ANY WAY. SHE SAID CLARA HAD SUFFERED ENOUGH. LUCKILY YOU WERE AROUND, THE HERO SWOOPING IN ALL OVER TOWN TO TAKE CARE OF EVERYTHING.
YOU HAD ONE WEAKNESS THAT WE USED IN OUR FAVOR.
YOUR WIFE.
THAT FAKE LETTER TO BENNY WAS DULCE'S IDEA. WE KNEW ONCE YOU GOT THAT LETTER, YOU'D DROP EVERYTHING AND GET YOURSELF TO SAN FRANCISCO AS FAST AS YOU COULD!
YOU SHOULD FEEL LUCKY. HOW NICE TO LOVE SOMEONE SO MUCH THAT YOU'D RISK IT ALL, GIVE UP YOUR LIFE TO SAVE THEIRS. I HAVE NEVER LOVED ANYONE THAT MUCH.

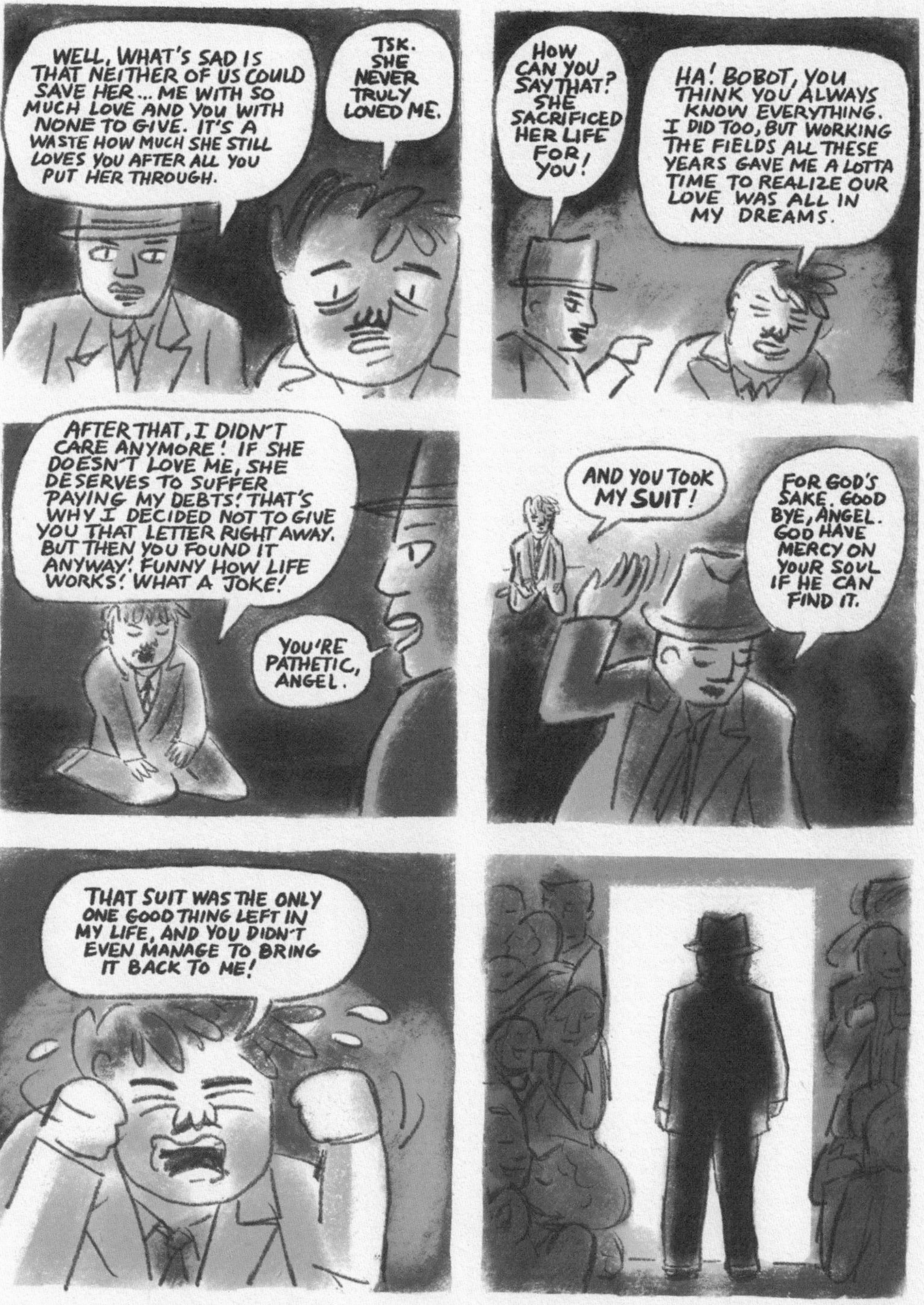
WELL, WHAT'S SAD IS THAT NEITHER OF US COULD SAVE HER... ME WITH SO MUCH LOVE AND YOU WITH NONE TO GIVE. IT'S A WASTE HOW MUCH SHE STILL LOVES YOU AFTER ALL YOU PUT HER THROUGH.
TSK. SHE NEVER TRULY LOVED ME.
HOW CAN YOU SAY THAT? SHE SACRIFICED HER LIFE FOR YOU!
HA! BOBOT, YOU THINK YOU ALWAYS KNOW EVERYTHING. I DID TOO, BUT WORKING THE FIELDS ALL THESE YEARS GAVE ME A LOTTA TIME TO REALIZE OUR LOVE WAS ALL IN MY DREAMS.
AFTER THAT, I DIDN'T CARE ANYMORE! IF SHE DOESN'T LOVE ME, SHE DESERVES TO SUFFER PAYING MY DEBTS! THAT'S WHY I DECIDED NOT TO GIVE YOU THAT LETTER RIGHT AWAY. BUT THEN YOU FOUND IT ANYWAY! FUNNY HOW LIFE WORKS! WHAT A JOKE!
YOU'RE PATHETIC, ANGEL.
AND YOU TOOK MY SUIT!
FOR GOD'S SAKE. GOOD BYE, ANGEL. GOD HAVE MERCY ON YOUR SOUL IF HE CAN FIND IT.
THAT SUIT WAS THE ONLY ONE GOOD THING LEFT IN MY LIFE, AND YOU DIDN'T EVEN MANAGE TO BRING IT BACK TO ME!

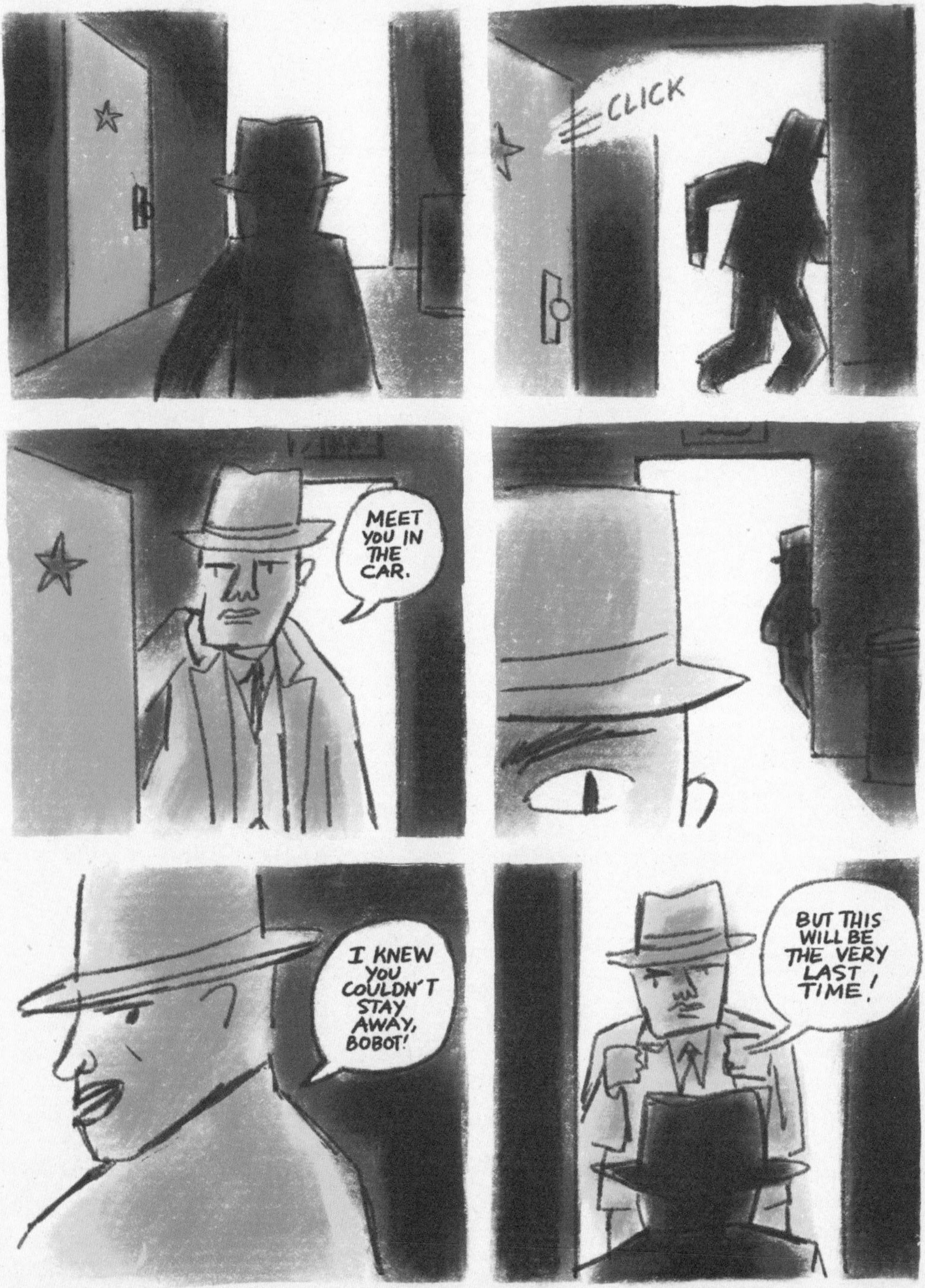
CLICK
MEET YOU IN THE CAR.
I KNEW YOU COULDN'T STAY AWAY, BOBOT!
BUT THIS WILL BE THE VERY LAST TIME!

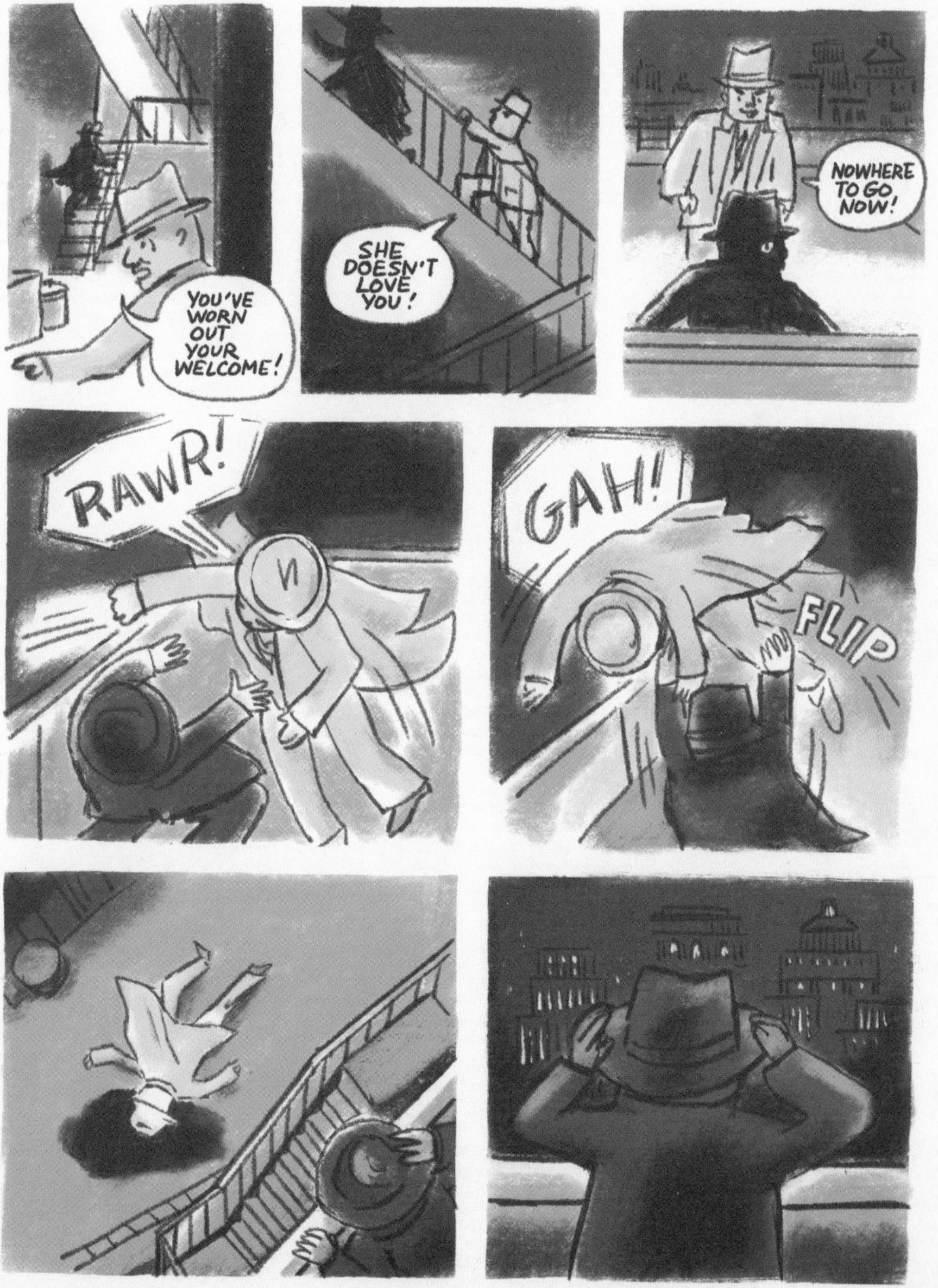
YOU'VE WORN OUT YOUR WELCOME!
SHE DOESN'T LOVE YOU!
NOWHERE TO GO NOW!
RAWR!
GAH!
FLIP

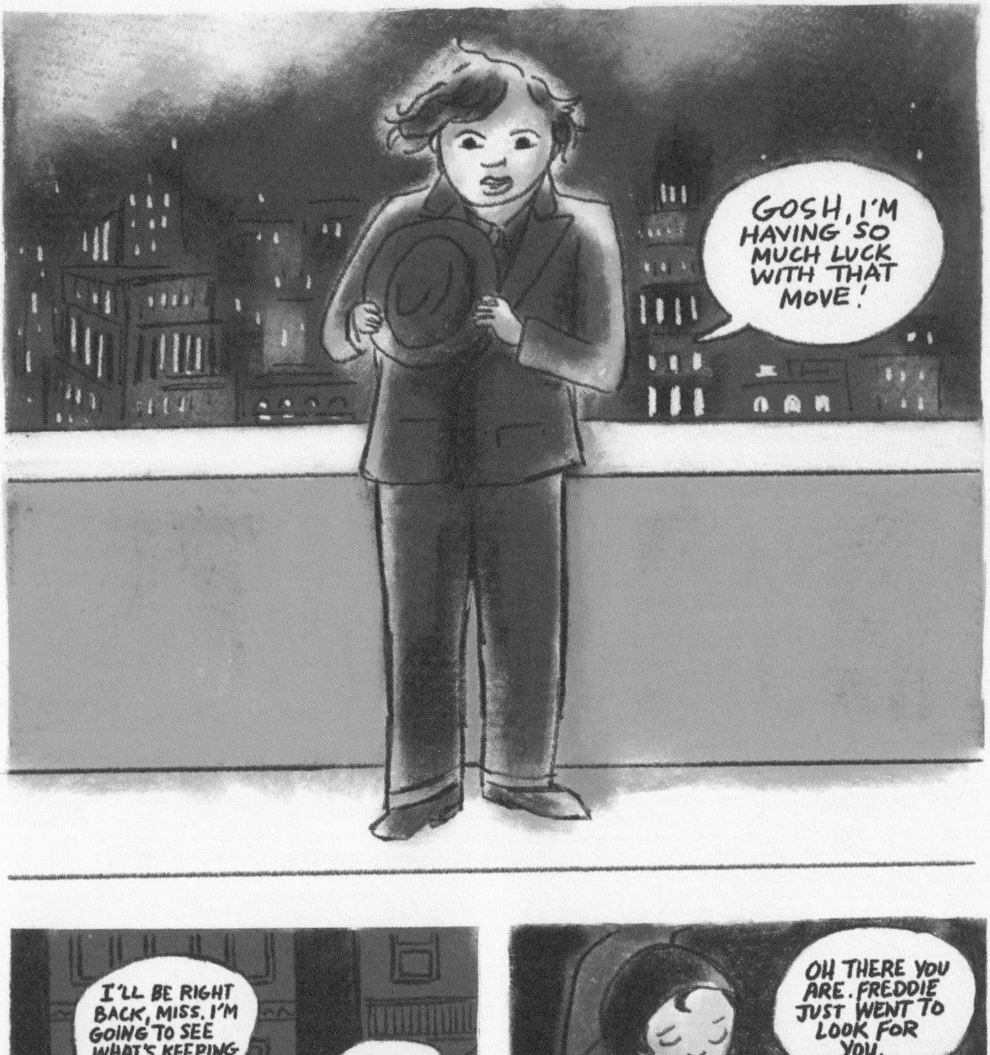
GOSH, I'M HAVING SO MUCH LUCK WITH THAT MOVE!

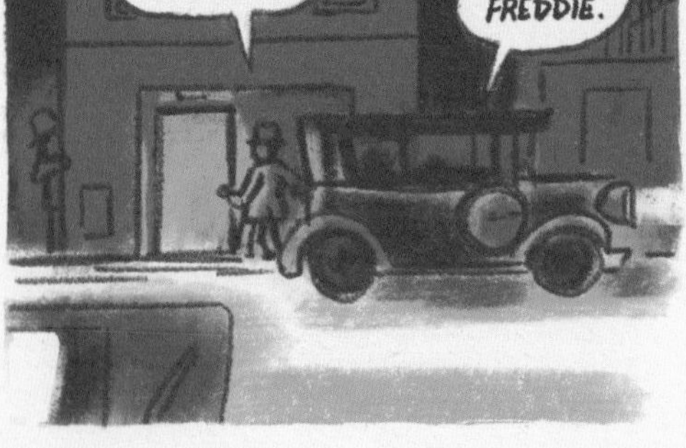
I'LL BE RIGHT BACK, MISS. I'M GOING TO SEE WHAT'S KEEPING MR. DIAZ.
THANKS, FREDDIE.

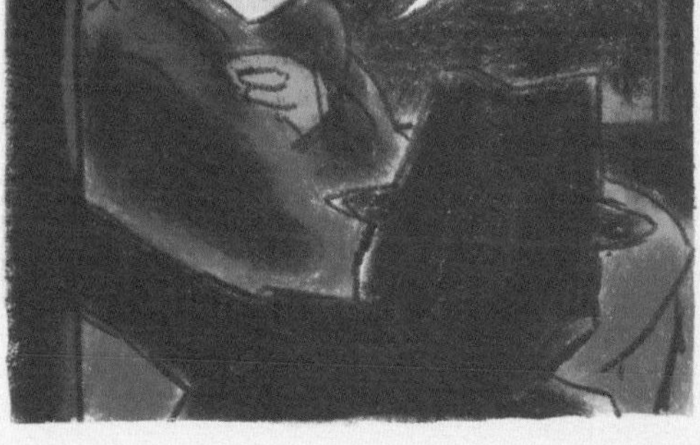
OH THERE YOU ARE. FREDDIE JUST WENT TO LOOK FOR YOU.

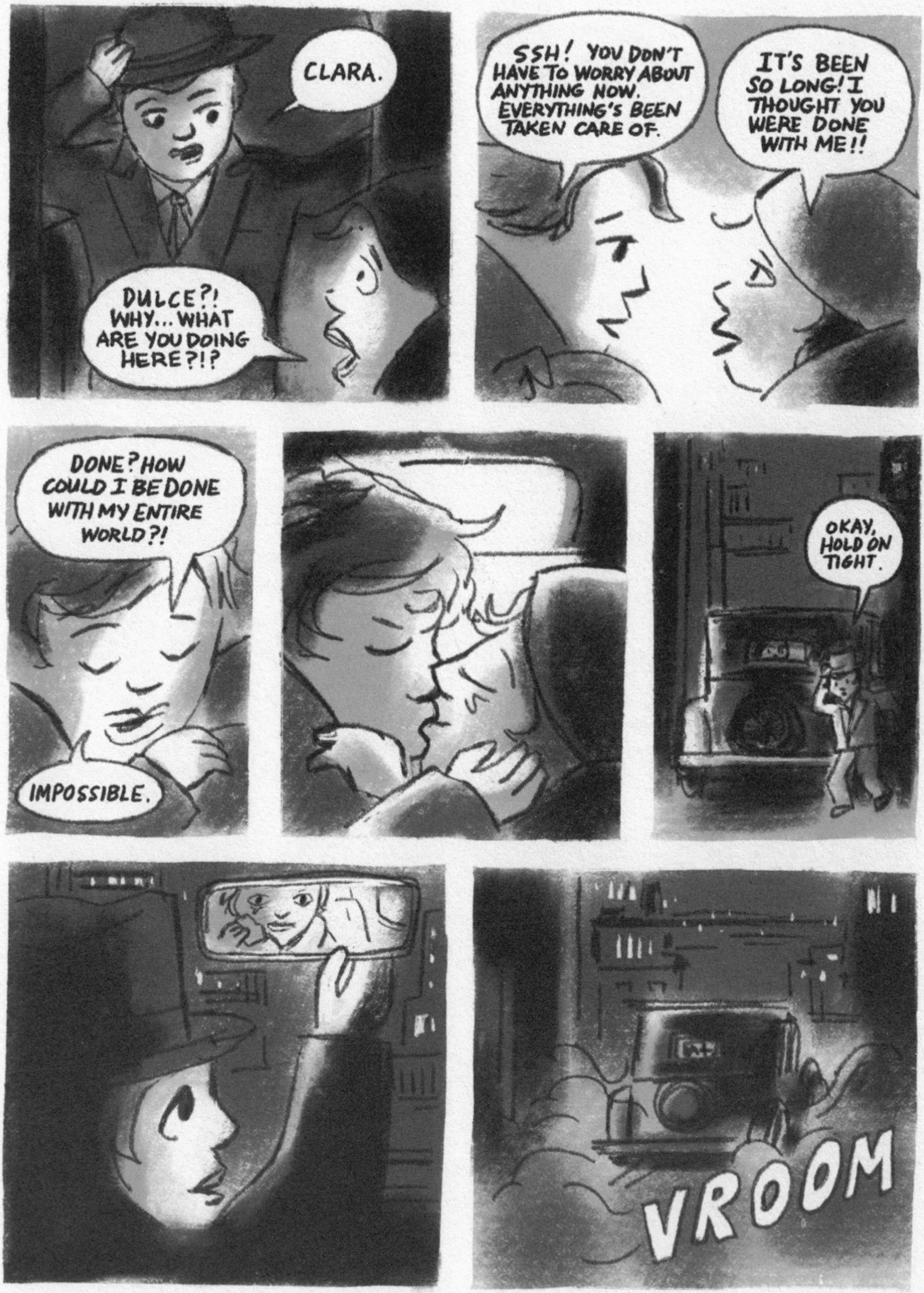
CLARA.
DULCE?! WHY... WHAT ARE YOU DOING HERE?!?
SSH! YOU DON'T HAVE TO WORRY ABOUT ANYTHING NOW. EVERYTHING'S BEEN TAKEN CARE OF.
IT'S BEEN SO LONG! I THOUGHT YOU WERE DONE WITH ME!!
DONE? HOW COULD I BE DONE WITH MY ENTIRE WORLD?!
IMPOSSIBLE.
OKAY, HOLD ON TIGHT.
VROOM

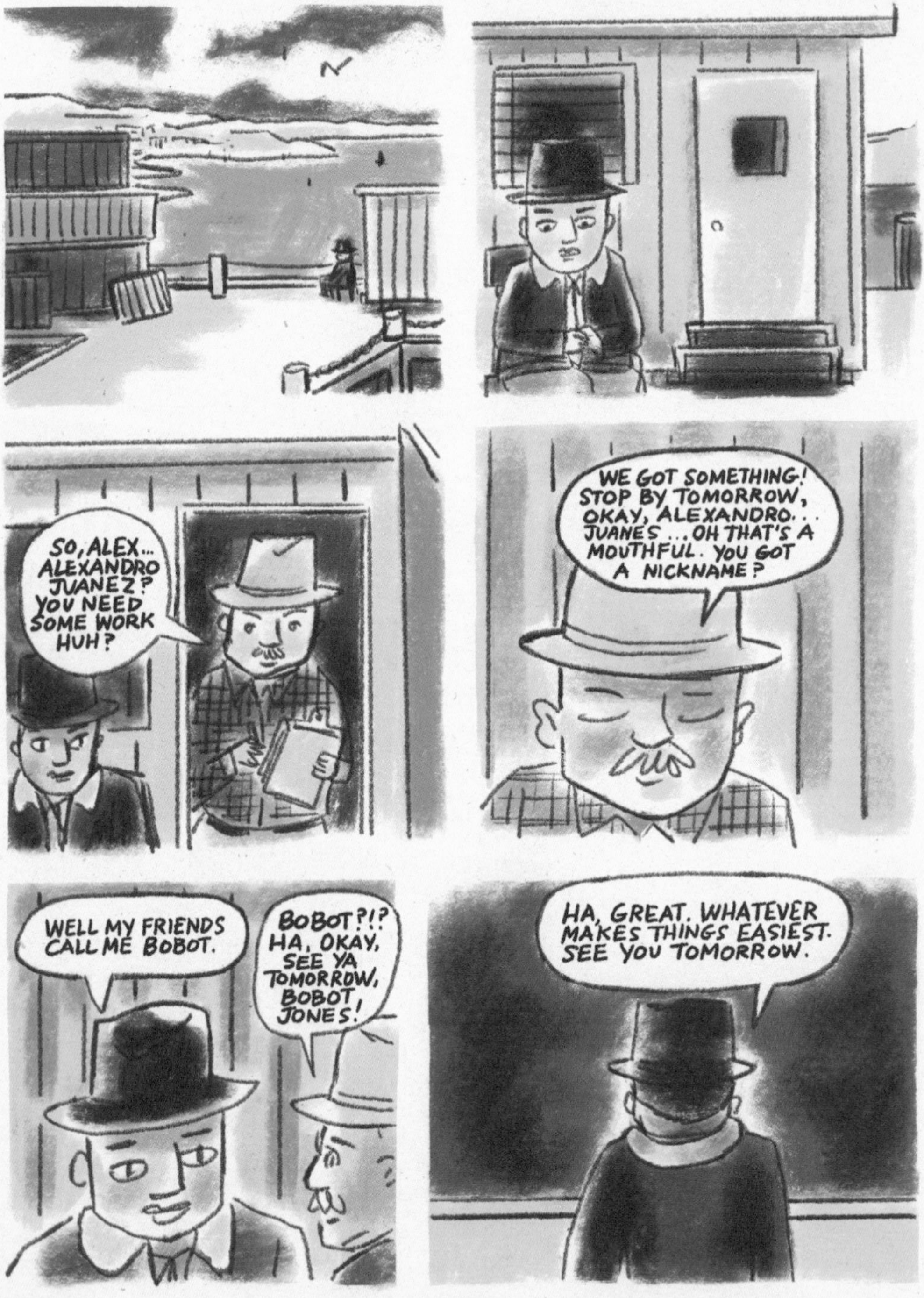
SO, ALEX... ALEXANDRO JUANEZ? YOU NEED SOME WORK HUH?
WE GOT SOMETHING! STOP BY TOMORROW, OKAY, ALEXANDRO... JUANES... OH THAT'S A MOUTHFUL. YOU GOT A NICKNAME?
WELL MY FRIENDS CALL ME BOBOT.
BOBOT?!? HA, OKAY, SEE YA TOMORROW, BOBOT JONES!
HA, GREAT. WHATEVER MAKES THINGS EASIEST. SEE YOU TOMORROW.

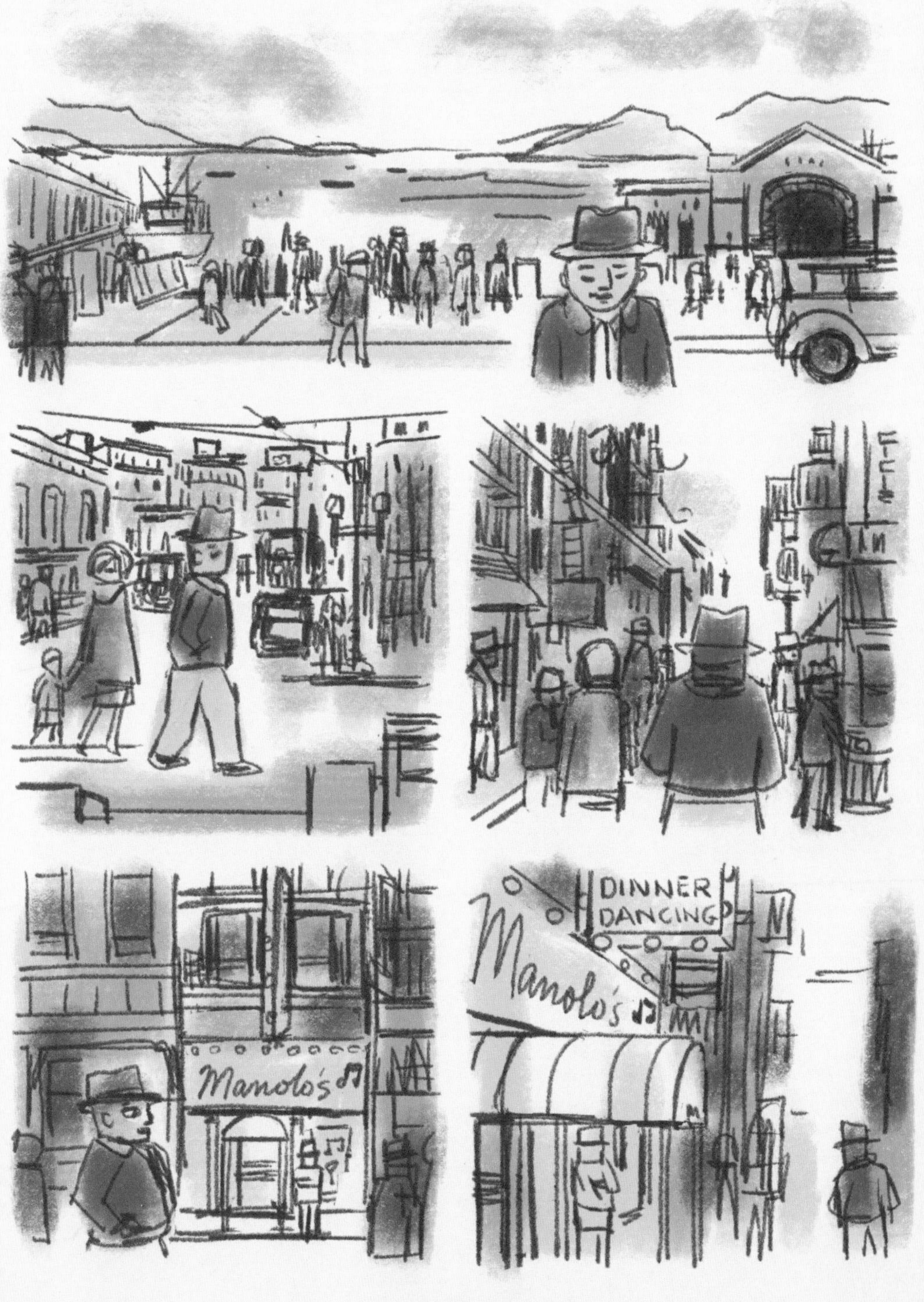
DINNER
DANCING
Manolo's
Manolo's

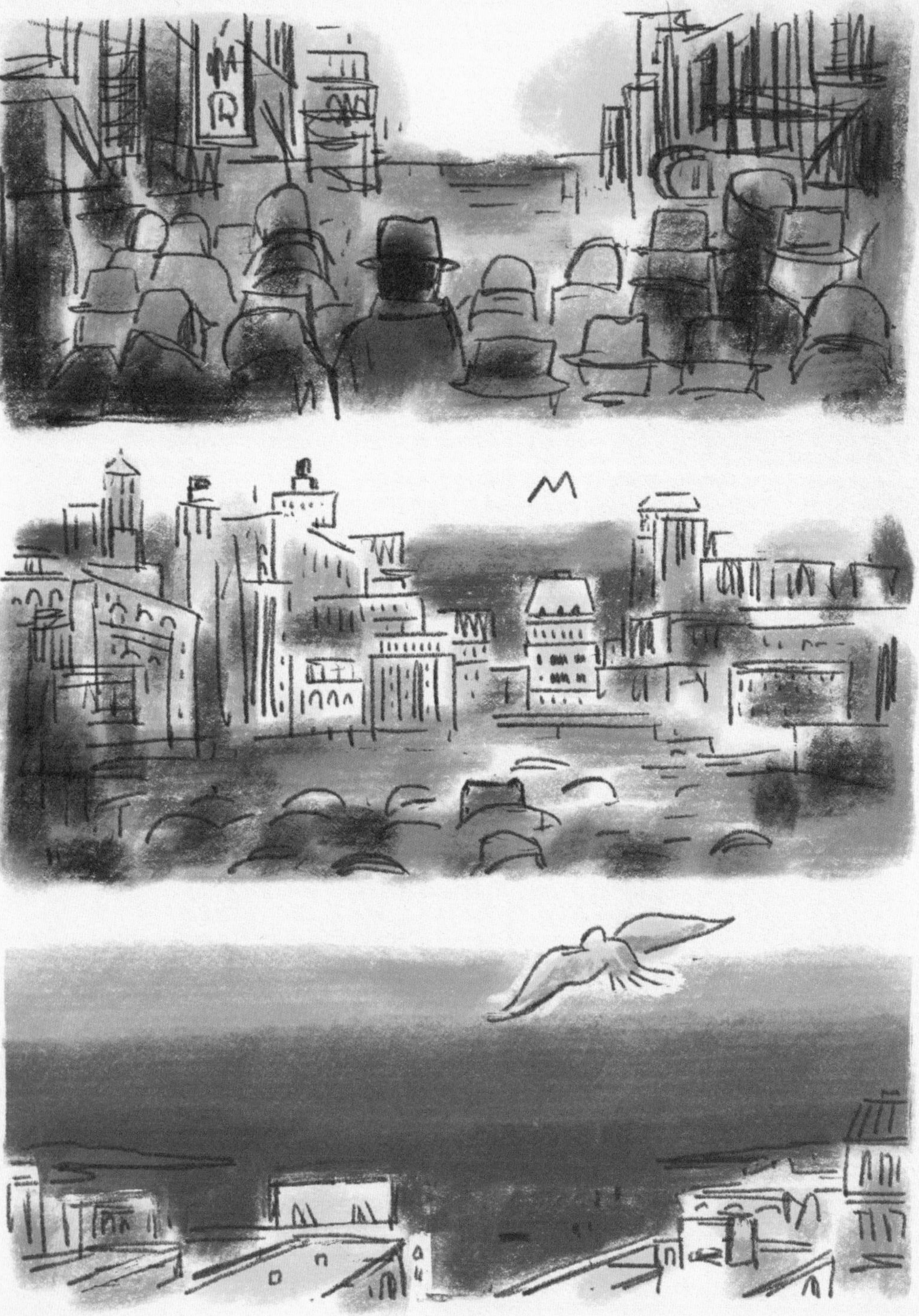

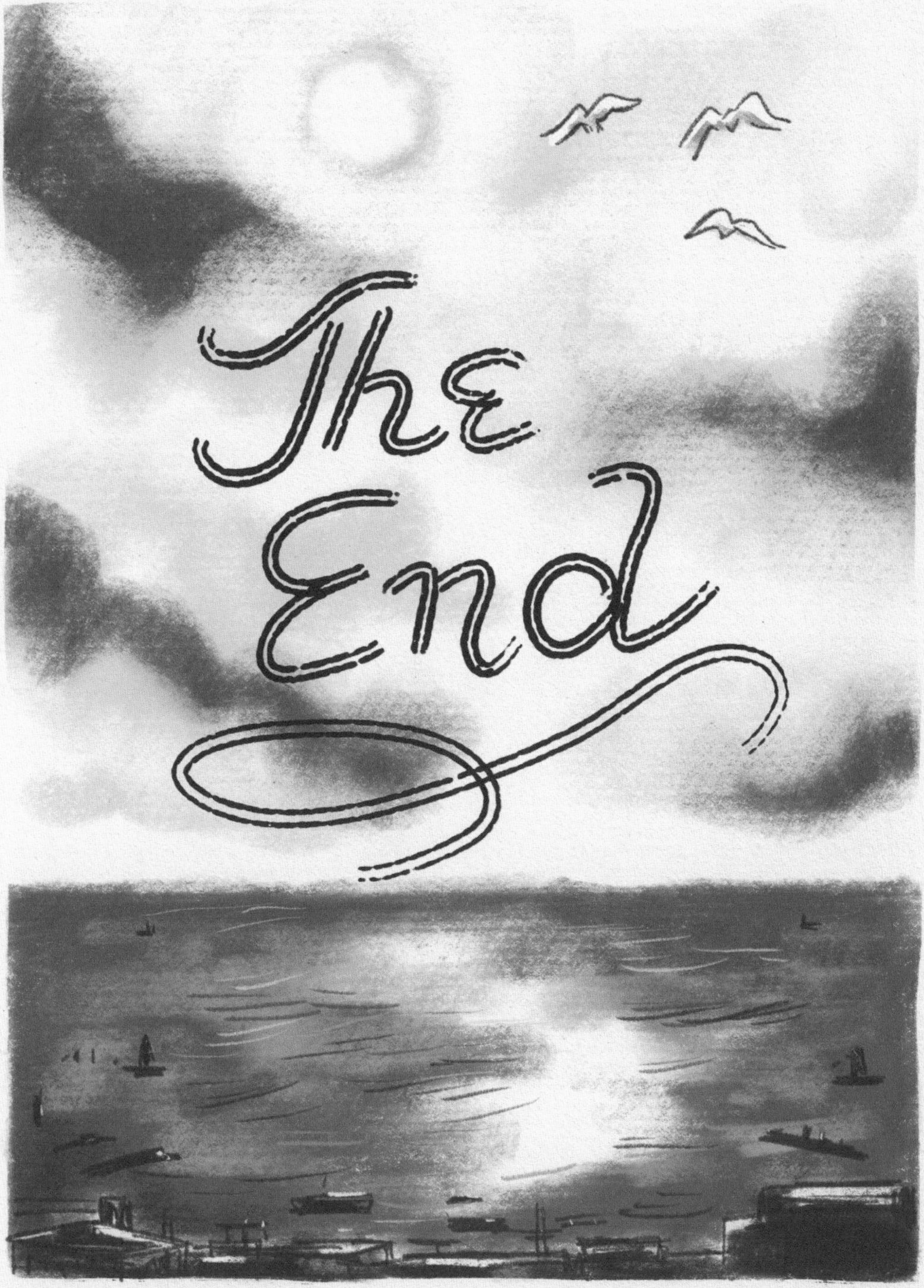
The End

For Dad

and to the
Manongs & Manangs

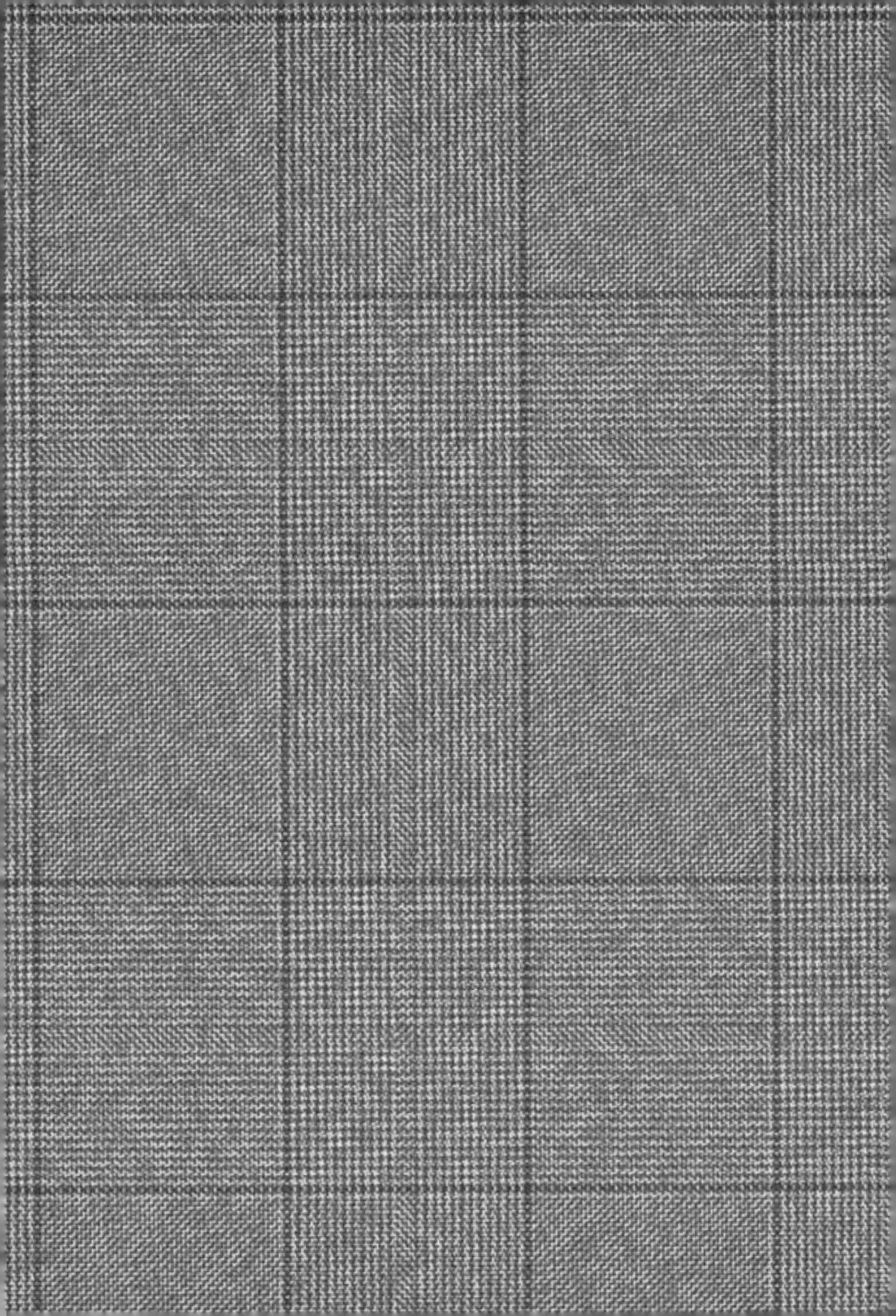

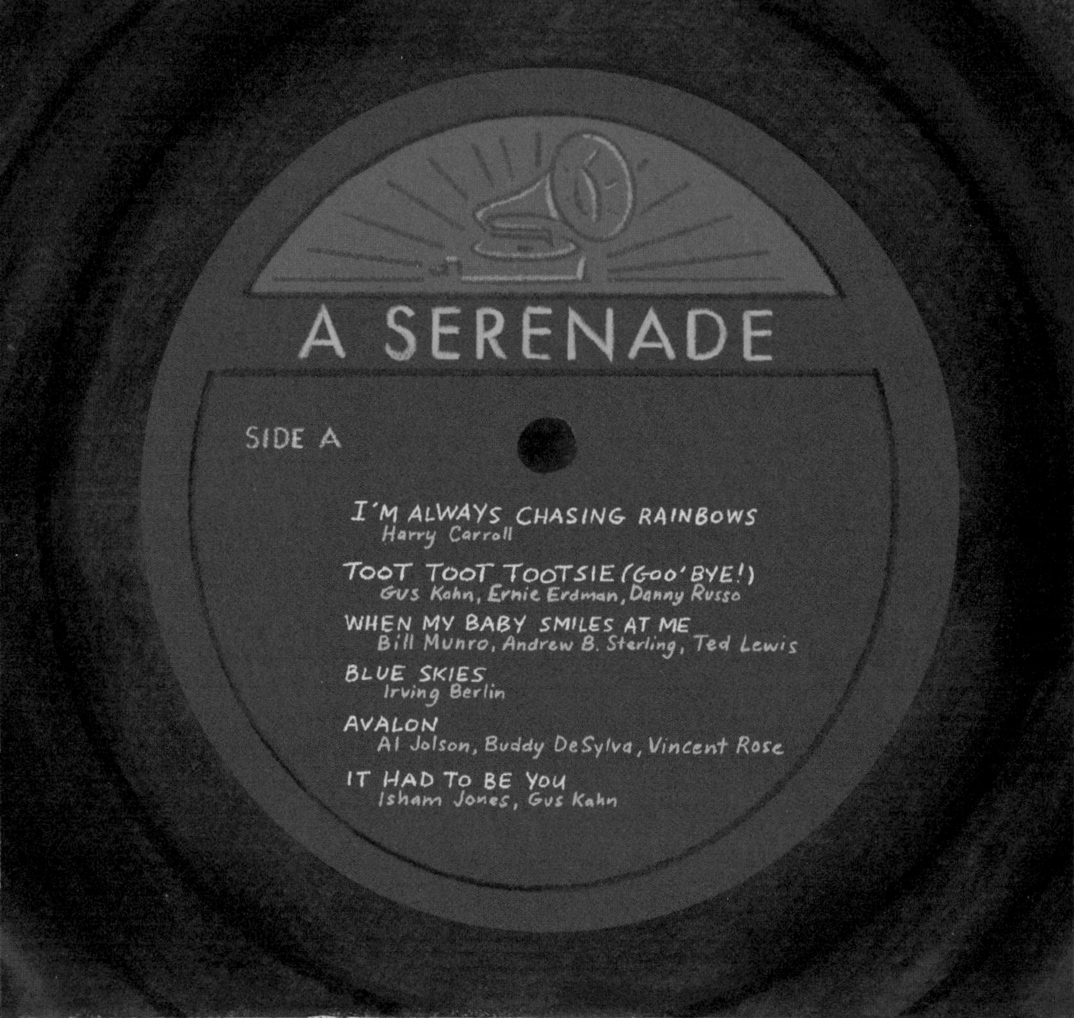
A SERENADE
SIDE A
I'M ALWAYS CHASING RAINBOWS
Harry Carroll
TOOT TOOT TOOTSIE (GOO' BYE!)
Gus Kahn, Ernie Erdman, Danny Russo
WHEN MY BABY SMILES AT ME
Bill Munro, Andrew B. Sterling, Ted Lewis
BLUE SKIES
Irving Berlin
AVALON
Al Jolson, Buddy DeSylva, Vincent Rose
IT HAD TO BE YOU
Isham Jones, Gus Kahn

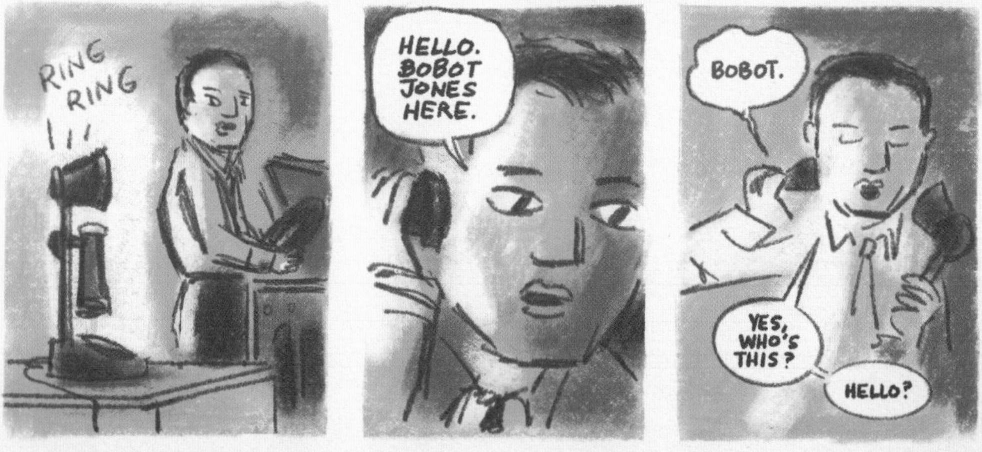
RING RING
HELLO. BOBOT JONES HERE.
BOBOT.
YES, WHO'S THIS?
HELLO?

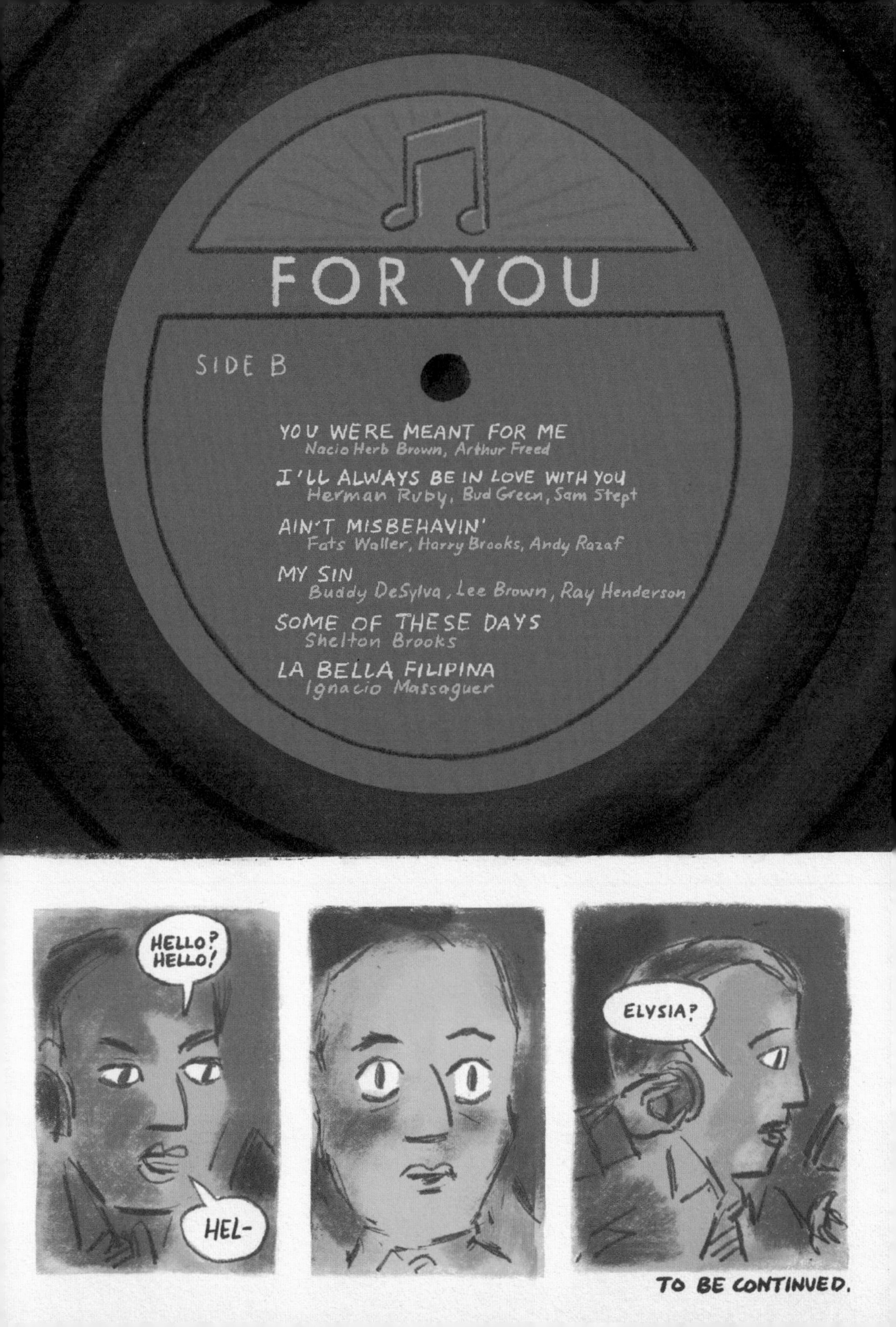
FOR YOU
SIDE B
YOU WERE MEANT FOR ME
Nacio Herb Brown, Arthur Freed
I'LL ALWAYS BE IN LOVE WITH YOU
Herman Ruby, Bud Green, Sam Stept
AIN'T MISBEHAVIN'
Fats Waller, Harry Brooks, Andy Razaf
MY SIN
Buddy DeSylva, Lee Brown, Ray Henderson
SOME OF THESE DAYS
Shelton Brooks
LA BELLA FILIPINA
Ignacio Massaguer
HELLO? HELLO!
HEL-
ELYSIA?
TO BE CONTINUED.

RINA AYUYANG was born and raised in Pittsburgh, PA. She was always inspired by the Sunday funnies and slice-of-life tales. Her short stories have been nominated for the Ignatz and Eisner awards and she has been honored with a MOCCA Arts Festival Awards of Excellence silver medal. Her comics have appeared in *Mutha Magazine* and *The Comics Journal.* Her first book published by Drawn & Quarterly was *Blame This on the Boogie,* which appeared on best of year lists from *Forbes, London Free Press,* and on *Publisher's Weekly's* Critics Poll. Ayuyang lives in Oakland, CA with her husband and son.